I pledge allegiance to the Flag of the United States of America,
And to the Republic for which it stands,
One Nation under God, indivisible, with liberty and justice for all.

To Mike
I hope you enjoy my story.
Best wishes for your own
good health.

George

HIGH FLIGHT

By

John Gillespie McGhee

Oh! I have slipped the surly bonds of Earth
And danced the skies on laughter-silvered wings;
Sunward I've climbed, and joined the tumbling mirth
Of sun-split clouds, - and done a hundred things
You have not dreamed of – wheeled and soared and swung
High in the sunlit silence. Hov'ring there,
I've chased the shouting wind along, and flung
My eager craft through footless halls of air . . .
Up, up the long, delirious burning blue
I've topped the wind-swept heights with easy grace
Where never lark, or ever eagle flew –
And, while with silent, lifting mind I've trod
The high untrespassed sanctity of space,
Put out my hand, and touched the face of God.

~~~~~~

MY STORY…
and I'm Sticking to it – I Think!

A Georgia Farm Boy's Dream to
Become a Fighter Pilot

By

GEORGE R. PARTRIDGE
Lt Col, USAF (Ret)

George Partridge
21 December 2017

MY STORY...AND I'M STICKING TO IT – I THINK!
A Georgia Farm Boy's Dream to Become a Fighter Pilot

Front Cover Credits
Top photo: Author as FAC in Vietnam 1965; US Air Force Photo.
Bottom left photo: Author on father's farm with plow-horse Rex, circa 1943; author's files.
Bottom center photo: North Georgia College circa 1950s; courtesy, of Special Collections and
Archives/University of North Georgia.
Bottom right photo: Author, F-100 Fighter Pilot, Cannon AFB, NM 1964-66; US Air Force Photo.

Back Cover
The author at his home in Prattville, Alabama circa 2014;
author's files.

ACKNOWLEGEMENTS

I wish to acknowledge all members of my family – and extended family – for their assistance in helping me *remember* the events in my life that I am putting to paper; and for any documents, photo, stories etc., that they may have provided. The validity of events as I remember them may be subject to the *fuzziness* of my recollection and are thus *noted*. But it's *My Story* and I'm sticking to it – *I think!*

I must thank my late sister Oreese for jogging my memory, and hers, particularly for my early years. My late older brother Harold could have provided so much fodder for my memories as he had to deal with his much younger siblings: my brother Richard, and me. We were about ten years younger than our older sister and brother, Oreese and Harold. Richard and I grew up together. I appreciate his "Partridge Family Tree" work which I referred to for this project.

My niece Melissa has expended countless hours, days, years, expense and shoe leather in researching our family genealogy, for which I am grateful. It is her work, and Richard's, to which I referred for listing the parents and siblings of my mother and father in Chapter 1.

My sincere gratitude to my late wife Pat for her calendar dairies and my letters she kept which prompted cherished memories. Also for her love and understanding as we spent days and years – holidays and special events – separated, due to my military commitments; and for her urging me to get on with *my story*. Had she lived, she could have added so much to this story. Thanks too to Pat's family for the memories and inputs. I also must thank my late son Norris, and my son Robert, for the cherished adventures we shared together as *we grew up together.* I missed so much of their lives because of the absences demanded by my military career – but Pat, their Mom, filled in *beautifully!*

My thanks to friends who reviewed my manuscript to determine general interest; to anyone who has provided inputs and memory joggers for my story; and to all whose footsteps have merged with mine as we walked together in good and bad times. You are an integral part of my life and this story, whether or not included in this work. Thank you.

Thanks to my USAF Pilot Training Class 56-V for the fond memories and the many photos provided. A special thanks to my aviation cadet buddies for the experience-of-a-lifetime we shared together.

Thanks too to my Air Force friends for the experiences we shared; especially my Vietnam combat buddies for our shared life-or-death experiences. You know who you are and our stories are told in this: *My story...*

Thanks to the University of North Georgia Special Collections and Archives for their permission to let me include on my story's cover, an early photo of the campus from the 1950s; the years I experienced on the campus which was then known as North Georgia College.

For my later years: Thanks to my devoted wife Margaret, who has provided me memorable inputs and assistance to bring my story up to date with our fun adventures. I am grateful for her love and care. She has really watched my health like a nurse (that she is). She has likely saved my life on at least two occasions. Thank you, Margaret for your caring and assistance in my writing of my "*My Story...*"

George R. Partridge

*****

CONTENTS

MY STORY... AND I'M STICKING TO IT – I THINK!
By
George R. Partridge, Lt Col, USAF (Ret)

DEDICATION

"*My Story*" is dedicated to my late wife, Pat, who died much too prematurely, and to our late son Norris who also died prematurely in his early middle age. My story is much too late for them and my promise to write it for my family. Procrastination: the nemesis of all of us humans!

I also dedicate "*My Story*" to my son Robert, who experienced many of my absences during his impressionable young life: my 15 months away in Goose Bay, Labrador; my deployments and alerts in the F-94C, F-89D/J, and the F-100C/D/F; my ejection from an F-100; my T-33 flights during the Cuban Crisis and my three temporary duties and combat time in Vietnam, to include Forward Air Controlling in the O-1 Bird Dog. He also was there with his Mom and me for our two years in the Philippines; for my Air Force retirement and my fiery T-34 crash and rescue. We also lived under the constant threat of a nuclear attack during the 'Cold War' in which major countries had nuclear weapons pointed at each other – and still so. I had so many fun times growing up with him, and the thrill of our aerobatic flying together. I hope he enjoys reminiscing with my story as much as I enjoyed writing it.

"*My Story*" is also dedicated to my late Mom and Dad. After all, without them this would be a *non-story*. My Mom would have been so thrilled to see "*My Story*" in print. With all her chores on the farm helping Dad make a living, she found some personal time to write short stories and do oil painting – her heart's desire. She tried so hard to get her short stories published but with only mediocre success – maybe one that never went anywhere. Although she had great talent, she was so humble that she would not try to sell her paintings because she said "Nobody would want them". She so wished her family would take an interest in her talent and hobby. But they all had other interests – especially Dad in making a living for his family. Mom wanted her sons to take an interest in the arts – especially with her talents – and me in particular with the little drawing talent I inherited from her. Now with "*My Story*," whether published or not, she would be delighted just to see my story in type. *I wish you could, Mom!*

To my wife Margaret, I also dedicate "*My Story*" for her enduring my many hours, days and years of work on my story. I hope she will find it entertaining and give her an appreciation and understanding of my life's experiences, and the kid that I used to be – and some people think I still am. We have had many fun times together including attending several of my military reunions. She always makes an impression on my aircrew buddies. In fact, she makes an impression on my friends wherever we go. I'm also sure she has saved my life on a couple of my life-threating medical emergencies. I must thank her also for her assistance in reading/editing and offering suggestions for my work. Thank you Margaret – I love you!

To the rest of my family and extended family I dedicate *"My Story"* for your reading enjoyment (I hope). My love to all!

George R. Partridge

*****

WARNING! This story contains no profanity; no trash-talk; no sewer-talk; no sexy scenes or secret affairs. So if those are your things, put it down now! There might be a slightly risqué spot here and there. It is also very politically incorrect! So if I write in terms common during my growing up years that today may be objectionable to some, get over it!

INTRODUCTION

Sometime around 1988 I put together a manuscript on my Dad's World War One service – 1917 to 1919. A couple of years after the war, he married and started a family. He and Mom produced my Sister Oreese, my brother Harold, then me and my younger brother Richard, in that order. He rarely mentioned the war, nor told any stories of his two years of service which included combat in the trenches of France as an infantry rifleman. My brothers, sister and I were told not to ask him about the war. His family only had a handful of his letters of those years. Although it was about twenty five years after his death, I had an almost spontaneous inspiration to try to reconstruct his service through any means available. I have so many times regretted that I was so late in suddenly deciding that his family needed to know *his story*. Visits to the National Archives in Washington, DC and Maryland; visits to the US Army Third Division's museum in Wurzburg, Germany; visits to Dad's frontline trenches and encampments in France; his German occupation sites; interviews with WW I veterans; studying WWI histories; WW I doughboys' personal accounts; and reading Dad's personal copies of his Third Division and 38 Infantry Regiment histories produced only fragments of his history and much speculation based on those documents. I spent a few years (days and nights) in researching and writing the manuscript for the benefit of Dad's and my family – not for publishing.

When all was done, my family said that they wanted me to do my story so that they would not have the frustration and years doing my story, that I had doing Dad's. My wife Pat and our sons Norris and Robert were my principal cheerleaders in getting this started. Thus, "My Story...." However, having promised Pat, Norris and Robert that I would do my story, I succumbed to that old nemesis of all good intentions: *Procrastination*. On December 14, 2008 I finally *got to it* and started to put my story to paper (make that 'computer'). Now it is with heavy heart that I regret not having completed my story prior to the death of my wife, Pat, and our oldest son, Norris. I hope my son Robert will enjoy it and fondly remember *our growing up together*. I also hope my wife Margaret will enjoy my story and find it worth the hours, days and years she endured while I was deeply engrossed in its production.

My story is also written in the hope that my family, extended family any anyone reading it, will enjoy it and find some parts humorous, some profound and some exciting and thrilling – as they were for me. Some of the parts written will be better understood by aircrew personnel, but I've tried to make it meaningful to all. There is no profanity; no trash-talk; no steamy intimate scenes; no intended racism and no intention to embarrass, harm or insult anyone; although some parts may not be *politically correct* they are written as I remember them unfolding in my life: A life in which I have been unjustifiably blessed beginning with my Mom and Dad. I count *everyone* who has played a part in my life as a blessing: Even the school bully that used me for his personal, and favorite, *punching bag*. Thus far God has granted my life's dreams, although not as I had planned and scripted them – which is probably a good thing. None-the-less I have no complaints. This is not to say that I have no more dreams. I do!

My story is too late for my Mom and Dad, of course. I know they could have added many tales such as the time when I was about three years old sitting on the edge of our porch by my Dad, when I leaned over and bit him hard on his leg for some undetermined and spontaneous reason. Dad reacted unthinkingly and started to back-hand me, but Mom yelled and startled him to his senses. It is also too late for my older sister and brother, Harold and Oreese. I think they would have enjoyed it. I know my sister would have been delighted. Before she died she had started her (unfinished) story and was a help in providing stories of early events in my life.

I count a few exciting events in my life – at least for the moments in which they occurred. There have been a few close calls along the way. But I don't pretend to suggest that I have had a more exciting, dangerous or adventurous life than many of my friends and fellow airmen. My stories pale before some of the events they encountered. One time, after swapping *"war stories"*, an Air Force pilot friend said to me: "George, I didn't know you lived so close to the edge!" This after he had just lived through a night convoy ambush by the Viet Cong in Vietnam, where there was some close-in fighting with hand-to-hand combat. I did acquire a few combat decorations and awards along the way but I wish to impress upon the reader that I did no great heroic deeds. There are many *real* heroes out there who truly deserve our gratitude!

I did thirty-three years, one month and twenty-six days of military service – all active duty Air Force except for the first seven months and twenty-four days in the U.S. Marine Air Reserve at the Atlanta Naval Air Station, Chamblee, Georgia, enlisting August 4th 1951. I intended to retire as a General (...didn't all my Air Force friends?), but somewhere along the way I misread my cue cards and retired as a Lieutenant Colonel in 1984.

I have written my story in a storytelling mode; not necessarily a grammatically and literal correct mode. But the only person who should be distraught over that, were she still living, would be my high school English teacher.

As a matter of note, it should be noted that my life was void of modern advantages (or curses) of electronics such as cell phones, laptops, computers, GPS etc. until well after retirement. But I wouldn't change a thing. Otherwise, who knows what might have been my fate? I acknowledge that it is by the *Grace of God* that I have been able to write my story, and pray that He will grant me the memory to remember it as long as he allows me to live on this earth. My story is related as I remember it, so some events may be *skewed* a bit, but the words are mine and I take full responsibility. To my dear family, friends and casual reader, I hope you enjoy my story and *growing up* with me on Dad's farm; sharing my dreams, disappointments, successes, stark terrors, and immeasurable blessings! I enjoyed living it with you and enjoyed writing and reliving it! I had forgotten that I had so much fun! If it's printed *I hope you bought a copy because I need the money!* ☺ (Just kidding!).

Disclaimer: My story is told to the best of my recollection. My veteran and combat buddies may remember some of the events differently, but that's *their story*. Even my family and friends may remember events slightly different. Anyway, this is *my story* and I'm sticking to it....I think! Enjoy!

(When Hollywood picks up my story, my wife Margaret has said that she reserves the right to select the actress who will play her part in the movie production of "My Story" ......and she's sticking to it!)

George R. Partridge

PROLOGUE

~~~~~

It was a cold winter day in January 1950 when the black 1939 model Chevrolet sedan pulled over to the left curb and stopped. Above on a modest knoll was the Commandant of Cadets Headquarters Building that overlooked the beautiful undulating campus of a small military college, *North Georgia College*, nestled in the foothills of the beautiful Blue Ridge Mountains of North Georgia.

I opened the left rear door of the sedan and slid out of the seat onto the curb dragging my luggage with me. I stood on the sidewalk awed by the beauty and the impressive buildings on the hills above me – wondering what my future holds. Mom got out of the front passenger seat and came around back of the car to the curb where I stood; Dad remained in the driver's seat. She hugged me and kissed me on the cheek, obviously distraught with emotion. Then she got back into the car and they drove away. I saw Mom teared up looking back and waving. She realized that for the first time in *his young life that* her second son was *out of her life!*

As a 16 year old wet-behind-the-ears Georgia plow boy, I was fraught with emotions, trepidation *and elation* at the first major step toward my life's dream: becoming a *fighter pilot!*

~~~~~

So many close calls...
Saved by the *Grace of God!*

CHAPTER ONE
THE EARLY YEARS

Before the Beginning.......

George Partridge, my father, was born in Georgia during the early 1890s, and died in the early 1960s. Lenna Gilbert, my mother, was born in Georgia during the late 1890s and died in the late 1970s. Fate brought them together in their young lives as husband and wife – my Mom and Dad.

Dad's parents were William and Carrie Partridge: Grandpa Partridge was born in Ireland in the mid-1800s and died in Georgia during the 1920s. Grandma Partridge was born in Georgia in the mid-1800s and died in the early 1920s. They had nine children, in this order: Arthur, Dora, Willie May, John, Kate, Annie Belle, George, Agnes and Percy.

Mom's parents were William and Minnie Gilbert, born in Georgia in the 1870s. They died in Georgia in the 1930s and 1900s respectively. They had two children in order: Lenna and Carl ("Jimbo").

Dad and Mom would be classed in today's culture as very poor, only they didn't know it: they were too busy struggling to survive. No one told them they were poor. After all, everyone they knew was in the same boat. However there was usually a small farm subsidy after the annual visit by *"the government man"* who told Dad what crops and how much to plant. Dad eventually met Mom and began their courtship in the style of the farming communities of those days: weekend dances, church socials, community events, etc. Before they married, "The War to End All Wars" (World War One) would interrupt their dating – but not their love for each other. Dad would be drafted and eventually see combat as an infantry rifleman in the trenches of France with Company F, 2nd Battalion, 38th Infantry Regiment of the U.S. Army Third Division. He would later march 250 miles with the Division into Germany for the post war occupation. I have covered Dad's World War One military service in a manuscript that I completed November 1988. Dad was the only one of Grandpa and Grandma Partridge's four sons to see military service in World War One – or any war. Uncle Arthur was too old for the draft, Uncle John had a club foot and was rejected, and Uncle "Pert" was too young. Uncle John did his wartime duty later during World War Two as a fireman on the Tampa, Florida Army Air Field, which was used for B-17 aircrew training. It is now known as MacDill Air Force Base.

It was a couple of years and two months after the November 11th, 1918 Armistice that Dad and Mom would be married on January 8th, 1921 in Tucker, Georgia. Dad then moved himself and Mom into a small two-room farm shack located on his Dad's (Grandpa Partridge) 40 acre farm. About one year later they would have their first child, my sister Oreese. Oreese died 2009 at age 87.

Grandpa Partridge's house was a four-room house located nearby where he lived with his daughter, my Aunt Annie. Grandma Partridge had died in 1921 about six months after Mom and Dad married. Grandpa Partridge died in 1925 about three years after Oreese was born. Dad and Mom then moved into Grandpa's house on the farm with Aunt Annie. Then in 1923, my older brother, Harold, was born. Harold died in 2007 at age 83.

The farm was located in Gwinnett County a few miles from Norcross, Georgia and near the old U.S. Army Camp Gordon firing range. It lay just east of the present day Interstate 85 route and north of the old Norcross-Lilburn Road (now Jimmy Carter Boulevard); and according to Oreese, it bordered Goshen Spring Road. Living was hard! Dad had injured his back lifting wagons during the occupation of Germany following World War One. For years he tried to get disability compensation through the Veterans Administration but was unsuccessful for many years. Sometimes he would go for days bent over in terrible pain. But, according to my sister, he would go on day-in and day-out bent over his plow without a word of complaint – he had no choice. He was doing what he knew he had to do to feed his family – pain or no pain. (Later, in my early life on another farm, I too would witness Dad in the same must-go-on pain as he labored in the fields). In December 1929 Dad could not pay off the $750 mortgage for the farm. Unable to get an extension or to borrow the money, he lost the farm. *Merry Christmas!* Thus Dad had to move his family off the old farm place. He found another four-room tiny shack of a farm house in the country on Pleasantdale Road, outside of Doraville, Georgia. Here, in order to provide for his family, he became a tenant share-cropper for Westbrook's Farm. Pleasantdale Road is off the Norcross-Chamblee Road, which branches off the Norcross-Lilburn Road at a little community known as Glover. Glover was a little two-store crossroads. Pleasantdale Road is actually less than a mile from a little community known as Pittsburg where the Tucker-Chamblee Road joins the Norcross-Chamblee Road. At that time Pittsburg was a one-store county road intersection. Most county roads of that day were unpaved dirt or clay – very treacherous and deeply rutted during and after heavy rains.

The Beginning!

In the beginning God created the Heavens and the Earth...and in 1933, me! He introduced me to the world at 12:45pm one afternoon in that little shack on a rural county road in Georgia. My first earthly home! A doctor in Chamblee, Georgia, made the introductions. *I remember it well! God gave me a choice of parents. I chose Mom and Dad;* a great choice, as I would later discover. However, I did not enter this world as a robust and happy baby. I was a very sickly infant. My mother and sister told me later after I was much older, that my continued early journey in this world at that very vulnerable time was somewhat uncertain. I seemed to be making no progress; in fact even deteriorating and unable to digest my mother's milk. My only food source provided no nutrition at all. What to do?! Alas! Thank the Lord for a wise old country family doctor and his medical wisdom mixed with plain old common sense. The doctor told Mom to put me on goat's milk. Eureka! It worked! To assure a supply of goat's milk for me, Mom and Dad got a "nanny" goat. This nanny had to be tied up to keep her from wandering the farm, and those of our neighbors, devouring everything edible, inedible and all of the above. Goats are programmed to do that you know. There was this large tree – oak probably – in our front yard. Nanny was tied to that tree. Did you know that goats are tree climbers? They are. This tree had two or three large low limbs. Occasionally Nanny would be seen in the tree on those limbs stretching to reach every possible leaf. One day Mom and Dad came home to find Nanny had accidently hung herself! Apparently Nanny was too high on a limb and likely jumped or slipped off on the side that did not allow the rope to let her reach the ground. Sad day! But, Nanny had apparently done her job. Anyway, we got a second nanny goat, somewhat smaller than Nanny #1. I guess I flourished well on goat's milk in my early infant years.

This four-room house was home for Dad, Mom and their children, Oreese and Harold. Also living there were Aunt Annie and Grandpa Gilbert, until he died in 1933. My younger brother Richard was born in 1934 (another farm hand) a few months before we moved in December 1934. We needed all the help we could get – I needed a younger brother to pick on – and Oreese needed another younger brother to help Mom care for. Grandma Gilbert had died years ago in 1901. To summarize: Oreese and Harold knew our grandfathers a few years before they died. Our grandmothers had died years before. Grandpa Gilbert died soon after I was born. Mom said that he took a look at me and said I would be a preacher. He missed that call; but I have been a deacon in the Southern Baptist Church for a number of years (currently inactive). Richard knew neither of our Grandparents all of whom died before he was born.

Our little home was set about 100 feet or so off Pleasantdale Road in a wooded area. Of course most everything was woods or farms then. Can't say I remember the home as an infant, but I saw it several times in my teen and adult years. As a teenager and during my young adult years, I hardly gave my infant years in that home a thought, although we never moved far away. When visiting Mom and Dad years later after I had moved away and had my own family, I would take my family on a nostalgic visit to see my first home before it was torn down and the property cleared for *progress!*

As was the custom in the south at that time, all of us kids were called by our middle names: Oreese, Harold, Robert and Richard. However, I am the only one who grew up with a nick name – Bobby. Actually, Dad and Richard called me Robert. My Mom, Oreese and Harold called me Bobby. Later when I would enlist in the United States Marine Reserve, and subsequently the United States

Air Force, all documents would require first name and middle initial. So, I became George. But when I would go home to visit, I was George, Robert or Bobby depending on who was addressing me. It's a wonder that I grew up to know who I was!

Second Home

We moved from Pleasantdale road in December 1934 to my second home on Chamblee-Tucker Road; probably about fifteen miles from Chamblee. I was one year and eleven months old at that time and I don't remember the move. Richard was three months old. *He might remember.* This home was located on the Warren's Farm where we lived until December 1936. I would have grown from a year and a half to about three and a half years old on this farm where Dad also did share-cropping.

This home is the first recollections I have of my life. It was located on a hill above a creek that ran under a bridge on the Chamblee-Tucker road below. The bridge had wooden planks lengthwise on the bridge for cars to traverse the bridge. We lived on a curve in the road about a quarter of a mile above the creek. The house was set upon a slope about 30 yards above the road; a paved road finally – uptown! Across the road from the house and down the hill was some rich farm land by the creek commonly called "bottomland". What I remember about the house was that it had a 'dogtrot.' For the uninformed, that is a long hall-like breezeway running through the house from front to back. Oreese tells me that the floor in the house had gaps between the boards. You could see chickens, dogs, cats and other critters through these cracks. I don't remember, but I'm sure it got rather cold in the winter time. I don't remember the heating system either but I'm sure it was fireplace and maybe a wood stove. There was a barn, which I remember little about, except that it was about 75 feet or so off to the side of the house towards the creek. It was connected to a barb wire fenced pasture where we had a couple of mules – which I also don't remember – but one of them was named "Nell", according to my sister. I remember very little about the house and farm other than what I've already mentioned. However, I do remember playing in the front sloping yard and on the front porch which, I think ran the length of the front of the house. The porch was also very high due to the slope of the yard. In addition to vaguely remembering our neighbors, I remember these four stories from that home:

First: One of our neighbors needed a well dug. I remember standing around watching the activity fascinated by the digging of that hole. Everybody pitched in, as was the custom of the day. Everybody helped everybody: Neighbor helping neighbor. *Those were the days.* The men descending into and climbing out of that monstrous hole in the ground was spell-binding. And finally the finishing touches to place the well curb over the finished well.

Second: The state or county occasionally would dredge the creek under, and on both sides of, the bridge. I would go down with my brother Harold and sit on the slope above the creek and watch the fascinating process for hours. I loved watching the tractors and heavy equipment at work. Some of the workers would occasionally come by and tease or try to scare me, much to the delight of my older brother, Harold.

Third: My mother was terrified of snakes, so my dislike of snakes is perfectly normal. She would occasionally take Richard, my younger brother, and me down to the creek to "fish" or just relax. At about three years old I can only imagine any "fishing" that I might have done. Anyway, my Mother told me this story. It seems that there was this small vine over the creek, which was only a few feet wide and maybe a foot deep at this point. At three years old I don't know how I managed it, but my mother said I crawled out on this vine. I must have crawled out only two or three feet when I saw a small snake in the water. I began screaming. My mother saw me and panicked at the sight of me hanging on that vine just out of her reach, and over that snake. Now, my mother was a Godly person and prayed to God and Jesus often – and tried to teach her children likewise. A kinder, gentler, meeker person never walked the face of this earth since Jesus. She told me she was praying for Jesus to save me from that snake. From the bank of the creek she couldn't reach me to pull me back. Stretch as she might, she could only touch the hem of my pants leg with the tip of her finger and thumb, not sufficiently to grip them; only barely pinch the hem. She said she was praying as she, with that insecure pinch on my hem, yanked. Instantly I was standing upright by her side. Small stuff, you say? Not so. My mother and I were terrified. Her Jesus answered her prayer. I was safe by her side. She then got a very small pebble – remember this was a small snake – and didn't throw it but gently tossed it at the snake. That pebble hit that snake square on the head and in a few seconds it was belly up, floating on the water. Amazing! Mom's prayers were answered and her son was safe.

Fourth: One day I was running from the barn toward the house when I tripped and fell. I fell onto the barbed wire fence with my mouth open. One of the barbs caught my tongue and cut a big gash on the upper surface of my tongue. Of course Dad quickly rushed me to the family doctor in Chamblee, Georgia about fifteen miles away. All was well eventually. How do kids grow up? I know parents wonder and worry all their lives about their children.

That's about all I remember and recall from family stories of the old home-place on Tucker-Chamblee Road.

Third Home

In December 1936 we moved to a farm on Rockbridge Road (also known then as the Norcross-Lilburn Road, but today known as Jimmy Carter Boulevard). It

27

was a 40-acre farm, bordered on one side by a red Georgia clay and gravel road, with adjacent farms each side and a forest on the back side. The farmhouse sat on a slight knoll a little less than a quarter of a mile back from the road in a field by some heavy woods. A small farm lane ran along the property line from the road to the front of the farmhouse. About a hundred feet before the house, the property line did a ninety degree left turn with a fence forming the boundary to the back corner of the pasture. My sister Oreese says that Dad bought the farm for $3,500 with the disability compensation that he finally received from the Veterans Administration (VA) after so many years. It was a beautiful farm of mostly pasture and field which is the norm for most farms of course. The back half of the pasture had a small wooded area of big pines on a hillside overlooking a small stream. The stream was always cool with slow running water. It traversed diagonally across a back corner of the pasture through a small hollow. On top of this hillside, at the upper edge of the pasture, there were two large structures about 100 yards from the front yard of the farmhouse. One was a huge unpainted barn with a large hay loft and tin roof. Next to the barn was a corn crib with a wagon shelter. They were reached from the house by a wagon path along the barb-wire pasture fence to the crib. A small structure next to the crib on the house side was a covered well with a rope-drawn bucket and windlass – the only source of water for the home. It was located at the end of this wagon path to the crib. A corner of the pasture came right up to meet the corner of the front yard. Often the stock (farm animals) could be seen grazing on the hillside near the yard. One horse, Rex, was a young and curious animal of very broad and huge muscular build. He would have made the Clydesdale Horses jealous. Any activity around the house would normally get Rex's attention and he would invite himself to the event in a trot restrained only by the fence and gate. The best way to describe his personality is *'hyper'*, 'type A'. He would trot up to you and almost walk over you expecting some kind of hand-out. He was so huge and robust – full of energy – as to be intimidating to me, and I think he knew it. However, Dad, Harold and Richard could handle him easily. The cows would let you know when you were late with milking time. They would come up to the corner of the pasture and stand around mooing until someone started for the barn. Then they would make haste for their customary stall and feeding trough.

It was here, this farm, that I call my growing-up home where I learned so many things about life: first grade; later a well-pump with cold running water only and piped to the kitchen – no water heater; electric lights with ceiling-hanging bare light bulbs; a four or more party-line telephone (with whom, you never knew) requiring you to check to see if the phone was free prior to dialing. You only hoped for short-winded party-line neighbors. Operator assistance was required for calling outside a very small local calling area. Also, ice boxes before refrigerators ("Frigidaire"); small black and white sometimes TV; and much later a small gas heater for the kitchen – but never one of those modern indoor private conveniences. I would have to wait until I went off to college to experience those. Uptown! Ours was a two-hole-er (outhouse) located about 40 yards from the back of the house. Talk about a visit to the outhouse on a rainy, freezing dark winter night! B-r-r-r! However, for the faint of heart, there was always a chamber-pot located under the bed during winter time.

In the back yard was the smoke-house where, after the fall hog-killing time, Dad would store and hang hams from which we would eat all the next year. There was some really *good eatin'* around home after hog-killing time: Biscuits and gravy, tenderloin and gravy, eggs and hog brains scrambled together with gravy, ham and more ham. Mom was the best cook ever. Dad's tool shed for large farm equipment and blacksmith shop was located at the other corner of the back yard. Dad could do or repair anything with those tools, blacksmith bellows and anvil. He also did a lot of his own automobile repairs.

Although I disliked farm life, I loved the farm. I wouldn't take anything for the experience – and we had a great and loyal friend on the farm: Butch, the best old beagle-hound-buddy a farm kid could ever want. Years later when I had my own family, I said so many times to my two sons Norris and Robert that I wish they could have grown up on that farm. This would be the last real home I would know before I left for college, the working world and a career in the United States Air Force. Flying was my thing – not farming. I know Dad felt deserted. His daughter left home early to get married and his three boys left the farm after growing up to pursue their own goals. Later Dad would offer to sell me 20 acres of the farm – I think in a father's desperate effort to keep some of his family at home. Of course it was a generous offer, but my heart and mind was set on flying – flying some of the military fighters that I would daydream about as they did aerobatics and mock dogfights over my head, while working in the fields. If I had taken Dad up on his offer, I would be a multi-millionaire today due to the commercialization and industrial explosion of northeast Atlanta and the surrounding farm lands.

But I'm not remorseful, other than the disappointment that I know Dad felt. Because later when Dad and Mom were not able to keep up the farm because of their health – and this hurt the most – they were able to sell the farm to a land developer for his building them a new brick house on a small portion of the farm – their first ever new home and first ever brick house! And later after Dad died, my sister and her husband were able to move in and take care of Mom in her seriously ill and final years – in her own home rather than in a nursing home facility somewhere. I feel that this is the way Dad planned it and would have had it in order to care for Mom after he was gone.

*****

CHAPTER TWO
SCHOOL – BEAUTIES, BUDDIES AND BULLIES

The New Home

As I said earlier, it was December 1936 that we moved to the farm on Rockbridge Road in Gwinnett County (Between Norcross and Lilburn, Georgia). I would have been about three and a half years old. Here is where I spent my young years that I will always claim as my home – although the farm and farmhouse have long since succumbed to progress. Except for the sketchy stories and memories that I related from my first and second homes in Chapter one, here is the essence of my growing up; thus the most memorable memories of my family and home before I left home to pursue college and a military pilot career.

First School – Glover School

About a quarter of a mile up Rockbridge Road toward Norcross was the Community of Glover. It was a two-store crossroads (Rockbridge Road and Singleton Road) and a school house, naturally called Glover School – my first school. The stores were very small and in adjacent corners of the cross roads. They carried limited groceries plus candy and soda pop. One room also functioned as living quarters in the back of the store for the owner and his family. The store across the street included a gas pump – and I mean *pump.* You actually pumped the gas from the underground storage tank into a glass tank on top of the tall pump. There was a gage visible in the glass tank that indicated the number of gallons you pumped. When the hose nozzle trigger was squeezed, gas was gravity fed into the car's gas tank. It was a simple life – one grade of fuel, no decision required as to unleaded, leaded; regular, plus, premium or supreme. Just pump!

Glover School: I don't remember much about the farm before I started the first grade in 1938 at the age of five. Normally first grade was entered at age six. However since I would be six in less than six months, I think I was allowed to begin at the age of five. Maybe Mom was just anxious to get me out from under her feet. Just kidding! The school was located about a quarter mile from our house and diagonally across a field to the corner of our farm. So it was just a short walk from home through the field to the school. It was a brick four room school containing grades one through nine, and served as the community's Sunday School and Church on Sundays. Two rooms contained student desks and a teacher's desk. A third room contained student desks plus a stage with dressing rooms behind the stage, one each side for his and hers. The fourth room contained student desks, a couple of tables that served as the lunch room, the kitchen and food counter. About all I remember of the lunch room is that they served bologna sandwiches, milk and lot of white beans – called navy beans, I think – which I now love but hated then. The rooms contained two to three classes – and one teacher. Heating was a potbellied coal stove. It was the boys' chore to keep coal brought in from the outside coal pile and to keep the fire stoked. In the summer heat and humidity, the only air conditioning was open windows. My sister Oreese, older brother Harold, younger brother Richard and I all attended school at Glover. After finishing the ninth grade in 1937 my sister got married, and did not complete high school. I entered the first grade at Glover in 1938, Richard entered two years later. Somewhere between the first and fourth grade I was promoted two grades ahead – thus skipping one grade. I don't remember which grade I skipped, or the reason. I sure don't understand this especially in light of beginning school one year early at the age of five when the customary beginning age was six. So it was in 1941 that I began my fifth grade (fourth year, having skipped one grade) – at eight years old. Thus through my school years until graduation, I was always the smallest and youngest boy in my classes. I don't remember the Japanese attack on Pearl Harbor but I should – I was old enough. I do seem to vaguely recall President Roosevelt speaking on the radio.

After I completed the fifth grade, Glover School closed – 1942. I don't know the reason for the closing. Harold transferred to Norcross High School where he graduated. Richard and I began the school year at Lilburn Grammar School, Lilburn, Georgia. The reason for splitting schools between Norcross and Lilburn was probably based on grade levels and number of students. So it was 1942 that I entered Lilburn School at grade six and Richard entered at grade four.

Back to Glover School: The school building sat on the back side of a leveled graded area on Rockbridge Road. The rear of the school was on the edge of a steep wooded hillside. At the bottom of the steep hill was a small stream about two feet wide and two to three inches deep meandering slowly through the woods. It was about fifty to sixty yards down the hill to the stream. (More about this small stream later). Because of the slope of the hill there was a crawl space under the school accessed by a small opening at each end of the rear wall of the building. It was very dark under the building, but with a moment for the eyes to adjust one could get about fairly safely by crawling or stooping– being very careful of protruding nails and other hazards to the head. There was a rectangular hole about four by ten feet and about three to four feet deep at one end of the crawl space. The reason for the hole was never known to me. But it added to the mystery and intrigue of the dark and scary cavern under the school building. Kids being kids, all kinds of scary stories emerged concerning that mysterious space: Mad dogs, snakes, wild animals, and occasionally a mysterious person – all allegedly seen by a student at one time or another. I'm happy to say that I never encountered any of those things, although I felt that I took my life in my hands whenever I entered that forsaken space many times during my four years at Glover School. My heart was in my mouth whenever I went under there and I was always relieved when I emerged safely into the light of day. For the life of me I can't remember why I ever went into that space. I'm sure it was during hide-and-seek games, curiosity, demonstrating my bravery, or some other dumb reason. But to a five year old kid, it was a life threatening venture.

In back of the school, just outside the right entrance to the crawl space (facing the back of the building), was a covered well. That was our water source. The school had no plumbing of any kind. The water tasted terrible. I couldn't tolerate it and I don't think anyone used it. On rare occasions one might find a dead rat or mouse in a drawn bucket of water. Remember that this was a rural county school – no luxuries! Speaking of no luxuries, it had no plumbing, and no nothing. Remember the small stream at the bottom of the wooded hill behind the school? That was our bathroom plumbing: an outhouse over the stream – upstream (boys) and one about thirty yards downstream (girls). Our toilet tissue was the Sears Roebuck catalog – if one was available. But not to worry, that's the way it was at home too – for all of us. When working in the fields, corncobs work well – a little rough maybe. You had to be careful if you used leaves. *Don't grab the poison ivy!* Can you imagine the absolute field-day that present day health departments, child welfare agencies, boards of education, environmental agencies and other such governmental bureaucracies would have over the conditions that existed at Glover School? We all grew up without such intervention – and survived. And to my knowledge most of us made it to senior citizen status.

First Grade

We had great teachers that I remember fuzzily. But there is one principal I won't forget! More on him later. The most frightening day of my tender life at that time was – the first day of school! But first I want to say that as traumatic as it was for me, there could not have been nicer teachers anywhere on this planet than I had at Glover School, the exception being the principal referenced above. Remember, school was only a quarter mile walk through the fields of our farm to the school – Glover School. Since my brother Harold was attending there in the ninth grade he took me to school on my first day. I don't remember the introduction to the teacher – but I think she was Mrs. Simpson. Nor do I remember meeting any of the kids in the classroom. For some reason soon after I was settled into the class, I became terrified. I jumped up and bolted out the door and down the short hallway to the school yard, with the teacher and a string of kids right behind her trying to catch or corner me. I ran all over that school yard crying and yelling for my brother Harold. That must have been a sight to see for anyone passing by – that little kid (and I was little) running and screaming around the school yard with an entourage running after him. Finally I was cornered and I guess Harold was summoned to help quiet me. But I don't think I would be quieted. Anyway, I don't remember the rest of the day but I'm sure that they let Harold walk me home. No memory of what Mom and Dad did.

I guess it's good that I don't remember. Apparently Mom and Dad were very persuasive though, because I think I was back in school the next day. Harold probably was required to check on me through the first several days.

I was a very timid kid. It was a policy to raise your hand and ask to be excused if you needed to go to the restroom – those outdoor "restrooms' that I described earlier. Anyway, I was in class and needed "to go". But I wasn't about to embarrass myself by raising my hand to ask to "be excused". So I sat there – and I sat there – and I sat there. Finally my bladder said: "OK, enough"! I wet myself good and provided a big puddle under my desk. I thought no one would notice. Then one of the girls (always a tattletale girl) said in a loud voice that I had wet my pants and puddled the floor. I don't remember what happened after that. I guess that's one of those moments so embarrassing that in self-defense your mind erases it from your memory bank.

As I moved up in the grades, one of the favorite pastimes for the boys was harassing the girls. The favorite harassment was pulling the hair of the girl sitting in front of you. Pig tails were a favorite. Of course it was all ways the cutest girls that got their hair pulled. Oh, the beginnings of love! I remember some of the kids' names, but no outstanding events related to them except for one. There was this guy three or four years older and much bigger than me. He had little tolerance for the younger kids but wasn't mean, and sometimes was downright friendly. He had a skin condition which made him somewhat self-conscious. But he played well with the kids at times. One day during a recess, the guys were out throwing rocks up into a locust tree trying to knock the locust down. Why, I don't know – just a sport I guess. But silly me, I decided to walk under the tree for some reason, to pick up the locust I guess. Anyway, this guy decided to launch a big rock up into tree about the same time. Of course down comes the rock onto my head. It was a fair sized rock. He could wield larger rocks than us smaller kids. To me it looked about the size of a softball – but I'm sure it was more like baseball or tennis ball size, and much harder than my head. I got a pretty good (bad) gouge in the top of my head. Of course my scalp bled profusely. Blood was all over my head, face, hands and chest. I thought I was killed! One of the teachers cradled me in her arms trying to calm me. Finally, with towels they got the bleeding stopped. They chastised the guy, but I was at fault as much as he was. He felt bad about it of course. *And I lived!*

About my *unfavorite* Principal that I mentioned earlier: He was a real disciplinarian and would not take any nonsense from the boys. His favorite tools for dispensing his discipline were a knee-high long narrow flat bench with no back, and his long, wide belt. It was long because he was long around. If you misbehaved (based on his rules) he would have you roll up one pants leg above the knee then climb up on the bench. He would slowly pull his belt from around his waist and instruct you stand one-legged on the bare leg, and lift the other leg about calf high. Usually he had three or four guys on the bench at one time. I think I remember a time when I was the only guy on the bench. His instructions were to not to let the raised leg touch the bench. He would slowly march around the bench, belt at the ready. These sessions would probably last about twenty minutes or at least long enough that your leg would get tired and eventually touch the bench. Each time your leg touched the bench, he would pop the bare leg with his belt. For some kids, having been subjected to this discipline at school meant they would likely also be severely disciplined at home. My Mom and Dad were not that severe with their discipline. For other reasons, I only remember Mom taking a peach tree switch to my legs a couple of times, and Dad maybe a little more substantial switch on one or two occasions. *(Imagine that happening in today's culture!).* After completing the fifth grade here, I entered Lilburn Grammar School the following year. Glover School was closed forever as a school.

One other story I remember about Glover School a few years later, although it isn't school related because it had been closed as a school for a few years. The building was used as a Sunday school and church and I often attended there. It seems that there was this girl that I had an interest in. I don't remember the reason for the event, but I seem to remember that there was some kind of play to be conducted on stage. I had a part in the play. Mom and Dad bought me a new pair of shoes for the occasion. I chose a pair of white shoes with the brown 'saddle' side panels. Saddle Oxfords, I think they were called. Man, I thought I was the "Cat's Meow" in those shoes! I just knew that this cute girl would find me irresistible in them. Not only did she not give me a second look, she didn't give me a first look! I think that about sums up my recollections of life at Glover School.

Second School – Lilburn Grammar School

I was nine years old as I entered Lilburn School, Lilburn, Georgia in the sixth grade – 1942. (Remember I skipped a grade at Glover). The school was located just outside of the town on US Highway 29 that ran from Tucker to Lawrenceville, Georgia. Lilburn was a small town with a couple of stores – a clothes store and feed store I think. It also had a small garage and a corner café. The main street through town was lined with the typical Southern small town homes, and split the town with the small businesses either side of the street. There was a large brick church located just outside of town on Highway 29, near the school. There was also a service station on the highway next door to the school that served as a favorite place for students during lunch, recess, and after school while waiting on your bus to return from its first route. It was reached by a short walk along the highway from the school to the station. My brother Richard and I rode the bus to school. The school bus ran Rockbridge Road and, since our home was about a ¼ mile off the road, if Richard and I were late it meant a dash from the house to the bus. Occasionally we would miss the bus completely and would have to wait for Dad to get home from his rural paper route to take us to school – about fifteen miles, which he was not very happy about.

The school building was a long one-story brick building with individual class rooms each side of a long hallway running through the building end to end. One of the rooms served as a lunch room for the grammar school. I don't think the adjacent high school was permitted to use the lunch room. Or maybe it was that the high school students were just too sophisticated to associate with us lower grammar school types. It was a great improvement over Glover School but not much. It did have running water (cold) for a hall water fountain and the lunch room. The restrooms were located at each end of the building, 'his' on one end, 'hers' on the other. They were just outside the double door entrances at the ends of the hallway. But no plumbing! They had a large pit under the fixtures.

I completed grades six through eight here without skipping a grade as at Glover. The teachers were great. The names I've forgotten but I can see their faces. I was not a troublesome student and tried hard to do my homework. And overall, I did pretty good work in grammar school – and tried my best to be teacher's favorite. It didn't always work.

There was this bully of a kid! A mean kid! And I seemed to be his target. He was ugly, tough, had a disfigured face and probably had a rough life at home. It may be an unfair assumption but you've seen kids that you just know have it tough at home. Whatever it was, he took it out on me. He was slightly bigger than me – most of the guys were. I was a small and skinny kid- *cute though* – and those are the types that the cowardly tough kids like to pick on. Recess, lunch time, after school waiting (about an hour) for the bus to return for my route home, those were his times to pound on me, but most of the time it was while waiting for the bus. We never got into any serious bare knuckles facial blows. It was always trading blows to the chest, shoulder or stomach – mainly shoulder – more or less a 'let's see who can hit the other the hardest or who got in the last punch.' He always got the last punch. Occasionally a flurry of fist would fly. That is usually the way we spent our time outside the classroom. Sometimes a teacher would see us and break it up. I don't know what happen to him but he never came back to school after a couple of years; probably a dropout. There was also another guy who seemed to enjoy using me as a punching bag. He was not as bad as the bad-bully however. We traded blows occasionally – nothing serious. It lasted for a couple of years. I believe he may have transferred to another school. In spite of being a punching bag, there was a lighter side to school: There was this cute blonde girl who lived on the county road behind our farm, who rode my bus. However she never gave me a flip.

Somewhere during my *very early years* I realized I had a desire to fly. I don't remember developing this interest in flying, nor suddenly one day deciding that I wanted to fly – it was sort of a latent thing and now began to manifest itself. 'Born wanting to fly' is what I tell everyone since I have no recollection of making a decision to do so. Drawing airplanes was my past time at home and in school. Somewhere in these years I began to build model airplanes. Initially my Mom would help me. Then, as the models got more complex, she sort of dropped out of the projects. As I got older and World War Two was on everyone's mind, my interests became more specialized: I wanted to be a fighter pilot! The first air show I ever saw was at Dobbins AFB, Marietta, GA. There was a B-29, F-80, P-51 and the Thunderbirds (F-84s). I was *drooling* over the fighters. Our home was filled with my models of war planes – especially fighters. The corn crib loft was filled with my models. Aviation magazines were a great source of pictures of all kinds of military planes. I started a scrap book of pictures of military planes. It must have been a couple of inches thick. Whatever happened to it I don't know, but I would sure love to have it now. The magazines carried recruiting ads. Many were for pilot training – especially Aviation Cadet flying training. There was one recruiting ad for pilot trainees that showed an Army Air Corps Pilot Second Lieutenant being pinned with his wings by his girlfriend. The pilot looked like me – *really!* The resemblance was uncanny. This was my omen! I would be a fighter pilot. This interest carried into high school, college and my Air Force Career. By the time I got in, the Army Air Corps had been made a separate service and became the U.S. Air Force on September 18th, 1947 – two years after the war. They were still wearing the brown, khaki and olive drab uniforms. The blue uniform, which new enlistees were issued, was being phased in over the next few years. Anyway, that's about all for grammar school. On to high school!

Lilburn High School

The high school building was a one-story, L-shaped concrete block structure and perpendicular to the grammar school. The grades were: Ninth, tenth and eleventh. Our high schools only went to eleven grades back then. This building had indoor plumbing in the bathrooms! Uptown! Of course, that building was constructed several years after the grammar school building. But it was still a small country school. My graduating class – May 1949 had only twelve students, I think. The high school had a boys and a girls basketball squad. Each squad was made up of a first and second-string team. A basketball team consists of five players, thus our squads had ten players. Our principal/coach didn't like losing and he let us know his real feelings when we were losing. He was also a World War Two veteran Naval Officer and regimented disciplinarian – his naval officer training, I guess. Our boys and girls teams won state championships on a couple of occasions as I recall. But Lilburn High School also had a third-string boys team: Me! Since ten players were required for the two teams, and we had eleven players, I often joked that I was the one-man third team. Because of my athletic prowess our coach allowed me to play for a few minutes three or four times during a season – when we were well ahead enough to ensure winning. We had no gym until later. Our basketball court was dirt – Georgia red clay! It wasn't until my senior year – I think it was – that we had a gym built.

Back then rural schools had six-man football teams rather that the eleven-man team that the bigger city schools had. Lilburn didn't have a football team at all, though some schools in adjacent counties did. We hounded the coach to form a six-man football team, but to no avail. Most of us followed our favorite college teams. My favorite was the Georgia Tech Yellow Jackets in Atlanta, whose stadium was Grant Field. Since we couldn't have a school team, some of us guys decided get together on weekends at one of our home's pasture for a fun football game. The favorite place to gather was in a cow-pasture by the railroad tracks below the home of my good friend John. He lived about six miles away so usually my brother Richard and I would bike to his home, where several other guys and John's brothers would gather for the contest. It was a large, level meadow pasture and was ideal for our games – with a few exceptions. Have you ever played football in a cow pasture? It's an experience! You haven't lived until you have been tackled on a fresh cow patty! Or catch a pass with that *specially treated* leather. But we all were big football fans and the opportunity to play outweighed everything else.

I considered all of my classmates as good friends. But there were three friends that I was especially fond of: One friend was captain of our basketball team and over six feet tall. He was our tallest team member, and therefore played center position. He was a fellow aviation enthusiast. We both swore that we would never get married until we finished military pilot training. At that time the Air Force and Navy required that their aviation cadet applicants be unmarried to enter their program and remain so until graduation. We both favored the Naval Aviation Cadet Program (NAVCAD). After high school however, he got married and joined the Navy. He went on to become a radar operator on the A-1E, as an enlisted aircrew member. After doing a tour in the Navy he was discharged and established his own electronic repair shop. He died many years later of cancer.

We guys would gather at the home of another good friend to play football. His father had a farm with a good pasture for our games. He played guard position on our basketball team and was a great player. On occasions, when we were playing late night games, Mom and Dad would let me go home with him overnight because I had no transportation to get home after the games. He was up about 4:30 to 5:00am to do the milking, feed the stock and get the other chores done before the school bus arrived. Of course I rolled out early to help him. His mom had breakfast ready and on the table before getting on with her chores. Wow! Does bacon and eggs ever smell good early in the predawn morning on the farm? One of the perks (?) of farm life! After high school he joined the Army and became a Tank driver. With his tour in the army over he went on to establish his own bricklaying or construction business.

Third but by no means least, was Charles Stone; one of my best friends through the years. His mom and dad bought the farm three farms over from our farm. They moved down from Connecticut. With their crisp New England accent, the kids thought they talked and acted funny. He was very brilliant, well-educated and a class-act *comic* which delighted some of the girls in the class. Initially, he was not well liked by the guys in our class and by a couple of the girls. I think it was his greater education and brilliant mind that made them envious. Today, I think he would be termed a 'geek-nerd'. I liked him right away and we became lasting friends. He had a car and we would go cruising downtown Atlanta and the nearby suburbs and smaller towns of Decatur, Buckhead, Brookhaven, Tucker, Lilburn and Norcross – *chick-hunting!* We weren't often successful, but occasionally succeeded in making some very nice acquaintances.

Lilburn High School being a small school, the curriculum was very limited. Charles' parents soon realized that he could not get the quality education and curriculum to which he was accustomed; and that they wanted for him. So he stayed only one year at Lilburn and then transferred to North Fulton High School in Buckhead (Northeast Atlanta area). We still got together frequently to do fun things like roaming the woods around our and our neighbors' farms. People weren't so skittish then and you could walk through a neighbor's farm and woods with hardly a notice by anyone. Charles, Richard, and I, and other farm buddies, would occasionally camp out in our pastures, build camp fires, tell stories (mostly ghost stories) and talk about girls, among other things. We slept on quilts, blankets or tarps under a bright yellow moon, countless stars and with God watching over us; no tents, no sleeping bags, no comforts. The sun would wake us all dew-covered from the night. Then we would sleepily wander to our homes and our Mom's kitchens for a delightful breakfast. Speaking of dew, I remember the motto the The Atlanta Journal-Constitution newspaper used when Dad delivered those years ago: "Covers Dixie like the Dew."

In some of our cow-pasture experiences Charles and I would often wrestle for fun but never seriously. My Dad loved to watch wrestling on the small black and white television set we had. Mom occasionally watched the wrestling matches and voiced her concern for the wrestlers. She was afraid that they were going to get hurt. All the grunting, yelling, body slamming and tossing about convinced her that it was a very dangerous sport. Charles and I tried in vain to convince her that it was all fake; that they weren't hurting each other at all, just acting – that they were performing a pre-rehearsed show. She wasn't convinced. We decided to convince her once and for all. We would do a fake wrestling match for her. So we told her that we were going to convince her that wrestling was a big fake. We squared off in the wrestling stance. Then we locked each other in *mortal combat!* We rolled and kicked, twisted arms, legs and necks. We yelled and grunted. We slammed the floor with our hands and feet. You would have thought we were killing each other. Mom did! She yelled for us to stop, that we were going to hurt each other. But we kept on punishing each other with our killer holds, leg and arm twists. Finally when we thought we had enough to convince her, we jumped up all smiles and said: "See, it's all fake!" I don't think she was ever convinced.

In 1949, after high school, Charles joined the Marine Air Reserves fighter squadron VMF 351 at the nearby Atlanta Naval Air Station, Chamblee, Georgia and served as an aircraft flight line mechanic on the F4U Corsair. He later completed Aviation Electricians School learning to maintain aircraft electrical and instrument systems. After assignments to El Toro and Cherry Point Marine Corps Bases he was discharged in 1953 as a Sergeant. He used his VA benefits to re-enter Georgia Technical Institute (Georgia Tech) Atlanta, Georgia and graduated with an electrical engineering degree. He went to work for an electrical engineering firm and would later establish his own electrical engineering company. While attending Georgia Tech he married a wonderful girl, Doris Findley, and now has a great family, grandchildren and great-grands. He and his family eventually moved away.   However, we continue to correspond.

In high school there were three girls that I really liked and tried to impress. Not only did I not get to first base with them, I struck out at home plate. They were older than me.   And they always seemed to date much older guys for some reason. Skipping that one grade back at Glover School condemned me to being about the youngest kid in my classes – and the smallest – The 97-pound weakling of the Charles Atlas Ad! Anyway, there was this one cute girl with long blonde hair who was about the cutest thing that I had ever seen in my young, tender and innocent life. There were four problems: One: My older brother Harold. She was Harold's girlfriend. Two: She was older than me. Three: She was a grade ahead of me. And four: I was a small, skinny kid. But not to be deterred: After school I would ask to carry her books to the store on her way home while I waited for my school bus to return for its second trip. She lived in Lilburn within walking distance of the school. She would humor me and let me carry her books. After all, they were heavy. Then she would tell Harold. I'm sure they got a great laugh out of it. Harold would tease me later. But I kept asking to carry her books until she graduated that year. I had a few other heart-throbs in high school, but they were all one-sided affairs: Older than me, and dating older guys. *Unrequited love!* One was the girlfriend of Harold's buddy. Boy, can I pick 'em! I'm sure they got a kick out of that too. Believe it or not, I even dated a couple of girls in my class. Those relationships never went anywhere either. Could have been the way I combed my hair. Anyway my real heart-throb was airplanes!

My interest in becoming a military fighter pilot caused me some concern because of the limited curriculum our school had. We had no trigonometry or geometry classes. With the emphasis on math, trig and geometry in flight training, I felt that I would be greatly disadvantaged if I didn't get the classes. I spoke to our principal about my interest in becoming a Navy Pilot. Remember he was a former Naval Officer. I told him that I would have to transfer to another school (probably Tucker High School) in order to get a foundation in the two courses that I would eventually need. All schools are interested in maintaining a high student population because it meant more funding for them. The principal quickly agreed to provide me a personal tutor for the two courses. She was a knock out! It's a wonder that I learned anything – but I did: *Trig and geometry I mean.* She was very wise. She would come in and assign sections for study, write problems on the chalk board, assign problems in a work book, then leave the room so I could *concentrate*. She would come in occasionally to see how I was doing, check my work, answer questions then leave. I really did enjoyed trig and geometry.

The rest of my high school years were pretty mundane. I had good teachers. We had the usual auditorium assembly before class each morning with announcements, invocation and the Pledge of Allegiance. We weren't politically correct; *just God fearing Americans* - thank goodness! Can you imagine the ACLU or our courts allowing that to happen today? I was in a couple of school plays. No Hollywood offers. But at the age of 16, I GRADUATED: May 1949!

*****

CHAPTER THREE
FARMING, FANTASIZING, AND GROWING UP – I THINK!

Home on the Farm

Dad had bought a 40 acre farm on Norcross-Lilburn Road (Rockbridge Road) in late 1936 for $3,500. He moved us into the farmhouse on the property in December of that year. My sister Oreese, the oldest child (11 years older that myself), completed the ninth grade at Glover School in June 1937. She married in September at the age of 15 and moved away with her husband. She later went to work for Lovable Brassiere Company, from which she retired. Am I allowed to say 'brassiere'? Anyway that was the name of the company. My older brother Harold transferred to and graduated from Norcross High School. A couple of years later he was given an all-expense-paid cruise to the South Pacific islands with free meals and lodging: courtesy of his Uncle Sam – and the United States Navy (WW II: New Guinea and the Philippines), Drafted in August 1943 and discharged December 1945. He later went to work for General Motors, from which he retired. Therefore, except for the few years with Harold while he finished high school and before being drafted a couple of years later, it was mainly my younger brother Richard and me growing up together on the farm. A year and some months separated Richard's and my ages but our interests varied greatly, especially as we gravitated into high school. I think the one common interest we shared was our determination not to be a farmer.

I remember growing up during the war years (World War Two) although I can't remember the actual Pearl Harbor bombing by Japan. I had an interest in being a fighter pilot and followed newspaper accounts of enemy shoot-downs by our pilots. I also watched the news accounts and news reels of how the ground war was going – or not going. Everyone endured rationing and shortages of everything. Farming was considered an essential occupation. So was the delivery of newspapers which Dad did throughout rural areas in several counties. So he was issued gasoline rationing stamps which provided a little more than the normal allocation. Luxuries were practically on hold – considering that we were never affluent enough to provide for much more than the necessary essentials. Everything was saved and collected for the war effort: Scrap medal, toothpaste tubes, rubber, tinfoil, paper and just about everything imaginable. We bought War Bonds and Savings Stamps. I remember taking my meager allowance and buying Saving Stamps until I filled a stamp book which was traded for a bond. The theme was: Use less, use longer! V-E and V-J Day: I vaguely recall them. But finally the war was over. We won! What a great relief! My brother would soon be coming home. Mom was overjoyed!

Richard and I shared the same childhood friends from neighboring farms, but in school our friendships pretty much revolved around our classmates. After high school and working a few months I entered North Georgia College at Dahlonega, Georgia to acquire the two years of college necessary to apply for Naval Aviation Cadet Pilot Training. My dream was to become a Marine Fighter Pilot. While in college I enlisted in the Marine Air Reserve Squadron at the Atlanta Naval Air Station, Chamblee, Georgia, the same Marine Reserve Squadron that my high school friend Charles had joined. Immediately upon completing the two years of college after cramming nights and days for the final exams, I applied for Naval Aviation Cadets. I was rejected due to a minor difficulty with the eye chart. I was totally devastated! That's putting it mildly. I will discuss more on that later. I have always felt that had I rested from my final exams a few days before applying for Naval Aviation Cadets I might have made it.

In 1952 Richard and I enlisted in the United States Air Force during the Korean War, but neither of us was sent went to Korea. Richard did not share my interest in flying. This interest took me through more than thirty-three years of military service. After one tour of duty with the Air Force, Richard went to work with Capital Airlines reservations and became involved in their early entry into computer operations. So he got a firm and early foundation into the computers of the future. Capital later merged with United and after retiring from United, he developed a keen interest in radio controlled model airplanes which he shared with his son, Stuart.

Dad and Mom

Before I get into my growing up on the farm, I want to talk a bit about the life that Dad and Mom had on the farm. They had a hard, hard, life and were very poor, and Mom was sometimes sickly. Today some people will fake being "poor" for the benefits they will receive. Dad and Mom were poor but didn't know it. All they knew was that they had to struggle to survive and knew everyone else was doing the same thing. What a difference in their and today's culture!

Dad

Dad struggled so very hard on the farm to put food on the table. And that was what his farming was all about – staying alive. Cotton was the primary crop, with corn, hay and hogs next, if hogs are a crop. A large vegetable garden was a necessity. It was not a commercial farm, although Dad would sell his cotton after it was picked and baled. The corn was for the dinner table and making bread and flour. Corn was also for the cows, for Rex and Nell – our plow horse and mule, and for the hogs. Every farmer knows that the luck of the draw, prayers and weather dictates the success he will have with his crops in any given year. Dad tried very hard to get his sons interested in working the farm. We worked, but our hearts were not in it. The struggle for survival was there hidden in the recesses of our minds, but it didn't manifest itself to the degree that we really appreciated the burden that Dad and Mom had on their shoulders until much later in life. Sometime around 1937 (I think) Dad took on a rural paper route as a carrier for the Atlanta Constitution in order to help make ends meet. I don't know how he did it and maintained any reasonable health – except for the necessity and his sheer determination. He would get up about 3:30 a.m. every morning, every day of the year, go get his newspapers, and drive for hours over country roads of all description, and through small towns delivering them. He would get home about 8:00 a.m., have a quick breakfast and then go work the fields until dark. After supper he would catch the news and then go to bed to start all over again at 3:30 a.m. the next morning – rain, shine, snow, sleet, blizzards or scorching heat – mostly country roads! You name it, and Dad delivered papers in it. Dad did this year after year for about 15 years. Almost never a vacation! I do remember one vacation that he and Mom took, but more on that later.

Oreese said that on the old farm where she and Harold were born, Dad had a Model-T Ford with curtains to keep out the weather. Later he got a Star with roll down windows. On this farm where Dad began the paper route, I remember a Ford Model-A four-door sedan with a clutch and gear shift lever in the floor; and later a 1939 Chevrolet with a vacuum gear shift lever on the steering column. Later, the automatic transmission would greatly relieve the work load on Dad with all the starting and stopping required. After I learned to drive and began dating, I loved that gear-shift lever in the floor. It was an opportunity to accidently brush the girl's knees while shifting gears. Alas, car manufacturers soon developed the gear-shift-lever on the steering-wheel column. Richard and I would alternate helping Dad on Sundays when the papers were too big for Dad to drive and roll. When we went to church, Dad would doze off and Mom would elbow him occasionally. Usually she would let him sleep. She knew how hard he worked, so would just let him be. He suffered from a back injury received during the occupation of Germany after World War One. It bothered him severely but I never recall him complaining except on very rare occasions. Mustard gas exposure during the war caused him respiratory problems in his later years but I'm sure his chain-smoking also contributed significantly. He spent many days in and out of the Veterans Hospital at Oglethorpe, Georgia for his respiratory problems. I believe that both of these conditions, mustard gas and chain-smoking, caused a premature end to his life at age 69. I also became a chain-smoker by proxy. Going with Dad on the Sunday morning paper deliveries during the winter months with the windows up, he would fill the car with his cigarette smoke. It would make me sick. I would roll my window down and stick my head out into the frigid winter air in order to breath. I don't know how Dad could breathe in all that smoke.

Mom
Mom was a frail, sickly and small woman. A gentler woman and greater Christian you would not find. If you knew Mom and didn't love her, there was

definitely something wrong with you. I could not have picked a better Mom. She would give you the last bite of food, the last of whatever she had if she thought you needed or wanted it. Never, never, would she utter an unkind word about anyone. She suffered with severe headaches and frequent 'smothering' spells. Her smothering spells were quite frightening for me, largely I guess because I was helpless to help her. They were very frightening for her also. After all, if you can't breathe, nothing else matters. Suddenly for no reason she would jump up, or quit what she was doing and grab her throat and yell: "I'm smothering! Get me some salt water!" She literally stopped breathing. She would run to the back porch, fling the door open, and we would hand her a salty glass of water. After swallowing several gulps she eventually would throw it up and all would be fine. To my knowledge there was never any medical diagnosis for this, or any medical intervention that cured it. But she 'out-grew' the problem later in her life.

Mom worked the fields too: I can see her now in the cotton field; back aching and crawling on her hands and knees; dragging her heavy cotton-filled pick sack by the strap over her shoulder. Every ounce of skin covered to shield her from the sun – and her big sun-bonnet for extra protection. Then the housework! How did she and Dad do it!? A couple of times a month Mom would do the wash in two large black wash pots over fires in the back yard. She later hired a lady to help her. The lady was the wife of a neighboring black farmer. She would bring her son with her on these wash days. He was about my age and we would play and roam the farm together while our mothers labored over the hot wash pots.

On top of all of this, Mom would somehow find time for her self-taught oil painting. She also did some short-story writing. She was a talented lady and loved these two indulgences of hers. To her dismay, she could never get anyone in the family interested in her talented paintings or writings, or even to encourage her. She could not find any publisher interested in publishing her works. In her later years she became interested in making ceramic items which she combined with her painting talent. She did sell a few ceramic pieces and paintings – but never for what they were worth. She never seriously attempted to market her ceramics and paintings because she was a very humble person and felt they were not worthy. Mom was as good a person, neighbor, friend and Christian as you could ever find! She agonized so much for her children's well-being, safety and Spiritual health! I remember sitting at her knee on the front porch while she read from the Bible and told Richard and me Bible stories. I know she cried floods of tears for all of us – her only daughter Oreese that had a marriage go bad, her oldest son Harold who was in the Navy in the South Pacific during World War Two, and her two younger sons Richard and me who enlisted in the Air Force in 1952 during the Korean War. I know Mom felt like life had dealt her another unfair blow, although Richard and I never went to Korea during the war. I remember during World War Two while Harold was in the

South Pacific, my interest in flying and wanting to be a fighter pilot and fighter ace (at about the age of 10) prompted me to say to Mom: "I wish I was old enough to be a pilot in the war!" That hurt her terribly, the fact that I would want to go away to war and maybe get killed.

Mom would do anything within her power to help her children and keep them from harm and all adversity, even to her death at 79. She was that kind of mother – a model for all motherhood.

After Dad sold the farm to a land developer who built them a new brick home on the farm, they lived alone until Dad died in 1963. Mom was 65 years old. She was never one to impose herself on anyone if she could help it. So a year later at age 66, my amazing Mom who had never driven in her life (maybe a horse and buggy), bought a 1955 Pontiac and hired someone to teach her to drive. My family was speechless! Actually though, I seem to remember years before that Harold had tried unsuccessfully to teach Mom to drive an old Model-A Coupe that he had – rumble seat and all. I used to love to ride in that old rumble seat. But I think Harold was mostly having fun with Mom. He would grab Mom out in the yard, pick her up and run around, with her squealing and yelling (delightfully) in fake horror. He would usually end up tossing her across his shoulder before he would put her down. She enjoyed it! In 1975 Oreese and her second husband, M.G. Couch moved in with Mom to take care of her. She still enjoyed her painting, writing and ceramics, and established a ceramic factory in the basement.

My Air Force Career had taken my family and me to many interesting places. From 1974 to 1977, Pat, Robert and I were at Eglin AFB, Florida. We brought Mom down to stay with us for a few weeks, or preferably months if only we could persuade her to stay. Pat arranged for painting lessons for Mom while there. She would take Mom to an art instructor's studio on the beach. Again Mom amazed us with her talents. She was in her earthly heaven! Never before in her life had she had painting lessons – one of her lifelong dreams.

Just as she enjoyed her son Harold's good-naturedly teasing in years gone by, Mom now enjoyed her grandson Robert's turn at teasing her. She reveled in it, all while faking disdain at his mischief. She was also going to get to see him graduate from high school. She had not been able to see her grandson Norris graduate from Dysert High School while we were at Luke AFB, Arizona. Alas, Robert's class graduation was held in the football stadium of Niceville High School, Niceville, Florida. Mom, Pat and I were in the stands with the families and guests, proud as could be, watching the ceremony. Typical of late Florida summer afternoons, a sudden thunderstorm developed with a terrific downpour. Pat and I had to get Mom under an overhanging eave to protect her. Robert received his diploma in a thunderstorm while we were scrambling to keep Mom safe and dry. She missed seeing Robert get his diploma. So did Pat and me.

Mom died at her home a couple of years later at the age of 79. I was not a bad son, but if I could do it again, I would try to be a better son for Mom and Dad.

My Life on the Farm

Where was I? Here, I think. My growing up on Dad's farm was a memorable and happy time – although I hated farm work. Richard and I had the usual sibling arguments, much to the consternation of Mom. We would sometimes argue over chores to the point that Mom would do them. Chores such as milking, feeding the stock, even cutting firewood. She would rather do the chores than have to endure our arguments. We knew that if we procrastinated long enough, Mom would do it. However, Mom drew the line at doing our plowing. If you wanted to get Dad's ire up, all that was needed was for him to come home from his wee-hours of the morning paper route and find Mom doing the chores that we should have been doing. I don't think he ever whipped us for that (although he should have) but his words and looks were a whipping in themselves.

Life on the farm was fun; I just didn't know it then. You learn a lot around the barnyard. I learned what farm animals were about! As a very small youngster watching roosters around a hen house I would ask some innocent questions for Mom and Dad to squirm and struggle with. It all became very clear to me one day however, when Dad said I could go with him to a neighbor's farm to get our young cow (heifer) serviced. I had no idea what that meant. He put a rope around the heifer's neck and let me, likely barefooted, bare-headed and in overalls, lead her as we walked to the neighbor's farm about a mile away on a dirt country road. We met the neighbor and he accompanied us into his pasture where he had a bull grazing. Wow! When that bull saw that heifer he forgot all about his grazing! He came over on the double (make that triple) and proceeded to get intimately acquainted with our heifer. He knew his duty and had no problem with what servicing meant! He acted as though it was a marathon. My young mind was sort of in a whirlwind for a moment, but I finally figured out what *servicing* was all about! I didn't have to ask Dad anymore questions. We were soon on the way home with our heifer following contentedly behind us at the end of a rope. You have heard of "contented cows;" I also then knew what that meant.

Why Everyone Should Grow Up on a Farm

Sometime around the early 1940s, I think we had one of the biggest snow storms that had occurred in that area during my time on the farm. I would have been 8 or 9 years old. There was about four to five inches of snow – deep for that area. Great fun for kids! The farm was great fun at a young age, playing in

46

the pasture, a dirt yard and in the woods. The woods came right up to the side of the house opposite the pasture. After I was old enough to wander the farm by myself, I enjoyed just walking through the woods and taking in nature with all of its beauty and wonder. It was a thrill to come upon a small stream in the woods. It would be lazily flowing along, six to twelve inches deep, with cool clear water. Most of these streams were on neighboring farms. Back then neighbors were neighbors and "no trespassing" postings were practically unheard of. Many times wandering the woods and steams I would get down on my hands and knees and drink the cool clear water right from the stream. I would take off my shoes, if I was wearing shoes, roll up my overall pants legs, get in the middle of the stream and just follow it to wherever it went for a mile or two; sort of my own Huckleberry Finn fantasy. Sometimes I would find an old pine tree and sit down under it, lean back and daydream; *just God and me*. I would fantasize about becoming a fighter pilot. I would talk to God! I made all kinds of promises to Him if he would just let me become a fighter pilot. I'm sure I haven't been as faithful in my promises to Him as He has been in His to me. I did become a fighter pilot – not quite as I had planned, but none the less, a fighter pilot! I'll elaborate more on this later.

After school it was usually to the fields and then homework after supper at night. I would occasionally have trouble with math problems. With Dad having only a sixth grade education, he was very sharp with math. I would get so upset because I couldn't understand the problems as he would explain them. Dad was no dummy. He was very intelligent. Later, as I got into algebra he gradually had to drop out of the tutoring. He had not been exposed to algebra. Although from the instructional material and sample problems, he could usually figure it out. Dad did not spell very well. Nor do I, and I have a master's degree. Heredity I suppose.

Sometimes when Richard and I would have some time we would visit our friends on neighboring farms. In addition to my "wrestling" buddy I've already mention, we had a friend on the farm across the road. Whenever we would visit each other, if one still had work to do, all would pitch in to get it done so we could have some play time. There were others who lived on farms a few miles away, so Richard and I would get on our bikes and head out. And of course Butch, our beagle hound, would be right there tagging along, or more likely leading the way. Whenever we jumped on our bikes, hitched the wagon, or started to leave the house, he was right there – always ready. Sometimes we would encounter unfriendly dogs along the way. I don't know the number of times that Butch came home all chewed up. There was one neighbor's dog, a very vicious Chow, who always seemed to have it in for Butch. Butch was his favorite chew-toy. And Butch usually came back needing a few repairs.

We would bike to nearby towns: Norcross and Tucker. For trips much further we would usually hitchhike – which was no problem back then. No way would I do any hitchhiking today except for dire necessity. There was another friend who later became a minister. A couple of farms over from us was the black family I mentioned earlier. They were really nice and Richard and I enjoyed playing with their son about our ages.

Summer, Barefoot, Buck-Naked and Slick Rock!

Summertime meant bare feet and Slick Rock! The first day of summer was a real treat when we discarded our shoes and went about barefooted in the dirt and sand. Another summer treat was Slick Rock. About two miles from home across a couple of neighboring farms in a densely wooded and hilly area was "Slick Rock!" There, secluded in the dense woods on some farmer's land, was this shallow small creek about four to five feet wide running rapidly down a narrow draw through the woods. It had a large, smooth and nearly flat formation of stone in the stream, that sloped slightly for about twenty yards then dropped over a waterfall about four feet into a pool that had been formed over the years from the waterfall. The pool was about fifteen feet wide at the waterfall and narrowed to rejoin the stream in about thirty feet. It was only about three to four feet deep at the waterfall and shallowed to about ankle deep as it joined the stream on its journey to *wherever*. This was not deep by anybody's measure but it was where I learned to swim – or attempted to swim. The sport was to go upstream about twenty yards, sit our bare bottoms down in the rapidly moving stream over the slick rock and ride the smooth but bumpy rock down to the falls to be tossed into the pool.

The water was cool, refreshing and always hurrying to its destination. We boys had our own personal and secluded waterslide before "waterslides" became cool. I say 'boys' because I never saw any girls there, although they were *always welcomed.* Could it be because we always played and swam buck-naked? *Reckon they ever tried to sneak-a-peek?*

Growing up in those 1930s, 40s and 50s years a kid could wander over the local farms, woods and streams (all fordable) and never elicit concerns from neighboring families. Our only concern was Mom's admonition to be home "by dark" – and in the summertime "dark" came late. There were rarely any posted lands. Farmers cared not that you wandered their land as long as you didn't destroy any crops, bother their livestock – *or their daughters*. You could wander as far as and wherever you dared. Of course, if you wandered onto pasture land you better be sure you could outrun any irate bull that you encountered! It was like that then! Everyone was everybody's "neighbor". Yes, those were the days. Never to be again!

Girls!

When I was very young and innocent, I didn't know much about girls although one of our neighbors had three girls, two about Richard's and my age, and a small daughter. Even then I was obsessed with becoming a pilot, which occupied much of my time. Mom and Dad didn't tell me about the "Birds and the Bees", and somehow always seemed to squirm out of my innocent questioning. I learned by what you might call "on-the-job training" but never *graduated.* However, the mysterious, magical, *wonderful and strangely curious* feelings between very young and innocent boys and girls at play are marvelous things. *God's gift!* The "you show me yours and I'll show you mine" revelation shocked me to learn that girls are different! *Thank you Lord!* I enjoy being a guy and glad I *know* which one I am. Thankfully I still have my originally issued equipment. Again, thank you Lord! I just couldn't figure out how girls could do with theirs what I could do with mine. Slow to learn as I was, I really didn't find out what girls were about until much later. By the time I figured out what girls were about, their moms had already warned them what boys were about! Alas!

A few years later, during my high school years with my friend Charles and me double dating, I learned much more about girls at drive-in movies! Nobody went to drive-in movies to watch the movie. Anyway, the windows were too steamed up to see the movies. How was it that those girls knew so much more than I did? How innocent I was! But I never went the course – intercourse I mean. That intimacy I reserved for my wife and me, whoever she might eventually be. It is so sad that many young people today do not have that reserve. Anyway, I still wanted to be sure to remain single in order to later apply for aviation cadet pilot training.

Big "Harley!"

Later, after Richard and I got our driver's licenses, Dad would occasionally let us use the car for greater excursions. Harold had taught Richard and me to drive. After returning home from the Navy, he bought a big Harley-Davidson motorcycle. He let Richard and me ride it alone occasionally – to Mom's chagrin. He had an old Navy Pilot helmet with goggles. I would put that helmet on and fantasize that I was a navy pilot – and tried to drive like one occasionally. There was this steep hill nearby with a sharp crest, which I loved to go over at high speed. (Stupid)! It would lift me lightly out of the seat and was a great sensation – like flying! That Harley was a big hunk of steel for a skinny weakling like me. If I ever let it fall over I could barely get it upright.

Atlanta Airport

I don't know when I developed an interest in flying. I tell people that I was born wanting to fly because I don't remember a point in my life when I said: "A pilot! That's what I want to be". It was always there, for as long as I can remember. The airport at Hapeville, Georgia (Now Atlanta International Airport or,

Hartsfield-Jackson International) was just southwest of Atlanta. At that the time it was called Candler Field, or Hapeville Airport. There was a big aviation event scheduled there and Dad took his family to see it – although I only remember Dad and me. I think it was the arrival of a new airliner: the Douglas DC-3, which most airlines purchased. I recall seeing it land on what I think as a large grassy area, about 50 yards in front of the crowd. It was a huge silver twin-engine airplane. After landing it taxied back and did a sharp turn toward the crowd. I thought it was going to run over us, but it stopped suddenly and shut down the engines. Later we were walking the airport flight line and came upon a guy selling airplane rides. I begged Dad for a ride. He relented but I think he was as curious as I was. He paid the guy and we climbed on board. I'm not sure Richard was onboard. All I remember is Dad and me. I don't remember the type of airplane but it was high-wing, single-engine, tail-wheel and with a radial engine. It had several seats. I was ecstatic as we took off and climbed over Atlanta and I looked down on the small people, small buildings and small world. The flight probably lasted about 10 to 15 minutes. Flying was definitely what I wanted to do. It was at Candler Field that Harold took flying lessons in the Piper Cub J-3 with his GI Bill after being discharged from the Navy. He quit flying shortly after he soloed, and to my knowledge never flew again – except with me years later. It was a Piper Cub that I soloed at the age of 16 at a small clay strip near Lithonia, Georgia in 1949. More on that later. When Harold was flying at Candler Field, they flew with radio receivers only, no transmitter. Tower instructions were by lights, and acknowledged by wagging the ailerons or rudder. Imagine that at the Atlanta International Airport today; the old Candler Field.

Making of a Fighter Pilot

Very early in my life I began building model airplanes. Then, models were made of balsa wood sheets with printed parts that had to be cut from the sheet with a razor sharp knife. My fingers were always cut up from using double and single-edged razor blades. Building models from balsa sheets was very tedious: Hundreds of pieces, some so small they were difficult to hold. I built them on the floor or kitchen table since we had no spare space to use as a work bench. When my mess was spread out over the floor, everyone had to carefully step around my area. Mom helped me with the difficult pieces. In fact she did a lot of work on my first rubber-band wind-up flying model. It flew! About ten feet, I think. I believe it was a T-6 military trainer. But as time progressed, so did I in my model building. I only built military models, mostly fighters of course. None of them flew well, but I kept building them. Later on I chose to build non-flying scale models which had to be cut from solid wooden blocks. I had them hanging from the ceiling, on shelves, desks – plus covering the ceiling in the old corn crib. A neighbor's son who was a few years younger than me loved the piano. He practiced his piano more seriously than I built my model airplanes – if that was possible. He commented to my Mom that he didn't know why I spent my time building those "silly old airplanes"! Of course I couldn't understand why he spent his time practicing on that "silly old piano". But he went on to become an extremely talented and much sought-after professional musician and teacher, and has had several students attend and win awards at the Julliard School of Music in New York. Unfortunately he died in 2014. He was a fabulous piano player – a real Master of his art!

Back to farming! I guess I hated harvesting hay the worst, mainly because of the dusty field, burning hot sun and stifling hay loft with dust so thick you could bite it. The hay would be raked into long rows by a ride-on rake pulled by Rex and old Nell. After raking into these long rows we would pitchfork it into larger piles for pitching into the wagon – also drawn by Rex and Nell. Pitching hay into the wagon would often result in a face full of hay if you didn't pitch the hay just right. Dad would pile the hay high onto the wagon to the point where I couldn't imagine it remaining on the wagon for the trip to the barn. But it always did. At the barn, the wagon would be pulled up to a permanent opening to the loft. Usually Richard and I would climb into the loft to keep the hay moved to the back, keeping the opening clear as Dad pitched the hay into the barn. It took both of us to keep up with him. With the sunlight shining through cracks in the wall and small holes in the tin roof, the rays would illuminate the air with sort of an eerie display of rays and swirling dust. Honestly, the dust would be so thick you could almost bite it. I couldn't imagine anyone breathing that air. I usually tied a bandanna around my neck and over my nose and mouth. We might be working in outside air temperatures of 95 degrees plus. In the confined spaces of the loft and under the hot tin roof, I know the temperatures well exceeded 110 degrees – more likely 115 plus. You came out of that loft literally drenched with sweat. Often, when working the farm, I would daydream of when I would leave the farm for pilot training. After a day behind the plow, looking at the *south end of a north-bound mule*, I tried to correlate how this was preparing me for those eventual days when I would be a fighter pilot flying those fighters I saw doing maneuvers over our farm: aerobatics, in trail formations, or just plain flying overhead. I was especially thrilled when one would fly extremely low over the farm. When in the house and I would hear an airplane approaching, I would drop whatever I was doing and run outside to see it. Sometimes there would be an unusual airplane fly over, that is one that was not stationed at the nearby Naval Air Station. Other times there would be an Army Air Corps fighter fly over – or a big bomber. I got to where I could identify most of them by their engine sound. The Atlanta Naval Air Station was located at Chamblee, Georgia about 15 to 20 miles from home. Harold did his Navy Reserve time there after discharged from active duty.

There was another chore that I hated almost as much as pitching hay in the barn loft. In fact there weren't too many farm chores that I liked. Every few years, or when fertilizer was needed for the fields, Dad would decide that we needed to clean out the barn stalls – down to ground level! There were three stalls! Having accumulated for a few years, the manure was a foot or more deep. After shoveling it into the wagon or on to a sled, it was then hauled out to the field for spreading as fertilizer. I could hardly wait for the Saturday night bath! Just kidding. Seriously though, except for unusually dirty conditions, bathing was usually reserved for Saturday night – unless you had a big date.   But dates, too, were usually reserved for Saturday nights. Bathing was done out of a wash basin or big galvanized wash tub. Water was brought from the well and kept in a couple of water buckets on the shelf of the screened back porch. An aluminum dipper was hung nearby for dipping water and for drinking – as a community dipper. If you wanted hot water, it had to be heated in a kettle on the stove. Or you could heat the water in the water reservoir in the old wood stove. We bathed in the kitchen or on the back porch. In the summer time you could bath outside and hope none of the neighbors or visitors showed up.

More farm tales: Plowing wasn't really unpleasant for me, although it got very tiring throughout the day. As always, I usually eased the pain by daydreaming of when I would leave the farm to become a fighter pilot. I rather liked plowing with a 'turner', which was used early in preparation of the fields for planting. The 'turner' was a sharp plow point from which a large curved 'wing' curved upward and outward. The point would dig into the ground and the wing would plow up the ground and throw it over – practically upside down, thus the name 'turner'. This was done to loosen the ground, aerate it, and turn the old crops or weeds under to provide nutrients for the soil. It was a big plow but usually moved along rather smoothly since you were plowing old fields. Plowing new ground is a different story totally.   I'll discuss plowing new ground later. Another thing that I rather liked about turning ground was walking barefoot in the freshly plowed cool sod.   The first day of summer, us kids were usually allowed to throw off our shoes and go barefoot for the remainder of the summer. It was always a great feeling and sensation for the soles of our feet for the first few days while our soles toughened up. Following behind the plow and in the deep furrow was a treat. Of course, a day of staring at the rear end of old Nell or Rex left a lot to be desired. Walking barefoot behind the plow and the deep furrow also had its hazards. I remember the time that I was plowing merrily along – barefoot of course – and suddenly the plow turned up a snake about a foot and half long, right in the furrow I was walking and about to step on! I would love to have a video of that event. Of course videos were unheard of in those days. My feet surely flew up above those plow handles and I came down about as straddle-legged as I could get. You can believe that the rest of the day was spent head down and eyes on the ground where I was stepping behind that plow. I don't think the snake was poisonous, but a snake is a snake. I'm sure I killed it. But I'm hard-pressed to relate that snake incident to my preparation for flying. Maybe it's the hours of boredom with moments of stark terror attributed to flying.

Mom would often bring us water and a biscuit. Or if Dad was in the field, she would send us to him. Generally when we would stop plowing for dinner (lunch), or at the end of the day, we would unhitch Rex or Nell and take them to the barn for watering and a few bites of hay or corn for lunch or supper. Usually I would climb upon Nell and ride that old boney ridge of a backbone to the barn – bareback of course. Rex was too high-strung, big and muscular for me to ride him. He was always ready to leave the field for the barn. Sometimes you would literally have to hold him back. I would lead him, and still it seemed he would try to walk over me. One day I led him into his stall – as was the procedure for Rex. You could turn Nell loose and she would go into her stall. Not Rex! As I led Rex into his stall, I had to turn him around so I could get back to the door. Of course, this placed Rex between the door and me. As he turned he leaned against the wall and I had to duck under his stomach to keep from being crushed, then I dashed for the door. To this day I think that was a deliberate attempt on his part to pin me against the wall. Dad, Harold and Richard seemed to handle him OK.

Plowing new ground: New ground was a new field carved out of a woody or scrub brush area. For years it was identified as such and had roots, rocks (all sizes), sprouts, and stump remnants underground. Being underground and out of sight of course, you usually found them when the plow tip encountered them. Roots were the worst and they were so numerous. Plowing new ground behind old Nell was generally no problem. She was so old and slow that the plow tip encountering an immoveable root was no big deal. But Rex! Now that was a different story. He was young, strong, and as I said earlier, hyperactive. So he moved right alone at a rapid pace pulling a plow. He could sense when it was near quitting time and the closer we got to quitting, the faster and more anxious he got. Moving along quickly behind that plow with it handles about waist-high would provide a painful jab in the gut when the plow tip snagged an underground, unyielding root. I recall a time when I was working our new ground behind Rex. Of course you anticipate the unseen roots, but that doesn't help much. Rex was at his usual impatient and quick pace. Suddenly the plow grabbed a humongous underground root! I thought the plow handle had ruined me when it stabbed me in the gut. Fortunately it didn't. But the sudden snag jerked Rex back so quickly it sat him back on his haunches. But it didn't deter him. He was right back up and pressing on like the locomotive he was.

Another of the chores I really hated didn't involve Nell or Rex at all. And that was chopping cotton and hoeing corn. Cotton was planted by a planter pulled by either Rex or Nell that planted the cotton in a continuous row. Chopping cotton was done when the cotton was young and tender and out of the ground about a couple of inches high. A hoe would be used to chop excess young cotton plants out of the row leaving the best plants a few inches part for growing room, and at the same time digging out grass and weeds that had grown among the cotton. Weeding would have to be repeated several times until the cotton stalks were couple of feet high. The corn was planted also by a planter (or by hand) a few inches apart. It required weeding with a hoe often, to keep the corn stalks healthy and free of weeds. Both the cotton and corn also required fertilizing – sometimes by hand.

Picking cotton: Picking cotton was a back-breaking job. I've already described how Mom would be bent over or crawling along on hands and knees. She would occasionally call out in pain from her back. I've done the same. What I describe as occurring on the farm pretty much applied to Richard and me; but most of my comments will be my experiences. Oreese and Harold had similar tasks while they were working on the farm. Oreese married young, so she was not on the farm while Richard and I were farm-hand age. Harold was there with Richard and me only for a short time, since he was much older, having been drafted into the Navy and later left home to work in industry – General Motors.

I hated picking cotton second to harvesting hay. Probably pulling fodder (from corn stalks) was third. Extreme heat, high humidity and heavy cotton pick sacks made for a miserable time. Additionally, I was constantly on the alert for the large green worms on cotton stalks. There were two types: one stubby and fuzzy like a large caterpillar and the other a long, green, segmented worm with horns at each end. It had eye-like patterns along each side of its body and was very mean-looking. Both types of worms stung and hurt severely. Thus my apprehension as I constantly searched the cotton stalks while I picked the cotton from the bolls. The worms were well camouflaged. Just like when I was plowing, I would stop and gaze up in awe and fascination whenever an airplane would fly over. This also gave me an opportunity to pause a moment from the back-breaking cotton picking. Occasionally Dad would admonish me for slacking off on the job. At the end of the day the cotton picked by each one of us would be weighed by Dad. Sometimes he would give us a few cents based upon how much we picked. My cotton never seemed to weigh very much on the scales. The reward for picking cotton was rolling and playing in the cotton piled into the corn crib loft or on the front porch. Also, after the cotton had been taken to the gin and compacted into large cotton bales, they made great mountains to climb and forts from which to fend off imaginary enemies.

About the corn crib: I've already discussed the fact that I had numerous model airplanes hung from the ceiling and around the wall. I clipped airplane pictures and kept in a thick scrap book that I also kept in the crib loft. The loft also had a window about 10 feet above the hard-packed Georgia terra firma below. I would stand in the window and survey the surrounding fields and imagine that I was flying over them in my airplane. Or I would be a paratrooper and bail out of the window. On occasion I would be Superman, with a towel-cape about my neck and jump out of the window as though the cape would enable me to fly. It never worked! I also tried umbrellas as a parachute. They never worked either. As for daydreaming, there were some very tall trees behind the crib at the lower edge of the pasture along the fence. I would climb those trees to the top. There I would sit or stand on the limbs while the trees swayed in the breeze. My imagination would run wild again in my *airplane*.

Heartbreak for Mom

Let me divert here for a couple of stories from my younger years when my Mom's only sibling, her brother, came to live with us for a while. I don't remember, maybe it was a year or two that he stayed with us. He went by the nickname "Jimbo". We never referred to him as Uncle Jimbo – only as Jimbo. Why, I don't know. All my other aunts and uncles were address as just that – "Aunt" or "Uncle". He was an alcoholic. Back then we call them "drunkards". I've mentioned that Mom was a sickly person with several health problems. One of her problems was that she worried a lot – especially about her children. Now she had a drunkard brother at home to add to her "worry list". He had married a first cousin, which didn't last too long, and was now divorced. They had a child. Uncle Jimbo never had a job while with us, that I know of. But he always seemed to have money for booze. A very likable guy he was, drunk or sober – sort of a comedian, especially after a few drinks.

Uncle Jimbo would go away for days without a word. Then Dad and Mom would get a call to come get him out of jail. Generally the police would pick him up drunk – they would find him drunk-out-of-his-mind lying in a water-soaked or muddy ditch somewhere along some road. He sometimes would be roughed up. Other times he would be minus his clothes and wallet. Mom would worry herself sick about him while he was away: Worrying about where her brother was; what kind of trouble he was into. When would he return? Was he dead? And on and on. She knew the inevitable: the call from the police. Jimbo always promised her it wouldn't happen again; that he was going to quit drinking. Mom had heard it hundreds of times before. Alcohol had as tight a grip on him as I have ever known it to have on anyone. He was helpless! I think that experience of seeing my Mom *die a thousand deaths* over her drunkard brother – and what it did to her health – is why I swore that I would never, never take a drink. Exposure to my Dad's chain smoking and his smoke-fog filled car likewise convinced me never to start the habit.

I said that Jimbo was usually a jolly character, drunk or sober. Thank goodness he was not mean when he was drunk, as so many alcoholics are. But I did witness a terrible scene between Dad and Jimbo. I think Jimbo came home drunk –that's a pretty good bet as he was usually drunk or drinking. Mom and Dad didn't allow him to bring any alcohol home, but he usually sneaked it in and hid it. A terrible argument developed. The reason, I don't know. Maybe Dad found Jimbo's liquor. They began to scuffle and moved into the kitchen. Jimbo grabbed a butcher knife from a drawer and started at Dad. Dad was able to disarm him and sent him away. I was amazed because Dad was not a big man. Jimbo was slightly larger and much heavier than Dad. I guess it was due in part to Dad's military training and to the fact that Jimbo was drunk. Jimbo later died from TB – probably complicated by the frequent exposure to the elements spent overnight in ditches filled with mud and water, or lying along the road in a drunken stupor.

Long Lost Uncle!

Another more delightful story: One day when I was probably nine years old, Dad and I were sitting together on the front porch of the farmhouse with our legs dangling over the side. A strange car turned off the road and came down the small one-lane trail to our front yard. Dad jumped down off the porch and went to meet this stranger, who was alone. They talked for a minute or so then Dad yelled excitedly to Mom who was in the house: "Lenna, it's my long lost brother!" They began to laugh and hug. It was Dad's brother, John, who had left home about 25 years earlier without a word – and no word until that moment! He had left home in 1917, the year Dad was drafted for World War One. They came in and as you can imagine were sharing some joyous times. That evening, Uncle John told us many stories of his experiences over the years. One that I recall was about *real* Indians when he was living in Oklahoma. He had me sit on the floor cross-legged like Indians in their tepees as he told the stories and simulated some of their dances and chants. His family was back in Virginia waiting for him to come back and move them all to Florida for his health. He would later bring his family by to visit us during their move to Florida.

My wife, Pat, told me a few years after we married, that her Dad (my Uncle John) had told her he left home for Oklahoma after discovering his first wife (not Pat's Mom) was having an affair with another man.

After Uncle John left for Oklahoma he changed his name. The name change was probably to establish anonymity and sever connections with his family over his hurt. This is all such a family tragedy. However, had this not have been, he would not have met and married Pat's mother, Vennie, who was born in "Oklahoma Territory" before it became a state. There would not have been Pat and my sons Norris and Robert. Yes, Pat and I were first cousins. When Uncle John and his family came by our farm on their way to Florida, Dad's family met Uncle John's family for the first time. Pat was about 14 years old, me about 9. But I was infatuated with her and I never forgot her. Pat's younger sister Carrie and younger brother John, Richard and I played together in the trees by the house, we would climb the trees and swing down yelling like Tarzan. We would let go of the trees when we touched the ground and they would snap back upright. Great fun! Pat was the oldest at 14 and too "grown up" to socialize with us kids. I was disappointed that Pat would not play with us, but I really enjoyed my newly discovered cousins. I remember that John the younger brother could mimic a machine gun terrifically. He was great in our war games! I was amazed. When we visited them in Florida a couple of years later, I still had that feeling for Pat – and I never lost it. It would be some ten years or so later before I saw her again – 1954 when I was home on leave from the Air Force. *I still had that feeling for her!*

To the Fields and Chores Again

Back to farming and pulling fodder: When the corn was harvested and the stalk leaves ready for fodder, I would pull the leaves off the stalks until I had an arm full, then tie them with a strap of corn leaves into a bundle as fodder. The stalk leaves would sting and cut my arms and hands. Many times this would be done in the blazing sun and the sweat in the cuts would sting terribly. This would be done bare-handed, bare arms and bare-backed. In fact, Dad and we boys never wore gloves for farm work. We didn't have them. Sometimes I would wear long sleeves and button up the shirt collar, but this was so stifling in the heat. Like the hay being pitched into the barn loft, the bundles of fodder were flung into the barn loft opening. They would have to be pulled back into the loft and stacked to be fed to the animals later. As with hay, the dust and heat in the loft under the tin roof was punishing.

There was never *nothing* to do on the farm. After plowing was laid-by, when the final plowing is done prior to harvesting and the fall harvesting done, farmers generally relax somewhat through the winter until time to begin preparing the fields for next year's crops. There were continuing chores to do such as daily caring for the animals, milking, the ever present need for equipment and building repairs – and for Dad, the 24/7, 365 days a year rural paper route. The farmer and the weather are either the worst of enemies or the best of friends. Rain is necessary for the crops of course. But when it comes at the wrong times it can be disastrous, such as on unharvested crops still in the field. Rain storms can ruin cotton still in the bolls on the stalk and hay left in the fields. Drenching rains can cause erosion – always a problem. Blistering sun and droughts can burn up crops. Farming is not without its hazards. Farm equipment is nothing to be careless around – nor the farm animals. I've mentioned my near miss in the stall with Rex. We also had this young bull by the name of "Buck". He liked to show who was boss, occasionally. One time I thought he was going to come into the feed room after me while I was preparing to feed the cows prior to milking. But a pitchfork in the face is a pretty good deterrent. Sometimes he would lower his head, tuck in his chin as though he was going to charge you and roll those round menacing eyes up at you. Fortunately he had no horns. Speaking of milking, how does a urine-soaked cow's tail laced with manure swished across your face while milking sound? Well, it sounds: "swish" and "splat"! It also stings terribly. What about a cow sticking her foot into the milk bucket after it's nearly full or the cow literally kicking the bucket? Or stepping on your foot? Fun on the farm!

Uh Oh! Are They Still There?

I've mentioned my falling on barb wire and one of the barbs splitting my tongue. Oh yes! Hay has another hazard. When the barn was full of hay, the spill-over would then be stacked outside. It was stacked on a tepee-styled frame. For support of the hay and the tepee structure, pine stakes about an inch and a half in diameter and three feet high would be driven into the ground and attached around the frame. After the hay was stacked onto the frame it looked like a large hay dome – the frame and stakes not visible just under the surface of the hay. Well, it was great sport to climb to the top of the stack and slide down the side. (You know what coming, don't you?) One day, when I was about 10 years old, I slid down the side of a hay stack. I was snagged abruptly about two-thirds of the way down the side by one of those hidden beveled stake ends – not by my overalls, not by my leg, but my very private parts. Yes, my scrotum and testicles! Now, this flipped me forward and left me hanging upside down by my private parts. Dad heard my yelling and came running over and un-snagged me. I thought I was ruined. He rushed me to our family doctor in Norcross. The doc extracted about an inch long sliver of a splinter from my private parts and applied some antiseptic. He said there was no damage done. I have the scar to prove the incident if anyone is interested. Yes, they are still there, both of them! I also have a great son, Robert, for proof.

Another rather scary summer event would be a mad-dog scare. It seems that during the summer there would be a few sighting of mad dogs – real or suspected. This always caused me to stick close to the house for a while until I got the courage to venture out again. Biking or walking the country roads and spotting a strange dog always got the hackles up on my neck. I don't know if I ever saw a mad dog, but I saw a few stray dogs that could have very well have been mad.

A Tractor!

After a few years, Dad got a small farm tractor: a Farm-All Cub. Uptown! It made farming a bit more tolerable. Harold, Richard and I enjoyed using that tractor. Sure beats following behind a plow! The sad fact was that it reduced, and eventually eliminated, the need for Rex and Nell. Dad sold them both. I didn't really hate seeing Rex go – well I did too! He was going to another farm. But our mule, old Nell! Her usefulness as a farm mule was all used up. She was so slow. I was really sorry to see her go, because I knew she was going to the "Big Glue Factory in the Sky"! Mom was kind of broken up over seeing her go, too. That very much sums up my farming experiences, although there are many more events if only I could remember them.

The Wild Blue Yonder!

Extracurricular activities: Dad would give Richard and me an "allowance" weekly – about 25 cents, I think. On the Sundays that we helped him with the paper route, he would usually give us and extra quarter. Finally I had enough allowance to buy one hour of flight instruction in a Piper Cub J-3 at the Lawrenceville airport about 30 miles away. I logged my first hour of flight instruction on September 15th 1948 at age 15 in a Piper Cub J-3 number NC7366H. I would hitch-hike to the airport or go with a friend. You could take flying lessons at any age the instructor would take you. But you were only eligible to solo at age 16 or above, when your instructor thought you were proficient enough. Age 17 was the minimum age that you could acquire a pilot certificate. The airport was located west of town on the left side of the present Georgia Highway 20/124, just before they split. The runway was a short, clay/dirt strip and ran perpendicular to the highway, with one end of the strip at the highway. There was a power line along the highway, right at the end of the runway. I witnessed my first aircraft crash there. This single-engine, high-wing airplane approached the runway on final approach over the highway. He was just low enough that his tail wheel caught the power line and it slammed him onto the runway, nose first. The plane's engine cowl and wings were bent slightly and the pilot was rendered unconscious for about 2 to 3 minutes when his forehead hit the windshield. His forehead was bleeding moderately but he seemed OK after he recovered.

Somewhere in the same time-frame, plus or minus a year or so, I saw the results of another aircraft crash but did not witness the crash. The crash occurred in a field about half way from our farm to Norcross. It was either a T-6 from Dobbins Air Force Base, Marietta, Georgia, or an SNJ from the Naval Air Station at Chamblee. (The T-6 and SNJ are the same aircraft; except the Air Force and Navy designate them as T-6 and SNJ respectively). This aircraft's fuselage had separated from the wings. Except for some dings, a bent prop and broken canopy, the fuselage and wings seemed mostly undamaged. It must have hit the ground in a relatively level flight attitude. Hearing of the crash, I went up to see the crash site. The two pilots had already left or had been taken away. I didn't know their fate or status. There was no sign of injuries. And no one was guarding the crash site! No taped off area! You could walk right up to the fuselage and look into, or climb into, the cockpit or walk on the wings. Imagine that happening today!

Back to the Lawrenceville airport: The airport was owned and operated by a World War Two P-51 fighter pilot, who was also a Georgia Air National Guard pilot (P-47s). I think his name was Martin. He was my instructor, and signed my log book as "SAM". Like thousands of World War Two pilots, after the war he bought an airplane and airport and stayed in the business. He didn't seem to take much interest in instructing. But knowing that I could only fly about 30 minutes every other month or more on my allowance, I think he knew that I wouldn't be flying often enough to make the training effective. Anyway, I enjoyed the opportunity just to fly. I loved it! Flying lessons were $3 an hour.

Back then flying regulations were very relaxed, especially away from populated areas. We did the basic maneuvers: turns, climbs, descents, takeoffs and landings. Occasionally we would do tight turns and lazy-eights, which I loved. The lazy-eights were done at 90 degrees of bank, not the 30 degree banks that the FAA limits them to today. It's a different FAA today! Being new to aerial maneuvers, it seemed that the world was the major factor and would maneuver around the airplane. As I developed more experience in flying, the airplane became the major factor and would maneuver about the world. The difference is acclimation and flying experience. There is a saying among pilots that you're not really a pilot until *you* fly the airplane, rather than the airplane flying you. Landings are the most troublesome for most student pilots. I was no exception. I just couldn't get the hang of it. Of course, flying every other month or less for only 30 minutes a lesson didn't help. Normally the optimum is three times a week at about 45 minutes to an hour the first few hours and then an hour to an hour and a half each lesson thereafter. The average dual flight instruction before solo is six to eight hours. On April 25, 1949 after 12 hours of dual instruction and still no solo, I decided to try another airport and instructor. On May 15th I switched to a small airstrip south of Stone Mountain, Georgia, near the town of Lithonia, where they also had the Piper Cub J-3. The J-3 was the primary student pilot trainer those days. As at Lawrenceville, the airstrip was a short dirt/clay runway. It was carved into a slight knoll and known as Gunn Field, named for the owner and operator of the strip. That 800-foot high chunk of Stone Mountain granite was a great landmark! Hard to get lost! But that was back when the skies were clear and not obscured with haze and air pollution. You could see forever!

World's First Flight Simulator

In the meantime, I had built the world's *first airplane cockpit simulator* – at least as far as I was concerned. I got some old boards, lumber, nails, broomstick and some cord. The floor was made of boards. Then I made an instrument panel and glued pictures of aircraft instruments on it. The rudder pedals were attached to the floor and pivoted fore and aft, which allowed them to operate like actual aircraft rudder pedals – i.e. when one pedal was pushed forward, the other would move back. They were attached by a closed cord that allowed them to operate in this manner. The control stick was a broom handle, attached to pivot fore and aft in a box that was pivoted to rotate left and right, which allowed the stick to move in all directions. An old straight-back chair was my pilot seat. I would sit for probably 30 minutes to an hour imagining that I was actually flying a fighter plane in the skies over Europe or the South Pacific, against German or Japanese airplanes and shooting them out of the sky. Those

German and Japanese pilots didn't know how fortunate they were that I was still a youngster on the farm, because in my vivid imagination I would have shot them all out of the sky! Harold had a Navy pilot's khaki helmet with goggles that I sometimes wore. It was not unlike "Snoopy" in his pilot's helmet, sitting astride his dog house, in his *Sopwith Camel fighter plane* of World War One fame, always looking for the notorious German Ace, "The Red Baron". Snoopy was Charlie Brown's beagle hound in Charles Schulz's comic strip: "Peanuts". If you're not familiar with it, you've missed one of the most hilarious comic strips ever. In my cockpit simulator I would practice loops, rolls, spins, lazy-eights, tight turns, take-offs and landings. I could imagine the "Gs" as I did the maneuvers. To me, my cockpit was a work of art. But to my musician friend it was a monstrosity of the highest order.

Solo at Last☺!

Back to Gunn Field, Lithonia, Georgia: My instructor there was J.M. Criswell, also a World War Two fighter pilot in the P-47s and flew them with the Georgia Air National Guard at Dobbins AFB. Sometimes he would fly his P-47 over Gunn Field and circle a time or two – then do a couple of high speed low (very low) passes down the runway – and pull up and away sharply. Man, I could hardly contain myself! What a beautiful sight. I would drool at the thought of someday flying one of those. But I was born about eight years too late. Today the FAA and surrounding neighborhood would have a fit! Those were the days! I wouldn't change my young years for all the wealth in the world. After a few more hours with my instructor, he finally soloed me – the customary three takeoffs, patterns and landings: Piper Cub J-3 number NC78413. What a thrill! That was on July 3, 1949 after a total of 17 hours dual instruction. As was the tradition after the solo, the guys grabbed me and cut off my shirt tail. Why I did not keep that treasure, I don't know. It was probably tacked up in the operations shack and I left it there. After the very unceremonious shirt-tail cutting, I asked my instructor if I could take the Cub up again and fly out to the practice area about 15 miles for about an hour. He OK-ed me, so I was soon off again – in my glory! Not walking on cloud nine, rather flying on cloud nine! I was no longer under the critical eye of the dreaded instructor nor tethered to the airport traffic pattern. I did loops, spins, lazy-eights and turns – all the things I had been taught – having a ball! Coming out of the bottom of one of my loops, which pulls about three to four "Gs", I was startled by a very loud "bang"! I thought maybe I had pulled a wing or tail off. But I was still flying so that wasn't it. I leveled off and began to check all the airplane parts. They all seemed to be there. Then I noticed that the door's rear latch had popped open. Apparently I had not fully secured it before takeoff and the extra stresses on it from the high "Gs" caused it to let go with a loud "bang". I told the guys about my big scare on my first solo out of the traffic pattern. They got a big charge out of that. Mr. Gunn, the owner, told me he had never seen a student pilot take an airplane out and do those maneuvers on their first solo away from the field. I loved doing them! I seem to remember that Richard went with me to Gunn Field and got some pictures of me in the Cub. But I don't know where they are. I went on to fly out of Gunn Field a few times after that, but it would be some five years later that I would get my Private Pilot Certificate, once I had some money after enlisting in the Air Force. Not long after my solo and a little time in the local area, I seem to recall flying over to our farm. I'm sure I got Mr. Gunn's OK. It was only about 25 miles and I couldn't get lost. That 800 feet high chunk of granite (Stone Mountain, Georgia) was a landmark you could see for miles and miles. There was no haze and smog such as we have now. My memory of the event is rather fuzzy. Why, I don't know because it would have been a major event for me: away from the airport navigating solo to the farm and back by old fashion "pilotage". Pilotage is navigating by roads, railroads, landmarks, towns, lakes etc. I seem to remembering identifying the farm while still about five miles away. Wow! The excitement factor probably went off the scale. I made a few circuits around our house – low but not low enough to scare myself. I'm not clear as to whether anyone came out to see me or not. I sort of think Mom did. Now to navigate back to Gunn Field. Just "lock on" to that big chunk of granite then about twenty-five miles south and I'm there. What a great feeling! No radio, no control tower, no air traffic control, no Terminal Control Area (TCA) around Atlanta just to the south of Stone Mountain, no special rules air space. This was flying as God meant it to be! One thing that has not changed with flying over the years is that it is still expensive. Three dollars an hour was expensive for me on my allowance when I started flying. It's still expensive!

Years later, after retiring from the Air Force, I did some flight instructing at the Maxwell Air Force Base Aero Club, Montgomery, Alabama. This included teaching the ground school class to student pilots. After the Principals of Flight class on the how and why an airplane flies, I would ask someone to tell me major principal that without which, an airplane would not fly. Invariably they would guess: air, propeller, wings, engine, etc. I would then pull a dollar bill from my wallet, hold it up before the class and announce: "This is the principal thing that makes an airplane fly". However, that joke did not originate with me.

Dreams and More Dreams!

I actually had two major dreams in my young boyhood. Although flying was my first big dream and ultimate goal, and remained my interest and hobby throughout my life, I also had a cowboy hero: Gene Autry, America's favorite singing cowboy! As a really young kid I wanted to be a singing cowboy in the movies, like Gene Autry. In fact I bought a small hollow-body "Gene Autry" guitar and learned a few chords. I thought I looked like and sung like Gene. Occasionally someone would humor me and actually say I looked like him. And of course I believed them. I sure thought I could sing like him. I guess you could say that I wanted to be a singing cowboy superstar and fighter pilot ace! I wasn't asking for much, really. I enjoyed watching the Gene Autry TV and so did

Dad. He would sit up close in front of the TV absorbed in the show and other westerns. We enjoyed watching westerns together. One of his favorites was The Lone Ranger and Tonto.

The date was January 1948. I was just a young teenager. Gene Autry brought his show to the Atlanta City Auditorium. I begged Mom and Dad to take me. Of course they enjoyed Gene Autry also. We went. We were in the lobby before the show when suddenly Gene appeared. I wanted his autograph. All I had was my Gene Autry Friendship Club card. Mom and I went over to him and I asked him if he would autograph my club card. He was gracious enough to do so, and held out his hand and asked for a pen. (Cowboy heroes don't carry pens in their form-fitted cowboy outfit). Of course I didn't have a pen. Mom fumbled around in her purse for what seemed like ages while Gene waited patiently. She finally came up with a stub of a dull pencil (about two inches long). Gene signed my club card without batting an eye and acted as though it was a privilege to do so. I still have that club card today – my hero! They don't make heroes like him for kids anymore. Shame!

As fate would have it, Gene Autry enlisted in the Army Air Forces (AAF) during World War Two, as did many movie stars and famous personalities. He went on to become a Flight Officer in the AAF and flew one cargo mission in the China, Burma, India (CBI) Theater. After returning to the movies following the war he continued to fly privately, and named his ranch the "Flying 'A' Ranch". I guess you could say he was my double hero: a cowboy-pilot. Gene died at the age of 91 in October 1998. My favorite fighter pilot ace during the war was Joe Foss, a Marine Fighter Pilot Ace. He went on to become the Marine Corps' greatest fighter ace of World War Two with 26 enemy aircraft to his credit, winning the Medal of Honor. After the war he became the 20th governor of South Dakota, and the first commissioner of the American Football League. He died at the age of 87 on New Year's Day 2003.

Back to the farm: I think I forgot to mention earlier when I was talking about the coal burning pot-bellied stove in one of our bedrooms, that it was the main source of heat. Of course during the winter that was the favorite place in the house. All the other rooms were shut off to retain the heat in that one bedroom, which also served as a quasi-living room. However, adjacent to that bedroom, was the kitchen with its wood-burning stove, containing a water reservoir for heating water. It also served as a room for bathing since the hot water from the reservoir could be transferred right to the old tin washtub used as a bathtub. One of the chores for Richard and me was keeping coal brought in for the coal stove, and wood for the kitchen stove. Our wood pile was slab wood, which is long plank-like strips of outer wood cut from tree trunks prior to cutting the trees into lumber. We would saw the slab wood into stove wood lengths and then split them to accommodate the stove. Snakes were always a threat around the farm, and the wood pile was no exception. One day I saw Dad grab a three-foot snake by the tail from between the wooden slabs and whip it like a whip. It broke that snake's neck. I don't think that snake ever knew what got him.

Sometimes, when time allowed, I would go off by myself into the woods, find a big tree, sit beneath it for the longest time and just dream of someday realizing my dream. I also did a lot of praying about this too, and begged God to let it be so. I was not a Christian at that time. I believed then, and still do, in God and Jesus. I believed in them but I had never acknowledged Jesus as my Savior. I also believe there is a Devil adversary who is very alive and well, even today! At church I always resisted the preacher's call at the end of the sermon by holding on – white knuckled – to the back of the pew in front of me. I know you're not supposed to make deals with God. But during these dream sessions in the woods, I promised God that if he would let me become a fighter pilot – a Marine fighter pilot – I would accept Jesus as my Savior. Now, I know that such a salvation experience is not real salvation. It doesn't work that way. But at that time that was my offer to God. Along with this prayer to God, I also asked that He would let me find a great Christian girl to be my wife, and that we would have a great Christian family. I sort of outgrew my dream to be the next Gene Autry. God would later alter my dream to be a Marine Fighter Pilot somewhat – but he gave me a great wife and family and allowed me to become an Air Force fighter pilot.

Talent Wasted – Maybe

I spent a lot of time in class and at home drawing airplanes. I had some talent for drawing, but never painting. My Mom couldn't draw, but she could surely paint! I could draw but not paint. I tried oils and water colors later in life when Pat, Robert and I decided to give them a try. Pat and Robert did very well. But me, I could never quite get the hang of the colors and blending. Give me a pencil, pen or charcoal – fine. When I was in high school, I saw one of those "Draw Me Girl" ads in a magazine. It was an ad which encouraged you to draw (duplicate) the simple profile of a beautiful girl and send it in for "evaluation". The come-on was that if you won the contest you would be given "free" drawing lessons. I don't know if I decided to enter the "contest" or if Mom urged me to do so; she was always sort of interested in my drawing talent because of her painting skills. Of course I "won" the "contest", probably along with thousands of other contestants. I remember that I was in the field plowing, when Mom and this stranger in a suit came to where I was, to tell me that I had "won the contest". But guess what! I had to pay for the correspondence course. It was about $500 dollars as I recall. There was no way Dad would ever agree to anything like that. But Mom had some very modest savings and she insisted that I enroll in the correspondence course. Well, I did – for about a year. I did learn a lot and shared some of it with Mom, but I never finished the course. Sort of lost interest, especially when it got to commercial advertising drawings. This was not the type of career I wanted. I hated to quit, because Mom so wanted me to be a successful artist. But she never showed her disappoint in me. Funny, Dad wanted me to be a farmer; Mom wanted me to be an artist; I wanted to be a pilot! Years later, while in the Air Force as I indicated earlier, Pat and I bought Mom art lessons with a beach art instructor at Fort Walton Beach, Florida. I know she enjoyed those lessons we bought her with a "real" art instructor – a life's dream come true for her. She was in her earthly heaven. I rationalized that these lessons compensated her somewhat for paying for my art lessons.

Well, I finished high school and began preparations for college to acquire those two years necessary for Naval Aviation Cadet (NAVCAD) Pilot Training. Goodbye high school; Goodbye farm, and Hello college!

*****

CHAPTER FOUR
COLLEGE BOY; SHATTERED DREAM; NEW DIRECTION

Pre-College

After graduating from high school I needed a job to earn money for college. Mom and Dad could not afford to pay the entire tuition and expenses. I know Dad would have loved for me to stay around and work on the farm. Mom wanted her kids to have a college education but I was the only one interested – and I was only interested in the two years necessary to apply for Naval Aviation Cadet Pilot Training. I found a job as a grocery store bag boy in Decatur, Georgia. I don't remember how I managed to commute from our farm to Decatur – I didn't have a car. The pay was pitiful. Most of my earnings were probably from customers' tips. This was insufficient for my needs. So I continued looking for more substantial work. I found a job with a prominent bank and trust company in downtown Atlanta on the renowned Peachtree Street. At the job interview I mustered up my best "interest" in working with a very successful firm. Not once did I mention that I planned to leave at the end of the year for college. Did I lie? Maybe yes, by omission. After I was hired, I discovered that a longtime friend of some relatives was working in the same department that I would be assigned to. I really felt bad about the fact that I would be leaving after about four months. Still I never mentioned my plans to leave for college.

My job was to process cleared checks through a photocopying machine, then collect the checks and sort them into groups based on the local banks that they would be couriered to. I would then either walk or take a trolley to those banks, pick up their checks destined for my bank, and return with them. I also was a mail distribution clerk who would pick up various mail from the mailroom and distribute it to the designated departments. It was a great job, good pay, nice co-workers and a good supervisor. "Fess up" day finally came and I told my supervisor of my plan to quit the job for college. Needless to say, he was not very happy about the fact and cited the time they had spent training me, and implied that I was less than honest and upfront with them about my plans. But I would not have gotten the job otherwise – and I needed the money for college. I don't think he even wished me luck nor offered to hire me back if ever I wanted to come back.

Somewhere along the way I also worked as a stock boy in one of Atlanta's very prominent department stores. I think it may have been after the two years of college. There I met a real "knockout" of a beautiful girl employee. In spite of my attempts to date her – she didn't give a "flip" about me. What was I not doing right?!

North Georgia College, Dahlonega, Georgia

I had selected and applied to North Georgia College (NGC) at Dahlonega, Georgia. It was my choice because it was a military college and was known as the "West Point of Georgia". I figured that the military training would give me a valuable head start, leading to my Naval Aviation Cadet Pilot Training and military career. The buildings were located on hills surrounding a large sunken stadium-like hollow – that served for drill practice and parades - and was nestled in the foothills of the beautiful Blue Ridge Mountains of North Georgia – about sixty miles north of Atlanta. The campus was located adjacent to downtown Dahlonega, a two or three block small Georgia town. There were neither traffic lights nor stop signs. Dahlonega had been a gold mining town in its early history, with "crawl through" gold mines dug into the surrounding mountain sides following the gold veins.

NGC was a 24/7 military college. (The name was changed to University of North Georgia in 2013). The U.S. Army uniform was purchased and worn at all times by male students, so civilian clothing requirements were minimal. The list of items to bring from home was very limited so I had little baggage. Academics were on the quarter-system rather than the semester system. Having worked the summer and fall of 1949, I entered the Winter Quarter in January 1950. Dad and Mom drove me from the farm to the campus and dropped me off on the concrete sidewalk in front of the ROTC Commandant's Office. (ROTC: Reserve Officers Training Corp; upon graduation you would be commissioned as a Second Lieutenant in the Army Reserve). We said brief goodbyes. Dad's goodbyes were always brief. Mom looked back and teared up at me standing there on the steps with my bags and waved. She later said I looked so forlorn and lost that she broke down and cried. I really don't think that I was sad, I was really glad to be getting on with my plans. I admit that after a week or two I did get homesick but it was only temporary.

In addition to the normal college campus rules and regulations there were the military regulations. All male students were required to participate in the ROTC cadet program. It was a co-ed college (a few female students) but there were no female ROTC cadets. The uniform was the World War Two style regulation Army uniform with ROTC insignia, shoulder patch and rank. The ROTC program was comprised of a Cadet Corps Staff, Group Staff, and two Battalions of two Companies each. We were assigned a fully operating M-1 army rifle which was kept in the armory. We would be permitted to take the M-1 to our barracks (yes, barracks, not dorms) on occasions for cleaning and to practice the manual of arms. Can you imagine anything like that being allowed in today's college dorms? Our barracks were not the open-bay style normally associated with early army enlisted quarters. Rather, we had two-man rooms – much better for study. However, our latrine (bathroom) was centrally located in the barracks with open area community-style accommodations: i.e. no partitions for shower, commodes, sinks or urinals. No privacy!

We had drill, manual of arms, and parade practice on the parade field two or three times a week. Normally parades were held on weekends. Once a year there would be Parents Day, when there would be a Corps-wide parade with the parents, public and students attending. Mom and Dad came up for a couple of parades. We always formed up in company formations at our barracks and would march by our parents on the way to the parade field. I felt great pride as I would march by Mom and Dad and caught their eye. I would recall Dad's World War One military service with the US Army Third Division as a rifleman. But Dad never let on that it brought back memories (happy or painful) of his army service. I did get a chance to show him the M-1 rifle and how it operated. It was semi-automatic, 8-round clip-fed, whereas the Springfield 1903 rifle he used was bolt operated and 6-round clip fed.

Once a year we would have "maneuvers and war games" in the Georgia mountains north of Dahlonega. It was an all-day event where we would have the "good and bad' guys opposing each other. The maneuvers were complete with map reading, mountain climbing, "prisoners and captors", blank ammunition for our M-1s rifles, and flanking and frontal assaults. We had the necessary umpires of course. I had purchased a World War Two bayonet from an Army and Navy store while home, for about $3. Today it would go for about $100 – $150. I used it on my M-1 occasionally, just for the familiarity and novelty. I kept it in my barracks. Imagine that today! Of course I didn't use it in our war games. I loved those drill sessions, parades and war games. I also enjoyed the ROTC classes about battle-field combat formations, map reading, hand signaling, etc. I guess I was looking forward to my training as a Naval Aviation Cadet. I could hardly wait!

And of course, don't forget the "spit and polish" uniforms, stiffly starched shirts and khaki pants, neatness, and standardized organization – everything in its place. I have always been one for neatness and organization. Of course my Mom would probably have a different take on that. Our khaki pants were so stiff with starch that you had to open the legs with force. We would stand on a chair and put them on. Of course you had to then jump down from the chair practically stiff legged, so as not to break the crease. I guess about the only thing I really didn't like was the frequent "GI Parties". (GI Party: Scrubbing floors, washing walls, cleaning windows and latrines, and general preparation for a "white-gloved" inspection by the upper class or Army staff). All lower classmen had a standing invitation to the "party".

I mentioned that we wore the regulation US Army uniform. We did not wear the dress coat. Our uniform was the khaki uniform for summer and the wool Olive Drab (OD) pants and OD "Ike" jacket in winter. The cap was the army OD cap with the ROTC insignia. On some weekends when we were allowed off, I would hitch-hike home – in uniform of course. Back then hitch-hiking was safe and you usually didn't have to wait long for a ride – especially in our ROTC uniform where most people mistook cadets for real soldiers. I've ridden in the back of pickups; in stake-bed trucks; in 18-wheelers, and in passenger-filled cars. I've been picked up by old farmers; women; young adults. On one occasion, I was picked up by a guy who attempted to make uninvited and unwelcome advances. I quickly 'identified my stop' and let him go on his merry way. Would I consider hitch-hiking today? Not on your life! Nor mine.

My best friend at NGC was a kid even smaller than me, who lived at Tucker, Georgia several miles from Dad's farm. He was also interested in becoming a Naval Aviator. However, after college I lost contact with him. I hope he went on to realize his dream. For diversionary activity there were intramural sports. The one-block downtown area had a courthouse, one small theater, a "juke joint" and a restaurant. The famous "Smith House" restaurant was just around the corner from the court house. Students would hang out at the juke joint, which was located on the corner just outside the campus gate to downtown. Many college romances were formed over Coca-Cola or ice cream sodas at that "social center". I never developed a crush on any of the good-looking co-eds during my two years at NGC. Mainly, I guess, because none of them would give me a second look. Anyway, I had no time for them; working on my Navy pilot career, you know. Naval Aviation Cadets had to be single. Sorry, girls!

"Thar's Gold in Them Thar Hills! Whar?"

Another diversion was weekend exploring of old abandoned gold mines in the mountains around Dahlonega. On some weekends two or three of us would climb over the mountains looking for abandoned mine sites. They were usually identified by small holes dug into the sides of the mountains, sometimes hidden by the foliage. Keep in mind that these mines were small crawl-through caves dug into the sides of the mountains, following the gold vein into the earth. Most mines were rather horizontal, but occasionally they would descend or climb steeply. Many would go for fifty or a hundred yards or more, into the mountain side. They had been abandoned for many years and not maintained. *Really unsafe!* The mines were really dangerous and I would hope that they have been sealed off so that present day "stupid" students would not have access to them. If you were ever trapped no one would know, or even where to look for you. Of course, we never told anyone where we were going because we really didn't know; just exploring. Recklessly, we would craw through these mines to see where and how far they went. Of course, we had to use flashlights. Sometime we would find places where the ceiling had given way and there would be a pile of crumbled dirt and rock semi-blocking the mine. Did we turn back? No! Again, stupidity prevailed as we proceeded to crawl cautiously over the rubble and through the narrowed passage way. Occasionally we would come upon a vertical ventilating shaft. If the surface was near enough, you could actually see light up through the shaft. There was one mine which even today when I think of it still gives me the willies! This one mine had a rather large chamber in which you could actually stand. The chamber had a large dark hole through the floor probably about 15 feet in diameter. In order to continue into the mine you had to negotiate a narrow ledge about a foot wide for about fifteen feet, in the dark, underground, around this hole, with only a flashlight. In addition you could hear running water at the bottom, with no idea of the depth of the hole, nor how deep or swift the water. But, press on we did! We're stupid, remember! Occasionally you would lose sight of each other, especially if there was an extremely narrow access or bend in the cave. Nobody would dare be the first to suggest a retreat. For safety we had to remain together. Nobody thought of flashlight failures, or cave-ins behind us. That is, nobody except me! But we always emerged none the worse for the experience – and none the wiser either.

One weekend, three of us were climbing and exploring the mountains and came upon a sight that disturbed us greatly. Now, we knew that mountaineers lived scattered about in those mountains; but you rarely saw a cabin. We were also aware that we could accidently discover a mountaineer's illegal "moonshine still" in those hills, and would be very unwelcome intruders. Of course we were confident that our youth would convince the moonshiners that we were not Federals (revenuers). We never thought that, youth or not, they may not chance our telling someone of our discovery. Anyway, one day we were sort of lost – with a general idea of what part of Georgia we were in. We came upon this small cabin in the mountains, away from civilization; away from anything: roads, trails, neighbors, etc. There were a couple of small, dirty, and raggedly-dressed children playing in a small clearing that sufficed as a yard. The cabin was like something thrown together in a loosely make-do manner – a mountaineer's cabin like you would see in movies such as 'Deliverance'. It had large spaces between the planks, which were nailed together to form the outside wall. You could actually see into the cabin through these spaces. As we approached the front door to inquire of our location and directions, a thin, dark-haired young woman whose dress and hair looked unkempt, as though they had not had much attention in a few days, met us and stood in the doorway. She looked at us suspiciously, and she stood as though trying to block our view into the house. We had a partial view beyond her, however, at what seemed to be a skinny, dark-haired young girl in a makeshift wooden *cage* of some type.

Of course we said nothing about it then. After getting some sort of "over yonder" directions, we thanked her and left. As we left we looked at each other with a concerned look on our faces. When out of sight, we began to discuss

70

what we thought we had seen – a young, girl about 12 years of age, imprisoned in a makeshift *jail*, hidden away in this remote mountain cabin.

Upon eventually finding our way back to Dahlonega, we proceeded to the Sheriff's office and told him what we had seen – or thought we had seen. He seemed more interested in chastising us for stupidly wandering the mountains than in what we had to say. He showed no interest at all in our story. In fact we were encouraged to forget the whole thing. We surmised that he was already aware of the situation and that maybe the young girl was a mental case who had to be contained to keep her from wandering off – or hurting herself or someone in the family. Anyway, we felt that we had done our duty. But I still think of it today. It was truly a scene that one would only expect of a poor isolated mountaineer family, or in a movie setting.

There was another time we were exploring the mountains again. We never learned! We came upon a lone individual with a rifle. No one else was in sight. Of course we approached him cautiously from a distance, calling out that we were lost. We weren't really lost, but felt that we need a reason to make him not feel threatened. After getting directions to the campus, we sort of eased ourselves out of the area, never looking back – expecting to feel the bullets in our backs at any moment. We surmised that we had wondered upon the perimeter guard for a mountain moonshiner's still. I've always heard that the Lord takes care of drunks and stupid people. *I don't drink!*

Tragedy!

There was one tragic event that occurred during my two years at NGC. This co-ed, whom I thought was one of the best looking girls on the campus, was very friendly with one of the professors and his wife, both of whom I thought were sort of weird-looking for no reason other than that they both were stick-thin, tall, very "hard" looking and never smiling. The professor seemed to always have a scowl on his face. As I remember the rumors, the co-ed was known to spend some time in their home occasionally. Anyway, one day she was reported to have allegedly killed herself in their home with his .45 caliber pistol. I never heard any more about the situation. But years later, searching the internet, two newspaper articles were found that covered the tragic event. The December 1, 1951 St. Petersburg Times quoted the detective investigating the case as saying there were "indications of suicide". That she was found on the sidewalk outside of her apartment with a .25 caliber bullet wound to her heart, and a pistol nearby. Shortly afterwards her English professor was arrested on suspicion of her murder. The professor stated that she shot herself as she stepped from his car at 2:30 a.m. following a drive-in movie that they had attended together.

The Sunday Press, Binghamton, NY Dec 2, 1951 stated that the police released the professor after a pencil-scrawled "suicide letter" was found in the co-ed's belongings. The letter asked for the professor and his wife's forgiveness for the things she had done.

The Sunday Press went on to say that the college had asked the professor to resign because of his romantic affair with the co-ed, and that the parents had withdrawn the co-ed from college shortly before the tragic event. She was such a beautiful girl.

Summer Break – Summer Job

After the Spring Quarter I needed to go back home for the summer (1950) and find a job to enable me to return for the Fall Quarter at NGC. My brother Harold was working for the General Motors Plant at Doraville, GA between Norcross and Atlanta. It was a Buick, Oldsmobile and Pontiac assembly plant – BOP plant as it was known. He had been there for a few years and had a management level position in plant maintenance and housekeeping. He helped me get a summer job in the plant as a yard laborer – good pay for a kid looking to make some money for college. It helps to know people in "high places". My job was manning a shovel, pick and jack hammer – digging and busting concrete. I really worked hard – honestly. I had to work hard because I wanted to show those men I could carry my weight – and my weight wasn't much. Also, I wanted to make sure Harold was justified in helping me get the job. Some of my co-workers told Harold what a hard worker I was. It truly was hard work, especially breaking up concrete with that jack hammer. The jack hammer was about as big as I was – or so it seemed – and felt as heavy. It was about all I could do to handle that thing. After a few minutes on that thing my whole body stung from the vibrations. But I acclimated to it and handled it OK. After a day on the job, I had no trouble sleeping at night.

There was one guy on the crew who was a person that would go out-of-control if you touched him, or even gestured at him as though you were going to touch him. He is the only person I have ever known with that affliction. He would helplessly fling his arms or strike anything or anyone that was in front of him and within reach. It was a completely involuntary reaction on his part. I really felt sorry for the guy, although I did partake in his torment a time or two. I hope he has forgiven me. Others would touch him often, in order to see his reaction. The guy must have lived a miserable life. One day he was standing near one of the vehicles on the assembly line, and he had a hammer in his hand. Yes! Someone touched him from behind and he barely halted his swing before slamming the car. You could be talking to him and if someone touched him, you were the target. We all knew to duck. Imagine the unaware stranger talking to him and someone touched him. Poor guy! Poor stranger! I can't imagine going through life with that affliction.

Back to North Georgia College

Having done the 1950 winter and spring quarters, and with summer over, it was now back to NGC for the 1950 fall quarter. My plan was then to do the next four consecutive quarters: Fall, winter, spring and ending with the summer quarter of 1951 so that I could apply for NAVCAD (Naval Aviation Cadet) pilot training as soon as possible. I could hardly wait to get into pilot training. I just knew I would be the Marine Corps' next highest-scoring fighter ace, surpassing Joe Foss of World War Two fame! If I didn't hurry, the Korean War would be over before I got there. I didn't have to commit to a major course of study until the junior year. Since I only planned to do the freshman and sophomore years, I didn't have to commit, but I elected to concentrate on math. I liked math although I wasn't a math whiz. But I preferred it over history, English and literature. I did entry and next level Algebra, Trigonometry, and Analytical Geometry. Analytical Geometry stopped me in my *math tracks.* The professor told the class if you don't get an "A" in his class, then don't even think about Calculus. I was lucky to squeak by analytical geometry with a "D". This math professor was a character. He was an old guy and looked like a farmer right out of the fields – as "country" as you could get – however, instead of overalls he wore wrinkled shirts and pants. But, you paid attention in his class! He definitely was a professor that loved his math. No nonsense! Formulas and proper procedures to problem-solving were more important to him than the correct answer – if your wrong answer was simply due to a careless miscalculation. If he caught you dozing he would hurl a piece of chalk or an eraser at you. He would do the same if you offered a dumb answer to his questions. He would let you know if you were a "dummy", in his words. Imagine that in today's college classrooms.

I tried Chemistry, man what a mistake! Once again, I just squeaked by. I loved it but I was afraid it was going to be my demise. I also tried Physics and did fairly well with it. I really loved the math and physics classes but I just didn't have the mathematical insight and moxie to do the advanced stuff. It convinced me that I would never be a rocket scientist.

I hated literature but my professor happened to be a former Navy Corsair Pilot. Man, that bit of information sort of perked up my interest in literature. The Corsair is my favorite all-time airplane. But even his being a Navy Corsair pilot couldn't make Shakespeare palatable. He never discussed his Navy experience, World War Two, I think. The rest of my professors/instructors seemed rather normal.

During the 1951 Summer Quarter (my last Quarter needed to complete the two years of college) I had a couple of electives that I could choose to complete my required hours. I chose what I thought would be "crip" courses – a "piece of cake". Although I had absolutely no interest in music appreciation that was one that I chose, because I thought I could glide right through the course. Wrong! My appreciation of Gene Autry's Western Classics didn't qualify me for appreciation of classical music. Bored, bored, and more bored! I had to struggle to keep myself awake and engaged in the musical classics in order to respond to exams and the professor's questions. I did manage to pass the course however. No, it did not enhance my appreciation of classical music – although some of it is really nice and easy listening. It did make me more appreciative of Gene Autry's Western Classics.

One class that I did enjoy was physical education gymnastics. It was mandatory but did not make me a gymnast by any stretch of the imagination. The instructor was your typical gymnastics instructor: Muscles on top of muscles; no fat; average height; broad shoulders; narrow waist and hips – and serious. We did the usual: Tumbling on mats; the horse; parallel bars; suspended rings; and rope climbing. On the mats we would do the three-point hand and head stands, running assisted flips, summersaults. I managed these well enough to avoid the instructor's wrath, and not to break my neck. I did fairly well on the horse and parallel bars, just Gymnastics 101 stuff, that's all. To my surprise I managed to do the knotted-rope climb, because I have never been a muscular type. The rope was suspended from the high gym ceiling (no short distance) all the way to the floor. We were required to do the hand-over-hand (no feet) climb to the ceiling, and lower ourselves back down. I think I enjoyed the suspended rings the best. These were two rings, about eight inches in diameter, attached to two straps about shoulder width apart, suspended from the ceiling. The rings were hung about a foot above your maximum reach while standing upright on the floor. You would jump and grab a ring in each hand then begin to pump your body (as in a backyard swing) until at the zenith of your swing you were about 15 feet high. Then, while swinging, you would swing your body up (as in the child's skin-the-cat maneuver) and place your legs between the straps, with knees bent and lower legs outside the straps over your hands. Then, on the peak of your back swing you would release your grip on the rings and grab them again (hopefully), as your legs cleared the rings; and repeat the exercise a couple of times. Another fun thing was where someone (a mat-person) would lie on their back on the mat, with knees drawn up and hands in the air, palms up. We would then get a running start, place our hands on the mat-person's knees and our shoulders in their hands, as we flipped into a summersault over them, to land on our feet. After the first few practices, we did all these gymnastics things without safety persons or safety nets, only mats.

Dream Shattered!

Having just completed the 1951 Summer Quarter at NGC, with all the final exam "cramming" into the early morning hours for the last couple of weeks, I was home – a two year college-educated (military college mind you) farm boy. I was so elated. Now I was eligible to apply for the NAVCAD pilot training program. *Lookout world, here comes the next greatest Marine Fighter Ace!* After collecting all the necessary paper documents to prove that I was: Born; old enough; and had the required two years of college- (and had eaten all the carrots that I could hold – fighter pilots must have eagle eyesight you know) – I went to the nearby Atlanta Naval Air Station at Chamblee, Georgia to sign up. I was excited beyond description! All I had ever dreamed of becoming was about to unfold. I don't recall how I got to the NAS. But I completed the application and was sent to the station hospital for the necessary physical. I passed all the physical exam stations, with only the eye exam remaining. To say I was nervous and excited is an understatement. Here in the eye exam room it would be make-or-break time. The room contained a Navy Corpsman who put me at ease. Every aspect of the eye exam went OK until the very last test, the eye chart. I missed one letter. I struggled with that one letter for a time but was never able to identify it for the Corpsman. He called the Flight Surgeon to the room. The Flight Surgeon was a grumpy old Navy Captain, rather gruff speaking, who looked like he had been at sea all his life. I still couldn't read the letter for him. To his credit however, he gave me several opportunities to identify that letter and actually tried to pull it out of me. Finally, he said for me to go home and come back in a week for another try. He was doing his best to get me in! Again I stuffed carrots into my body and slept all the hours I could, in order to get my eyes rested for the next try. A week later I hitchhiked to the NAS and was to hitchhike back to the little junction of Pittsburg, where I would meet Dad doing his paper route bill-collecting. He would then drop me off about three-quarters of a mile from home, where I would walk through the woods to home.

At the NAS I entered the Flight Surgeon's office and reminded him that I was there for the repeat eye exam. He told the Corpsman to take me back to the examining room to read the chart. I read the chart OK. I was elated. The Corpsman went to the Flight Surgeon and told him I had read the chart. I heard the Flight Surgeon, in his course and gruff voice, tell the Corpsman to put up another chart because I might have memorized the old one. My heart sank! I'm sure it almost stopped beating in fear of missing another letter. Sure enough, I missed one letter on the new chart. The Flight Surgeon came back and tried me one more time. No luck! He then said that was it! He made some comment under his breath about my probably having gone through life looking at pictures rather than letters and words. How could he have known that he just cost the Marine Corps its next great fighter ace?!

I cannot describe what I felt as I made my way back to Pittsburg to meet Dad. My whole life was shattered, my life's dream of being a fighter pilot. It had to be the lowest feeling I had ever experienced. Everything in my life had been done and planned around going to NAVCAD pilot training. DEVASTATED! That was my life at that point. What now? A new direction was needed in my life. The thought had never crossed my mind before. I met Dad and he gave me a ride to my drop-off point. Of course I told him I had failed the eye exam again. Dad never talked much or showed emotion, and true to form he said little now. Just as well because I wouldn't have been able to talk without breaking up. I'm sure he felt bad for me, because he had to know how badly I wanted to be a Marine pilot. As I walked through the woods toward home, I felt lower than a worm. I couldn't hold it any longer. I sat down at the base of a big pine tree and bawled my heart out for about 45 minutes to an hour. I got home and of course had to tell Mom. She showed no real emotion, but I feel she was sort of relieved that her second son would not be flying in those airplanes.

A New Direction – US Marine Reserve

The Korean War was about a year old and in full bloom. Things were not going well for the United Nation forces (read *American* forces). One thing I knew for sure was that I did not want to be drafted into the Army as a "grunt" infantryman. I still favored the Marines and the Atlanta NAS had a Marine Reserve flying squadron – with Corsairs that they shared with the Navy Reserve flying squadron. I figured the next best thing would be a Marine Reservist working with Corsairs, my favorite airplane – knowing full well that Marines are sometimes cycled into their infantry on a rotational basis.

On August 4, 1951 I enlisted as a private in the Marine Fighter Squadron VMF 351 at the Atlanta NAS. We had weekend drill once a month. I was an apprentice level Corsair plane captain. In Navy and Marine lingo "plane captain" is the same as what the Air Force calls an aircraft crew chief. We fueled, serviced and cleaned them; changed tires, did minor flight line maintenance, and the morning preflight prior to the first mission of the day – which meant starting the engine, checking all systems and doing an engine run-up. Man, I was in an almost heaven in that cockpit doing the engine run-up; noisy and powerful – about 2000 horse power. At full throttle, which was a required check for max power, you could not physically hold the stick back far enough against the prop blast to keep the tail on the ground, or from bouncing. The procedure was to strap the seatbelt around the stick and cinch it back into your stomach. Inevitably the thought of "hi-jacking" a Corsair would cross my mind. And I knew I could fly it! But knowing what I know now, I would have killed myself. I enjoyed assisting pilots with their preflight and helping them strap into the cockpit. My mind would imagine that it was me strapping in for the mission. During lunch breaks I would go to the hangar and climb into a Corsair cockpit and just let my mind go wild with imagination and emotion. I got to meet some of the Marine pilots of course, and one of them took me up in an SNJ, a World War Two Navy trainer. *My first flight in a military aircraft!* Another flight was in an SNB, I think it was – a twin engine Beech aircraft used as a light bomber and navigation trainer during World War Two. It was known as a C-45 in the Air Force. After a few weekends of military drill, classes and written exams, I was promoted to Private First Class. Honestly, I thought I looked like a real Marine in that uniform.

I think it may have been about this time in my life that I had that major department store stock-boy job in Atlanta that I mentioned earlier. Richard had graduated from high school now and we were both subject to the draft. I don't remember if my being in the Marine reserve would have kept me from being drafted. If my draft number came up I probably would have been required to go on active duty with the Marines, or be drafted. Neither Richard nor I thought much of a draft prospect whereby we might be drafted into the Army. Seeing our patriotic duty (tongue-in- cheek) Richard and I enlisted in the Air Force on March 29, 1952. Richard wanted to do his four year enlistment and get out – his commitment completed, except for mandatory eight years of inactive reserve service. Me – I thought it might be an avenue to getting into Air Force Aviation Cadet pilot training. He, I and other enlistees went through the usual battery of exams and were bussed to Macon, Georgia (I think it was) to complete our processing. We returned and were flown out of Atlanta commercially to San Antonio, Texas – Lackland Air Force Base – for basic training. Goodbye to the farm once again – and now for a new direction. I don't remember, but Mom was probably beside herself with her two sons in the military while the war was raging in Korea.

*****

CHAPTER FIVE
BEGINNING CAREER – THE UNITED STATES AIR FORCE!

US Government Property!

Following the battery of testing and examining, the Air Force determined that Richard and I could walk into the room without stumbling or tripping over the door threshold, and were thus potential *US Government* material. So on that March 29th day of 1952, we raised our right hands and were declared "US Government Property".

From Atlanta, there was a small group of new enlistee "government properties" being sent to Lackland Air Force Base, San Antonio, Texas for basic training. Being the only one with any military training (ROTC and Marine Reserve), I was placed in charge of the group and given all the enlistment and personnel records to deliver to the personnel processing center at Lackland. Hot dog! My first for-real "in command" big military assignment responsibility! I'm sure the purpose in collecting all the records and giving them to me as courier was to prevent some of the enlistees from losing or forgetting them along the way. *I would ensure that this did not happen.* We were flown to San Antonio by commercial airlines with one brief stop along the way – where, I've forgotten. Soon we were on our way again. I'm sure all us were contemplating what we had just done and with apprehensions about the future we were soon to encounter. After a few short hours we arrived at the San Antonio air terminal and were met by a "friendly" Air Force *welcome committee* to herd us onto awaiting buses for Lackland. Of course the first question asked was who was in charge. I responded that I was. The next question: "Where are the records?" Man, I could have melted into the floor – in fact I wished I had. *I didn't have the records!* Somewhere along the way I had put them down and forgot to pick them up when I left. It had to be the stopover. I did remember laying them on the counter as I coordinated with the airline personnel behind the counter for our continued flight. I can't describe how I felt. I only knew my Air Force career was ended before it started. *My first responsible task and I blew it –big time!* The Air Force Processing Center was very understanding. Obviously, this had happened before. They contacted the airline at our stopover point and they had them. They arrived there in the processing center in the next day or two. Our processing proceeded as though this glitch had not happened. Nothing else was ever said about the incident. I'm sure those guys whose records I left behind would have had something to say about it if they had to repeat all the enlistment testing we had just completed before we left Atlanta. From his point on we were not a person, but a *thing* to be despised by the drill instructors (DIs). We were government property and our DIs constantly reminded us of that fact.

O-Dark-Thirty!

Richard and I were assigned to the 3720th Basic Military Training Group, 3722nd Basic Military Training Squadron, Flight 496. All of us were enlisted at the lowest possible rank of "Airman" – that is, no rank; no stripe, a "slick sleeve" and in the popular vernacular: "Airman No Class"! Stark reality hit on the first morning of basic training: *Reveille!* Five-thirty in the morning, or in military time: "O five-thirty hours" (0530hrs), commonly referred to as "O dark-thirty". In fact any time before sun-up was commonly referred to as "O dark thirty". "FALL OUT"! was usually the next sound bellowed at us from the door of our open-bay barracks, by our DI. Everybody scrambled into their fatigue uniform (green mechanic-style coveralls) and stumbled over each other getting out the barracks door to fall-in at our designated formation position on the street. You did not want to be the last man out the door, which always brought the wrath of the DI down on that poor soul. Roll call, then fall out to the barracks for thirty minutes to shower, shave and other "duties" associated with morning rituals. Then it was "FALL-OUT" to form up and march to the mess hall; then back to the barracks and into the uniform-of-the-day, i.e. fatigues or physical fitness uniform. Then off for the day's activities, which ended about Twenty-Two hundred hours (2200hrs, or 10:00pm).

We had classroom activities to learn: Air Force Doctrine; Air Force History; famous Air Force personalities; policies; regulations; military law; military courtesy; rank, and respect for same. We viewed training films on numerous subjects; including personal hygiene and protecting ourselves from *social diseases* especially when encountering *women of the night* if and when we were turned loose on the local unsuspecting population. Then drill, drill, drill and more drill; field exercises; firing range (M1 Carbine – I fired "expert"); calisthenics: run, run, run! Even at this time of the year – April and May – the tar in the asphalt would melt and stick to the bottom of your brogans (heavy GI ankle-high shoes). After it rained, that black Texas mud was sticky, gooey, and very tenacious. It would build on the bottom of your brogans to the point where you were marching an inch taller than you really were. Removing it was a real chore.

We had open-bay barracks with double-decker GI bunks. I'm not sure, but I think today they have small two-man cubicles or rooms. Each recruit had one narrow metal clothes locker and one wooden GI foot-locker. Of course, everything had its place. Woe unto the recruit who had an item out of its designated spot. Bunks were made up in the standard GI fashion, tight enough to bounce a quarter pitched onto the blanket. The typical "make work to keep us busy" was the order of the day. When the schedule allowed the inclusion of a "make work" activity, the DIs were quick to insure that we did not become bored. A favorite anti-boredom ploy was: moving a pile of large heavy rocks in front of the barracks..... to another location, a few feet away, in front of the barracks. The next day we would be ordered to move them back to the original spot in front of the barracks. The proverbial "digging of holes in order to fill them up again with the same dirt you just removed from them", was a favorite. Oh yes, the infamous trip to the barber shop soon after arriving at basic training was an event to behold. You could almost see the gleefulness in the eyes of the civilian barbers when a bunch of new recruits arrived. I know those barbers must have been barber school wash-outs. Then there was the battery of immunizations! I never knew there were so many immunizations in the world. Nor, that the arms could absorb so much vaccine. We had this gauntlet of medics to proceed through and they got you in both arms simultaneously. I saw one medic with his palm open and three, repeat, *three* syringes in one hand, held between his fingers. He would jab you with one syringe and hit the plunger with the other hand; then rotate his palm to position the second syringe to repeat the performance, and so on.

There were guys from all across this great land of ours. For a Georgia farm boy, I never realized there could be so much diversity in humanity. I became friends with a kid (we were all kids) from Minnesota. His name was Ed. He looked like what today would probably be described as a "nerd": black horn-rimmed glasses, sharp features, skinny, and the picture of a seriously intellectual "nerd"! One day Ed and I were talking about our home towns (I guess) and the subject of my farm background came up. I discovered that he had never seen a real live pig or cow. He did not know what an ear of corn looked like. He wasn't pulling my leg either. I think I may have felt that he needed a buddy. When we did have a little free time, Ed, Charles from South Carolina and I would wander off into the mesquite grove a couple hundred yards from the barracks and explore the area. I was amazed at the number and size of the various cactus plants. I have some snapshots of us with the cacti and mesquite. During Basic Training we were given the opportunity to apply for Air Force Aviation Cadet Pilot Training. *Another chance at becoming a fighter pilot!* My third! I passed the eye chart with no problem! I thought: "I'm in!" Then came the depth perception portion of the eye exam. I had no problem with that during the NAVCAD exam so I thought this would be a piece of cake. Not so! I couldn't distinguish the difference in the bars. I must say that I think the medical technician was administering the test wrong. The box was dark and unlit and he held it very far away. Of course as an Airman Slick-Sleeve basic trainee, you never questioned authority. My third strike! It appeared that I was not destined to be a fighter pilot; *another sinking feeling.* It was back to Airman Basic Training. Finally the graduation parade! We were promoted to Airman Third Class (one stripe) for simply surviving the training – no more slick-sleeved Airman No Class!

First Assignment!

Many Airmen went on to technical schools for the specialty to which they were assigned. Richard and I, without benefit of technical school, were ordered to proceed directly to our assigned unit to report on May 28th, 1952 to the 772nd AC&W Squadron (Aircraft Control and Warning) at Claysburg, Pennsylvania. The 772nd was an air defense radar site of the 26th Air Division (Roslyn, New York). It formed a portion of the Air Force Air Defense Command radar network, protecting North America from an "over the pole" attack by Russia. Located on a mountain peak in Blue Knob State Park, it was an isolated location. Richard and I were given travel tickets via train to Altoona, the nearest large town. When we arrived in Altoona I looked out the window as we pulled into the station. I had never seen such a dirty, black, dingy place in my life. The coal-burning factories had turned the town into a blackened, dismal, gloomy blight. An Air Force bus from the radar site met us and took us to the mountain top for sign-in and processing. It was an extremely small site, which consumed the very top of the mountain. This made for a very close-knit group of personnel. There may have been seventy-five to a hundred personnel on the site. We would discover that one of the best features of this assignment was the mess hall. Great food, good mess sergeant! I guess they tried to keep the troops happy, since the site was so remote from civilization.

Richard was assigned to the administrative section and me to radar maintenance. Keep in mind that I went to the radar maintenance section without the benefit of the technical school course that would have been the normal route to such a specialized field. What I knew about radar – especially radar maintenance – would fit on a postage stamp, and leave very wide margins. The Non-Commissioned Officer in Charge (NCOIC) of the radar maintenance shop was a crusty old Master Sergeant; we didn't have Senior and Chief Master Sergeants in those days. I've forgotten his name, but he was still wearing the khaki and brown-shoe uniform of the World War Two Army Air Corps. "Old Timers" were authorized to wear the Army Air Corps uniforms until they were phased out over the next few years. The Air Force had become a separate service in September 1947, with its own blue uniform. The blue uniform was a winter uniform, so we still wore the khaki shirt and pants for summer. In order to distinguish us from the army, we wore a blue hat/cap; blue belt with silver buckle; black socks and black shoes, and silver brass. The brass was silver oxide with a dull finish, not bright and shiny.

I met the sergeant in charge of the radar maintenance shop. He tossed me a radar maintenance manual that must have weighed seven or eight pounds and told me to read and *"learn it"*! It was no less than three inches thick, hard cover, and so thick that it used those long silver bolt and screw fasteners to keep the pages and cover together. I don't remember, but it was probably classified as a secret document, and therefore not permitted to be taken out of the shop or work area for study. I remember flipping through that manual and seeing the voluminous technical data: electronic formulas; ohms; resisters; wave lengths; charts and graphs in hieroglyphics and other totally foreign stuff. Then I felt a sickening feeling in my stomach. There was no way I would ever grasp the stuff in that manual without some formal technical training. I guess I mulled over this for a week or two, and then I mustered up the courage to tell the Sergeant that I was in the wrong career field. After a short time, he was convinced.

I was then assigned to the administrative section mail-room, assisting a Staff Sergeant (I think he was), and with other administrative duties. One of my jobs was printing typed documents on the old purple ink stencil machine. This procedure was where the document was typed onto a blue stencil sheet that was attached at the top of a page-sized backing pad. The stencil sheet and pad were then inserted into the typewriter for the document to be typed. The typewriter keys cut the letter into the stencil sheet. When finished the stencil sheet was removed from the pad, which was discarded. The stencil was then attached to a rolling drum affair that contained the printing ink. As the drum was rotated it fed paper into the machine, where the ink was squeezed through the cut letters of the stencil onto the copy paper, to complete the printing process. Messy, messy, messy – and time consuming. The blue stencil sheet would last for only so many copies – maybe 30 to 50 – before it begin to come apart. For more copies, a second stencil had to be typed. Ah, the convenience of modern technology!

Because of no commercial transportation between the radar site and civilization, and the fact that many lower grade airmen could not afford cars, the squadron would run a bus to Altoona and Claysburg on Saturday and Sunday mornings, and return about midnight. There were the usual favorite juke-joint/soda-shops where the girls and guys gathered. I dated a couple of good-looking girls for a short time, but never allowed myself to get "thick" with them. I still had a dream of someday going to Aviation Cadet Pilot Training. Sorry, girls! Claysburg usually had a Polka-Party, comparable to the old Saturday night Square Dance. The polkas were new to me and I rather enjoyed them as a spectator: I could not dance. Sometimes I would walk a girl home before catching the Air Force bus back to the radar site. One of the more romantic moments that I experienced was walking a girl home arm-in-arm, in a foot of newly fallen snow, with snowflakes as large as nickels and quarters slowly drifting down into our faces while making small talk – totally lost in the moment and oblivious to the cold. The street lights were diffused with halos from the falling snow, which also gave the scene a truly picturesque setting.

Later Richard and I bought an old Nash; 1950 model I think it was. It had one of those inverted bathtub bodies. One night we were returning to the radar site after an evening in Altoona. I was driving. We were passing a high embankment to our right. *Then I saw it!* It was already airborne. A deer had jumped from the bank onto the highway below. It landed just in front of the left front fender. No great damage was done to the Nash, but the left headlight and fender were history and so was the deer. Had I been a split second earlier, that deer would have been in my lap and I would have been wearing antlers; and probably the nickname "Rudolph" if I had survived. Richard and I pulled the deer onto the shoulder and, upon arriving at the radar site, reported the incident to the Air Policeman gate guard, who in turn reported it to local authorities, as was the law. We never heard any more about it. It sure would have been nice to throw that deer over the hood and take it to the mess sergeant.

There weren't that many airmen in the area, so when we would go to town on Saturday nights in uniform, we were usually very popular with the girls. It couldn't have been just the uniform though because many times when I was in uniform, it didn't work for me at all. The new Air Force uniform being blue, and the Air Force having more or less demilitarized it, it looked very much like a bus driver's uniform – especially a Greyhound bus driver. This provided the local male population great sport: They would often stop an airman in blue and ask when the next but was leaving. Some of the more physical types would make a real issue of it. Being the coward that I was, I would usually respond with a fake time and keep walking. Most guys hated the new "civilianized" blue uniform. For some reason the Air Force had decided that there would be no military patches on the uniform: No Air Force patch and no Command or unit patches, as was done on the old Army Air Corps uniforms, and it only contained the metal Air Force insignia, silver buttons and sleeve chevrons. Of course any ribbons awarded could be worn (optionally). So it was no real surprise that one day a friend and I were walking along the sidewalk and approached a car parallel-parked along the curb, apparently illegally. Suddenly this little old gray-haired lady ran out the door of a shop we were passing and pleaded with us not to give her a parking ticket; that she only parked there for a moment to go into the store. We assured her that we would not give her a ticket – that we were airmen from the local base. She seemed so relieved.

Technical School – Jet Mechanic

This administrative stuff was not to my liking either. It had nothing to do with airplanes. I applied for, and was accepted for, aircraft jet mechanic school. My TDY (temporary duty) orders directed me to report on December 9th, 1952 to the 3320th Technical Training Wing, Amarillo Air Force Base, Texas for sixteen weeks of Aircraft Mechanic General Jet Course starting December the 11th. TDY meant of course that I would be coming back to the radar site. I said so long to Richard and was on my way, back to Texas. At Amarillo I would be assigned to the 3320th Tech Training Group's 3339th Student Squadron. Unknown to me there was a guy, Airmen Third Class by the name of John, from the radar site who had applied for jet mechanic school also. We were both on the same orders, although I have no recollection of him until we were reassigned to the same fighter squadron following completion of the jet mechanic course. John was one of the sharpest, most intellectual and conscientious guys I have ever known. I was to discover this at our next assignment together.

I had always heard that guys in uniform had to be vigilant for the following: drunks looking for another drink; street women looking to make another dollar; *and guys playing on the other team.* One of my early encounters with one of those *other team* members was in the Altoona Train Station, awaiting my train to Amarillo. I was sitting on the bench and he slowly walked up to me and, as though he had known me all his life, sat down next to me – I mean *close* next to me. As he did so he placed his hand on my thigh and began to talk to me, about what I don't remember, but I threw him my meanest look, shoved his hand off me and walked away. I held no animosity toward him and his *team,* but I don't play their game. Rather, I should have tried to talk to this guy about the Biblical condemnation of his life-style.

I rather enjoyed the cross-country train trip to Amarillo. This is a beautiful land that we have. I wish Americans would appreciate it more! There was a conductor on the train, with whom I became acquainted. He was about early middle-aged and from Amarillo. When he found out where I was headed he invited me to attend his church while in Amarillo, which I did. What a switch from the stranger I had just met in the train station. The conductor and his family, and other families, invited me into their homes for dinner. It was great. There was this girl in his church who was a real Texas knockout! Cowgirl or not, I don't know. I could never connect with her – not that I didn't try. Anyway that wasn't what Uncle Sam sent me to Amarillo for. Back to Texas! Anyone in the Air Force will find themselves in Texas at least a few times. The jet mechanic course was fun. Although Dad would have me be his "gopher" while doing backyard repairs to his car, I didn't learn a lot about mechanics. I had a foundation in the basics of auto repair and tools, but little in the way of trouble-shooting and actual repair. The hands-on class work and practical exercises in jet mechanic school taught me a lot. However, today my auto repair skill is still rather limited to simple repairs. Of course, as the name of the course implies, this was a general jet mechanic repair course. I think I was most fascinated with the electrical system and its relays, solenoids, switches and such, although I did enjoy jet engine work, especially the engine run-ups.

Amarillo: Certainly not a San Antonio! Amarillo is in the Texas Panhandle: Desert, flat, no trees and scrub growth. The unhampered wind was relentless at about 30 to 40 miles per hour day and night! That was the first time I ever got a tan from wind burn. Amarillo was what I pictured a small Texas town to be. The base was about 12 miles away, and you could look out the barracks window and see the Amarillo skyline unobstructed. At night the city lights made it look as though it was just a couple of miles away. Driving those straight, endless Texas highways at night a town can look like it is a mile down the road, although it may be 20 miles or more away. You had your choice of weather if you only waited for it: On one particular day I remember it was clear and dry. Soon there was a blinding sandstorm depositing dust and grit on everything, including in your hair and in your ears. Then not long afterwards it clouded up, followed by a light rain and mud; not to be outdone by a follow-on light snow fall, then clearing. All this in one day – true story! We had one-man rooms in old WW II wood-constructed frame barracks. Not airtight by any stretch of the imagination. Wintertime was cold of course, on that Texas plain. As I recall, we had those old steam pipe radiators with a knob to control the heat that went "clank", "clank" during the night. Dust storms were frequent and it was not uncommon to get up in the mornings in a cloud of dust, as you rolled out of the bunk. Shaking the dust out of your blanket created another dust storm that filled the room. Dust on everything: in your toothbrush; in your hair; in your coveralls; in the sinks and showers. You have to wonder why people live in those climates. Of course I guess many people wonder why people live in hot, humid, sweaty Alabama.

A Jet Mechanic *Grease Monkey*

I graduated as an honor student on April 3rd, 1953 and returned to the 772nd AC&W Squadron at Claysburg, Pennsylvania on April 10th. Remember, I was on TDY orders from the 772nd. Back at the 772nd I was reassigned to the administrative section. Soon I had orders to report to the newly reconstituted 332nd Fighter Interceptor Squadron (FIS) at New Castle County Airport (NCCA), Wilmington, Delaware on May 20th. The NCCA is now known as the Greater Wilmington Airport. The 332nd had a long and honorable history. In World War Two it was the P-51 squadron of the Tuskegee Airmen. In forming new squadrons, the Air Force usually designated the new squadron with the squadron number of a previously deactivated squadron, in order to carry on its traditions and history. Upon arrival at the 332nd, I was surprised to learn that it had no airplanes. There were only a handful of pilots, maintenance and other squadron personnel; but personnel were arriving daily. To support the pilots' requirement for mandatory monthly flying hours, the squadron had on loan: One B-25, one P-51 (both of WW II fame) and one T-33 from Dover AFB, Delaware. Within a few days we begin to receive our newly minted F-94C Starfires. The F-94C was a new aircraft just coming into the Air Force inventory – right off the assembly line at Lockheed. It had newly designed radar for its fire-control system. Its firepower was twelve 2.75-inch folding-fin rockets in the nose, which fired around the nose radar dome (radome). The wings had an exaggerated dihedral and were super thin, which made it capable of supersonic flight. And it had a drogue chute (drag chute) which was deployed upon landing to aid in deceleration, and thus save wear on the tires, wheels and brakes. A designated pickup truck crew would retrieve the chutes and deposit them at the aircrafts' parking spot. The crew chiefs would then re-pack and re-install the drag chutes. The F-94C Starfire was a newly designed aircraft and bore little resemblance to its predecessors, the F-94A and B, which were basically T-33s on steroids (radar and an afterburner). The "A" and "B" had 50 caliber machine guns in the nose, whereas the "C" had the aforementioned rockets. All models had tandem cockpits with the pilot in front and the radar operator in the rear. Although a totally new aircraft design with a newly developed engine, the F-94C retained the designation as an F-94. The story was that Congress would not authorize funds for the development of a new aircraft, so the Air Force had one developed anyway; bought it, and gave it an existing aircraft designation: The "F-94", to circumvent the *new* aircraft development prohibition.

In those days a squadron was complete with all functional sections, i.e.: operations; maintenance; administration; security; messing, etc. Operations, the main function had the mission of the Squadron and *"drove"* the other sections, which were solely to support the Squadron mission: Combat flying proficiency, training and Air Defense! Today the other functional specialties are formed into separate organizations. I was assigned to the flight line "A" Flight as a flight line crew chief, with my own F-94C – number 531 – for flight line maintenance, servicing, preflight, etc. My Flight Chief was an old World War Two veteran Master Sargent; a great guy to work for. Standard procedure for a squadron accepting an aircraft, even from the factory, was to do a thorough "acceptance check" of every system. This required several days. Of course, we expedited the inspection as much as possible. The acceptance check is probably the most thorough inspection that an aircraft will receive short of depot maintenance and overhaul. Aircraft began to arrive regularly. As with all new airplanes there were many maintenance problems to be dealt with. Personnel were still being assigned – most of whom were new guys fresh out of tech school. A few old-head veterans were available to supervise and assist. I quickly learned that there is no such thing as a "9 to 5" day in the Air Force – especially maintenance and operations. If an aircraft was schedule to fly the next day, you stayed with it until it was ready – if it required all night. You would likely be back to work at 0600hrs the next morning. Because of the shortage of personnel, we were working 24/7 with a short break for a quick nap and meals. I'm not exaggerating when I say that it must have been five to six months before things begin to resemble a somewhat normal schedule of 12 to 14 hours, and before I finally had a day off. Aircraft maintenance sections worked as long as it took to have airplanes ready for the next day's missions.

Working the flight line and crewing my F-94C was fun. Those F-94Cs were beautiful airplanes; bright and shiny, just off the assembly line. I met many fine guys there. When you needed help, you didn't have to ask. Everyone on the line pitched in and helped each other. I can still recall many names of guys I worked with or for. Funny thing though, I noticed that the older veterans in the maintenance section all had the same first name: "Sergeant"! Some of the other first names I recall are: "Lieutenant", "Captain", "Major", and one guy with the first name of "Colonel". I was promoted to Airman 2nd class on June 1st, 1953 (two stripes). This wasn't necessarily a reward promotion, but an *on schedule* promotion; as long as you had done a good job and stayed out of trouble. All aircraft had a six digit number on their tail, which was a combination of the factory contract date and the production sequence. The last three digits were painted in large numbers on the nose. I have a picture of old "531" with her assigned pilot in the cockpit. The right side of the aircraft under the pilot's cockpit was painted with the names of the pilot, radar operator and crew chief.

Sometime after we became operational with our F-94Cs, we were sent to Dover AFB, Delaware to conduct our air defense alert commitment while the runways at NCCA were repaired. Since we had no alert hangars at Dover, the crew chiefs had to sleep on the ramp at night under the wings of their aircraft. The aircrews were in a nearby line shack. Those summer nights were hot, humid and miserable, made more so by those monstrous mosquitoes coming in off the bay for midnight chow: *us!* To protect ourselves, we would wrap up in the thick, heavy, padded aircraft canopy covers – which made the night even more miserable. Still those mosquitoes found their way into those covers to get to us. I have never been made more miserable by mosquitoes in the States than by those home-grown Delaware mosquitoes. They were huge, and their numbers had to be in the millions!

I mentioned John, who was also from the 772nd and had attended jet mechanic school along with me. He was also now assigned to the 332nd as a crew chief. I also previously mentioned what a sharp and intelligent individual he was. There were not many maintenance problems that he could not solve. He was chosen to be the crew chief for the 525th Air Defense Group Commander's F-94C. Quite an honor! The Group Headquarters was located at NCCA, and the commander chose one of the 332nd F-94Cs as his personal aircraft. I was not surprised at John's assignment as crew chief for the Group Commander's aircraft. The aircraft had four diagonal stripes around the aft fuselage – I assume representing the four squadrons of the Group. Two of the squadrons were located at NCCA: the 96th FIS and the new 332nd FIS. The 96th was still flying the F-94B. I'll have a little more to say about the 96th later in my story. John kept the Group Commander's aircraft shining like new silver. At one time I tied with another airman as "Airman of the Month", which usually earned a ride in the back seat of an F-94C on a maintenance flight test. I did get a couple of flights in the F-94C and in the T-33. One flight was on a cross-country trip, when the squadron deployed to Wright-Patterson AFB, Dayton, Ohio on September 3rd, for open house and a fly-over. Man, was I thrilled! I was determined to try for Aviation Cadets again after I had done a couple of years in the Air Force.

Our barracks had four-man rooms; two double-deck GI bunk beds, and the usual centrally located community latrine down the hallway. The rooms were crowded, but generally we were a congenial group of guys. One of my roommates was an Italian from one of the rougher boroughs of New York City. He was about five-five, thin, and with long shiny black hair combed up in the back into the flared-up "duck tail" style of the day. I never did understand how he got away with that haircut. When off duty he usually wore pegged pants (tight around the ankles) with pleated full legs – the style of the street gangs of that time. To round out his outfit, he wore his shirt collar turned up against the back of his neck, and a long chain loop dangling from his belt loop and pocket down to his knee. He would usually walk about twirling that chain in gangland fashion. What was at the end of that chain was anybody's guess; and he was never without his switch-blade. No doubt he was street smart and street tough – and he played the role. I had seen him with a pair of nunchakus – a martial arts weapon. My other roommates were two black guys; from where, I forget. But we all got along fine. In fact the entire squadron was a fine bunch of guys. I don't know of any real problems. The over-loaded work schedule we were on probably had a lot to do with that. After the end of a 12-14 hour day there wasn't much energy for a ruckus. For a time we were moved into an open bay barracks with single GI bunks; pot-bellied coal heaters at each end; and a latrine in a separate building. The reason for the temporary barracks, I don't remember. It could have been renovation of the other barracks.

Needed: "Chick-Magnet!"

As the work schedule began to allow more free time on weekends, I decided I needed "wheels" if I was going to be able to chase "chicks". I went to downtown Wilmington on car-dealer row. I found this 1949 black Oldsmobile convertible, (it was now 1953), with a beige top and interior. Bound to be a "chick- magnet"! It was the big Olds, a Delta 98 with 350 horsepower, and a "muscle car" of those days. Oh yes, and a 4-barrel carburetor. A real gas guzzler! I don't know what I was thinking – an Airman two-striper. But I had more money than I had ever had before – I don't remember how much, but my pay was probably $50-75 a month. However, I made my payments. I dated two or three local girls a few times – and a Navy nurse Ensign from the Philadelphia Naval Hospital. More about her later; just hold on! But that big Olds never seemed to be the magnet I thought it would be. Just as well. I still had to keep myself unattached in order to qualify for Aviation Cadets. Sorry again, girls! However, my buddies seemed to think that my big Olds, with the top back, was great for us cruising the streets of Wilmington, New Castle, and Newport together, giving the girls a *thrill*. One particular Tech Sergeant apparently thought it would be a great "date chariot". He was one of our maintenance chiefs. One day he asked if he could borrow my

Olds for one night. I told him I would have to think about it. I knew he drank regularly, so I had some reservations. He knew that I did not drink. Finally, I told him he could use it for one night if he agreed not take a drink while he had the Olds, and no reckless driving. He agreed. I loaned him the Olds and there was no incident, accident or situation. Whew!

New Castle, which was just about three miles from NCCA, had some public tennis courts. Some of us guys discovered that the local girls would be on the courts during weekends – in their cute, short tennis skirts. We decided that we needed to polish up our game of tennis. There was this one cute girl who I tried to connect with, but without success. She didn't seem to believe that I was interested in her tennis game. And my girl-magnet Olds was parked right by the courts. I told you it didn't work for me. And my tennis game never improved either. I still have that tennis racket and frame today. But I enjoyed that Olds. It had a hydraulic system, to raise and lower the top, which was always giving me problems. It was what is known as an electrically-powered, hydraulically-operated system. That is an electrical motor powering the hydraulic pump to rise and lower the top. The hydraulic system occasionally had a hydraulic leak (which used brake fluid – separate from the brake system) that I would repair whenever I had time. Dating a girl in a car that smelled strongly of brake fluid did not make for the most enchanting evening. On April 1st, 1954 I was promoted to Airman First Class (three stripes) – and it was not an "April fool" joke.

There was a girl I dated only once, who sort of shook me up. It was in Newport, about a two miles west of NCCA in the opposite direction from New Castle. Newport had a drive-in hot-dog/soda shop, where the car-hops were girls on roller skates in short (really short) sexy-flared skirts. You know, those kind that sort of lift up when you twist or twirl. The drive-in had this one really cute girl car-hop. I've just realized what a role that cute girls played in my young and tender life! Anyway, I drove into the drive-in a couple of times with my big Olds, top back, and would request of whoever came over to wait on me if they would send this cute girl over for my order. It got to the point that I didn't have to ask. She would come skating over whenever I drove in. I don't remember her name. She probably doesn't remember mine, either. I finally asked her for a date and she said yes. Wow! I picked her up and I think we went to a movie. We were on the way to her home when I parked on one of Newport's lonely isolated roads. We were sort of hugged-up when I noticed it! *She was wearing a ring!* I asked her about it. Yes, she was married! I told her that she did not wear it at the drive-in soda shop; but she insisted she that she did. I know I would have seen it had she worn it. To this day, I think that she had it in her pocket and slipped it on when we parked. It was probably her subtle way of easing out of a relationship she was not particularly interested in. (Maybe it was the smell of brake fluid permeating my Olds). Anyway, I took her home to her apartment complex. She asked that I stop a couple of apartment buildings from hers to let her out, which I did. Was I glad to get her out of my car! I just knew that I was going to be killed by an irate husband. We never dated again although we had a couple of chance cordial meeting later in Wilmington.

DuPont Airport

Back to more important things. I decided to resume my flying to acquire my Private Pilot Certificate – now that I had some money in my pocket. Just west of Wilmington was a small airport with two perpendicular grass runways. It was DuPont Airport and had very nice facilities: A hangar; operations office; briefing rooms, and a couple of Piper PA-18s for student flight training. The PA-18 was a Super Cub, about 85 horsepower and the engine was enclosed in a cowl. The Cub had 65 horses and exposed cylinders. I signed up for flying lessons and met my instructor. He was a really nice guy. My first flight at DuPont Airport with him was on December 5th, 1953 in Piper PA-18 number 1202A. This was about four years after my last Piper J-3 Cub flight at Gunn Field, Lithonia, Georgia. I really liked the PA-18 because you could solo it from the front seat. Because of weight and balance, you had to solo the Cub from the rear seat. Almost a month later, the day after News Years Day 1954, I was re-certified for solo flight. I had more local dual flights, plus two dual cross-country flights with my instructor. On the second cross-country he noted in my log book: "Great Navigation". On this cross-country he also introduced me to main-wheels only landings (in a tail wheel airplane).

My instructor cleared me for my first solo cross-country on August 7th, 1954. This was a simple flight from DuPont to Bader to Cape May then back to DuPont. To complete my solo cross-country requirements, before being recommended for my Private Pilot Certificate flight check with an FAA inspector, I had to do a solo three-leg cross-country. One leg was to be at least 100 miles or more, and to include landing at three airports – one of which was to be DuPont Airport, of course. At each of the airports, you were to take your log book into operations and get it signed, as proof that you actually landed there. Otherwise you could have flown a few miles out and went sight-seeing for the planned duration of the cross-country, and returned at the designated time. *No student pilot would ever consider doing that of course.* My instructor designated the airports: DuPont to Quakertown, Pennsylvania; then to Lancaster, Pennsylvania, and back to DuPont.

On November 4th, I planned and scheduled the solo cross-country, got my instructor's blessing, and was on my way. It was a great feeling being alone and navigating on a long cross-country, with three destinations in mind. First destination was Quakertown. The airport there was a small, grass, single strip airport. Every checkpoint was falling into place right on time. Great feeling! Finally I arrived at Quakertown – *but no airport! I could not find it!* I flew around the place where I knew it should be for about 30 minutes. All landmarks in the area around where the airport was supposed to be were right where they were supposed to be. The airport's airplanes were probably in the hangar or flying. I could see no airplanes on the ground anywhere. The grass strip must have blended right into the surrounding fields, and I was not experienced enough to look for the right indicators. After the 30 minutes of orbiting and searching, I decided to press on to Lancaster. En route, all checkpoints again fell into place and on time. So I know I had been over the Quakertown airport – just couldn't find it – too obscured in the surrounding landscape. Lancaster airport had three hard-surfaced runways so I had no qualms about being able to find it. Landing on that big, long, hard-surfaced runway at Lancaster, I felt like "big stuff"! I got my log book signed and was on my way to DuPont, which would be my 100 miles-plus, leg. No more problems, until I faced my instructor about not being able to spot the Quakertown airport. He gave me one of those looks, and was probably wishing he hadn't made that "Good navigation" comment in my log book on the second dual cross-country. But, he was finally satisfied with *my story (and I'm sticking to it)*.

On November 25th, my instructor gave me a rehearsal FAA flight check and on November 30th, 1954, I passed my flight test and received my Private Pilot Certificate! Oh, Happy Day! It so happened that he had just received his designation as an FAA Flight Check Examiner and he gave me my flight test in Piper PA-18 number 3683A. *You don't think he would fail his own student do you?* I don't know whether he was afraid to put me up with another examiner for the flight test, or if he was confident enough that I would pass and was comfortable with it. I'm not particular – I passed! Soon afterwards I checked out in the Piper Colt (two-seater, side-by-side), and then the Piper Tri-Pacer (four-seater); both had nose wheels (tricycle gear). The Piper Cub J-3 and PA-18 were tail-wheel airplanes and the seats were tandem (front and back). Naturally I was soon flying some of my squadron buddies, and showing off my newly acquired pilot certificate.

If at First You Don't Succeed.....!

Early in 1954 I decided to try for Aviation Cadets again – my fourth try to get into either Navy or Air Force Aviation Cadet Pilot Training. After completing the necessary application and submitted the required documents, I was sent to the base hospital for the dreaded physical. I passed all the eye exams with great relief; then the inevitable in-the-cup specimen. The doc suspected kidney or urinary tract infection. Man, it seemed that I just was not destined to be a fighter pilot. I was sent to the Naval hospital in Philadelphia for a thorough (really thorough) check-up to determine what the problem was. After about a week, several specimen samples, and multiple exams by the doctors, I was pronounced healthy. The diagnosis was that there was a false negative on the first specimen sample taken at NCCA.

About that Navy nurse I mentioned earlier! I told you I would tell you about her later. It's now later. She was an Ensign (2nd Lt to the other services) and nurse on the ward at the Naval hospital where I was admitted for the urinary tract evaluation. Very friendly she was – and really great looking. Aren't they all!? I was wishing I had passed that Naval Aviation Cadet exam. After two or three days we were on very friendly terms. I must say that she had that kind of personality. She knew I was from NCCA of course, and she knew my rank and service. Anyway, as I was released to return to NCCA I asked her if I could call her and come up to see her. Surprisingly she said yes. This was 1954. There was much more discipline in the services then than there is now. So I was truly surprised. It was not only something that was not done – but an absolute "No-No"! It was positively against regulations for an officer to date or otherwise fraternize with an enlisted person. Court marshals and officer career terminations have occurred because of lesser transgressions. We dated a couple of times and she seemed very interested in me. I was sure interested in her. I told her of my intentions to go to Aviation Cadet Pilot Training, but would like to continue our relationship and I would come back to her as a 2nd Lieutenant. It was like turning off a switch. She never would take my calls again and I called – several times. *(Maybe it was that cursed brake fluid again).* I finally got the message and figured that either she was never *really* interested in me; did not desire a long-term relationship; or some of her friends got to her about the officer – enlisted thing, and she wised-up as to what it could mean for her if she should be found out. It was less than chivalrous of me to have even considered asking her for a date – knowing the potential repercussions for her if she was discovered dating an enlisted man. Anyway she was sure a cute thing; and this three-striper dated her, a Navy Ensign. *Something to remember!*

Back to the 332nd FIS: I was pronounced physically acceptable for pilot training by the flight surgeon. Thank you God! Ahead lay the Aviation Cadet Examining Board at Andrews AFB, Washington, DC; and if successful, the Aviation Cadet Stanine Testing at Sampson AFB, New York. I forget the location of Sampson AFB, but it was upstate New York. I think it may have been Utica. It was a training base similar to Lackland but much smaller.

On July 19th 1954, I was ordered to Andrews AFB, Washington, DC to meet the Aviation Cadet Examining Board. This was a Board of three or four Air Force Officers assembled to grill you on everything imaginable, to include current events; job knowledge; Air Force Doctrine; and why you wanted to be an officer and pilot. Not the least was your military bearing; personal appearance; how you handled the questions, and interacted with the Board members. Of course they had reviewed your complete military record beforehand. Before appearing before the Board you insured that you had shaved close enough to remove the outer layer of epidermis; had just left the barber shop with their best military haircut ever; every hair was in place; had rank and insignia precisely in place, and had climbed upon a chair to get into your board-stiff starched khaki pants. The interview went well I thought. Soon they informed me that I had satisfied them as to my sincerity, bearing and officer qualities. Thank you God! One more hurdle hurdled.

Next was the final hurdle in the long list of applicant requirements. It was the Aviation Cadet Stanine Test at Sampson AFB, New York. The stanine tests were a battery of three-day exams, to include educational, mental, psychological, and motor skills. I was not home free yet, and ordered to report to the testing center at Sampson on August 2nd 1954. I can only attempt to convey to you my apprehension at this, the final potential barrier to my being appointed as an Aviation Cadet. There was nothing else to do but to do my best – and pray – which I did a lot. After arriving for the testing, some of the things tested were: Reading comprehension; English; spelling (don't know how I passed that one); math; science; physics; and what I would classify as common sense stuff. You were asked questions about your family relationships while growing up. There were also the typical square-peg-in-the-round-hole tests, plus sketches of blocks and diagrams all skewed up, in which you had to identify the most matching figure to the test figure. I only remember a couple of the motor skills tests. One was a record player type turntable with a nickel-sized metal disc on the outer edge of the flat surface. You were given a five inch metal pencil-sized rod, which had a stylus on one end. The rod was electronically wired to the turntable device. As the turntable rotated at a rather moderate clip, you were to hold the tip of the stylus over the disc – not quite touching. Your score was the amount of time that you kept the stylus tip over the rotating disc. You should try it! The other motor skill test I remember was where you were sat in a chair with a panel in front of you representing an aircraft instrument panel. You had a stick and rudder pedals for controls. The panel had three sets of double parallel rows of lights; one red row and one green row in each set. One set of double parallel rows was arranged vertically, representing pitch control with the stick. A second set of parallel rows near the bottom of the panel was arranged horizontally, representing yaw control (left and right) with the rudder pedals. The third set of parallel rows in the center of the panel was arranged in an arc representing left and right roll. The machine controlled and illuminated simultaneously one red light in each of the three sets of double rows. You controlled the green lights in the other rows with the stick and rudders, to match the illuminated red lights. Once you made a match, the machine would randomly present you with another set of red lights to match. Your score was the number of matches you made in a given time, about one minute. There were other types of motor-skill tests, but these two are the only ones I remember.

Before leaving the testing area I was told that I had passed all the exams, and I was to return to my squadron and wait for orders. It was about a one mile walk back to the barracks. Those people I met, either walking or driving, had to think

that I was nuts, drunk or high on something. Actually I *was* high on *something* –
I felt like I was walking a foot off the ground, and was wearing the biggest,
widest grin that I had ever mustered in my life. The grin wouldn't go away. I
can remember very distinctly forcing myself to stop smiling but it automatically
sprang back. I kid you not. I don't remember how long that lasted but I know it
lasted while I walked the mile back to the barracks. I could hardly wait until I
got back to my squadron to kid my buddies that in a little more than a year they
would be saluting me.

Back at the squadron it was business as usual. Really, I didn't flaunt my
acceptance for Aviation Cadets. The guys knew that I had planned for a long
time to do this. They seemed genuinely happy for me. While awaiting my
orders, we made several short deployments to various bases for various
reasons. Back on July 24th 1954 I was sent with an F-94C pilot to Suffolk County
Airport on Long Island, New York to provide a static display aircraft for a public
"open house". I think I was flown in the back seat of the F-94C to Suffolk. On
September 10th the squadron sent our F-94Cs to Wurtsmith AFB, Oscoda,
Michigan for Hurricane Edna evacuation. On October 1st we were sent to
Langley AFB, near Norfolk, Virginia for a rocket meet – competition between
F-94C squadrons from around the country.

Home with my New Pilot Certificate!

It had been a couple of Christmases since I had been home to see Mom and Dad.
I never wrote as often as I should have, and Mom begged me time and time
again to write more often. I submitted a Christmas leave request, and it was
approved. So I saddled up my '49 Olds and headed south to Georgia – with
"Georgia on my Mind"! I drove straight through, with stops only for the
"necessary" – and coffee. It took me a bit over 24 hours as I recall, and that was
in the days of no Interstates. Climbing out of the Olds was a slow, creaky event
even at my age then: 21. It was great seeing all the family again. I don't
remember if Richard was there or not. He may have been on his overseas
assignment to Germany. Soon I was showing off my newly minted Pilot
Certificate. I chose to go to Charlie Brown Airport (now Fulton County Airport)
just west of Atlanta, where they had an Aeronca Champ: a tail-wheel, tandem
seats, fabric covered, and 65 horsepower trainer, similar to the Piper Cub. I
checked out in Champ number 4198E on December 7th 1954 – (that "Day of
Infamy" when the Japanese attacked Pearl Harbor in 1941). Of course I asked
Mom to go flying with me, my first family member to fly with me. She agreed to,
but I don't think she was very thrilled with the prospect. I think this was to be
Mom's first airplane ride ever. At the airport, I could tell she was just a bit
apprehensive; not bad, however. We got airborne on December 9th for a few
minutes around the area. As I was climbing out, she was concerned about
something – I forget what – but it was nothing. I told her in my best voice of
confidence to just sit back and enjoy the flight and the view. She did – sat back

and said nothing else. I flew her over northeast Atlanta and around the country side, pointing out places of interest. Was she enjoying the view? I think so. Anyway, after landing she seemed to have enjoyed it. Maybe she just enjoyed being back on the ground. I would love to have taken Dad flying. I don't remember asking him, but I can't believe I didn't. After all, he bought the first airplane ride I ever had; and he went along on that one. Earlier in my story I said that Harold never set foot in an airplane again after he soloed the Piper Cub on the GI Bill, following discharge from the Navy. I stand corrected. I asked him to fly with me. He did, on December 12th. We flew over to Norcross and around Dad's farm. I think that was Harold's last airplane ride.

December 1954: The *Christmas Present* of Christmas Presents!

While I was home Mom told me that my cousin Pat, whom I had met when she and her family came by our farm on their move to Florida about 1942, had recently moved from Florida to live with her mother who was now in Doraville, Georgia – about ten miles away. My heart had done flips-flops over Pat during her family's visit to our farm in 1942, although she was 14 and I was nine. It happened again when we visited them a year or two later in Florida. Pat had gotten married after high school. I remember thinking at the time that I would never have a chance with her now. Mom told me that she was now divorced (in 1953) and had a four year old son, Norris. I know this will be difficult for you to understand, but when I heard that she was now divorced, that old feeling came back. Would I now have a chance with her?   I invented a reason for Mom and me to visit Pat and her Mom. My invention was that I had not seen Pat's mom (my aunt) in several years and maybe we should go visit her. Of course Mom was quick to accept my *thoughtful* offer. I don't think she ever caught on to my real motive – to see Pat again after all these years. Hiding my real motive was, I think, one of my greatest performances. As I walked into the room and saw Pat, *I knew she was still the one!* She had kept her married name, Wells, probably for Norris's sake. I met Norris. He was a good looking kid, and well behaved. Pat and I got acquainted again and of course the subject got around to my flying, my new Pilot Certificate, and my selection for Aviation Cadet Pilot Training. She had flown in light aircraft before with a former boyfriend. I asked her if she would like to go flying again. "Yes!" *Our first date!*

So, on December 19th, we went to Charlie Brown Airport. The weather was dreary and sort of snowy-looking – cool too. I was thinking our flight may have to be postponed. The visibility was hazy, barely enough for visual flight, but I decided to launch and stay in the traffic pattern so we could land immediately if weather worsened. As we took off it began to snow lightly, reducing the visibility to barely enough to keep the airport in sight. The snowflakes were dazzling splattering against the windshield and they looked like white horizontal streaks as they zipped by the side windows. We commented on just how beautiful the snow was as we flew through it. I was barely able keep the airport in sight for three traffic patterns and landed. After the third landing I decided to terminate the flight since the snow seemed to be increasing. Pat seemed to really enjoy the flight, as short as it was. Years later however, she became a "white-knuckles" flyer. Part of that was my fault, and I'll expound on that when I get there. Back at Pat's home we talked more and I played with Norris. Upon my leaving, I asked her if I could take her to a movie. She said "Yes"! Thank you Lord God!

We went to a movie. Now, you know I don't remember the name of the movie. But I seem to think it was an Elvis Pressley movie "Love me Tender". Anyway the movie was playing at one of the four big theaters in downtown Atlanta on Peachtree Street, The Rialto, Lowes, Paramount or Fox. I think it was the Paramount that we went to.

Afterwards we went to the Varsity, a drive-in restaurant on Spring Street – a favorite of dating couples. The car-hops would jump on your bumper or running-board (we had them in those days) as you drove in, and direct you to their assigned area; or a darker, more private area if you choose. There was never an abundance of parking places; it was always nearly filled to capacity. The Varsity was a favorite place and especially for the Georgia Tech students, whose campus was just a couple of blocks away. After eating, we stayed, and stayed, and *stayed*. We were there *all night*. I told Pat how I, as a nine-year old, she fourteen, had flipped over her when she visited our farm with her family on their move to Florida from Virginia. I reminded her that she paid me no mind. She said she hardly remembered me at all. I also told her of my continued infatuation with her when my family and I visited them later in Florida. Again, there was not much recollection on her part. I'm sure then she was absorbed in things that young teenage girls are absorbed in at that age; certainly not a young kid five years her junior. When I told her of my suggesting to my Mom that we visit her Mom in Doraville, and that my real motive was to visit her, she was delightfully amused. Then I told her of the rekindling of my feelings for her, and the heart flip-flops I experienced when I walked into the room and saw her again; for my third time ever. She confided to me that she experienced similar heart flip-flops when she saw me. Later she told me that while we were flying she could not understand the wonderful and puzzling attraction she had towards me; a much younger guy. Before the night was over we had pledged our hearts and lives to each other. Engaged on what was our first *real* date, date! Engaged to the girl I had wanted ever since I first met her when I was a nine-year old kid; a girl like I had asked God for since I was a young teenager on the farm. *What a Christmas Present!*

She understood that I first had to finish Aviation Cadet Pilot Training – about 16 months. And that we would rarely see each other during that time. None of our families voiced any serious objections – not that it would have mattered. Her mom did comment briefly on our family relation – first cousins. Pat confided that her first husband had been unfaithful, and after their divorced in 1953 she told her family she would never marry again – and never again trust another man. Thankfully she had a change of heart towards me. A few years after we were married I learned that her first husband was also physically abusive to her. Thank you Lord that she had gotten herself and Norris out of that abusive situation!

We saw each other as much as possible before I had to return to NCCA. She and her mother had to go to Florida for a few days while I was home. When they got back Pat told me that she was miserable the entire time while there, wishing to be back with me. We called each other often. I felt guilty about the late night hours that I kept her out (wee morning hours) because she only had time for a couple of hours sleep then to work. But we were trying to make the most of the little time we had because we wouldn't be seeing each other for months at a time. I went to church with her, Brookhaven Baptist Church, Brookhaven, Georgia. She was a strong Christian – and loved her Jesus! As I said early in my story, I knew Jesus and believed in Him but I had never proclaimed him as my Savior. I told her that as an Air Force pilot's wife, long separations would be the norm. She understood. Over the years the separations, fears, dangers and job stresses would be trying for both of us, but especially for her. However, she proved to be a real *trooper* and a very understanding military wife. Many military married couples didn't make it, largely due to the stress of frequent and long separations. Some wives gave up based on fear and stress alone. The time finally came that I had to return to NCCA. I couldn't stall my return any longer.

Back to New Castle and Wait

The drive back was lonely, but with a happy-heart. I never knew that a person could miss someone so much. I was soon back on the job but with a renewed enthusiasm. The wait for my Aviation Cadet class assignment went so slowly. Not only did I now have the goal of completing Aviation Cadet Pilot Training, but the additional goal of making Pat my wife. Time went by "so slowly" as a popular song of the day lamented: "Unchained Melody", it was. *Our song was "Melody of Love".* Waiting for one of her letters to arrive was almost unbearable. At our GI mail-call I learned the real meaning and heart-break of the words "no letter today" as it goes in the song. If a letter didn't arrive as anticipated, I almost went nuts. The emotions heightened with each missed letter and the mail clerk's: "No letter today, Partridge". I am sure that burying myself in my job was a saving grace.

My last deployment with the 332nd prior to my orders to Aviation Cadets Pilot Training was on April 1st, 1955. It was to Moody AFB, Valdosta, Georgia for our aircrews' rocketry proficiency training. Our squadron pilots broke all records for F-94C squadrons. Somehow I managed to acquire a few days leave. I let Pat know. I told her about a good buddy that I planned to bring home with me, Sam. Sam was one of the most bashful guys I had ever met, a nice guy; very much the silent type. He would take most anything without getting upset. Pat said she had just the girl for him, one of her best friends, Betty. I don't recall a lot about that leave except that Pat planned for the four of us to go to her church on Sunday. Now Sam was a devout Catholic. When he learned that we planned to go to Pat's church; a Southern Baptist Church, he balked. He said as a Catholic, he could not go to a Baptist church. He wouldn't. So we didn't go to church. We did a couple of double dates but Sam and Betty just didn't click. Good times, but nothing clicked. Now back to NCCA.

Finally my orders arrived to report for Aviation Cadet Pilot Training. I was ordered to report on June 7th, 1955 to the 3700th Air Force Indoctrination Wing, Lackland AFB, Texas for entry into Air Force Pilot Training Class 56-V – Preflight. Oh Happy Day! As I said "So long" to my 332nd squadron buddies, had I known the future I could have proclaimed: "I shall return"., quoting General Douglas MacArthur of World War Two and Philippine Islands fame, promising to retake the Philippines from the Japanese. I had read many stories and seen movies about Aviation Cadet Pilot Training. I had a pretty good knowledge of what to expect during the course of the training. I had decided that I would treat the upper class' ridiculous hazing as a big-boys' *game*; the rules; regulations and discipline; the rigorous physical training; and the ground school. I would not allow myself to take personally the intimidation, the demeaning, and the in-your-face upperclass haranguing. It's a game! My aim was to give the training my best shot and to graduate, if it was within my power to do so – with a lot of prayers, of course. I knew that Pat would be praying for me. If I was successful I would have acquired the two greatest prizes that I had ever prayed for: Being a fighter pilot and having a great and beautiful Christian wife – not necessarily in that order.

I drove home to see Pat, Norris and my family. I left the "chick-magnet" '49 Olds with Pat. It had done its job well. I'm kidding of course. I know that Olds did not attract Pat – *I did*☺! I would not need the Olds at Lackland, and she could use it since she didn't have a car. On to Lackland, with another heart-heavy departure as I left Pat. It was with great anticipation that I proceeded to Lackland. Before me lay the opportunity that I had been dreaming of all my life. My fourth attempt at pilot training to become a fighter pilot had finally been successful; thus far. Thank you, thank you, Lord!

*****

CHAPTER SIX
US AIR FORCE PILOT TRAINING CLASS 56-V

Following is a short biography of U.S. Air Force Pilot Training Class 56-V that I wrote for our 2008 reunion, which never occurred due to a threatening hurricane.

WE ARE USAF PILOT TRAINING CLASS 56-V

Class 56-V began preflight training in June 1955 at Lackland, AFB, Texas, a couple of years following the Korean War, with approximately 350 students. The class was comprised of officers, civilians and enlisted personnel from a cross-section of America. Those who were not officers were entered into the aviation cadet program. Following preflight, students were assigned to three primary flying training bases: Bainbridge AB at Bainbridge, Georgia; Bartow AB at Bartow, Florida; and Spence AB at Moultrie, Georgia. 56-V graduated 13th September, 1956 at five basic flying training bases: Bryan AFB, Bryan, Texas; Goodfellow AFB, San Angelo, Texas; Greenville AFB, Greenville, Mississippi; Reese AFB, Lubbock, Texas, and Laredo AFB, Laredo, Texas. Following graduation many of us would eventually be introduced to little known places like Vietnam, Laos, Thailand, and Cambodia! One member of our class, that I am aware of, would become a POW guest of North Vietnamese hospitality in Hanoi. Another member, that I am also aware of, would be shot down in North Vietnam and again in Laos; fortunately rescued both times. The type of combat missions 56-V members were directly or indirectly involved with throughout North and South Vietnam and into Cambodia and Laos, included: Ground attack supporting friendly forces; bombing designated targets; air combat; air refueling; enemy ground fire and missile suppression; surveillance; forward air control; resupply; search and rescue, and others.

All would be caught up in what would be labeled "The Cold War", a nuclear confrontation with Communist forces, worldwide. Some would conduct long hours of nuclear and air defense alert duty in alert facilities around the world. Others would deploy to worldwide trouble spots in order to thwart potential enemy attacks on America; to include driving Soviet missiles out of Cuba. All the while our families remained at home, fearful for our safety, while we worried about theirs. Other members would, after their Air Force tours or careers, go on to distinguished civilian careers in: Aviation; education; finance; agriculture; government; business, and more – or simply retired to private lives.

Our first "all 56-V" reunion was held in Prattville, Alabama, September 1999. The second reunion was to have been at Wright-Patterson AFB, Dayton, Ohio, on 13-15 September 2001, but was cancelled by Osama bin Laden's cowardly and infamous September 11th attack on America. Our third reunion was held in

Seattle, Washington 14-16 September 2004. The fourth reunion was held 13-15 October 2006 in Eureka Springs, Arkansas, site of the Aviation Cadet Museum. This was 56-V's fiftieth graduation anniversary! Our fifth reunion was to have been at Randolph AFB, San Antonio, Texas on 12-14 September 2008. However, it too was cancelled at the last moment because of a hurricane bearing down on the Texas coast.

Although 56-V reunions have been few over the years, all members and their families can look with pride upon 56-V's contribution to fighting America's wars for freedom. No doubt our brothers and sisters who followed us – and those who continue into the future – can be proud to be counted among those banded together to protect America and preserve our freedoms. The freedoms that we enjoy today were not bought by draft dodgers, deserters, and those ignorant of the Price of Freedom! They were bought by 56-V and our brothers and sisters in arms! *"Freedom is not free!"* God Bless America Forever!

George R. Partridge

Hello Lackland AFB, Again!
Leaving Atlanta, I was not sure when I would be returning home. Pilot training would be about sixteen months, and I had no idea to which primary flying base I would be sent following Preflight. Several Primary flying and subsequent Basic flying training bases were located through the U.S. I have no recollection of my travel to Lackland AFB from Atlanta. I know that I surely had to have been in a state of conflicting emotions as I left the most wonderful girl in my life; that I had recently asked to marry me; and she had said: "Yes"! And I was on my way to a dream that I had had since before I could remember: Pilot training, to become a fighter pilot. I knew it was going to be difficult to keep focused on the training with Pat constantly on my mind. I thought of one of my fighter ace heroes, and his stories of his pilot training days while being engaged to his future wife: Brigadier General Robert L. Scott, a former Flying Tiger pilot in the China-Burma-India (CBI) Theater during WW II, and author of "God is My Co-Pilot."! I had done a book report on his book for a high school book report assignment, and many years later had a chance to meet him, with Pat and Robert. A few years ago I got him to autograph a copy of his book for me, while he was visiting Maxwell AFB, Montgomery, Alabama. General Scott was from Macon, Georgia and drove between Georgia and Texas many times while in pilot training, to see his fiancée. Of course, I knew I would not have that opportunity to see Pat while at Lackland AFB for Preflight Training.

Preflight!
Lackland AFB was the only preflight base in operation at this time. A second one had been closed a few years earlier. Both Aviation Cadets and Student Officers in flight training attended preflight at Lackland. Student Officers were

commissioned officers from the military academies; college ROTC; Officer Candidate School, or other commissioning sources. Aviation Cadets were from civilian life or the enlisted ranks. They (Aviation Cadets) were required to have at least two years of college. I had three stripes, Airman First Class; some cadets were Sergeants. Once entered into Aviation Cadets, enlisted members kept their pay grade, but their rank was removed from their sleeves, and their status was changed from enlisted to "Airman Detached" (AD). This meant that our serial number prefix of "AF" was changed to "AD". There have been many personal stories written in great detail about military pilot training, by those who have been there. There are so many thing of interest pertaining to military pilot training that could be, and have been, told. But since this story is about my life and my training experiences, much of which I have long forgotten, I will attempt to limit it to just that – with a few asides. My experience has taught me that there are three categories of people you cannot please: Drill Instructors (DIs); upperclassmen; and flight instructors. DIs were the instructors in Air Force Basic Training, which was also conducted at Lackland. As Aviation Cadets we had an Air Force Tactical Officer as our officer-in-charge; but our military training, and most functions, were conducted by upperclassmen. Of course, after Preflight and for flying training, we all experienced both civilian and military flight instructors.

I don't remember my arrival at Lackland, and little about the in-processing. But I was soon again reintroduced to the sticky Texas asphalt tar, and the clingy, gooey, practically irremovable black Texas mud that I had experienced in Basic Training as an Airman. It must be the inherent oil in the Texas soil. Our upper class was 56-T. They had just received their upper class status and were feeling their freedom *and power*! Their upper class had just moved on to their Primary Flying Training bases. Classes were designated by the number of the scheduled year of graduation plus an alphabetical letter, designating their sequence for graduation in that year. 56-T met us, to make sure that we understood that they were in charge and we were "dirt"! They of course wanted us to feel *welcomed* properly. In-your-face shouting, insulting and intimidation was the order of the day. Understand, there was no profanity, obscenities, nor touching (without permission). Once the training got started, I constantly had to remind myself that it's only a game. For the first few weeks, our uniform was the green mechanics fatigues; black combat boots; and the blue Air Force officer's cap with the silver eagle and shield. The green fatigues were popularly referred to as "green tuxedo". These were only worn by the underclassmen. Upperclassmen wore the uniform with the Army Air Corps of World War Two propeller and wings insignia on the collar.

The military drill was essentially the same as basic training. But there was so much more harassment, humiliation, intimidation and stress applied by the upperclassmen. Our military training and Cadet Corps discipline was administered by upperclassmen who seemed to delight in their status, and control over the underclassmen. It was as expected: a game, remember? We had a Cadet Council to consider serious violations. There were some washouts, and a couple or so of SIEs (Self-Initiated Elimination). We were required to evaluate our peers on an occasional basis. There was only one Cadet recommended by the Cadet Board for elimination. That was a guy who had such a quick and violent temper that no one would have anything to do with him. I think he actually struck a couple of cadets in anger. We were, of course, on the Honor Code to report any and all violations of the Code, and to report anyone who showed personality traits of being unfit to lead; command; or characteristics undesired in a military officer. Of course our Air Force Tactical Officer oversaw all of our activities. Washouts were considered, evaluated and acted on by a board of Air Force Officers. Our classroom, physical fitness and firing range activities were conducted by military instructors. Actually, firing ranges were supervised by Air Force sergeants. We fired the M-1 Carbine, as I did in Air Force Basic Training. As a kid on the farm, I never was good at shooting a rifle. However, in basic training and here in Preflight, I qualified as "marksman". Later in my career I would qualify as "sharpshooter", and once qualified as "expert", with the 45 caliber semi-automatic pistol. This is ironic, because the 45 caliber automatic pistol is notorious for its inaccuracy. Throughout my Air Force career I would qualify as either marksman or sharpshooter with the M-1 Carbine, the M-16 and the 38 caliber aircrew snub-nosed pistol.

As we proceeded from our Preflight, Primary, and Basic flying training bases, the upper class haranguing would decrease respectively, as we got on with the more serious business of learning to fly the Air Force way. It seemed that Preflight was to be the initial weeding-out process. I was determined to do my best; and not to give anyone any excuse for wanting to eliminate me from the training program – to just suck it up and take whatever harassment came my way. Remember it's a game!

Milk and Bananas – *"The Staff of Life"*
Pressure, and little or no time to respond to changing schedules, was the order-of-the-day. Reveille at "O" dark-thirty (5:30am); back-to-back schedules; and go, go, go until Taps at 2200hrs (10pm). No lights or moving about was allowed after Taps. Many hours were spent under blankets, with flash flights to study by. Our barracks were the WW II open-bay style, with double-decker GI bunks. Each cadet had one wooden GI foot locker; metal clothes locker; and a shared clothes bar, on which to display our uniforms in the prescribed manner. At the end of the barracks, built into the wall, was a huge exhaust fan which would come to be a big part of the Aviation Cadet's Preflight remembrances. Let me just say here that the Student Officers (commissioned officer pilot trainees) were housed in Officers' Quarters, and not subjected to the Preflight training

rigors, as were the Aviation Cadets. My experiences related in my story will be from the Aviation Cadet perspective.

After Reveille sounded we had about five minutes to be dressed in our green tuxedos and formed up on the street for roll call. Then back to the barracks to prepare for the breakfast formation march to the mess hall. We had about fifteen minutes for a shave, shower, and other morning activities before breakfast formation. Our latrines were at the end of the bay and, if I remember correctly, three sinks, commodes, and showers. With only the fifteen minutes to be back in formation on the street in uniform, shaved, showered, with our bay and individual areas in inspection order, there had to be organized chaos. One minute for a shave, same for a shower, and a few moments for other duties; then clean up and prepare your area and the bay for inspection by the upper class while you were at breakfast. Whether you were in or out of the barracks you, your personal area and your barracks were subject to a personal and detailed inspection by any upperclassman at any time.

Our march-route to the chow hall for our meals took us by our Student Officers' Quarters, most of whom were college ROTC graduate commissioned officers. For the breakfast march it was about 5:45am. As we passed their quarters we did our best to insure that they were awake and did not miss their first class schedule. We would sing marching songs at the top of our voices – any song, but the favorite of ours was: "**Rrrr**-Oooo-**Rrrr**-Oooo, Oh it's R-O-T-C for **me**, for **me**!" Then we would repeat it several times. We always had three "square" meals a day. Food was forked or spooned, then brought straight up vertically from the tray to the level of your mouth, then brought forward, square to the mouth; thus the "square" meal. The utensil was returned to the plate in the same manner; repeated over and over, in a robotic "square" action. The food was good – when we were able to eat. An upperclassman was assigned to each of our tables, and sat at the end so he could observe everyone for any infraction of the "rules of Cadet etiquette". We were required to sit at attention looking straight ahead, without letting our eyes wander. Everything we did was by peripheral vision. Everything we did, other than the actual act of feeding yourself from your plate, had to be with the requested permission of the upperclassman. Time for the meal was very tightly limited, due to the long chow line. So many times you had to be up and out for formation before you could get more than just a few bites. There were many times when I had barely sat down and it was time to fall out and form up for the march to the next activity. However, there was no limit on the amount of milk you were allowed to drink, or the number of bananas you were allowed to eat. So you would gulp down all the milk and eat all the bananas you could. You were allowed to take back to the barracks all the bananas you could carry in your hands. If it were not for milk and bananas many cadets, including yours truly, would have practically starved to death. Nothing at any time was allowed to be in your pockets, except the "gig slips" which were carried in the left shirt pocket. If an upperclassman suspected you of carrying a banana in your pants pocket, he would approach you and ask if that was a banana in your pocket. Of course the cadet code (Honor Code) precluded you from lying, cheating, stealing or quibbling; either of which could get you washed out of the program. It also required you to "rat" on cadets who violated the Code. This was probably the most violated code. So, if you were carrying a banana in your pocket, your answer was always: "Yes Sir!" Then the upperclassman would ask for permission to touch you, which was always granted. He would then slap your pocket, resulting in a squishy pocket depending upon the ripening state of the banana.

Physical Conditioning – Project 'X' and ....Confidence Building

The physical training program was one of the best I have encountered. It was geared to stamina, endurance, general fitness and confidence building – not great strength. I think after Preflight I was in the best physical condition I had ever been in my life. I know there are more rigorous and demanding physical training programs, e.g. Army Ranger training, Navy Seal training and Marine Boot Camp, just to name a few. But they are geared for a more specific type of conditioning and career. Part of our conditioning was what was known as "Project X". This was a confidence building obstacle course. I don't remember all the problems designed to challenge the individual, and challenge team cooperation. But there were a couple of the individual obstacles that I do remember. One was a "ladder" of large logs, which formed the rungs of the ladder between two vertically mounted columns about ten feet apart. The log rungs were about six to twelve inches in diameter and were spaced at increasing intervals, as you ascended the latter. The ladder being vertical, you couldn't climb them as you normally would a ladder. You had to climb it vertically by hugging the higher rung and pulling yourself up over it; then stand up on it to reach the next higher rung. By the time you reached the last two rung logs, they were spaced far enough apart that you had to jump and grab the higher rung. By now you were about 30 feet above the ground. There were no safety nets or ropes. Once you were on the top rung there was only one way you were going to get down: The way you got up there, but in reverse order.

The other confidence building obstacle that I remember, and wonder why I am still alive, was a type of inverted square cone, probably about forty feet high. It was constructed with square platforms, supported at each corner by columns angled out to form the inverted square cone. Each platform was slighly larger than the lower, and placed at increasing intervals as you ascended the "cone". This also helped to give it the inverted cone shape. I think we had stairs to the top platform because I don't remember having to climb the cone. Maybe we did, and the descent was so much scarier that it was indelibly inscribed in my mind at the expense of occluding the ascent. Anyway, from the top platform we would lie on our stomachs facing out and look down over the edge of the uppermost platform. Imagine looking over the edge of the cone from 40 feet or more above the ground and seeing a narrowing structure to a small base at ground level below you. The rim of each platform had a steel pipe about an inch and a half in diameter, and supported by brackets to hold the pipe about a couple of inches from the edge of the platform. You were to grab the pipe with your wrist inverted, and slide over the side and swing yourself onto the edge of the next receded platform below and behind you. Because of the increased interval between the higher platforms, you had to be sure you swung back far enough in order to drop onto the lower platform. Again, there were no safety nets or ropes. The young and indestructible don't need them!

A part of Project 'X' was team problem-solving. It consisted of several different types of problems centered on simulating small group travel on foot in an "escape and evasion" environment. Problems would be presented whereby the group would be faced with an obstacle to their progress such as simulated bridge out, raging stream, quick sand, high wall, etc. Each problem would have materials available such as lumber, poles, rope, blocks, etc., which, with some thought, could be used to overcome the obstacle presented. No team leader was selected. Each problem was designed to allow a "leader" to emerge during the process of everyone trying to come up with suggestions as to how to best use the materials available, to solve the problem. There was no pass/fail. It was observed by upperclassmen and Tactical Officers to evaluate ones cooperation, team spirit and mental savvy at arriving at a workable solution.

Upper Class Delight!

We marched everywhere and sang marching songs: The nice, not so nice and the less nice. As an underclassman you marched even when you were alone – which was very rare. And of course there was the weekend walking tour marches. These were punishment tours for demerits received during the week.

While cadets with excessive demerits were walking tours – Saturday and Sunday – other cadets were doing free time at the Cadet Club, or studying. Remember the "gig" slip, or demerit slip? It was a pink slip, on which you preprinted your name and cadet info. You were required to have five of these in your left shirt pocket at all times. Whenever an upperclassman nailed you with an infraction, he would demand in his sternest voice: "Post me one, mister!" Whereupon you would immediately loudly slap your left shirt pocket and retrieve a gig slip and hand it to him. These were collected by the upperclassmen, and on Friday they were tallied up. I think a cadet got one hour on the tour ramp for every five demerit slips he had surrendered during the week. The tour ramp was the walkway around the quadrangle in front of the barracks, or on the street by the barracks. They were started early Saturday morning and continued all day or until you had walked off your demerits; rain or shine, cold or hot. Unfinished tours carried over to Sunday. An upperclassman could gig you for even the smallest infraction. Some things qualifying as demerits were: Not having your shirt buttons lined up with your belt buckle and fly line (called the 'gig' line); or a button unbuttoned; even a fraction of a thread exposed from the stitching. Others were: Moving or looking around while at attention or parade rest in formation. Allowing your eyes to wander from the straight ahead was called "gazing". If the upper-class caught you "gazing", they would shout: "Are you gazing Mister? Post me one!" Where upon you would slap your chest and produce a gig slip. Excessive wrinkles in your uniform; incorrect responses to upperclassmen; reciting required cadet knowledge incorrectly, all would require surrendering a gig slip. And on and on; the list is endless. An entire barracks bay could get sufficient demerits, requiring the entire bay to do time on the tour ramp. Bunks and barracks had to be in inspection order at all times. Upperclassmen could walk in and inspect at any time. While underclassmen were at class or other functions, upperclassmen would usually do a walk-through of the barracks. If an item was out of place it would be a demerit for the offending underclassman. We were also required to have the gig slips available in our area by our bunk. One favorite was to inspect footlockers, which were required to be unlocked. If a required item was missing or out of place, the upperclassman had a choice of pulling a gig slip or, as often was the case, set the can of Rise shaving cream (required item) upright in the top tray of the footlocker and close the lid. The can of Rise was just high enough so that when the lid was lower on an upright can, it depressed the button on the can to release the shaving cream. The cadet would return to a footlocker full of shaving cream. If your bunk wasn't made proper and tight – really tight – tight enough to bounce the proverbial quarter, then the upperclassman would pull off the bedding, sometimes to include the mattress cover, and leave them on the floor.

Remember the large exhaust fan at the end of the bay that I mentioned earlier? If the upperclassmen inspected the bay while the lower class was out and found the fan running – which was strictly against safety regulations when no one was in the bay – they would tear up every bunk and drag the bedding to the end of the bay against the fan (after they shut it off), and turn over every footlocker. When the underclassmen returned, the upperclassmen would announce to them that they had left the fan running, and it had "sucked" all the bedding to the end of the bay and turned over all the footlockers. The lower class would then be given a few minutes to have everything in inspection order for another inspection. Fun and games!

Whenever an upperclassman approached you, whether inside or outside, you were to get into an exaggerated position of absolute rigid attention, until he passed. If you were inside near a wall, you were to slam your back against the wall. Your chest would be out as far as possible, your stomach and chin in.

When walking, all turns were done as square corners. Walking was at attention, as in marching. Sometimes when meeting an upperclassman, the upperclassman would order: "Double-time, mister!" whereupon you would double-time until out of sight or hearing of the upperclassman. There was a thing called "Space Brace". A couple of upperclassmen would order you into a space brace. You would stand at rigid attention and fall back into the hands of one upperclassman, who would catch you by the back of your head. While you were still at attention, another upperclassman would grab your heels and hoist you up into a horizontal position. You would then be at attention while suspended between two upperclassmen – thus "Space Brace". Drills; drills; parades; white glove inspections; academics; calisthenics; all the while just waiting for the upper class to move on to their primary flying training bases – and then we would become the upper class!

Happy Days are Here – *Upper Class I are!*

Finally! Our upper class moved on to their Primary Flying Training bases. We were now the upper class. This would be mid-way through our Preflight training. I don't recall what Aviation Cadet rank I was promoted to, but I seem to think that I was designated as a flight commander, probably Aviation Cadet rank of major. Everything continued as normal. Our underclass had arrived, and the indoctrination started all over again. However, we (56-V) were now the indoctrinators rather than the indoctrinated. The underclass designation was 57-C. There was a guy in the class from Tucker, Georgia, about 15 miles from my home. I sort of took him under my wing and gave him a little extra help learning military formation, procedures and maneuvers. I think he was one of the well-known players on the Tucker football team.

As upperclassmen we were still subject to the demerit system, for walking tour hours. However, it was usually a Tactical Officer who gigged upperclassmen.

There were a handful of cadets who made it through Preflight without having to walk a single demerit tour. I was one. I was doing my best to not give anyone an excuse to eliminate me from the program. Of course the big tests lay ahead: Primary Flying and Basic Flying training. I felt a little comfort in having my civilian private pilot certificate, but that didn't save some who had theirs. I never mentioned to anyone that I had a private pilot certificate, for fear that I would be targeted by flying instructors as flaunting it; or maybe be targeted for extra attention. After all, military flying instructors felt that civilian flying training taught you all the bad habits of flying, and that you had to be de-programmed!

Finally Preflight was over! I had my Primary Flying Training Base orders for Spence Air Base, at Moultrie in southern Georgia – about five hours from my home. My orders read that I was to depart Lackland about September 2nd and report by September 8th 1955 to the 3302nd Pilot Training Squadron for about 20 weeks of training. This gave me five days between Lackland and Spence. I don't remember how I traveled but I must have flown by the airlines with a stopover in Atlanta, to visit Pat, her mother and Norris, and my Mom and Dad. In fact throughout my Aviation Cadet Pilot Training, I don't remember much about extracurricular activities or my travel between bases. My schedule was so orchestrated and tight, and my mind was full of training. I'm sure I must have gotten home to see Pat at least a couple of times during those 20 weeks, but my mind is blank regarding any trips home.

Primary Flying Training – Spence Air Base, Moultrie, Georgia

After sign-in and barracks assignments, I was ready to get into the air! We had two-man rooms, converted from WW II barracks. Spence was a training base during WW II, as were probably most every airport in the country. After Preflight; open bay barracks; and the upper-class; now with a two-man room and a roommate, I felt like a human being again. My roommate was Don. I've never run across him again since Primary. I heard a few years ago from someone that they though he had died. Like at Lackland, we were the underclass until our upper class finished Primary, about half way through the 20 weeks of training. At Primary, both upper and lowerclassmen, were occupied with absorbing the volumes of material in ground school, and learning the aircraft systems and flying procedures. So, upper class harassment was minimized. We still carried gig slips and walked weekend demerit tours. Again, I got through Primary without having to walk a single demerit tour.

We would do one week with ground school in the morning, then flying in the afternoon; then reverse the order on alternating weeks. Primary flying training was conducted by civilian instructors from a civilian flying school contracted by the government to provide the training. At Spence Air Base the flying school was Hawthorn Flying School; owned and operated by Bevo Howard, a world class competitive aerobatic pilot. The school had military pilots assigned who were the check pilots for all student flight checks at the end of each flying phase; and the final check-ride prior to completion of Primary training. They also conducted evaluation check-rides for students who were having difficulty with the training. The check pilots would make a recommendation for additional training or for an elimination check flight with another military check pilot. Before being eliminated for flying deficiency, a student would have had at least three check-rides to determine his potential for retention and successful completion. The phase check-rides were to evaluate the civilian instructors as much as the students. This way, the Air Force kept a check on the training that the civilian instructors were providing – to ensure that the training was standardized to Air Force standards. So, unknown to the student, his instructor probably was sweating the student's check-ride as much as the student – maybe more so. After all, it was the instructor's livelihood on the line.

108

Generally each instructor had three or four students, a mixture of Aviation Cadets and Student Officers. At Spence we had about a 50% mix. One of 56-V's Primary bases, Bartow AB, Florida, was Student Officers only. At Spence we had the relatively new T-34A and T-28A for training; first the T-34, then later transition to the T-28. Each was a tricycle-geared airplane with a nose wheel. At Bartow they had the Piper PA-18 Super Cub and the T-6 Texan, both of which were tail wheel airplanes – "tail draggers". The T-6 was a WW II basic trainer, and used by some countries for ground attack. I would love to have trained in and flown the T-6. Many years later, after retirement, I did get 15 hours dual time in the front cockpit of a friend's T-6. It is a beautiful and fun airplane. I think 56-V Bartow was the last class to fly the PA-18 and T-6 before they converted to the new T-34 and T-28. The PA-18 was the aircraft I got my Private Pilot Certificate in at DuPont Airport, Wilmington, Delaware.

My instructor at Spence was a slightly chubby guy with a reddish complexion, sort of reminded me of an Irish Redneck! But he was really a nice guy. I liked him very much. He was very calm, cool, and level-headed; never got excited or raised his voice. The squadron had flights designated by different call signs. My instructor's flight call sign was "Fireball". I only recall two other flight call signs: "Gopher" and "Polecat". Instructors were assigned a two-digit number ending in "zero" e.g. "Fireball one-zero," "Fireball two-zero" and so on. Students at an instructor's table were assigned their instructor's call sign and a number based on their position at the instructor's table. My instructor was Fireball nine-zero; his four students: Fireball nine-one, Fireball nine-two, Fireball nine-three (me) and Fireball nine-four. My table had three student officers and me – the only Aviation Cadet at the table.

Hello T-34A "Mentor" and the *Wild Blue Yonder!*

Finally! Before beginning flight training, we were required to log several hours (six, I think) on the ground in the T-34 cockpit, familiarizing ourselves with the layout, controls and instruments. The weekends would find students in the cockpits on the flight line, doing their required cockpit time. We had been introduced to the T-34 "Dash 1" (T-34A Flight Manual) in ground school. This is the equivalent of the civilian aircraft operating manual. The squadron operations section would initiate and maintain a civilian flight log book for you, for a fee. Of course I and most guys signed up. I don't know of anyone who didn't. The first big day arrived: My first flight in the T-34 on September 16, 1955! The T-34s flew out of Spence, then to one of three auxiliary fields for the day's flying activities: Thomasville, Tifton and Moultrie Airports. We would depart Spence and fly to our designated auxiliary. My flight usually operated out of Thomasville. On October 8, 1955 I soloed the T-34. I think I was the first of my instructor's students to do so. But remember, I had my private pilot certificate, Shhhh! Upon returning to Spence I was unceremoniously tossed in the base swimming pool, which was the traditional custom for one's first solo

109

flight. The T-34 was not a very complex aircraft. It was built by Beech Aircraft and was a civilian single-engine aircraft, modified to meet Air Force specifications. The greatest modification was military-styled tandem cockpits with a control stick in the floor; and the throttle, mixture and prop controls on the left console. It had a clear bubble-styled canopy, in three sections, which enclosed both the front and rear cockpits. The front and rear sections of the canopy slid to the rear, just enough to allow entry and exit for each cockpit respectively. The mid-section was stationary.   I enjoyed it as the first for real military airplane that I soloed, although it was a civilian airplane in military uniform. It was a replacement for the PA-18 in Primary training. I logged 40 hours and 30 minutes in the T-34A.

The T-28A "Trojan" and the *Wilder Blue Yonder!*

Sometime around the first of November, we began our transition into the T-28. This was a super thrill. The T-28 was a joy to fly and a piece-of-cake to land. It was a newly designed military trainer and looked like a fighter aircraft – inside and out.   It was built by North American Aircraft Company, who built the famous WW II fighter the P-51 Mustang, and the 1950s F-100 Super Sabre. You could actually see similar lines in the T-28 design as that of the P-51, complete with bubble canopy; except for the T-28's radial engine and nose wheel. The canopy was a three-piece canopy similar to that of the T-34, where the front and rear canopies slid back to uncover the cockpits for entry and exit. The center section of the canopy was stationary. It had provision for guns and bombs, with the appropriate armament control panels in the cockpit. In fact, some countries bought it as a ground attack fighter.   It was used extensively by the South Vietnamese Air Force throughout the early years of the Vietnam War. My first flight in the T-28 was on November 17, 1955, and my first solo on November 29th. Man, I felt like a real fighter pilot in that cockpit! I know that I must have gone home over the Christmas Holidays, though I don't remember them. I also know that I spent every minute I could with Pat, and getting to know Norris more. As mentioned before, I felt so bad about keeping her out late then leaving her with so little sleep to go to work. I would hate myself for that. But she was a person who could do with about four hours of sleep or less a night, then get up and go, full of energy as always. It never ceased to amaze me how she could keep going that way. This carried on through her life; right up to the day she died instantly of a massive cardiac arrest, at the age of 73 – *while at work.*

Instruments, Navigation, Attitude and Vertigo!

Somewhere in our training we were introduced to instrument flight in the stationary, bellows-mounted, 360 degree rotation, three-axis's motion, and enclosed LINK trainer. Later we would fly actual instruments, under a hood in the rear cockpit of the T-28. I'm sure the instructors enjoyed this, as it gave them a chance to fly in the front cockpit for a change. The LINK was rather rudimentary and had a control wheel rather than the control stick. I didn't have a very difficult time with instruments. In fact, except for the pressure by the very nature of the rigidly structured program, I rather enjoyed instrument flying. It was quite a confidence builder – the fact that you could "take off"; navigate; do instrument approaches; and land; all enclosed in that wallowing box with a blacked-out interior, except for very dim instrument lighting. The instruments, radio navigation and communications were reminiscent of early instrument flying days. It really made you appreciate what the early aviation pioneers had to contend with – and the hazards. For pilot readers, we were taught radio range navigation and approaches with the old "coffee grinder" – an archaic "crank" for tuning and finding (hopefully) the correct radio frequency.

The radio reception was subject to interference and static noises, making tuning and audio quite difficult. We also had ADF (Automatic Direction Finding) for navigation and approaches. It was early aviation – and subject to many errors, especially radio frequency interference, and was unreliable near thunderstorms or in heavy rain showers. How about that .... an instrument approach system that was often unreliable due to heavy rainstorms or nearby thunderstorms?........ just when you needed it most! Of course, vertigo was always a very serious contention for the instrument pilot. If it was severe enough, it could actually incapacitate the pilot to the point where he would lose control of muscle coordination and his sense of up or down – and subsequent loss of aircraft control. Fortunately I was never prone to – and never experienced – severe vertigo attacks, except for deliberate vertigo induced in vertigo trainers. Mild vertigo could usually be overcome by intense concentration on the instruments, and eventually it would pass. But a pilot's vertigo, in an airplane on instruments, can be a killer! Years later I would fly Air Force aero club or private rental aircraft. Often I would take my son Robert flying and teach him instrument flying procedures and techniques. I was amazed how adept he was at the basic fundamentals of instrument flying. With more concentrated instrument training he would have been a great instrument pilot. Like me, he seemed not to be very prone to vertigo.

I never experienced an in-flight emergency while in Primary training, and I don't recall anyone having any emergencies in the T-34. Not so of the T-28 however. One student lost his propeller on a T-28. It just spun right off the airplane. He landed in a field and was OK. Another student had partial engine failure at night, but landed OK. It seems one of the pistons decided to "bailout" and exited right through the engine and engine cowling. We lost one student, an Aviation Cadet, through what was determined to be sheer pilot error. Some said "stupidity". He had spun straight into the ground. The after-accident investigation disclosed that he had been bragging about how many spins he could do before initiating the recovery procedure. The T-28 spun very easily and rapidly. The usual procedure was to initiate recovery after three to five spins. Upon recovery, however, the T-28 would tend to spin a bit faster for about a spin-and-a-half, before it decided to comply and recover. In order to do the number of spins this student claimed to have previously done, he would have had to climb well above 10,000 feet. Air Force regulations prohibited flight above 10,000 feet without oxygen. The T-28s we flew did not have oxygen. Actually flight above 10,000 feet without oxygen is no real threat unless you spent considerable time well above that altitude. Of course no one knew how high, nor for how long, this student might have flown above 10,000 feet, if at all. At the time of the accident, one T-28 student (probably flying between three and five thousand feet, which would be the norm) observed the T-28 spinning down through his altitude, all the way to the ground. Of course it was a fatality. Speculation was that the student waited too late to recover and became disorientated; or that he actually had gotten hypoxia (oxygen deprivation) and passed out, due to flying too high and too long with no oxygen available. With his bent on proving his invincibility, he may have actually climbed to an altitude where the lack of oxygen became a major factor. Of course, the cause could have been something totally different – one of those "we'll never know" accidents.

Night Cross-Country (X-C)

After receiving a few hours of night flight training, and some day and night cross-country training, we were cleared for solo night cross-countries. On the night of the scheduled solo cross-country, we were all cleared to fly the same route - a three-legged cross-country at the same altitude - taking off at three minute intervals. An instructor in a T-28 would be orbiting at each of the two designated turn points, to observe and insure that the students were at the correct turn points when they radioed their position reports. And, of course, to insure that there were no unauthorized short-cuts. Another function of the orbiting instructor would be to find and retrieve "lost pilots" in the event that became necessary. Although each student was responsible for planning his own flight, it was such a clear night that you could see the aircraft lights of the preceding T-28. You could actually "navigate" by following the lights of the aircraft ahead of you; but if you had not been doing your own navigating, and lost sight of the preceding T-28, you could be in trouble. Or if the preceding pilot got lost, and you were counting on him to do your navigating, you could also be in trouble. Actually, not necessarily this particular night, I recall that a couple of students did get lost and had to be located and led back to Spence. Upon completing primary flying training I had logged 89 hours and 30 minutes in the T-28A.

On to Basic Flying Training

The 56-V Primary Pilot Training Class graduation roster at Spence AB showed 63 Student Officers – all First or Second Lieutenants – and 52 Aviation Cadets. For Basic Pilot Training, Aviation Cadets would be sent either to Bryan AFB, Bryan, Texas for Single-Engine Jet Training or to Reese AFB, Lubbock, Texas for

Multi-Engine Training. Those Student Officers selected for multi-engine training would also be sent to Reese AFB. For Single-Engine Jet Training, Student Officers would go to either Goodfellow or Laredo AFBs in Texas, or to Columbus AFB in Mississippi.

Basic Flying Training – Single-Engine Jet (T-33) – Bryan Air Force Base, Bryan, Texas

I now had in my hand the assignment I had been hoping and praying for (not necessarily in that order) all my life: Single-engine fighter pilot training! The dreaded fear that I would get multi-engine school was over. Of course the Air Force could always change its mind. But for the moment I was ecstatic beyond belief. Bryan, Texas was between Houston and Waco; and it was right next door to Texas A&M and all those co-eds. *Sorry girls, I'm spoken for!* I had logged 130 total hours; now on to Bryan AFB and the T-33A.

My orders read to proceed on/or about April 5, 1956 and to report to the 3531st Pilot Training Squadron, 3530th Pilot Training Wing, Bryan AFB, Texas on April 12th. I don't remember traveling to Bryan, but I must have found a way to spend a day or two with Pat between assignments. I would be flying the T-33A "Shooting Star", built by Lockheed. Lockheed also built the WW II P-38 "Lightening" of South Pacific Theater fame, and it was called "The Forked-Tail Devil" by Japanese pilots. The T-33, as I mentioned earlier in my story, was the same as the P-80 used in the Korean War. However, the T-33 had a rear cockpit added for the instructor; and had fuel tanks mounted on the wing tips rather than slung under the tips, as with the P-80. As for the upperclass, there was less and less emphasis on the status between classes as graduation neared. Ground school and flying was split between morning and afternoon, and reversed on alternating weeks, as was done in Primary. Those T-33s sure looked nice on the ramp. I could hardly wait. The students spent several hours in the cockpits on the ramp getting acquainted with the T-33. I felt a little advantage since I had done a little work on my squadron's T-33 while at New Castle. Additionally I had a couple of flights in the rear cockpit with our squadron pilots. And in jet mechanic school at Amarillo, the engine we worked on and ran up for engine tests was the J-33 jet engine built by Allison, the same engine that was in the P-80 and now the T-33. However, I now viewed all of this in a different and highly motivated perspective.

Our barracks were WW II barracks again! We had two-man rooms, a little bigger than at Spence but more austere. Our latrine was a community building outside in the middle of the barracks complex. My roommate was John. John was sort of a comic – a good guy with lots of friends. His favorite comment was: "Why yes, I fly jets!" This was also a favorite phrase we used with the local girls. John would go on to Fly F-100s after graduation, and later fly for Braniff Airlines.

113

Upon completion of Basic Flying Training, all Cadets would be commissioned as Second Lieutenants and sent to an Advanced Pilot Training base for specialized aircraft type training. Following advanced training, those who came from active duty or civilian life would begin a four-year active duty commitment; and those from the Air National Guard would be returned to their units. The top ten outstanding graduates for each Basic Flying Training Base would be designated as Distinguished Graduates and, in descending order of class standing, be given their choice of aircraft and/or base from those available to the class. I sure wanted to be in that top ten – I wanted an F-86, anywhere; the F-100 would be my second choice.

Basic training was very much a repeat of Primary, except for the T-33 and formation flying; new aircraft systems; emergency procedures; aerobatics; night flying; cross-countries; the works. Previous classes got more T-28 time, before transitioning into the T-33 jets. At Basic, our instructors were Air Force Pilots – no more civilian contract flying training. Each instructor generally had three aviation cadets at his table. At my instructor's table were Ed, Carlon, and me. Ed went on to own and operate his own flying service. In fact he had his own aircraft with him at Bryan – not at the base however. I don't know if our instructor was aware of Ed's airplane or not. I was not made aware until years later. Carlon went on to be a Senior Judge in a state court system. Then there was me: an enlisted Airman who went on to become a fighter pilot, and retire with over 33 years of service. *Fighter pilot;* the greatest job in the world!

New Stuff!

I think Bryan AFB Basic Pilot Training (56-V Aviation Cadets) was the second base to go to all-jet basic. There was no T-28 before transitioning into jets, as was done with previous basic pilot training classes. Entry into jet pilot training required introduction to many new training requirements, some of which were: Ejection seats; oxygen masks and systems; altitude chamber flight simulator; and the physiological hazards of flying in rarefied air and an oxygen-deficient environment. Ejection Seat Trainer: This was a pilot seat mounted on a near-vertical track, inclined slightly to the rear, simulating the seat ejection track of a jet aircraft cockpit. The seat sat on a huge compressed coiled spring; at which time, after assuming the correct ejection posture, the instructor shouted "Eject, Eject!" When the ejection seat trigger was squeezed, the spring was released and you shot up the track for about 15 feet. Correct posture was critical, to prevent back, legs and arm injuries during ejection from an actual aircraft. Oxygen Systems: The T-33 oxygen system was the A-14 pressure-breathing, diluter-demand oxygen regulator, which directed oxygen from the oxygen tank to the pilot's oxygen mask. It simply meant that oxygen was mixed with normal air in the cockpit, by the oxygen regulator; the ratio being dictated by the cockpit "altitude", maintained by the cockpit pressurization system. Upon reaching 30,000 feet pressure breathing was required, and the regulator had to be manually set to provide 100% oxygen under pressure. This required the pilot to reverse his breathing process and forcefully exhale against the pressure, which was very exhausting after a short time. A few of the training flights would be at 30,000 to 37,000 feet.

Altitude Chamber: This was a huge ground-bound tank, similar to what deep-sea divers are placed in when suffering "the bends" after a deep dive; except, divers are subjected to prolonged high pressures, whereas pilots are subjected to low atmospheric pressures. The chamber accommodates about 10 students. Students are paired together, and a couple of instructors are on board the chamber. After having the chamber air pressure rapidly reduced, to simulate climbing to about 35,000 feet, one student would be required to remove his oxygen mask while the second student acted as a safety monitor. The object was to acquaint students with their own particular symptoms leading up to hypoxia (oxygen depletion). Symptoms are not necessarily the same for all individuals. At these altitudes, useful consciousness is about three to four minutes. Small task were assigned to demonstrate to the observing oxygenated students just how quickly, *and unaware*, an oxygen-deprived pilot can become incapacitated, even before losing consciousness. The roles were then reversed. After all students had a chance to experience hypoxia, we were individually placed in a small sealed off two-part compartment of the chamber. One part was depressurized to simulate 45,000 feet; while the adjoining part of the small compartment with the student was depressurized to 5,000, simulating normal pressurization in the cockpit. The connection between them was a thin disc, which was punctured at a moment not known to the student, resulting in a rapid decompression; simulating instant loss of cockpit pressure, such as would occur from a failed canopy seal, battle damage, loss of canopy, etc. The student had only seconds to don his oxygen mask and signal to the instructor outside the chamber that he was OK. The student was then "landed", and hopefully had learned a valuable lesson in the physiology of flight.

T-33A: First Flight; First Solo!
My first dual flight in the T-33 was on April 26, 1956, and my first T-33 solo was May 10th. I don't think I was the first one at my table to solo the T-33. I remember clearly my first T-33 solo. Our practice area was about 20 to 30 miles west of Bryan. Right after takeoff and gear up, I think I had as big a grin on my face as my oxygen mask would accommodate – at least as big a grin as I had that day I knew I was accepted for Aviation Cadet Pilot Training. I entered the practice area, and did the routine stuff; turns; stalls; climbs; descents, etc. Then the aerobatics: Wow! Wow! Wow! What a thrill – thrill – thrill for me! I really hated to return to Bryan. Shortly afterwards we began formation flying. This was also totally new stuff for me. But again, it was such a thrill being in formation with other aircraft; two, three, and four-ship formations. My instructor said I took to formation like a "duck to water". He sent me up as solo

wingman on his wing, while he was dual with another student. My first dual formation flight was on May 16th 1956 and my first solo formation was May 21st.

High Altitude Formation: "Look Out! Here He Comes!"
Another new experience was high-altitude flying – especially formation flying. Formation flying is extremely intense; 110% concentration. In the summer time, I would land looking like I had just stepped out of the shower in my flying suit. When flying a wing position, your attention is focused on the aircraft you are flying on. The more aircraft in the formation, the more concentration required. Being number four on the end of a four-ship formation, is like being on the end of a whip. The slightest movement the leader makes is amplified with each succeeding aircraft down the line. If the leader or the other aircraft aren't smooth and steady, then number four can be all over the place as the "whip cracks". There isn't enough space here to go into detail about formation flying, but I will discuss high-altitude formation briefly. The automatic fuel controls of jet engines in those days could not handle rapid throttle movement, as they can with today's state-of-the-art. The fuel control in those days was essentially the pilot's hand on the throttle. You had to carefully and slowly advance the power (throttle) as the engine "spooled-up"; otherwise you would over-temp the engine and risk buckling, cracking, or warping the tailpipe, which would mean an engine or tailpipe change. One instrument on the instrument panel, called Exhaust Gas Temperature gage (EGT), gave the pilot an instant readout of the tailpipe temperature. As the pilot initially advanced the throttle for more power, he had to be very careful not to over-run the EGT with the throttle. In essence, he had to follow the EGT with the throttle as the EGT rose, and use caution not to exceed the limit. Just a little impatience in advancing the throttle would send a tremendous spike to the EGT. Due to the higher density of the air at low altitudes, the engine was a little more responsive than it was at higher altitude, where the air was super thin. This required a lot of thought and advanced planning in high-altitude formation flying, where throttle-jockeying was necessary to maintain position in the formation during maneuvering. During a landing phase, where a go-around or touch-and-go may become necessary or planned, this slow engine response and high EGT was a "must plan ahead" situation – commonly referred to as "stay ahead of the aircraft"! Propeller aircraft are a little more forgiving, in most instances. But you definitely had to plan your moves well ahead in the state-of-the-art jet engines of those days. A late decision to go around from an aborted landing attempt required finesse in nursing the jet engine to 100% power.

The same situation occurs at high altitude where, in the thinner air, the engine response is even slower. Likewise, reducing power has less instant effect than that of reducing the throttle on a propeller aircraft. Because of the thinner air at high altitudes, reducing power did not produce the immediate deceleration as experienced with a power reduction at lower, denser air altitudes.

Planning ahead was crucial. It was quite comical watching inexperienced students doing a formation join-up. If you are some distance away when the join-up signal is given by the leader, initially closure is not readily apparent. Of course, for join-up, your speed and cut-off angle had to be adjusted in order to close the distance properly and timely. Not until you are relatively close-in, is the rapid closure rate visually apparent to the pilot. Suddenly you realize that you are screaming in toward the leader or his wingman. To compensate, you rapidly reduce the throttle; but due to the phenomenon just explained above about thin air, the aircraft doesn't immediately decelerate. The results of all this is that you go *hurtling by the leader,* leaving him in your "dust". It's called an "over-shoot"! Fortunately the wingmen didn't see all this, because their eyes are "glued" to the leader in close formation. But the instructor saw it. He is puckered, hoping you miss him and the wingmen. He is now yelling instructions at you, to your embarrassment. In order to make a quick recovery from the over-shoot and regain your position in the formation, you leave the throttle retarded as the aircraft finally begins to decelerate. The formation is now *rapidly catching up to you.* Too late, you realize this; so you advance the throttle in an attempt to match his airspeed. Guess what? The formation now goes screaming past you again, as your engine is trying to wind-up to the thrust demanded by your throttle. So the seesaw, yo-yo maneuvering begins all over again; until you are finally able to regain your position in the formation. Fun and games! *Instructors are brave souls!*

If a solo formation student is having a really bad day at formation flying, the instructor may direct him to break off and return to the base. This very situation resulted in one of our student fatalities. This student was having a bad day in formation; so the instructor broke him off, with instructions to return to base. By the time students reach this stage, they have had considerable time, both dual and solo, in the local flying area. Anyway, this student became lost returning to the base and finally ran out of fuel. He chose to crash-land rather that eject, thereby killing himself. Attempts to locate and to orient him by radio, and provide a heading to fly to the base, were all futile. He was an extremely nice guy; very gentle; and had a girlfriend to whom I believe he was engaged.

Formation aerobatics were great fun, especially in-trail. In doing loops, the air and jet engine idiosyncrasies I've described above came into full play again. In all the aerobatics, the leader sets his throttle and leaves it there throughout the aerobatic maneuvering. During in-trail (follow-the-leader) aerobatics, when the leader starts a pull up into a loop, gravity naturally begins to slow him down. You must anticipate his slowing. The instant you see his nose come up to begin the climb, you must reduce your throttle slightly to maintain matched airspeeds and position. Your aircraft nose is only a few feet from his tailpipe. As he comes over the top, inverted, his aircraft will begin to accelerate; and continue to do so down the back side of the loop, until leveling off at the bottom. Again, you must anticipate this and advance the throttle to maintain your position. The leader's maneuvering will result in speed changes, even though his throttle is set. This must be constantly anticipated by the wingmen, and throttle adjustments made accordingly. Remember the poor number four wingman? Every movement of the leader is amplified by each succeeding wingman – the last guy in the formation feels like that end of the whip.

Hot and Cold!

Instrument training was flown under the hood, in the rear cockpit of the T-33. It was more of the procedures we learned in Primary – only much faster and at higher altitudes. The T-33 had a reasonably good air conditioning and heating system in most circumstances – if you anticipated its limitations. Under that canopy in the hot summer sun and high humidity, it was like a greenhouse; a sauna. At high altitudes, in the thinner and dryer air, the system did a fair job of keeping the windshield and canopy defrosted. However, if you forgot to turn on the defroster prior to a rapid descent to a lower altitude, the moisture at the lower levels would completely fog over your windshield and canopy. The moisture content of the lower levels and condensation inside the canopy and windshield were just too much for the marginally effective defroster. Even if you should find yourself in clear weather, you still couldn't see outside the cockpit, due to the heavy condensation on the inside of the windshield and canopy – and even frantically wiping with your gloved hand would not clear it! You were forced to fly instruments for a few minutes until the condensation evaporated and cleared the windshield and canopy for you – hopefully before you reached the runway for landing. Another odd thing about the air conditioning system was that it would throw *snowballs* at you. The cooling air was forced out of a pipe, with the outlet just behind your right shoulder about head high. Quite often, with the right atmospheric conditions, it would spit tiny snowballs at you – about pea or marble sized. But even with cockpit air conditioning, after landing you would climbing out of the cockpit in a sweat-soaked flight suit. Just how critical and how hot enclosed jet cockpits could become, even in winter time, would be brought home years later when I transitioned into the F-100. Until I get to that part of my story, just know that they can get seriously and sometimes fatally hot!

Formation aerobatics are intensively hard work. Sweating is the order of the day. Naturally, we wore jet helmets, with the necessary oxygen mask which contained our radio microphone. When flying formation aerobatics on a wing or in-trail, sweat would run down into your eyes; you barely had a chance to wipe them, and sometimes you couldn't – you couldn't afford to take your eyes off the aircraft you were maintaining position on. When pulling high "Gs" with your sweat-soaked face and mask, the "G" forces would pull the mask down almost off your nose – even my big "schnoz" wouldn't hold it in place. It couldn't be tightened sufficiently, without being painful, to prevent it from being pulled down. When doing air-combat maneuvers, this was even more critical while trying to keep your "enemy" in sight. Losing sight of your enemy would almost certainly give you a pain in the rear, literally the 6 o'clock position on your tail, and ruin you day.

There was another tragic fatal accident while I was at Bryan. It happened in another training squadron during night flying. Two T-33s collided, with each having an instructor and student aboard. One T-33 was making a straight-in approach to the runway. The other was making the normal circling descent from an overhead traffic pattern altitude, to a short final approach. The circling T-33 descended onto the lower T-33 just short of the runway. Apparently neither saw the other. Four fatalities! I never had any in-flight emergencies at either Primary or Basic. Thank you, Lord! There was only one close call that I saw. There may have been others, unseen. I was entering the traffic pattern when a T-33 already in traffic went whizzing by my nose – not startlingly close, but close enough. I don't think he saw me. My instructor never saw him either. For most civilian and airline pilots, if they *see* another aircraft, it's a *near-miss.* For military pilots, close proximity and close calls are very much a routine, and part of the flying day.

We flew one dual high-altitude Round-Robin cross-country (no stops) from Bryan AFB, to Austin, on to Waco and return to Bryan. I forget the date. On August 26th, I flew my last Basic Flying Training cross-country with an RON (remain-over-night) to Williams AFB, Chandler, Arizona and returned to Bryan the following day. This too was dual. I don't recall any solo cross-countries in Basic Pilot Training, but my military flight records show four hours of night solo time at Bryan.

Graduation Approaches!
About a week before graduation, the Advance Training assignments arrived. I had made the top ten ranking in the class – I don't remember my exact ranking – but it meant Distinguished Graduate designation. In addition to being able to pick my choice of assignment, among those remaining when it became my turn at selection, Distinguished Graduates were given the chance to apply for a Regular Air Force Commission. Would I? You bet I would! I had hoped to make the Air Force a career with a Regular Commission. Although not a guarantee of retention for the twenty years necessary to qualify for a full military retirement, it would give you an advantage in promotion selection; and meant that the Air Force would be less likely to terminate your service in an across-the-board military RIF (reduction-in-force). If you should happen to be RIF-ed, it likely would occur during your 14th to 18th year of service. An officer could be RIF-ed with as little as two years to go until retirement. If this occurred to a Reserve Officer, the officer had the option of reenlisting as an enlisted man at the highest

enlisted rank he had held, in order to finish his 20 years for military retirement. Or he could remain in the inactive Reserve forces and attend monthly drills until the age of 65, whereupon he could draw his military retirement. Once RIF-ed, the Reserve Officer also had the option of seeking government employment – sometimes in the same job from which he was RIF-ed, and at the higher civilian pay scale. Weird World! *A Regular Officer had none of these perks or options, like the Reservist did. A Regular Officer, if RIF-ed, could not reenlist, regardless of how little time he had left to do for a 20 year retirement; could not hold a government job; and could not join the inactive Reserves. Go figure! For a RIF-ed Regular Officer, all those years were useless toward a retirement program!* Still, I gambled on a Regular Commission and being kept on for retirement. It would be about a year before the Regular Application would eventually be approved. Actually, the date of Regular Commissioning would be back-dated to the graduation date of September 13, 1956. *Things were looking up – thank you Lord! I was one week from graduating as a Distinguished Graduate from Air Force Aviation Cadet Pilot Training, with a choice of assignments; commissioning as a Second Lieutenant; receiving my wings; a chance to apply for a Regular Commission; and best of all, five days after graduating I would be marrying the girl of my dreams!* All of this was almost too much for my mind to absorb.

Assignment Selection: I would have loved to get an F-86 assignment. But there were none, as I recall, when I got my chance at selection. However, there was an F-100 available – my second choice. But, there was also an F-94C assignment to an F-94C squadron *at New Castle County Airport (NCCA), Delaware* where I had been a crew chief on the F-94C for two years, before being selected for Aviation Cadet Pilot Training. Man! What a dilemma! I wanted that F-100. And I wanted that F-94C assignment back to New Castle. The F-94C assignment was to the 96th Fighter Interceptor Squadron (FIS), a sister squadron to the 332nd that I was in at New Castle. We had two F-94C squadrons and a Delaware Air National Guard F-86 squadron. I thought if I selected the F-94C assignment, I might be able to wrangle for a transfer to my old squadron once I got back to NCCA. I wanted that F-100, but also wanted to fly the F-94C that I was so familiar with. And it would also be nice to get back to New Castle and the old gang, so I could *flaunt* my new Silver Wings and shiny-gold Second Lieutenant's bars. Really it would be quite an oddity if I got back and was able to fly my old "531", the F-94C on which I was a crew chief for two years. What should I do? What should I do? Why did both assignments have to be there staring me in the face? Why couldn't it have been one or the other? Who in their right mind would give up an F-100 assignment? Silence! *Thinking, thinking!* What will I do? Finally – I chose the F-94C. I picked my old aircraft and base over the F-100. My classmate next in order behind me picked the F-100 that I passed up. Years later at one of our reunions, he told me that he picked my F-100 assignment. I told him that he didn't pick it, I gave it to him! I explained why I forfeited the F-100. But years later I would finally get into the F-100.

I logged 95 hours in the T-33A at Bryan for a total of 225 hours at Graduation. My orders read that I was to report on October 9, 1956 to the 3550th Combat Crew Training Group at Moody AFB, Valdosta, Georgia for Class 57-A, USAF Combat Flying School (Interceptor). This was the F-94C All-Weather Interceptor School. It would be instrument intensive (all-weather) in addition to learning the F-94C weapons control system and intercept procedures. Here I would be crewed up with a Radar Operator (RO) trainee graduate from Navigator School. We would do the training together and be assigned as a crew to the 96th FIS at New Castle. Hot Diggity! Moody AFB! I would be going back to Georgia – South Georgia – just north of the Georgia-Florida line! Completion of the course was scheduled to be February 12, 1957 then to New Castle, with a reporting date of February 15th. Of course I still had to get through graduation at Bryan which was scheduled for September 13th 1956.

Deal With God!

One day I was lying on my bunk thinking of the nearing graduation. The thought that, barring any tragedy, I was just about to realize my lifelong dream of becoming a fighter pilot – and shortly afterward would be marrying the girl that I would sometimes think of through the years, since I first met her when I was nine years old. I remembered as a youngster discussing with God my dreams of being a fighter pilot and having a great wife and family– and my promise that if He would give me my two dreams, I would give my life to Jesus and try to live accordingly. As I revealed earlier in my story, I had always known Jesus (so has the Devil), but I had resisted giving my life to Him – while holding onto the back of the church pew in front of me and resisting the preacher's invitation to "Come to Jesus"! I realized too, that my life could end any time before I made my profession of faith in Jesus public and acknowledged Him as my Savior, as the Bible teaches us to do. After all, we had lost two class members earlier during training and recently had four night flying fatalities just off the end of the runway. Except for the Grace of God......! I knew Jesus; I believed in Jesus! Why was I hesitating in doing what I knew I should do? "No excuse, Sir". as we were taught to respond when an upperclassman asked why we did a dumb thing or violated a regulation. I decided it's time! I went to talk with the base Chaplain about my decision to publicly announce my belief in Jesus as the Son of God who died for my sins, and to be baptized. The Chaplain suggested that I go to the First Baptist Church in Bryan and talk with their Pastor about my decision, and my wish to be baptized into their Baptist Church.

The following Sunday I attended the church service at the First Baptist Church in Bryan. I went forward at the end of the Pastor's sermon during the invitation and told him of my wishes. The church accepted me into the church membership and scheduled the baptism. The base Chaplin baptized me into the First Baptist Church, Bryan, Texas on September 9, 1956 four days before I graduated from Air Force Pilot Training Class 56-V. Of course my Mom and Pat were delighted when I told them. NOTE: From Pat's 1964 calendar she had entered that she had joined the First Baptist Church of Zephyrhills, Florida on April 3rd, 1952 – (after professing her faith and belief in Jesus Christ as her Savior) – and was baptized into the church on April 8th. Interestingly, I had enlisted in the United States Air Force on March 29th, 1952.

Mom and Pat were great Christian ladies, along with my sister Oreese. Pat was a relatively new Christian. Her best friend and co-worker had led her to accepting Jesus as her Savior. Can you believe in today's *enlightened society* that her friend and co-worker would have been permitted to talk to her about Jesus? Progress? Pat was very active in her church, The Brookhaven Baptist Church of Brookhaven, Georgia in northeast Atlanta – active in church, young adult activities and Sunday evening training programs. She was very instrumental in keeping me church active and centered. I credit her with my Christian focus. You did not have to know her long until you knew she was a Christian. She *walked the talk*; but did not wear her Christianity on her sleeve; nor carry a Bible; nor quote Scripture; nor corner you with her Christian testimony; nor flaunt her church or beliefs. *But her Christianity was loud and clear!* She was outstandingly humble and sincerely concerned about people – especially the elderly, the feeble, and young children; a people person who loved people, and they her. Pat told me that she was a very shy young girl growing up and in high school. It was not until she became a Christian, and attended Sunday night church training sessions, where members were asked to study and do presentations on various Biblical topics, that she came out of her shell. She became a great presenter, and developed a great "people personality", which she later passed on to our sons, Norris and Robert. I put her up along with my Mom and my sister Oreese in their love of Jesus. Thank you Lord! It was not long after we married that I realized this, and that God had given me the greatest gift He could have at this stage in my life; renewing my faith and Christianity, and beginning a new career with a new wife and new family. Norris was now six years old, whom I would later adopt, and try to make sure that I did not cause him to stumble along his way while growing up. Pat was a great help in guiding me to a mature Christian life.

Once when I was visiting Pat and accompanying her to her Sunday night church training group, the group leader asked Pat to introduce me. Pat introduced me as "Robert" Partridge, which is how she knew me. And so did my friends and family except for Mom, my sister and older brother who called me "Bobby". But I had been called by my first name "George" in the Air Force, for about four years by now. When someone in the group asked me to repeat my name I, without thinking, responded "George" Partridge. There was wholesale laughter. They thought Pat didn't know who she was with. *From that moment on Pat began to call me "George".*

GRADUATION DAY – September 13, 1956☺!

We went through the necessary processing, uniform purchases, tailoring and other preparations for graduation. Being an airman on active duty, I had to be discharged from the Air Force in order to accept a commission as a Second Lieutenant in the Air Force Reserve (active duty). My honorable discharge date is September 12, 1956. I now had two honorable discharges: One from the Marine Reserve on March 28, 1952, the day before Richard's and my enlistment into the Air Force; and this one from the Air Force in order to accept my commission on September 13th. Pat, Mom and Richard flew out for my graduation. I was getting more and more excited as the day I had waited for all my life approached.

Graduation Day: Exceptional spit and polish was the order of the day. The underclass would do the graduation parade for the dignitaries, VIPs and 56-V graduates. The instructors would provide a 16-plane T-33 formation flyover – twice. The graduation guest speaker and presenter of the wings, bars and commission would be "fighter ace" Brigadier General Robert L. Scott of WW II China, *Flying Tigers* fame. You will recall that I mentioned earlier in my story that General Scott was one of my boyhood heroes, and that I had written a high school book report assignment on his book: "God is my Co-Pilot". About some forty years later I met him again, at Maxwell AFB, Alabama and got him to autograph a copy of "God is my Co-Pilot". I mentioned the Bryan AFB, graduation to him. He had immediate recall, and began naming base personnel there at that time. He loved to talk and tell his stories and was a frequently invited guest speaker at events around the country. At that time at Maxwell he would likely have been in his late 80's. A few years after this meeting at Maxwell AFB, I took Pat and Robert to the Museum of Aviation at Robins Air Force Reserve Base, Warner-Robins, Georgia to meet "my hero" General Scott, who was the museum's Public Relations Officer – at 90 years of age, I believe! General Scott died soon afterwards at the age of 93. He drove his own car, and played golf weekly almost up until he died.

What a fitting climax to my pilot training, leading to a fighter pilot assignment: One of my boyhood ace fighter pilot heroes would be the graduation guest speaker; present my graduation certificate, Silver Wings, and conduct the commissioning ceremony! Man! What else wonderful could happen to me? Oh yes! Following the ceremony, Pat pinned my Silver Air Force Pilot Wings on me! Mom pinned on my gold Second Lieutenant's bars, assisted by Pat! Then I returned my first salute received from an enlisted man, and then handed him a new, crisp one dollar bill – a tradition for the first salute received by a newly commissioned officer. Richard was filming it all with his 8mm movie camera. My thanks and gratitude to Richard. Without him and his camera I would have no record of Pat pinning my wings, Mom pinning my bars, and receiving my first salute. My feet were off the ground! What a day to remember as long as my memory lasts! Now, to home for my next great commissioning: Husband to Pat and Dad to Norris on September 18, 1956. Soon we would be on our way to Moody AFB, Valdosta, Georgia and a search for our *first* home. Could anyone have been more blessed than me? I think not!

*****

ADVANCED PILOT TRAINING – MOODY AFB, VALDOSTA, GEORGIA; F-94C
(September 1956 – February 1957)

F-94C All-Weather Interceptor School Class 57-A – Course 112103B

I have already described the F-94C previously, as a totally new aircraft with a new weapons system for intercepting and destroying enemy bombers; new radar and rockets instead of guns. The Cold War against Communism was constantly percolating, particularly with regards to Russia. In the years following WW II, through the destruction of the Berlin Wall in 1989, with the subsequent dismantling of the Union of Soviet Socialist Republics (USSR) in 1991, nuclear war was always looming on the horizon. There were many potential *WW III* fuses just a heart-beat away from being lit. A case in point was the summer of 1962 nuclear confrontation with Russia, over the installation of nuclear missiles in Cuba.

Fighter-Interceptor squadrons and long range ground radar units were assigned to the Air Forces of the Air Defense Command (ADC), across the northern tier of North America and along America's east and west coasts. The northern-most defense early warning radar line, referred to as the DEW line, would provide early detection of enemy bombers coming in from over the North Pole, attempting to penetrate the American and Canadian defenses. There were other radar lines of defense below the DEW line. The ground radar controllers would direct the interceptors toward the enemy bombers, until they came within range of the interceptors' radar. The interceptors' radar operators (ROs) would then take control of the intercepts and direct their pilots into an advantageous position; whereupon the pilots would use their radar scopes to obtain a firing position on the enemy bombers. This is a thumbnail sketch of the fighter-interceptor operations of the North America Air Defense Command (NORAD) against enemy bombers of those days. There were also, of course, the Intercontinental Ballistic Missiles and submarines. Thus was the training into which I was about to enter: All-Weather Fighter-Interceptor Pilot. Intercontinental Ballistic Missiles (ICBMs) came on the scene about 1954. Russian bombers still remain a threat today, frequently testing our detection and intercept capabilities. Intercepting and identifying unknown aircraft approaching our national air defense identification zones (ADIZ), would remain an ongoing mission throughout my assignments within the Air Defense Command.

First Things First

En route to Moody AFB from Bryan AFB, I had an authorized delay. (leave) to take care of a priority matter: Making Pat my wife! Actually, there were several days between my September 13th graduation at Bryan and having to report to

Moody on October 9th. Since the time interval was more that the few days of authorized travel time, I had three options: Remain at Bryan until my travel time to Moody; proceed to Moody with my authorized travel time, sign-in and await my class start date (57-A); or take leave time, over and above travel time, as a delay en route. Any casual time spent at either Bryan or Moody would have meant pulling menial details while awaiting either my departure from Bryan, or proceeding to Moody and await my class start date. With the priority matter to take care of at home, which do you think I elected to do? You're right! Leave time! While at home, Pat and her girlfriends were in a flurry getting ready for our wedding on September 18th. I won't even try to recount all the activities going on. Of course wedding dress, cake and photographer were high on their list of things to do. I'm just glad they didn't forget the groom: Me!

Pat still used her married name of Wells. Perhaps because it was for Norris's sake, since he also shared the name. Norris was excited too. He was going to have a dad again! Pat's Pastor at First Baptist Church, Brookhaven, Georgia, would not perform the ceremony, because she was a divorcee. If he only knew the love that would grow and endure from that marriage, he would have been honored to perform the ceremony! How could he though? But he would permit us to use the church. We asked a cousin who was a pastor to do the ceremony, and he agreed: Frank Singleton. Pat was in her wedding dress, Norris in white tux as ring bearer, and me in my Air Force Silver Tan (Class A) uniform with white shirt and black bow tie. This combination of uniform was considered by the Air Force to be a formal uniform. Pat had her sister Carrie, friends, and family as her attendants. I don't recall much of the preparations; but, I remember the event and the day – September 18th, 1956! I think Carrie was the bridesmaid. My brother Richard would be my best man, and my brother Harold would be one of my groomsmen. Pat's family and mine were very supportive of us and I think all were present at the wedding.

We had no time for a honeymoon. I had planned and reserved a cabin at Gatlinburg, Tennessee. But the time between Bryan and Moody did not permit us to take advantage of the trip. In all of our 45 years together before she died – we never got there. There were many honeymoons however; here, there and half way around the world. For the time being Moody AFB would have to be our first honeymoon.

Never Ask Directions!

Pat's Mom Vennie would keep Norris while we used our honeymoon time searching for a house/home in Valdosta, Georgia, before getting down to learning my new trade – Fighter-Interceptor Pilot. We would try to find a house and go back to get Norris a few weeks later, when I had a break in training.

I had made reservations in Atlanta at the Cherokee Rose Tourist Court Motel, 1387 Northside Drive (Cabin No. 15) for our trip to Moody, immediately following our wedding. After the reception we were on our way. I can't remember but I think Richard allowed his car to be "decorated" as our decoy escape vehicle, and he would be the driver until we could get to my car for our trip south. My car was the "chick-magnet" Olds '98 convertible that I had left with Pat while I was in pilot training. Of course I no longer needed it as a chick-magnet. I think it had long since been demagnetized, even before I bought it. After transferring to the Olds and heading south, I couldn't find the Cherokee Rose Motel. I drove around for a little while looking for it, but no luck. I was getting exasperated, but I think Pat was amused. Then I did a guy's "No-No" thing! I stopped and asked for directions. Finally we found it! *To be continued – later!*

On to Valdosta!

The next day we were on our way south again. I left something back there at the Cherokee Rose which I don't regret – and I never went back for it. Pat and I arrived at Valdosta and arranged for a motel while we looked for a home. We found a room in the Pines Camp Motel on Ashley Street in Valdosta on September 19th. Finally we found a wood frame house, a duplex as I recall, with a second story. We had the left side of the duplex. After checking out of the Pines Camp Motel on September 21st, we moved into our first home at 1513 N. Slater Street, Valdosta. Our first church would be First Baptist Church of Valdosta, with Reverend James P. Rodgers as Pastor. I have no recollection of the Pastor or the church. Since my reporting date was not until October 9th, there was some time to discover Pat, Valdosta, Moody AFB, and settle into our home as *2nd Lieutenant and Mrs. Partridge.* I knew that once I signed-in, I would have little free time after I did the required in-coming clearances for personnel records; supply; hospital; squadron; and a host of other base facilities......and - oh yes - Base Finance, don't want to forget them. Pat and I were enjoying the time we had together before I had to get serious with learning to be an all-weather interceptor pilot. I was so preoccupied with all that was happening that I recall very little of our personal time at Valdosta. I think we had neighbors in the other half of the duplex but I don't remember them.

All-Weather Interceptor Training Begins – T-33/F-94C

Flying training for the first few weeks would be in the rear cockpit of the T-33, under-the-hood (*lovingly* referred to as "the bag"), flying on instruments. This was to get you to peak proficiency in instrument flying – the all-weather portion of the training. The latter part would be the F-94C checkout and transition, followed by the interceptor pilot training. For most of those instrument flights in the T-33 I never saw daylight, except for about five minutes during each flight for takeoff and landing. The instructor did the takeoffs and landings. You would go under the "bag" immediately after takeoff and remain there until just before landing. The rest of the flight, normally 2 to 2½ hours, would be under the hood on the gages (instruments). If we were in actual weather, the instructors would allow you to slide the hood back for some actual instrument weather experience. The hood was made of white canvas and suspended on cords strung overhead in the rear cockpit. When pulled forward, it blocked all forward and outside visibility, except for the instrument panel and interior cockpit. Actual weather instrument flying is really easier than instrument flight under the hood. The hood was confining, and sometimes sagged down onto your helmet. Shadows and light beams from the light coming in around the hood would move round the cockpit, and could be very distracting and vertigo-inducing. Fortunately I was never very prone to vertigo. The F-94C had a rear cockpit, but no pilot controls. It was strictly for the Radar Operator with his radar scope and electronic control panels. Therefore, the rear cockpit could not be used for the instrument training, pilot training or aircraft control of any type. Anyway, the T-33 was much less expensive to operate.

Getting her Feet wet!

As I said, I don't remember much of Moody except some of our training events. Pat was probably wondering what she had gotten herself into. Most of my time was spent flying or in the books and manuals. But she took it like a "trooper". While we were dating, I told her that being a military wife had demands about which civilian wives had no clue: Military career demands; frequent separations, both short and long term; military rank hierarchy; frequent studies to maintain knowledge and proficiency in the aircraft; wee-morning-hour no-notice practice alerts; and on, and on. Generally speaking, military wives share a common bond. They are a close-knit group, understanding each other's stresses and demands; supporting each other during their husbands long TDYs (temporary duty) away from home; deployments stateside or overseas; combat; and the ever-present potential fatality of close friends. I told her that she would sometime encounter a high-ranking officer's wife who "*wore*" her husband's rank. But not to worry, I soon learned. Throughout my career, Pat was the best military wife one could have. She was comfortable with everyone: High or low status; military or civilian; officer or wife; general or airman. She had no formal education beyond high school at that time, and she was her natural self with everyone – nothing fake; no airs; and an outstanding people-person. Everyone loved her – officers, wives and our civilian friends. If I had been as good an officer as she was a wife and mother, I would have retired as a four-star general rather than Lieutenant Colonel. Throughout my career I tried to impress upon my bosses that I should be a general, but they were never convinced. They all felt that Pat should have been a general.

It was soon after training started that we had an opportunity to return home to get Norris. I don't remember just what phase of training I was in at the time, but I must have had a weekend free. The only incident I recall at Moody, which was a non-operational incident, occurred in the base barber shop. I didn't witness it, but heard of it later. This is essentially the story according to what I was told: There was a black officer; the services had now been integrated for a few years, but remember this is South Georgia in the late fifties, and plenty of racism still abounded. The officer went into the barber shop, and when his turn came for a haircut he sat in the barber's chair and the (white) barber took his clippers and cut a swath through the officer's hair, from front to back. The barber told the officer that they didn't do haircuts for his kind there.

(Note: according to retired Major General Jesse M. Allen - as he recounts *his* memory of the same incident in his book 'From Jeep Driver to General' - the black officer was Major "Chappie" James, who went on to become a four star general in the Air Force, and Vietnam combat veteran.)

By the time my training was finished in early February 1957, Pat was getting a close-up and personal orientation into what Air Force life was about. There would be more to come: Some very tragic events for our friends– not at Moody, but later in my career.

Gages, Gages and More Gages!

The T-33 was a good instrument trainer. Instrument flying requires continuous 100% attention for scanning the gages (cross-check) to insure that you maintain the proper altitude; airspeed; attitude; heading; and a host of other things – including talking on the radio; recording Air Traffic Control instructions; and dealing with a disgruntled instructor. Instrument approaches required 150 % of your attention. And so did moderate to severe turbulence.

The state-of-the-art electronic navigation and approach aids of that time usually were: an Automatic Direction Finder (ADF); Radio Range (aural system); and, if lucky, a VOR (an advanced electronic navigation and approach system). The VOR did not contain all the problems encountered with ADFs and Radio Ranges which were low frequency radio bands and subject to static and weather interferences. Instrument Landing Systems (ILS) were available at some bases, but the usual type of approach was the verbal instructions issued by a Ground Controlled Approach (GCA) operator, issuing you headings, altitudes and descent instructions to the minimum altitude authorized for the type of approach flown.

Automatic Direction Finding (ADF): The ADF was an instrument with a pointer that pointed in the direction of the ground radio station transmitting the signal, but was not as automatic as the name implies. Theoretically it was a simple procedure to use. But it was fraught with outside interferences. It was generally short-ranged for instrument approaches, unless the station was a very powerful station used for navigation. It worked great in clear weather - when you usually didn't need to rely on it. If there were heavy rain showers or thunderstorms in the area, the electrically-charged air created static and noisy reception, resulting in a very erratic pointer; sometimes unusable -when you really need it. A thunderstorm could actually cause the pointer to point to the thunderstorm. Near a thunderstorm, you could never be sure if the pointer was pointing to the storm or to the station. More than a few pilots have been lost due to this phenomenon.

Radio Range: This was an aural-only, ground radio facility, with four radio range beams radiating outward, that formed four quadrants – a north; east; south, and west quadrant. These quadrants were separated by the four beams - or legs, as they were usually called. The range quadrants and the four beams were charted on aeronautical maps. Each quadrant was identified on the map and aurally by either the letter "A", or an "N", in international Morse code. The "A" code was identified by a dot and a dash (.- dot dash) and the "N" by a dash and a dot (-. dash dot). The opposing quadrants of the range were identified by the same letter, i.e., the north and south quadrants might be identified by the letter "N". The east and west quadrants would then be identified by an "A". The borders of the quadrants would overlap so that the "N" and "A", with opposite dash and dot signals, would merge to create a steady tone; thus forming the beam, or leg, of the range. Of course, the four beams projected outbound from the radio range, so that the beams could be flown aurally – to or from - the radio range (station). The station signals would fade gradually as you flew outbound and, conversely, increase in volume as you flew inbound. Passing directly over the station would be indicated by a momentary silence. There was a prescribed procedure to orient yourself geographically, relative to the radio range station - that is, to find which of the four quadrants you were in - then intercepting and identifying the beam. This was very time and fuel-consuming. It also added to the multi-tasking required to monitor the range aural signals; communicate with Air Traffic Control; maintain control of the aircraft on instruments; and conduct a radio range instrument approach to the runway. All of this was done under the hood of course. Fun and Games!

By the time I completed the T-33 instrument training portion of the all-weather training, I felt that I was qualified to fly in all kinds of weather; and to do an approach and land in any conditions, including zero visibility and zero cloud ceiling -"zero-zero" conditions. The ultimate confidence builder was the instrument approach with a *landing under the hood,* simulating these "zero-zero" conditions. Remember, this was all manual hands-on flying; no electronic marvels or auto pilot to fly the approach, and land the airplane. This *landing under the hood* occurred on one of my last few instrument training flights: I was under the hood doing a GCA instrument approach to Moody, for a full stop landing. About half way down final approach, the instructor in the front seat said for me to take it all the way to the runway *"under the hood",* unless he took control or instructed otherwise. Normally, during the final approach, the instructor would have you slide the hood back at about 200 feet above the ground, and he would take over to land the airplane. I made it all the way to touchdown without seeing the ground, and then made small heading corrections to follow the runway heading, until the instructor took control of the aircraft to taxi to the ramp. It was a great feeling to know that if it had been actual weather I could have made the approach and landed on the runway, without seeing it. Ironically, and sadly, when new pilots arrive at their new assignments from this training, they are immediately restricted to higher weather minimums, established by their higher headquarters. I thought, and still do think, that this is counterproductive for proficiency and confidence. I completed the T-33 instrument portion of the course with 19:45 hours of hood time; 2:40 hours of actual weather; and 18 hours of instruments, in the C-11 instrument trainer. The C-11 is a stationary (no-motion), generic, single-engine jet aircraft instrument trainer – a sophisticated Link Trainer on steroids.

F-94C Checkout and Interceptor Training

At Moody, pilot and radar operator (RO) trainees were paired up as a crew. Pilots had just completed pilot training, and the ROs had just completed navigator training. They completed the all-weather interceptor training together as a crew, and were then assigned to their first operational squadron together as a crew. Upon completion of the F-94C interceptor training, my RO and I were assigned to an F-94C squadron at New Castle County Airport, near Wilmington, Delaware. He and his wife would become very good friends of Pat and me.

While the ROs were learning the radar system and operations, pilots were checking out in the F-94C and learning its systems. After the required F-94C ground school came the traditional "dollar ride". The "dollar ride" was a familiarization flight in the back seat, with an instructor pilot in the front. It was mainly for you to "feel" the aircraft in flight, and to familiarize you with the flying area. Remember, all of that time in the T-33 was under the hood. Since the F-94C had no controls in the rear cockpit (radar only), there was no dual flight with an instructor. Your first front seat flight was for real – solo without your RO. If you killed yourself, they didn't want to have train another RO as well. This first F-94C solo flight was a "get acquainted" time for the pilot and aircraft. In other words, go out and have fun!

The F-94C was billed as a supersonic Air Force operational aircraft. That's true, but it had to be in a 45 degree dive with full power and afterburner. Afterburners were used for extra thrust for shorter takeoff rolls, and faster climbs to altitude, to intercept an unknown aircraft. The afterburner on the F-94C was unique for afterburners of that day. Only interceptors had afterburners then. On takeoff, you would hold the brakes and run the engine up to full power (100%). Jets don't use tachometers measuring engine revolutions per minute – RPM; instead of RPM, the "tach" measures the percent of power the engine is developing, as determined by the throttle setting. At 100% after checking the engine instruments, you released the brakes, then selected afterburner with an outboard movement of the throttle. The unique thing about the afterburner on the F-94C was that it used a "hot-streak" ignition system. This meant that once the afterburner was selected, which injected raw fuel into the tailpipe, a streak of ignited fuel was then released into the tailpipe, which exploded this extra fuel with a tremendous "BANG"! This provided a few thousand pounds of extra thrust and a hard "kick" to the seat-of-your-pants. You felt it! Quite a thrill!

The F-94C also used a drogue parachute – commonly called "drag-chute". It was deployed during the landing roll to reduce landing distance, and to save wear on the brakes. If the chute failed upon landing extra braking was required. This caused extreme overheating of the brakes. After clearing the runway, the drag chute was released for the runway crew to retrieve. If you had "hot brakes" you warned the ground crew to stay clear, because the extreme heat was capable of blowing the tires and could severely injure or kill the ground crew. Cooling air was applied to the tires and brakes until they were safe to taxi into the parking area.

One of the required maneuvers on that solo F-94C flight was to go supersonic. Supersonic flight (1950s) was still relatively new, so all the kinks had not been worked out and it was still somewhat of a mystery. When you went supersonic at Mach One (speed of sound), all the instruments went crazy for a moment, and the controls would reverse briefly. The elevator control was a high-boost system; otherwise you would not have been able to apply enough force to the stick to recover from the dive. There was also an aileron boost system that was controllable from the cockpit, up to an eleven-to-one ratio. For supersonic flight you had to set the boost at the highest ratio in order to have control of the ailerons. The rest of the interceptor training would be the serious business of learning my new trade.

Intercept Procedures

The normal mission was to takeoff, and contact the ground-controlled intercept (GCI) radar controller. The "target" aircraft would be another F-94C simulating an enemy bomber, and working with the same GCI controller. The intercepts would normally take place between 25,000 and 35,000 feet. The intercept controller would direct the interceptor into a near perpendicular collision course (called a beam-intercept) with the target. When the interceptor had the target within its radar range the interceptor RO would take control of the intercept. The RO would then provide the pilot with range, azimuth and altitude of the target, while directing the pilot into an intercept position on the target aircraft. This was usually a 90 degree beam (90 degree angle off) approach to the target. At a close-in range, where the target information was presented on the pilot's radar scope, the pilot would then assume control of the intercept. This was about thirty to forty-five seconds before the aircraft's fire control system would fire the rockets (simulated for training) – providing that the pilot had the trigger depress on the control stick. The pilot's scope presented him with a "steering dot" and small circle, about one quarter inch in diameter, in which to steer the dot. His scope also presented him with closure speed of the interceptor and target which, on a true beam intercept, could be approximately 800 miles per hour. The rockets would "fire" about three to five seconds prior to the merging of the interceptor and target flight paths. Upon rocket firing, the pilot's scope presented him with a large "X" (splash) indicating that the fire control system had fired the rockets. At the time of the "splash," the interceptor and target were about five seconds from a collision, if on a 90 degree beam intercept. The interceptor pilot is essentially on instruments, receiving guidance from the GCI controller; or from the RO using his own radar scope. The target pilot is the safety pilot in these training intercepts; therefore responsible for insuring that there is no *actual intercept* (collision). An actual collision course would show no relative movement, only the target getting larger and larger at the same relative spot on the canopy. Therefore, since the interceptor radar fires the rockets predicated on a collision course between the rockets and the target, the interceptor passes only feet behind the target; which, were it a real enemy target, would be exploding in bits and pieces. Thus, the safety pilot must sit tight during the last few seconds of the intercept, in order to determine the relative movement of the interceptor on his canopy. To sit out these last few seconds and overcome the pressing urge to take evasive action, takes an inordinate amount of "guts" and other appendages.

The fighter-interceptor's primary mission, such as the F-94C, was intercepting and destroying enemy bombers. There was of course the interception and identification of unidentified aircraft; aircraft that might be early, late or off-course according to its filed flight plan; or aircraft without a flight plan at all. The identification procedure is essentially the intercept procedure converted to a stern approach and closure, for the identification.

The F-94C All-Weather Interceptor training was uneventful. My last F-94C flight at Moody was on January 31, 1957 with a total of 40:55 hours in the F-94C that included 8:25 hours of "hooded" instruments and 50 minutes of actual weather time. How can you log "hooded instrument time" in a one-pilot-seat fighter where there can be no safety pilot onboard? Easy! When you log instrument time while in visual weather conditions, there is always a second aircraft with you as a "chase" aircraft providing safety surveillance for other aircraft. You concentrate solely on flying instruments in your cockpit.

Additionally, I had logged 10:30 hours in the F-94C simulator; which is instrument time, since you have no visual reference to an outside horizon.

Training Completed – Now, Back to New Castle, Delaware

My advanced pilot training as an F-94C All-Weather Interceptor pilot was complete; thus ending my formal US Air Force Pilot Training. Now it was back to New Castle County Airport at New Castle (Wilmington), Delaware which would be my *first* operational fighter pilot assignment and Pat's first *assignment* as a fighter pilot's wife. I don't recall a formal graduation at Moody; or a class roster and class book, as was done at some of the Primary and Basic Flying Training bases. After doing the required base clearing; checking out with the landlord; and arranging with base transportation for shipment of household goods (very little at this stage), Pat and I said "So long" to my RO and his wife, noting that we would be getting together at New Castle. So long, Moody! Hello again, New Castle!

*****

CHAPTER EIGHT
OLD BUDDIES, OLD SQUADRON – NEW NAME; F-94C (1957)

Settling In

Upon signing in with the 96th Fighter Interceptor Squadron at New Castle County Airport (NCCA) on February 15, 1957 as ordered, I was given a few days to do the required newly-assigned personnel check-ins with all base facilities. The housing office assigned me to temporary family quarters for a couple of weeks while I located a place for my family off base. The quarters were very small, of course, but very nice and equipped with essentials for short-term stays. Years later Pat and I revisited NCCA, which was then basically a civilian regional airport with an Air National Guard unit. Active Air Force flying units had long since been deactivated. The Air Force family quarters had been turned over to the city as project housing. Many of the houses were vacated, broken down and dilapidated, with windows broken out, doors hanging on one hinge or gone completely, wood rot, needing paint and yards grown over etc. It was heartbreaking and sickening. They had been so nice!   We also visited Wilmington General Hospital where our son Robert was born – remembering those happy times.

I finally found an apartment complex on the major highway between Washington, DC and Baltimore, MD; US 40, which ran north and south on the east side of NCCA. The apartment complex was on the left of US 40, about two miles north of the airport. It had many two-story apartment buildings, each containing four apartments. I moved Pat and Norris into the lower right apartment (two-bedroom) of one of the buildings, our new home and one of many over the years. It would be Robert's first home, although he had not yet arrived. It was small but adequate. There were many young families in the complex, so Norris had many friends – of many colors – to play with. The yard in front of the apartment was always full of noisy, happy playful children.

My New (Old) Squadron – the 97th Fighter Interceptor Squadron (FIS)

After orienting Pat to the base and its facilities and getting Norris in school, I proceeded to my squadron to begin the necessary squadron check-in and orientation. My orders assigned me to the 96th Fighter Interceptor Squadron (FIS). This was not the squadron from which I departed for Aviation Cadet pilot training in 1955. The old squadron that I was in as an F-94C crew chief when at NCCA was the 332FIS, and was located just across the ramp from the 96th. However, while I was away in pilot training, the Air Force re-designated the 332nd as the 97FIS. I think the powers-that-be do these things to confuse the enemy: Russians and Chinese. If it confuses them as much as does the personnel in the units being jerked around, then it works. It was still the same old gang: pilots and crew chiefs that I knew before I left. Once I had settled into the base and the 96th, it was time to get serious about my new assignment. I discussed my previous enlisted assignment with the 97th (formerly the 332nd), and my present assignment to the 96th, with their respective commanders; and the possibility of my being reassigned to my old outfit, now the 97th. Both commanders were acceptable to the idea. The base personnel office published the necessary orders for the transfer, effective March 4, 1957. Thus, the 97th Fighter Interceptor Squadron (FIS) became my *real* first operational flying assignment after F-94C Advance Pilot Training at Moody AFB, Valdosta, Georgia. My assignment to the 97th was largely uneventful, except for one incident a few weeks later that probably made the 97th commander wish he had not been so quick in accepting my assignment; and the 96th commander glad he had agreed to the transfer.

The 97th was undergoing extensive intercept training for its current F-94C pilots. Since I had not yet had my squadron checkout in the F-94C, I was given a quick T-33 evaluation and check-out. I had flown the T-33 extensively in Basic and Advanced training, so this was not a big deal. T-33 pilots were needed to act as targets and target tows for the squadron's F-94C pilots involved in an operational exercise. I, along with another newly assigned pilot, were designated as Instructor Pilots (IP) in the T-33, in order that we could fly with each other and each officially log the entire flight as pilot time. We could do this by alternating the IP time. It was an authorized way of building flying time. This also gave me an opportunity to get familiar with the local flying area.

From a record I found, noted years later in Pat's 1964 calendar, Pat and I had attended our very *first* Air Force Squadron party together on March 1st, 1957.

NCCA: The Airport

New Castle County Airport (NCCA) was a joint civilian/military base. In addition to civil air carriers operating from NCCA, it was also the home base for two active duty fighter squadrons; and the Delaware Air National Guard, flying F-86s. You also had the local pilots and their general aviation aircraft. Normally, civil air carriers had priority handling for traffic because of their schedules. Of course, emergencies always have the right-of-way over all air traffic. Other than emergencies, actual air defense scrambles of F-94C aircraft from the alert hangars (located just off the end of one of the runway), had priority over all other traffic. NCCA was a very nice airfield from which to operate. But, lying along a major US highway – US 40 – and a few miles south of Philadelphia, the airport was surrounded wall-to-wall by industries, business and homes. In fact there was civilian housing, just across the highway from the end of the runway where the alert hangars were located. Those people got the full measure of F-94C afterburners at all hours of the day and night – "The Sound of Freedom!" Middle of the night active air defense scrambles to intercept an "off course" airliner were common. And when we had exercises, frequent scrambles were normal. All F-94C takes-offs were with full power and afterburner. In the still air on cool dense air nights, you could hear those afterburners for miles and miles. The rumble and vibrations were terrific. You can acclimate to it. The airport had a couple of other features that made takeoffs and landings a little dicey. The north end of the north-south major instrument runway had a sheer embankment at the end. No overrun! The ground just dropped near vertically, for about 35 to 40 feet; almost like landing on a carrier deck. You definitely didn't want to run off the end of the runway upon landing; nor land short on final approach. The south end of the runway had an overrun; but also had a gas station, located directly on the centerline, about a quarter of a mile off the end of the runway.

Back at the Squadron

Back at the squadron, many of the old gang that was there when I left to go to pilot training was still there: Pilots, crew chiefs, maintenance and other support personnel. We had a new squadron commander. The pilot and radar operator assigned to my old aircraft F-94C #531 were no longer there, but #531 was. I got to fly it later, which was one of the highlights of my career. My old flight-line chief ('A' Flight), a master sergeant World War Two veteran, was still there. Pat and I were invited to dinner with him and his wife in their home, sometime later. My old flight instructor from the nearby DuPont Airport, where I got my private pilot certificate, was still there. We also had dinner with him and his wife in their home. It was real "old home" week. The fact that I returned as a 2nd Lieutenant officer/pilot, having left as an Airman First Class, was no problem at all. After all, a 2nd Lieutenant is *lower than dirt* in the eyes of young enlisted troops!

I have never consumed alcoholic beverages; never smoked; and do not use profanity. Some of my buddies I grew up with told me that I would never make it in the military, since I did not drink, smoke or "cuss". When single, I did chase girls occasionally – generally unsuccessfully! I'm here to tell you that after more than thirty-three years in the military, and at my present senior citizen status, I have never drank, smoked, nor yet use profanity – although I confess I have at times felt like "cussing" a bit. I am not boasting or playing "Holier than Thou", but simply stating a fact. A few times as an enlisted airman, some of my buddies tried very hard to break me – especially to get me to take a drink – "Just one. It won't hurt you". I have stated earlier on, in my growing up pages, why I chose not to indulge: My Mom's distress over her alcoholic brother! And I made that fact known to my enlisted friends who had persisted in trying to indulge me. After a while my friends realized that I wasn't going to change, so they accepted me as I was. I did go to bars and clubs with them, and would have a soda with my meal or snacks. Once or twice I pulled my 'Bob Hope act' on them and asked for milk in a "dirty glass", as Bob did in one of his movies; just kidding, of course. Later, as a squadron pilot – and throughout my flying career

– most of the days flying activities were rehashed at the Officer's Club "Happy Hour". So this was a time of comradery and learning, by listening to the "old heads". I would usually leave early to get home for dinner and have some time with my family. Later in my career, when I got into tactical fighters, deployments/exercises were frequent and long, and the times home with my family were even more cherished times.

As an officer, I did find that my friends were much quicker to accept my choice of lifestyle. I had one officer friend once tell me that he wished he had my "will power" not to drink – as he hung over his glass of beer, at the bar. I gently told him that it didn't take will power on my part, because I didn't wish to drink; but that it might be a big test of will power on his part, since he had such a drinking habit. I don't know whatever developed from our discussion. The squadron was soon deactivated, and our paths never crossed again.

Squadron F-94C Checkout

The day soon came for my initial squadron checkout in the F-94C, which all newly assigned pilots underwent. Since the F-94C is one-pilot in the front seat only, and a radar operator in the rear cockpit, the squadron senior RO generally flew in the rear cockpit as an evaluator of the newbie pilot; and as someone on board who was familiar with the area. Also, a squadron instructor pilot was assigned to fly in a second F-94C as chase-pilot, for safety and evaluation purposes. The flight would terminate in an instrument approach and landing, which would require me to fly solely with reference to my instruments. The chase-pilot acts as look-out for other aircraft. All this is standard operating procedure (SOP) for newly assigned pilots. I'm thrilled! This is my first F-94C flight in an operational squadron after my formal training course.

All went well until the instrument approach and landing. The primary runway was a north-south runway, which was the instrument runway. It just so happened that day that the active landing runway was the secondary east-west runway, due to the existing surface wind that required landing to the east into the low, early morning sun. On final approach to the east for landing on the active runway, a dump was burning with thick smoke obscuring visibility in the area for miles. It was not uncommon for smoke, haze and smog to prevail over the area due to industry, traffic and other pollutants. This was the late 1950s when those things were not a major environmental emphasis for clean air, as they are today.

After a pre-briefed and planned instrument approach to the north, on the primary runway with a low approach only, we would reenter the traffic pattern for landing to the east, on the active runway into that low morning sun, smoke and haze from the burning dump. You know that looking into a low-over-the-horizon sun through smoke and haze can reduce visibility to almost zero.

I'm Landing! Get Out of my Way!

During the northerly approach to the instrument runway everything looked good – until I reached minimum altitude -200 feet. I was doing an Instrument Landing System (ILS) approach, which is flown on the instruments in the cockpit without any ground controller assistance. The F-94C had what is known as a "Zero Reader". It's essentially an ILS; but rather than the instrument visually presenting the direction you need to fly to get on course and glide path, the "Zero Reader" would give you an on-course indication when you had a proper turn established to fly an intercept curve that would bring you to the center line of the runway. Thus keeping the Zero Reader's vertical indicator bar centered, you would constantly be correcting to, or maintaining, the runway centerline.

Upon reaching my minimum altitude of 200 feet the runway was nowhere in sight, although we were in visual flight conditions. There were other reports by pilots that day that the ground transmitter for the electronic runway centerline was malfunctioning occasionally. The chase IP then directed me to get on his wing and we would enter the traffic pattern for landing visually on the east runway. The traffic pattern was to approach the runway at 1500 feet and over the approach end of the runway; do a 360 degree turn descending to the runway for landing. Over the runway the IP directed me to land first. By now we were both down to minimum fuel, which means that we have enough fuel for a couple of short traffic patterns in the event of a necessary go-around.

As I began my 360 degree turn descending to the runway, I lost sight of the runway; descending into the smoke and haze, and looking toward the morning sun. The pattern was flown largely on instruments, literally guessing about where the runway was supposed to be. Upon reaching a very short final approach position I finally spotted the runway, but I was too far off the centerline and too close to allow for a correction to land. The IP made a low approach and had me join up in his wing again for another attempt. Meantime the tower had turned the runway lights up to full bright. Fuel was now critical (emergency fuel) for both of us – maybe one more approach. The tower knew our emergency situation. I briefed the RO that the next attempt would be it! If I didn't make it I was going to head for the Delaware Bay about five miles to the east, and we would "punch out"! - Eject! This time I spotted the runway lights in the haze *before* sighting the runway – again just barely off centerline and too close to land. Spotting the runway lights before the runway indicates just how bad the visibility was. The tower had turned the lights up to full bright, but still I never saw them until too close in. This second attempt was a repeat of the first. *I had no choice but to head for the bay!* The fuel gage was tickling "0".

The IP had to land! As I started my second missed approach, I saw the north/south instrument runway as I flew over it. It was wider and more prominently marked for instrument landing purposes. I told the tower that I had a visual on runway "one-nine" and would pull hard around and land to the south (270 degree turn); and to clear any aircraft off the runway. I kept the power at full power to keep my airspeed, although I knew we were about on fumes. The   F-94C was "burbling" as I pulled hard all the way around the turn at about 100 feet – indicating that I was just on the verge of stalling. I did not intend to lose sight of that runway. The RO was screaming "Take it around!" I said "No way! We're landing!" I was a little fast on airspeed over the end of the runway, but we had it made. We may go off the end of the runway, but that's better than the Delaware Bay! I deployed the drag chute early and fast – risking a premature separation – but it held. With judicious and gingerly increased braking, the tires held. PTL! I managed to stop on the remaining runway. Other F-94Cs had just cleared the runway for us. After a "hot brakes" check we taxied back to the ramp, and chocked. The fuel truck put just about every gallon of fuel in the aircraft that it was designed to hold. I would have flamed out any moment. I don't think that RO ever flew with me again. *In fact I don't know if he ever flew with any newly assigned pilots again.*

Not much came of the incident. I did have to brief the squadron commander on what happened. He seemed satisfied with my explanation of the events and especially the successful outcome. This is what I meant earlier when I said the squadron commander may have regretted accepting me from the sister squadron, the 96th FIS.

One other incident occurred which was very minor as incidents go. My RO and I were on alert in the alert barn one day, and we were scrambled to intercept an unidentified bogey about one hundred and fifty miles off the east coast. Bogey was the term normally used for an unidentified aircraft, until identification was made. Very likely an off-course airliner, which was usually the case, but they all have to be investigated. After getting airborne and switching frequency to the ground control intercept (GCI) controller, we were vectored to the southeast with instructions to "Go Gate!" (full-throttle with afterburner) and climb to "Angels 35" (35,000 feet). About a hundred miles from the coast the GCI controller advised us that the bogey had been identified, and we were vectored back toward NCCA to "RTB" (return to base).

Within a few minutes it was apparent that we were bucking a tremendous headwind of probably about a hundred and fifty miles per hour, which is not uncommon at those altitudes, and is called a Jet Stream. Our ground speed with those headwinds would not allow us to return to NCCA with our remaining fuel. A lower altitude below the jet stream would have increased our ground speed, but at these lower altitudes our fuel consumption rate would have increased critically. Aircraft, particularly jets, burn fuel faster the lower the altitude you fly. *I had no desire for another near-zero-fuel landing.* My RO had the coastline on his radar and could identify Virginia Beach, Virginia and the Oceana Naval Air Station. It was the closest coastline military air base and we could reach it comfortably with fuel reserve. I made the decision to divert to Oceana Naval Air Station. The landing at Oceana and the subsequent return to NCCA were uneventful. However, if one military service uses the facilities of another military service, there is a means for cross-billing reimbursement of the support provided. By refueling at Oceana I obligated the Air Force to reimburse the Navy for the fuel they provide. This is no big deal, as it's done all the time. After returning to NCCA I briefed the squadron commander on the situation. Of course he understood that it was an Air Defense Command-ordered active scramble for an unknown aircraft; and being a pilot he was well aware of the jet stream and its characteristics. However he had to act upset, because of having to pay the Navy for their fuel while having his own fuel in the base fuel supply system. Again he accepted the explanation and nothing else said. It's ironic that a few months later the squadron deployed to Oceana Naval Air Station to pull Air Defense alert for a few weeks, while the runways at NCCA were being repaired. There would have been tremendous cross-billing involved in this situation.

First Known Post-Training Pilot Class 56-V Fatality

I was not aware that one of my pilot class members was also at NCCA, until he was killed in an F-86 crash two or three months after I arrived. He was a member of the Delaware Air National Guard on the other side of the base. After pilot training he was sent to F-86 advanced training, then returned to NCCA and the Delaware Air National Guard. Although my pilot class lost two members in training, to my knowledge this was the first known Pilot Class 56-V fatality after training. I don't know the details. Pat was aware of my class' fatalities in training and my ordeal with my F-94C checkout. Now she knew of this fatality. I knew it worked on her, although she never let on. She knew how much I loved my flying.

Early in my career I had told Pat that I would be very closed-mouth about most activities involved with my Air Force assignments – except for the social stuff. As Air Force personnel, the aircrews and ground support personnel were often exposed to classified information. In addition to being against regulations to discuss such information, I told her that by not sharing operational information with her, she would not have to worry about inadvertently disclosing the information to her friends or other contacts. Through the years she would occasionally complain that she did not know what I did, or where I went. I would remind her of the consequences for me if she should accidentally disclose information she was not supposed to know. This would usually suffice, until next time.

Active Air Defense Alert

After I was certified current in the F-94C, and completed combat ready training as an Air Defense Command Crew Member, I was assigned to a flight. I don't remember the flight designation but I seem to think it was "C" Flight. As a qualified air defense crew member, I was required to sit alert duty in the alert hangar on a recurring basis. We would pull alert duty by flights; maybe once a month – unlike the Strategic Air Command (SAC) bomber and tanker crews, which would go into alert facility bunker for weeks at a time. Our alert hangars were located on the end of the west runway. They were situated so that scramble aircraft would come out of the hangar at an accelerating taxi speed, onto a short taxiway that curved on to the centerline of the runway. If necessary, a running takeoff could be made without the normal engine run-up and check. An active air defense alert crew was allowed five minutes from the time of the scramble horn, to gear-up. Exceed those five minutes, and the North American Air Defense Command Headquarters in Colorado would be on the phone asking for an explanation – *and it had better be good!*

There were four alert hangar bays – two adjacent bays on each side of a centrally located crew lounge, control room, small kitchen, and upstairs sleeping quarters. There was an F-94C in each of the four bays. The two center bays (one on each side of the center lounge) were for the 'five minute alert' aircraft. The two outer bays were for 'fifteen minute alerts'. In addition to the four aircrews, an additional officer was assigned to receive scramble orders, and monitor and operate the radios and telephones. We normally scrambled in pairs: one interceptor to make the identification; while the other interceptor assumed an attack position, should it be needed. The first aircraft out of the hangar after the scramble horn was the lead aircraft. The scramble horn would wake the dead! It was an old klaxon. Once the 'five minute' aircraft were scrambled, the 'fifteen minute' crews would move up to 'five minutes'. Upon returning from a scramble, the two aircraft would go on fifteen minute alert.

During a scramble the ground crews assisted the pilots and ROs in strapping in; assuring that they had their seat belts and shoulder harnesses secured; removing the ground safety pins for the ejection seats; removing the chocks, ladders and ground starting unit cables. Sometimes a pilot would allow the crew chief on the ladder, assisting him, to start the aircraft. The ground crew would also insure that nothing impeded the aircraft coming out of the hangar. They generally came out at near full power like a bronco out of the chute, and then afterburner when on the runway. The duty officer in the alert hangar would take the scramble orders from the scramble authority and authenticate it if necessary. He would then transmit the scramble orders to the flight as they taxied out. The ROs would copy the info.

The ground crews also provided front and rear hangar security guards – in all kinds of weather and temperatures. I pulled my share of guard duty, as a crew chief when at NCCA previously; shivering and trying to stay awake on cold, snowy winter nights. An Air Force cook/chef was assigned to prepare and serve the meals. The chefs were great and the meals outstanding; one of the perks of alert duty.

As I have indicated, time is of essence on a scramble. The fifteen minute aircrews were allowed to strip down and sleep in the upstairs bunks. The five minute crews could risk semi-stripping, but they were still held accountable for the five minutes to gear-up tolerance on a scramble. Upon the *death-awaking* klaxon horn sounding off, there was usually a moment of panicked confusion as everyone gathered their senses and got moving. For years after my alert duties, whenever a horn would sound I would almost come out of my hide. I recall one hilarious incident – that could have been very serious – where a pilot on five minute alert decided he would strip down to his undershorts and undershirt. A real risk! And, sure enough, in the middle of the night that klaxon went off. The scramble got off within the five minutes allowed. But when he returned and shut down the engine, he climbed out of the cockpit still in his underwear! Had he had to eject, he would have been in serious danger. More than once I observed life preservers on top of canopies when the aircraft taxied out of the hangar. The canopy would open at the end of the runway, and the crew member would retrieve the life preserver. Hopefully he had an opportunity to get it on during flight. Since the life preserver was worn over all the other gear, it could be done – although very difficult. Most of our active duty scrambles and intercepts were over the Atlantic.

Sea Survival Training
Soon after arriving at NCCA I, along with about five or six others, was sent to the base sea survival training on the coast near Atlantic City, NJ. I remember it as three nights and two days learning sea survival techniques – all on the beach. What would you pay for a vacation like that?! About the only thing I remember of the training was that someone made sassafras tea from sassafras roots. I found it very bitter and practically unpalatable for me, although I thought it had a sort of root beer flavor. I drank it because of the thirst I experienced. But I found it so distasteful that for years afterwards I could not a drink root beer, which I enjoyed very much before the sea survival training.

Night Flameout Landing!
I recall that one of our pilots had a very successful, but certainly puckered, night flame-out landing. It was a night flight near Philadelphia. Suddenly the engine flamed out, and he tried the only two chances he had for an engine air start. Later jets had a continuous ignition air start system. However, the F-94C had two shotgun shells mounted to the combustion chambers, to provide a charge to

ignite fuel in the chamber for air start purposes. He tried both, in an attempt to achieve an air start. Nothing! Night time over this part of the northeast is literally wall to wall lights. No opportunity for an open area, in which to eject and let the aircraft go into an uninhabited area. He luckily spotted the Philadelphia airport among all those lights, and did the only thing he could do – set up a flame-out pattern for a forced landing. It was very successful, and he got a well-deserved "Well done!"

Pregnant Pat!

Not long after arriving at NCCA, Pat greeted me with the good news that she was pregnant. We both were excited – her second child; my first! Norris was seven years old at this time. He was excited too. Pat had the usual morning sickness, which made her feel terrible. I was so sorry for her – and there was nothing I could do. It was awful having to go off to the squadron and leave her feeling so sick. Pat had a couple of Air Force and civilian wife friends who were also pregnant, so they comforted each other. Our friends at church were also a great help. We had joined the Bethany Baptist Church in Newport, just west of the base. This would become our baby's first church affiliation. Not as a member, but as a regular attendee. Baptist churches do not accept anyone for membership unless they have attained the *age of accountability* and make their *own* acceptance of Jesus Christ as their Savior. Then you can ask for membership in a Baptist church. The age of accountability varies with each individual and is when one realizes their own knowledge of God and Jesus Christ. The decision is theirs and theirs alone. No one can do it for you! Pat chose a doctor in Wilmington as her gynecologist, and Wilmington General Hospital for the birth. She wanted a son for me, and I said I wanted a girl for her (while secretly hoping for a son – but I think she knew that). Time would tell!

Squadron Additional Duties – Administrative Officer

All pilots are assigned additional duties within the squadron. Just as the name implies, these are addition duties that must be done by those assigned to the unit, i.e., administrative; supply; security; classified document control, etc.

These additional duties must be accomplished over and above your primary duty: Aircrew. It meant many afterhours, nights and weekends – no overtime pay! I cannot begin to tell you the afterhours I spent in performing additional duties throughout my career. Soon after arriving at the squadron, I was designated on squadron orders as Administrative Officer; which also carried with it the job of Classified Documents Control Officer. Paper work, paper work, and more paper work! I hated it. I have always hated paper work. Throughout my career, I always seemed to be a magnet for an abundance of paper work. As the squadron administrative officer, I worked directly for the squadron commander. Generally, for most internal squadron memos, directives, etc., that the commander directed, I was authorized to sign as the administrative office for the commander. Thus, such documents always carried the notation "FOR THE COMMANDER" over my signature. Except for documents that he preferred to write, I had to prepare correspondence and documents going outside the squadron, for his approval and signature. A lot of writing! Of course, I'm referring to times when everything was done by hand; typed on manual typewriters, and in multiple carbons. The Classified Documents Control Officer duty was most critical. I was charged with the safe-keeping and authorized access to these documents. One may have the proper classified clearance, but the ultimate test was "The Need to Know"! All classified documents were signed for by me. Upon reassignment, each document would have to be signed over to the next assigned individual, or documented as properly destroyed. The security of all classified document safes was my responsibility. At the end of each day, all safes had to be signed off as secured and checked. And the first thing in the morning they had to be check as not having been tampered with. A security violation could ruin your day – not to mention your career! Although I hated the additional duties, I managed to handle them satisfactorily. They sure didn't tell us about additional duties in pilot training recruiting pamphlets. The one perk about being the squadron administrative officer was that most everyone thought you had more clout than you actually possessed. I just hated all the extra time that it took to do the job. Someone else, with a talent for that kind of stuff, could probably have accomplished the tasks in much shorter time than I. As my career moved on I would come to appreciate the opportunities I had to see the inner workings of a fighter squadron, from the administrative perspective.

A New "Pilot" Arrives

Pat's pregnancy was becoming more and more obvious. During all this time I experienced what all expectant fathers experience: *The kicking; movement; anxiety* – and sympathy for the wife. Sometime later, Pat put me on alert duty! This can't be. It's a month early! A few days later Pat insisted that it was time; that she was experienced in these things and "It's time!" After a "scramble" to Wilmington General Hospital, things seemed to settle down. In fact, things were so calm after several hours that the doctor told me to go on home for the night; that nothing was going to happen for a while. (What does he know?!)

Our good friends had invited me to their apartment for dinner that evening. As we were preparing to sit down for dinner, I got a phone call from the nurse to come on back. *It was happening!* When I arrived, Pat was in the delivery room. So I joined a couple of other expectant fathers in the anxiety-room (waiting room). Soon our son announced his arrival, weighting in at 4 pounds and 15 ½ ounces. The nurse brought him out into the hallway for our first meeting. He didn't seem impressed, but I was. In fact he seemed downright unhappy about the situation. Finally I was allowed to see Pat. Her first words to me were: "Isn't he cute?"! My first words to Pat were: "Sure has my big nose!" Pat was doing well. PTL! We had already decided on names. If it was a girl, her name would be Roberta. If a boy, his name would be Robert. Back home I was known as Robert (my middle name) and that's how Pat knew me before I switched to my first name of George, after entering the Air Force. Pat insisted that he have the name of Robert, as I was called while growing up. She let me give Robert a middle name. I had chosen Douglas, after General Douglas MacArthur of World War Two and Korean War hero fame.

Pat was home soon but Robert had to stay six days in an incubator, due to his premature birth. Norris was thrilled at having a little brother. Pat and I were blessed with both Norris and Robert. They grew up well together. Of course, they occasionally had their brotherly-love scraps as they got older. Meantime I was learning a new skill: laundry! We didn't have disposal diapers then, as today.

Our friends and squadron personnel were great. The squadron presented Robert with a silver memento box engraved with his name. Pat's friends would bring in meals until she was well and on her feet. I know she and Norris appreciated that – rather than my cooking. I now had a third reason for getting home after work. And another reason for assuring that I walked *the straight and narrow way!*

Second-Shortest Assignment
My assignment to NCCA and the 97th Fighter Interceptor Squadron was the second-shortest of my career: Ten months and 24 days. I had reported on February 15th 1957. On Sep 6th I had orders from Headquarters United States Air Force, Washington, DC, appointing me as a Regular Officer in the Air Force with the rank of Second Lieutenant. My date of rank was retroactive to my date of commissioning as a Reserve Officer upon graduating from Air Force pilot training, as a distinguished graduate, September 13, 1956. How blessed was I? A wonderful wife and son, and now a new son; a new Regular Air Force Commission; a great flying assignment flying a great airplane (one of the Air Force's newest fighter-interceptors); and great friends, both Air Force and civilian. Is that all, Lord? How many more blessings could I stand?

At some point in my 97FIS assignment my brother Richard visited us. He was in the area going to computer school for Capitol Airlines and getting in on the ground floor of computers, when people could not yet spell "computer". His stay was too short. But it was nice to have him visit. I don't know if he got a chance to meet his new nephew, Robert, or not. I think Richard visited us before Robert was born.

Then on October 15th, the 82nd Fighter Group (Air Defense), our headquarters at NCCA, received orders from the Eastern Air Defense Force inactivating all active

Air Force units at NCCA, effective January 8, 1958 This meant that it would be a busy Christmas Holiday season with all the actions necessary to prepare for the inactivation. *Merry Christmas!* All that would remain would be the civilian aviation operations and the Delaware Air National Guard with their F-86s. My last F-94C flight ever, was on October 16th 1957, having accumulated 131 hours in the aircraft. I soon had orders for my new assignment: The 84FIS at Hamilton AFB, California. I think Pat and I both were rather excited about the prospect of traveling across these great and beautiful United States to California. However I was not thrilled about the F-89 that I would be flying. It was old, slow, way underpowered, a monstrous airplane; *and it had two engines.* *"Oh, No!"* That meant two throttles. What kind of fighter aircraft would have two throttles? It too, like the F-94C, had an RO in the back seat. It's an old worn out joke that ROs and Navigators are always telling pilots where to go! Actually my ROs would later save my hide on a couple of occasions.

New Assignment

As the squadron administrative officer, I would be one of the last to leave NCCA. In fact, I think the Commander and I were the last two 97th squadron members to leave NCCA. There were several bases available for assignment of the squadron officers. Personnel officers at higher headquarters make personnel assignments. However, personal preferences were considered in making assignments whenever possible. The Commander had asked me for my preference. I told him I thought Hamilton AFB would be nice, in spite of the F-89. He said he would do what he could with the base personnel office. The F-94C, although having been in the Air Force inventory for only four years, was being phased out in favor of the new F-102, and later the F-106. At this time the F-89 was becoming the mainstay fighter-interceptor with its two unguided ballistic nuclear missiles.

I mentioned earlier that some squadron members thought that the administrative officer position I held in the squadron gave me considerably more authority than I actually had. And this erroneous thinking carried over into our pilots' assignments for the available bases. Squadrons don't possess that kind of authority. One guy got an assignment to Iceland – Keflavik AFB. He was very upset about having to go to Iceland and thought I was responsible for his assignment. I tried unsuccessfully to convince him that I didn't have that kind of authority. He was never convinced, and prior to leaving the squadron he said: "I'll get you for this!" Many years later I ran into him, after our careers were essentially completed. He never said anything about his promise to get me – *and I'm not reminding him!*

Happy New Year 1958!

All personnel had departed except for the squadron commander and me, plus a remnant to act as temporary custodians to lockup and turnover the keys as the final act to inactivation. On New Year's Day 1958 the Commander and I flew our last remaining aircraft, a T-33, to Dover AFB, Dover, Delaware to transfer it to the base there. The few household goods Pat and I had acquired were packed and loaded on a moving van. We had said our goodbyes and well wishes to friends. On January 8th we left NCCA singing *"California here we come!"* – although it wasn't where we *"started from".* I had thirteen days travel time, plus 10 days leave time en route with a reporting date of January 31st for the 84FIS, Hamilton AFB, California. Hamilton was about 30 miles north of San Francisco at San Rafael, and would prove to be the most beautiful base and the shortest assignment of my Air Force career.

*****

CHAPTER NINE
FROM EAST TO WEST! - SAME GAME, DIFFERENT BAT AND BALL;
Hamilton AFB, San Rafael, California; F-89J (1958)

En Route

January 1958: With our car loaded floor to ceiling and wall-to-wall, Pat and I stashed Norris and Robert into any space available. Norris was seven years old, and Robert four months. It's a good thing we did not have Puff, our cat of 20 years that Robert acquired years later, or we would have had *no room for Norris and Robert*. We were finally on our way from the east coast to the west coast, with a delay en route to visit our folks in Georgia. It was great visiting with family, but we were eagerly anticipating the trip across these great United States and seeing some of the fantastic handiwork of God and nature. After saying our "so longs" we were *"on the road again"*, as Willy Nelson would put to song years later. We chose to do the southern route, due to the winter season. What a beautiful country: Lakes, rivers, mountains, deserts, wide open spaces! Our trip took us through Baton Rouge, LA and across the Mighty Mississippi; and on into El Paso, Texas. I thought we would never get out of Texas. What a huge expanse of American turf! Is it any wonder that Texans brag so? Then on through Arizona and into California: Blythe; Palm Springs; San Bernardino and Los Angeles.

Los Angeles! Wow! This was my first experience with high-speed freeways; eight-lane traffic, all in one direction, and spaghetti junction exchanges. However, I made it without bending any metal. From Los Angeles we went up Highway One towards San Francisco. A fellow 56-V Aviation Cadet Pilot Class member was assigned to an F-89 fighter interceptor squadron at Oxnard AFB, Ventura, CA. I decided we would stop in to visit him and his wife. He was a great guy and I had not met his wife and children. Pat had not met either of them. It was a great renewal of pilot class friendships. He and his wife had two beautiful children.

Leaving them, we continued north up Highway One, a beautiful coastline drive, to Hamilton AFB at San Rafael, CA about 30 miles north of San Francisco. Hamilton AFB was one of the prettiest bases I ever had the pleasure of being assigned to: Green and meticulously landscaped; old Spanish architecture; a high hill containing a beautiful Officers' Club that overlooked the flight line, runway and San Pablo Bay. After getting Pat, Norris and Robert settled into a motel, I proceeded to sign in at the 84th Fighter Interceptor Squadron. It took two or three days to complete the required incoming personnel check-ins with base facilities – the most important of which was getting on the waiting list for base quarters. I was given the typical week or so to look for quarters for my family, and to get initial necessities taken care of. Almost immediately, base housing had a temporary family unit become available. So I got Pat, Norris and Robert settled into those temporary quarters. It was located at the end of a beautiful drive up the hill to the Officers' Club. So they had a beautiful view as they waited for me each day.

The 84th Fighter Interceptor Squadron (FIS) and the F-89J

In the squadron, things progressed normally: Introduction to and checkout in the F-89J and local area; studying the manuals; base, wing and squadron regulations to learn. The "game" was the same Cold War scenario as at NCCA in the F-94C: Air defense against enemy bombers, should that become necessary. The new "ball" was nuclear weapons! The old "bat" was the   F-89, which had been in the air defense game for a number of years. I believe The "J" model of the F-89 was the only interceptor (at that time) capable of carrying and firing the recently developed unguided nuclear rocket designated the "Genie", and designed to destroy high-flying enemy bombers. (Maybe the F-106 later). The F-89 carried two rockets externally, one on a pylon under each wing. It had been around a long time; and having just left the F-94C, a relatively new airplane in the Air Force inventory, I felt like the F-89 was a come-down. But, with its nuclear capability, the F-89 was the mainstay of the interceptor force for a few more years of the "Cold War". It was the only interceptor at that time which had the capability of destroying enemy bombers flying at higher altitudes than the F-89 could attain. The civil air carriers and bombers of that day could fly faster and higher that the fighter- interceptors, whose job it was to identify or destroy them respectively. In intercepting an unknown aircraft for identification, if the ground controller or the RO ever got the F-89 positioned behind the target aircraft, it was usually a futile chase – unless you used afterburner, which used an inordinate amount of fuel. The F-89J was usually directed into a head-on or a quartering head-on intercept course, and then converted to a beam approach when close in. Hopefully you could ID the offending aircraft before he started to pull away. It was very embarrassing flying a fighter and having civilian airliners pull away from you – or fly higher.

For the destruction of enemy bombers, the tactic was to approach head on at about 30,000 to 35,000 feet; the bomber at 45,000 feet, plus or minus. At a precise moment during the intercept, the pilot, with afterburners on, would zoom up into a 45 degree climb toward the approaching high flying bombers. Rapidly approaching the stall airspeed, with the aircraft starting to mush and wallow, the pilot gingerly steered his radar target dot to the center of the small circle on his scope. The weapon system radar would then fire the rocket at the precise time, seconds before the F-89 stalled. At this point there was just enough control left to roll the F-89 inverted, and pull the nose down and escape before the nuke detonated. The F-89 also carried enough fuel for a mission of two to two and a half hours; versus the F-94C, which was about 45 minutes to an hour. I came to love the F-89, as huge and lumbering as it was. With its large wing area it was a fantastically stable instrument airplane, and a solid platform from which to fire its rockets.

The F-89 was named the Scorpion, and built by Northrop who built the WW II night-fighter - the P-61 Black Widow. The F-89 had a long snout-like nose, close to the ground due to its big locomotive-like main wheels and short nose gear strut. The tail was swept up in scorpion like fashion, thus the name. The two engines were low slung and created problems by sucking dirt and debris into its engine intakes at high engine power, during ground operations. Endearing names given to the F-89 by pilots were: Lead sled; gravel gobbler; aardvark; and other less printable names. It carried a pilot and radar operator (RO), as did the F-94C; and was the heavyweight of the fighters and interceptors of its day, weighing in at a design weight of 40,000 pound and maximum operating weight of nearly 45,000. But new to me were the twin jet engines. Heretofore I had only flown single-engine airplanes. The rated thrust of each engine was 5600 pounds and 7400 pounds with afterburning. Thus, with afterburners for take-off, there was about a 25,000 pound thrust shortfall, making the F-89 extremely slow to accelerate. And its weight made it difficult to stop in the event of an aborted take-off. It acted as though it was emulating a locomotive.

The afterburners in the F-89 were soft-igniting; not the hard bang kick-in-the-pants like you got with the F-94C. In fact they were so soft-igniting that you had to monitor the tailpipe temperature when you selected "burner", to detect the almost imperceptible wiggle in the temperature needle. The burner could blowout, and you would never know it unless you happened to be looking at the temperature gage. It was such a critical problem with the F-89 that the "Supervisor of Flying" (SOF), located in a mobile control unit near the active runway, was required to monitor all F-89 take-offs with binoculars for an afterburner blowout. Fortunately such situations were a rare occasion. You could see the afterburner flame, and it was readily apparent if it blew out. If so, the SOF would immediately broadcast "Burner Out!" It was instant decision time for the pilot. He could abort the take-off, unless near liftoff airspeed, in which case it was usually best to continue with one burner; because stopping on the remaining runway was very unlikely. This was a critical decision because the F-89 was so underpowered. It would likely not get airborne on a normal runway if a burner blew out early in the take-off roll. With one-burner-failure at or near lift-off airspeed, you probably would get airborne, depending on the runway remaining; but if so, it would be a "pucker factor" and a very low-slow climb-out, while dusting off the wildlife in the process.

It was always an adventure checking in to a new squadron: A new squadron commander; new flight commander; new squadron mates; new challenges; a new community and civilian friends; and a new church. The Hamilton AFB area; San Rafael; Novato; and San Francisco were beautiful, and great places for sightseeing. I had a great flight commander. After completing the required ground classes on the F-89; nuclear weapons operations; security; safety; and weapons delivery, the F-89 checkout began. I don't recall any significant events occurring during the checkout. It certainly wasn't like my F-94C checkout at New Castle. I always felt sorry for Pat, Norris and Robert during times like this, when I had to be so absorbed in my work, dealing with new stuff. I was fortunate in that I was not assigned additional duties early on at Hamilton, as I was at New Castle. Pat and Norris seemed to be settling in well. Robert? At six months old, if he didn't miss feeding time, had a nap and diapers changed, he was a happy camper.

Tragedy: F-89 Crash on Base

Things were going well. I guess it was a month or so after we arrived and I was flying rather regularly, that the squadron experienced a fatal F-98 accident in the traffic pattern over the base. The accident occurred as the pilot executed the turn over the runway in preparation for the base and final turn to landing. One of the wing aileron control surfaces failed to operate properly, which put the F-89 into an uncontrollable spin. At only 1500 feet above the ground, there was no chance for the pilot and RO. The squadron recalled all flying, and the commander gathered all aircrews together. He briefed what little information was available at that time. This was more than an hour or so after the accident. The word of the crash was now spread across the base, the local area, and on the local news. The names of the crew were not yet released, although we knew. The commander told everyone to go home and console their wives, who would obviously be very emotionally upset and fearing the worst.

Pat knew I was flying that morning. We were still in temporary family quarters on the hill. As I drove up to the house I was wondering if she had heard of the accident. I went in the front door and knew immediately that she knew. She was standing in the middle of the front room bawling and crying her eyes out. We just clung to each other for a few moments. Of course, she was so relieved to see me; but it was sometime before I could calm her down. I suppose in my inept way I was not very effective in doing so. I can only try to imagine what was going through her mind at that time. There she was, not knowing if I was dead or alive. There she was, in a new environment; among strangers; Norris in a new school; household goods not yet arrived; a six-month old baby; in temporary quarters; maybe having to pull up and start back across country to Georgia with a husband to bury. But she now knew that I was alive; and for the moment, all these other things were unimportant. We both knew that soon a couple of wives would be receiving visits from the squadron commander, along with the base Chaplin. We both hurt for them.

New Home

After things got back to routine around home and the squadron, I soon had a notice that I had been assigned permanent quarters in Hamilton's military family housing. This was a pleasant surprise since in those years housing was assigned based solely on rank. Me, I was still a relatively new Second Lieutenant. The quarters were off-base military housing in San Rafael, between Hamilton and the town of Novato. Our house was located on San Jose Boulevard, with a Novato address. We moved in, settled in, and found a Baptist Church in Novato that Pat and I joined. I cannot recall the name of the church nor the pastor. Our home was a beautiful place near the end of San Jose Blvd. It ended in rolling hills which also bordered San Jose. A friend and his wife from the 97FIS at New Castle lived just up the street from us. They had a new baby girl about the same age as Robert, so Pat and she shared many mutual experiences.

I bought my first handgun: A Ruger Single-Six Black Hawk 22 Caliber frontier-style pistol. I have always enjoyed target shooting and plinking, and thought those hills at the end of San Jose would be a great place to teach Norris (seven years old) to shoot. We enjoyed it, although he never took to shooting as I did. Can you imagine such a scenario in today's anti-gun paranoia culture: owning a gun; target shooting in the hills just beyond base housing; teaching my seven year old son to shoot? I think not. Progress? I think not. Pat seemed to be enjoying her role as housewife and mother; our neighbors; and our church; we felt blessed. We watched Robert grow and experience new thing, and Norris playing the big brother role. It was great. Norris was great with the neighborhood kids and seemed to enjoy being the king (bigger kid) of the hill. I was enjoying flying; even the F-89J: good squadron; great guys and nice base.

Hamilton AFB Aero Club

I joined the Hamilton AFB aero club, located just north of Novato, which had a T-34A like those I flew in Primary Pilot Training: A two-seat (front and back), low-wing, bubble-canopy trainer. That was a fun time – being back in the T-34. I liked the T-34. (Not many airplanes I don't like). I took Pat and Norris flying on a few occasions. Norris seemed to enjoy it; Pat said she did too, and tolerated my play time at the aero club. Of course I had already flown her in the Aeronca Champ at the Charlie Brown (Fulton County) Airport in Atlanta, after I got my private pilot certificate at DuPont Airport, Delaware, before we became engaged. Since the aero club was just over the hills from the Pacific Coast, we flew short distances over the ocean on occasions. Beautiful! I never ventured more than three to four miles off the coast, and always made sure we had the altitude to guarantee gliding distance to the beach if necessary. I would teach Pat a little about flying; particularly being able to maintain fairly straight and level flight and mild turns. One day I inadvertently frightened her to the point that she would never again put her hands on the controls, no matter how hard I tried to persuade her.

What happened? We were flying about 3000 feet and approximately three miles off the coast. I let Pat fly, and was instructing her in maintaining straight and level flight. She let the nose down slightly and I told her to ease the nose back up and to check its relationship to the horizon. She didn't comply. After a couple more times of urging her to ease the nose back up without success, I, with my voice elevated slightly, told her to pull the nose up, that we're "diving". Wrong choice of words! We weren't diving – it was a slight descent, just enough to see the ocean over the nose. But the Pacific was visible over the nose and it scared her to death. She let go of the controls in panic. Try as I may to convince her that I really didn't mean diving – only descending slightly – she was thoroughly convinced that we were diving into the ocean! Never, never again in all of our years of flying together could I get her to put her hands on the controls of a plane that I was flying – even if my hands remained on the controls and seated side-by-side. She would fly with me, but that was it. Years later I learned that she was a white-knuckles flyer. I did persuade her to take a Pinch-Hitter course, designed to teach non-flying passengers enough to safely land the airplane in the event of pilot incapacitation. I used the safety aspect of the Pinch-Hitter course to convince her, since we would be flying often and with Norris and Robert aboard. Years later she flew the Pinch-Hitter course at the Maxwell AFB aero club with an instructor pilot friend, Win DePoorter – not me.

Alert Facility

The alert hangers were very similar to those at New Castle, with the exception that there was a "firemen's pole" for the aircrews to use in getting from the upstairs sleeping area to the first floor during scrambles. The F-89s were armed with two nuclear rocket-propelled unguided weapons. Security was at a high state at all times in dealing with anything nuclear. There was a complex and multi-layered system to assure the security of the weapons. We never flew with the weapons, except for actual scrambles. However, we did have dummy concrete rockets in the shape and weight of the real weapons. We used these dummies during exercises and squadrons training flights. For air defense competition meets, we had practice nuclear rockets with rocket motors and a small explosive spotting charge in their noses. Your accuracy could be scored visually and by radar. I did get to fire two of these practice rockets at a weapons competition meet at the Yuma, Arizona Marine Corps Air Base.

The squadron flights would rotate the alert duty weekly. We had the standard five-minute and fifteen-minute pair of F-89s on alert. Crews were allowed to sleep, provided they maintained near fully dressed status and flight gear immediately available. I could never sleep soundly when I was on five-minute alert status – and I slept fully dressed, even with my life vest and boots on.

There were a couple of guys who could sleep right through the klaxon scramble horn. *That horn would wake the dead!* These guys had to be dragged out of the bunk and stood on their feet. A middle of the night scramble was a sight to behold – right out of "The Three Stooges" movies! That horn would practically lift you out of the bunk. Guys would be awoken in a confused stupor. I have seen guys bound out of the bunk and run two or three circles around the room in a confused state, colliding with each other until they became fully awake and aware. Then they would leap onto the fire pole and down they would go. I have seen guys piling on each other at the bottom of the fire pole. But they miraculously made their scramble times.

Single-Engine Emergency

On one particular day I was scheduled to fly as number two in a four-ship training flight. My flight commander would be leading the flight and we each would be carrying two of the dummy nuclear weapons. Passing through about 15,000 feet, I began to feel a very mild vibration throughout the aircraft. A check of all engine instruments did not identify the problem. It seemed the vibration was slightly increasing. Retarding each of the two throttles individually, identified the right engine as the culprit. A vibration in an engine is not good! This was a common indication that the engine had thrown a turbine blade in the aft section, or maybe a compressor blade in the front of the engine. Many times the blade would exit through the side of the aircraft, taking with it fuel, oil, electric or even control systems. If it went through the engine, it could mean a fire, or explosion, or both. If not reduced immediately it could shake the engine loose. Immediately after identifying the offending right engine, I shut it down and notified the flight leader. Fortunately, the left engine contained most of the critical systems for normal aircraft operations. After assigning one of the other pilots to look me over, which showed no visible damage, he had the pilot escort me back to Hamilton.

The F-89 does not fly well on one engine – especially for take-off or go-around, where maximum power is required. Intentional single-engine take-off is prohibited by the pilot's manual. Single-engine go-around decision must be made while airspeed it still relative high, in order to permit acceleration, otherwise a go-around at high gross weight may not be possible. I was still at a high gross weight, having just taken off, and climbing to altitude. I dumped the wingtip fuel to decrease weight, but I was carrying two dummy nuclear weapons weighting 800 pounds each: 1600 pounds above our normal training weight. The procedure was to drop them in the bay, just short of the runway which ran right up to the bay. Full flaps could only be used if a landing was assured, because level flight and go-around was not possible on one engine with full flaps. To jettison the two dummy nukes required pulling two T-handles, one for each weapon, which were located on the floor to the left of, and slightly behind the pilot seat. On final approach, with gear down and partial flaps set, it

155

was "show time" for making it right to avoid a go-around. The plan was to drop the dummy nukes in the bay, just short of the runway. As the landing was practically assured, and the runway was at hand, I looked down to quickly locate the jettison T-handles, and pulled them one at a time. They jettisoned normally. As I did so, I apparently let my approach altitude decrease slightly, because the RO yelled "Pull up!" I looked up to be staring in the face of the seawall at the end of the runway. I eased the F-89 up slightly to the runway, for a normal landing and roll out. After clearing the runway I shut the good engine down, in the event there was damage not yet known. Saved by my RO! It was discovered that the right engine had indeed thrown a turbine blade. But it apparently went right out the tail pipe. Had it been a compressor blade at the front of the engine it could have either gone through the side of the aircraft, through the engine, or into the adjacent engine, either of which could have had disastrous results.

Another Tragedy!

Another month or two went by normally. Then the squadron got word that an F-89 out of Oxnard AFB was lost at sea during a night flight. It seems the F-89 crew was doing a normal high speed descent – called "penetration" in instrument flight terminology – in preparation for an instrument approach and landing at Oxnard. The aircraft disappeared off the Oxnard Approach Control radar during the penetration and was not heard from again. To my knowledge, no cause could ever be determined for the disappearance since there was no radio transmission to indicate trouble. I don't recall if search and rescue (SAR) aircraft ever spotted any signs of the crash or not. It was a dark night, which means the pilot would have been on instruments. It is common for pilots to occasionally experience vertigo in such situations, since you are descending at a high rate and turning from an outbound to an inbound heading. Vertigo, unless extremely severe, can usually be overcome. It will never be known if this was the situation or not. An in-flight explosion destroying the aircraft and radio is another possibility. Control problems possible too. But Pat and I were shocked to learn that it was my pilot training classmate, whom we had recently visited at Oxnard AFB with his family, on our way north to Hamilton. We of course communicated our condolences to his wife and his family. He and I were not close buddies during pilot training, but I saw him almost daily and knew him as a really great guy. He was quiet and unassuming; extremely friendly; blond; and good-looking enough to make the most handsome Hollywood actors jealous. Bad things do happen to good people! For a few years we maintained contact with his wife, but lost contact years later. I hope she had and is still having a good life.

Night Search Over the Pacific

I was on alert in the alert hangars one night, when we were scrambled. After getting airborne, our instructions were to proceed about 50 to 75 miles west

156

over the Pacific to look for any sign of a distressed boat or survivor. It seems that ground radar detected a radar target, almost stationary, which indicated a surface, rather that airborne object. It was believed that there had been a brief, faint distress signal. The combination of the possible signal and the stationary radar target convinced the scramble authority to launch us to investigate. Once in the area, we were instructed to descend to just over the waves and begin a systematic search pattern in the vicinity of the radar return – which kept disappearing and reappearing. One F-89 was to remain a few thousand feet high, in order to maintain radar and communications contact. Guess who the low-search F-89 was? Me! It was pitch-black dark. No moon. I was down to a hundred to two hundred feet over the water, with landing lights extended. The lights illuminated the white caps on the water, but I never detected any signs of a boat or a survivor. Maneuvering at low airspeed in the dark just over the white caps was not a casual "cruise in the park". It was a "100% plus" attention situation: Scanning visually outside, and monitoring the instruments inside – especially the airspeed, attitude and altitude. Of course the RO was scanning visually too. His radar was useless at this altitude over the water. Ground radar eventually lost all radar contact with the unknown target. After about 30 minutes of searching, we were told to recover to Hamilton. Nothing was ever found. In those years radars were very susceptible to false targets such as flights of birds, precipitation, temperature inversions, and many other things. There is no telling what could have cause the radar return on the ground radar; nor the perceived distress signal.

Dad and Mom's Visit

Lo and behold! Mom and Dad came to visit us while we were at Hamilton. It is a miracle that Mom got Dad off the farm. I think it was a miracle by the name of "Robert," their nearly one year old grandson that they had only seen a couple of times; and grandson Norris. I would hope they wanted to visit Pat and me also. I had never known Dad to take an extended vacation from the farm and his paper route – and only two or three times take a couple of days or so to go somewhere with Mom. I think it was around late summer or early fall – very likely after Dad had gotten the crops laid by for the winter – that they came to visit. Of course, it was an exciting time looking forward to their visit, and I had asked for a few days of leave to visit with them. There are many things of interest to see and do in and around the San Francisco area. We intended to show them a good time – regardless of their focus on Norris and Robert. But wouldn't you know it! The Russians, Arabs and other Middle East countries chose this very time to rattle their sabers, and to place the region in turmoil – and the rest of the Western world: *The 1958 Middle East Crisis!*

The United States military, State Department, and other US agencies worldwide were placed on alert – just in case something developed. And the consequences reached all the way to San Francisco; Hamilton AFB; the 84th Fighter Interceptor

Squadron; and the George Partridge family. All military personnel were restricted to the immediate area, to be contactable and available within thirty minutes. This was a prelude to many similar scenarios that would repeat themselves throughout the majority of my remaining Air Force career. We offered apologies to Mom and Dad and they took it in their stride. I think Mom was delighted to remain at home with her grandsons. Dad, being a WW I veteran, understood exactly what was going on. We did manage to get them some quick visits to some of the sites in San Francisco. I don't remember if the sightseeing was before or after the alert status. I don't even recall how long they were there. We did get to show them the Golden Gate Park. And of course we had to cross the Golden Gate Bridge to get to San Francisco. I'm sure we must have shown them Lombard Street – the crookedest street in the world! I don't recall showing them the squadron and flight line. I'm sure that would have been high on my list of things to show them. But with the heightened alert and security, I probably wasn't allowed to bring them onto the base. I know that the United States deployed fighters to bases nearer the crisis, to be readily available if needed and to show the "Flag". Anyway, we did enjoy their visit. I don't know if they were there for Robert's first birthday or not. If not, they were there shortly before his first. Norris hit his eighth birthday while at Hamilton. Unknown at the time of Mom and Dad's visit, they would soon have 15 months of visits from Pat, Norris and Robert.

Other Events and Squadron Fly-By

I recall three other events while at Hamilton. First was taking Pat, Norris and Robert up Mount Tamaulipas to show them the view, and the Air Force Radar Site on top of the mountain: the Mill Valley Air Force Station. This was the radar site where the ground radar controllers and 84th aircrews would exchange cross-training familiarization visits. We worked together daily as a part of the air defense network, and would occasionally fly the controllers on our air defense missions when they visited the 84th for cross-training. One day, one of my RO friends and I took our families to the top of Mount "Tam" together for an outing and to enjoy the view; a fabulous view of the mountains, the coast and the Pacific Ocean.

Another event was the first air show Pat, Norris, Robert and I saw together, soon after we arrived at Hamilton. It was at the Naval Air Station Oakland, across the bay from Francisco. It was the first time that Pat and Norris had seen the Navy's Blue Angels aerial demonstration team perform. Great show! I had seen the Blue Angles at the Atlanta Naval Air Station, Chamblee, GA as a kid, when they were flying the propeller fighter, the F8F Bearcat.

A third event was the only 16-plane formation fly-over that I ever participated in. It was at a Hamilton AFB Open House. The squadron commander decided that our squadron should do a 16-aircraft F-89 formation fly-over for the wives and the public. After much planning and briefing, the day came. I would fly the right wing of the second flight. There would be four flights of four F-89s, each in diamond formation, to form a squadron diamond formation of the 16 aircraft. The second flight would be on the left of the lead flight; third flight on the right; and the fourth flight behind the lead flight in what is called the "slot". Each wingman's attention is focused only on his flight leader, and *praying* that every other pilot in the formation is maintaining proper position. The fly-over would be done at about 2000 feet – not a low fly-by by any imagination. Looking up from the ground at the formation flying from right to left, the formation would be formed as shown in the following diagram:

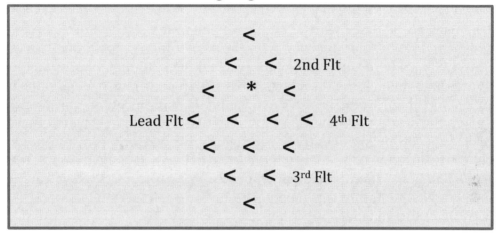

<------ Direction of Flight: 84thFIS 16-Aircraft Fly-by
"*" My position in the formation
(Viewed from the ground)

Orders Again – So Soon!

Hamilton was the shortest of my Air Force permanent change of station (PCS) assignments. On October 31 (Halloween) I received orders assigning me to the 59FIS at Goose Bay, Labrador for 18 months unaccompanied (without family). Travel time authorized was 13 days. I had 40 days of leave time so I asked for a delay en route. My reporting date was January 13, 1959 to the Air Force Air Traffic Coordinator at McGuire AFB, New Jersey, for air transportation to Goose Bay. This gave me a Hamilton departure date of November 22nd. Twenty-two days to arrange for pickup of household goods; clear the base; get Norris out of school and take care of other personal matters. Not much time, although I would have shorter assignment notices in my career. Theoretically, Command personnel make overseas assignments based on who is next in line. It must have been my turn. Pat would stay with her mother in Doraville, Georgia about 10 miles from Mom and Dad's farm. Having arrived at Hamilton the end of January 1958, and leaving the 22nd of November, gave me a nine month and 22 day assignment at Hamilton – one month shorter that my time at New Castle, Delaware. This time we would travel a more northern route. We traveled the famous Route 66 for many miles. Stopping at some of the remote (*really* remote) single-shack service stations along the way was interesting. You really watched the miles and your fuel gage very closely on those lonely desert highways. We stopped at Pat's mother's sister, Aunt Esther, in Paul Valley, Oklahoma. She was the chief Pack-Rat of all Pack-Rats – both her home and her car. All of her traveling was that way. Her husband had been killed in the "Battle of the Bulge" during WW II. She lived and traveled the country alone, visiting family and friends.

I saw the biggest snake of my life, outside of captivity, in her old unused backyard well. Try as I might, I couldn't get to that snake to kill it. It was a black snake. When I told Aunt Esther about my seeing it, she just sort of shrugged her shoulders and said something like: "Yes, he's been there a long time. He keeps the rats and vermin away". We finally reached Pat's mother's home and had a great time, and memorable Christmas 1958 with all our families. All of us tried to put the fact that I would soon be leaving for 18 months out of our minds and just enjoy the season. Foremost in my mind was the fear that Robert would forget me during the 18 months I was away. He was one year old now and would be two and a half when I returned. But Pat kept my picture readily available and kept him reminded of who was in the picture. I would call home often and talk with him to also help keep him aware. It seemed to work. I was not a stranger to him when I returned.

Some Reflections on Hamilton

In 2002, more than a year after Pat died on March 5th 2001, I took Robert to Hawaii for my Vietnam War Forward Air Controllers Reunion. On the way back we stopped at San Francisco. I wanted to show him where we lived in San Rafael while we were there at Hamilton AFB in 1958. He had his first birthday there. I took him to visit our old military housing area on San Jose Boulevard. The houses were no longer there but the streets, trees (much bigger now) and hills were still there. I took a picture of Robert – a grown man now – standing by the tree in our front yard where I had taken his picture sitting on the grass when he was less than one year old. Some change! I had him take my picture standing near the small stream behind our back yard, where I had my picture taken by Pat back then. It was so grown over now that it was hardly recognizable.

I took him by Hamilton (inactive now), but I don't remember showing him around the base much. We didn't have a lot of time to delay. We drove on up to Cloverdale to visit a pilot training buddy and his wife, a very lovely and fun lady. It was a great time reliving our flying training and career experiences. They really seemed to take to Robert. Of course most people he and Norris met really seemed to take a liking to them; I remember that they both made a big hit with my 56-V Pilot Training Class when I had them to our home in Prattville, Alabama for our first all 56-V pilot class reunion in 1999.

On our way back to San Francisco to catch our flight, Robert and I stopped at Belvedere to visit another pilot training buddy. We only had time for lunch and an hour or so to spend there; his wife was not home so we didn't get to meet her. I did years later. Robert and he swapped puns; and they connected each pun to the previous one just made by the other. It was Amazing! I never knew Robert was such a punster. He and my friend must have gone at it for about 20 minutes non-stop; each trying to out-pun the other. I think it must have ended in a draw as Robert and I had to leave to catch our flight. Otherwise it would probably still be on-going.

In 2006, a couple of years after my wife Margaret (Maggie) and I were married, we traveled to San Francisco to visit her relatives. Great visit! While there I showed her San Francisco, Mt "Tam" and Hamilton. Although an inactive base now, the old main gate was still there at Hamilton. We went up the hill to the old Officers Club. Deer were grazing on the lawn. They just looked up at us, curiously, as if to say: "What are you doing here? Can't you see we're having lunch?" Then, on to the flight line: I walked Maggie out to the old 84th hangar and onto the flight line. The hangar had much of the glass windows and skylights broken out. Sad! Many, many scenes from my memory of the 84th came flooding back. As I write this, I'm reminded of the World War Two movie, "Twelve O'clock High", with Gregory Peck. The opening scene was of this old guy in a civilian suit (not Peck), strolling slowly down an old abandoned runway in England, with grass and weeds growing between the cracks. He was obviously deep in thought, and glanced occasionally at the sky. Then the scene flashes back to the same airfield, with scenes of him in uniform; the airplanes; the air and ground crews; and the line shacks. It had been an American B-17 air base during World War Two. His World War Two story then unfolds.

While in San Francisco I phoned my pilot training friend in Belvedere, to see if Maggie and I could work in a short visit. We met him and his wife at a local pier restaurant for lunch. He is a lot of fun, and his wife was a very lovely and gracious lady. He invited me back again to go flying with him in his open cockpit bi-plane, the classic PT-17 Stearman; a World War Two military trainer. Unfortunately I never got back out there. Before we left San Francisco, he took us out to lunch at the old Army Post: The Presidio.

In a similar manner, I had taken Pat's sister Carrie to visit the New Castle County Airport, Delaware, sometime after Pat had died. I showed her NCCA; Pat's and my old apartment building (now project housing); and the hospital where Robert was born. I showed her the church we attended, which had been relocated and expanded over the years, and the tennis courts in New Castle where, as an Airman years before, I had tried out my Olds '98 "Chick Magnet" on the local chicks, but to no avail. As the old hymn goes: "Precious memories! How they linger and ever flood my soul". Next: "Loose on the Goose!"

*****

CHAPTER TEN
LOOSE ON THE GOOSE! - Goose Bay Labrador, Canada; F-89 (1959-1960)

Across This Great Land again!

With my 40 days authorized delay en route from Hamilton plus my 13 days of official travel time, I had 53 days with the family before I had to depart. This would have Pat, Norris, Robert and me leaving Hamilton around the third week of November 1958, having arrived there the 31st of January 1958. Robert was now about a year and two months old and will have traveled coast to coast twice. It's too bad he was too young to remember it because this is a beautiful country we have. I'm sure Norris remembered it. We were enjoying the sights and looking forward to another visit with our families. Things were going well. Robert was not yet old enough for him and Norris to play the "Mama, he's on my side!" – "Mama, he touched me!" game. However, Norris had the "Are we there yet?" line down very well.

We had a great time with family and friends. Since both grandmothers were within a few miles of each other; and Pat would be staying with her mother, I know both grandmothers were looking forward to an 18 month grand time with the grand kids. Foremost on my mind was the 18 month separation from my family. Heretofore I had only been gone a few weeks at a time. I've already stated my concern that Robert would forget me. Norris was old enough to remember me, however. Of course, I had warned Pat that there would be these separations during my Air Force career. I just didn't expect them so soon into it: Three assignments in just over two years; four if you include my advanced pilot training at Moody AFB following pilot training. I really didn't mind the Goose Bay Air Base assignment, as assignments go. After all, it was still on the North American Continent; and a Canadian base where they spoke English. Too, there was a likely chance that I could get home on leave during the 18 month tour. Only a few families of the higher ranks were concurrently assigned to Goose Bay with their service member sponsor, due to the lack of family quarters. Finally time came for me to depart. I would travel to McGuire AFB, New Jersey for military air transportation to Goose Bay. McGuire was the jumping-off place for military travel overseas to Europe and other places east. Mom and Pat would make sure I had adequate cold weather civvies. The Air Force would take care of the rest. Of course, it was always a heart-wrenching time saying goodbye to my family for long periods. Mom never got used to it. But, I was on my way! "Oh, don't give me a home where the polar bears roam – and the weather is frigid all day!" Sorry, I just couldn't resist.

Reporting to the passenger terminal at McGuire Air Force Base was the usual hassle of check-in; customs; wrestling my baggage along; and wait, wait, wait! It confirmed the old adage: "Time to spare; go by air!" Finally my departure time arrived. I would travel on an Air Force C-54, a four-engine propeller aircraft. Or was it C-118? They are both so much alike. After getting airborne, the plane captain came on the PA system and introduced himself, with the usual details of the flight. The name sounded familiar: James Williams. Of course there are many James Williams, but one of my pilot training classmates was a James Williams who went on to multi-engine flight training following Primary. What was the possibility? I went to the cockpit. You could do that back then. I asked the steward - they were stewards and stewardesses back then - if I could talk the pilot. You could do that back then, also. In fact, you could do a lot of things back then, before we ruined this great nation of ours with political correctness and security increases as the result of terrorism! Sure enough, it was the James Williams of my pilot class 56-V. We had a great visit. I jokingly chastised him for hauling me away on my first overseas assignment – unaccompanied at that. I have tried to locate James in the last few years for our 56-V reunions, but there are too many James Williams out there. And now privacy and political correctness have made it almost impossible to locate anyone, as you could back then.

Winter Wonderland!

James delivered me safely. We said our goodbyes, and I'm sure someone from the 59th Fighter Interceptor Squadron met me at the terminal. Snow! Snow! Snow everywhere – and deep! Many buildings were almost buried. Ice! Tunnels were dug under the snow, connecting adjacent buildings. Walking in certain places was very treacherous. The snow was so dry it was powder and blew with the wind like dust. Walking on the hard packed snow was no problem. Walking in knee-high and thigh-deep snow was difficult. But, you didn't get wet because it was so dry. It was not uncommon to be unable to see out your window for the snow piled up against it. Those lucky enough to have cars had to keep the engine (oil) heated with light bulbs under the hood, and connected to a power cord running from the building to the parking lot. Temperatures could easily get to 30 and 40 degrees below zero. Exposed skin would be frostbitten within seconds, and the wind which often blew quite strongly could seriously shorten the exposure time necessary for serious injury.

The squadron gave me the usual "new guy" days to get checked in around the base and settled into my assigned BOQ - Bachelor Officer Quarters; "bachelor" being any officer there without family. The rooms were very adequate and comfortable. The BOQ Next door had a bar and lounge in the basement that served as the after-duty happy hour get-together; and some "fighter pilot" antics, such as fighter pilots are known for. It was called the "Scramble Inn"! Scramble being the termed used for launching alert crews to check out unidentified aircraft.

As I would come to know very well over the years, homesickness would set in after a couple of weeks and last a week or so. Of course it never completely went away, but the symptoms eased off after a few weeks. The base was a Joint Royal Canadian/US Air Force and commercial air carrier civilian base. The RCAF and civilian operations were on one side, and the US Air Force on the other – all sharing the same runways. The US Air Force was, of course, a tenant on the Canadian base. The American side was primarily a Strategic Air Command (SAC) operation with the 59th FIS (ADC) being tenants of SAC.

Ernest Harmon AFB, Newfoundland

On February 3rd 1959, another pilot, two radar operators and I were ordered to Ernest Harmon AFB, Newfoundland for seven days of alert duty. The 59th at Goose was rotating crews there, to do Harmon's alert duty while they were transitioning from F-89s to the newer F-102s – the reason for our Harmon TDY (temporary duty). Nothing of significance happened at Harmon that I recall. I didn't know the exact arrangements between the Air Force and the Navy, but the Navy maintained a base there also. We were quartered in Navy BOQs and ate in the Naval Officers Mess. What I remember about Harmon is the great Navy mess and the luxurious BOQs. The Navy is much more formal than the other services, and dinner was always in class-A uniform. No one was seated until the Captain arrived and was seated. I have been impressed with the Navy mess from the time that I was a young Marine Reserve PFC at the Atlanta Naval Air Station, Chamblee, Georgia. *But the grass is always greener elsewhere*. I've heard Navy guys cuss Navy chow, as only sailors can – but I enjoyed it. Anyway, that's my Newfoundland experience. I think we did a couple of alert scrambles while there. Back to the Goose: It was a month later that I was scheduled for the Arctic Survival School.

Arctic Survival School

On March 16th 1959, I, along with seven other aircrew members, was scheduled for seven days of winter survival training. The training site was located a few miles from the base. On the first day we trekked to the site. During the previous night several inches of fresh dry snow had fallen. We were issued show shoes, my first ever. Heretofore I always thought that snow shoes enabled you to walk on the show. Not so! If the snow is hard packed or frozen, yes; if freshly fallen, no. Loaded down with about a 50 pound backpack, our trek was through the woods: Tall firs, spruce, and other specimens, reaching to the sky. Beautiful! That is, unless you are trying to survive with the barest of food and equipment. In the woods even the old snow was loose, with the fresh snow on top. There was no traffic or equipment to pack the snow. We were in thigh-high to waist-deep loose snow, sometimes higher, and took about 15 minute turns as trail-breaker. Tiring, exhausting! You didn't push your way through the snow, rather you had to lift your legs and feet as high as possible and tramp the snow down as you went – with your snow shoes of course. First survival lesson: If you crash or eject, don't try to travel unless absolutely necessary. Stay put, build a shelter, and try to find food. Above all – stay dry. If you get wet in those sub-freezing temperatures, you're done; unless you can get out of your clothes and into shelter and a fire. So the first priority is building shelter and a fire. All the other things then follow: Finding food; building signal devices; protection against the local wild inhabitants; wolves; bears, etc.

We had in our packs the usual survival items that were in our flying survival kits: Knives; fishing gear; signal devices; first aid kit; gloves; cap; Chap Stick; and limited food items. We also had a parachute canopy and harness; assuming that we would have these items in a bail-out/crash situation. So, upon reaching our survival site, we were singled out to survive on our own. We were in a quasi-camp site however, and had group training sessions. Temperatures would fall well below zero at night and sometimes during the day. We also had a sleeping bag which was contained in our flight survival kit. We were instructed to peel down to underwear or less at night, when crawling into the sleeping bag. This was to preclude sweating and getting your clothes damp; that would instantly freeze when you climbed out of the bag in the mornings. Of course, anything that you wanted to keep warm during the night you took into the sleeping bag with you. *No! We weren't issued any of those.* It was time well spent and the instructors were great; very valuable training, although I've forgotten most of it. The north woods and the snow were absolutely beautiful! In the summer time travel would become very treacherous: Loose and marshy tundra. And mosquitoes! There are horror survival stories of mosquitoes literally driving a survivor mad, if he had no mosquito netting and protection.

No Polar Bear's Lunch!

Flying up north beyond the Goose, on a rare occasion you would see a polar bear. I think I saw one. Of course being naturally *camouflaged* as they are, I probably flew over more that I saw. The base had an indoor underground pistol range. I was already interested in target shooting, as I have related in my Hamilton AFB story. Deciding that I did not want to become a polar bear's lunch, I purchased the largest handgun that the Base Exchange had to offer: a 357 Magnum revolver, with great penetration and stopping power. While at home en route to the Goose, I had purchased a World War Two-style pilot/aircrew survival vest, which had a shoulder holster. I flew with this vest; it's several pockets stuffed with survival items – *and my 357 Magnum.* I target practiced often. At first, shooting indoors was a strange feeling; but I came to enjoy it. Years later, at the first 59th FIS reunion that I attended, a 59th buddy came up to me and inquired if I was George Partridge. I recognized him right away: A really nice guy. He said he remembered me flying with that huge *cannon* in my shoulder holster, which had given him many chuckles. I told him it was my means to avoid becoming a polar bear's lunch. Of course, had I had the occasion to use it on a polar bear I'm sure I wouldn't be here writing about it. But it gave me a little bit of confidence.

What am I doing here?!

As a North American Air Defense (NORAD) fighter interceptor unit, we were always practicing scrambles and intercepts of "bogeys" (unidentified aircraft); or playing "war" and practicing the interception and "destruction" of enemy bombers. Sometimes we would do coordinated joint exercises with SAC bomber wings. This provided realistic detection and tracking by the NORAD ground radars; with scrambling of fighter units against real bombers, on simulated runs against major "targets". Most often however, our squadron would practice unilateral training missions: that is, using our own fighters to simulate bombers. We had a couple of T-33s in the squadron which, in addition to being used for instrument proficiency and other support, would also be used to simulate bombers on these practice air defense training missions. Being small as it was, the T-33 carried an underslung radar reflector to more realistically indicate a larger bomber on the radar screen.

The simulated incoming enemy bomber profile would usually be something on this order: We would fly high altitude outbound over the North Atlantic for 150-200 miles; then let down to about 200-300 feet over the water; turn inbound, and play *enemy bomber* – and wait for the intercept. Occasionally I flew one of these T-33 'enemy' bomber sorties. Now it is a well-known axiom for pilots that an airplane engine – especially in single-engine airplanes – will go into *automatic rough* mode, or develop unusual noises never before heard, the moment you leave land for flights over water. The T-33 is single-engine. Night flights have the same phenomenon, but not nearly as severe as over water. Now, the cold, rough, North Atlantic Ocean is not a friendly place to be. Air temperatures could be well below freezing and the water temperature very close behind. While clipping along about 350 miles per hour, 100-200 miles out to sea, I could look down a couple of hundred feet to those huge, angry waves and wall-to-wall whitecaps, and ponder – *what am I doing here?!* The only thing between me and instant death is that one jet engine that I am riding: thus the *automatic rough* engine, and unusual noise syndrome.

Funny how your senses seem to play games with you, in such situations. If you crashed into the cold raging sea you would likely not survive the crash. If you ejected and parachuted into the sea, you wouldn't live long enough to climb into your raft. Hypothermia would be almost instantaneous at those temperatures. To combat this, we were issued thermal exposure flight suits. These were rubberized (not insulated) suits, with wrists and neck bands that sealed you into the suit to prevent water entering. They were thus called "poopie" suits - for obvious reasons. We did wear quilted thermal underwear under the suit. With the wrist and neck seals, the suit was sort of a full-body flotation device in itself. The boots were an integral part of the suit. Gloves and a hood were in the pockets. It was almost impossible to prevent at least a trickle of water from entering the suit. Once enough water had entered the suit it would become like an anchor and tend to pull you under. The suit would enable you to survive the water temperature long enough to inflate and board your one-man dinghy. Then you could freeze to death at your leisure in the dinghy, rather than in the water. I'm convinced that the suit was simply a morale factor; it did offer you a life expectancy in/on the water of about ten to fifteen minutes. However, if your hands were exposed they had a usefulness of maybe five minutes or less.

The T-33 cockpit was very small. With winter flying clothes and underwear; exposure suit and hooded parker; you practically had to be shoe-horned into the cockpit. One or two brave (?) souls chose to fly without the exposure suit; realizing that its value at extending life was practically nil. It was extremely uncomfortable and cumbersome. While flying over those raging waves and whitecaps I would wonder then, later, and even now – what manner of men were those early Vikings, Norsemen, Whalers and explorers to sail those seas. I wondered if they – like me – ever wondered: "What am I doing here?"! They went out for their survival – and to war. I, likewise, was out there for survival; yours and mine – and it was a *war:* The Cold War era; Russia and China against the United States.

Alert Hangar

My flight commander was a few years older than the other guys in the flight. I think he was a little sensitive about that, and a couple of the guys teased him without mercy. He was stocky, muscular, and was always showing off his strength when he could. He went by the call sign "Boxcar". During alert duty he would often be seen chinning himself while wearing his parachute.

I have described the scenes around and in the alert hangars earlier in my story. The Goose alert hangar, like Hamilton, also had a "fire pole" from the second floor crew sleeping area. A real "Three Stooges" show: The scramble klaxon horn awaking confused and disoriented aircrews who would run around the room colliding with each other until they became awake and aware; then sliding down the pole on top of each other, on the way to their aircraft. The unwritten rule was that the first one to taxi out of the hangar was leader. Boxcar was usually the first out. Once, during one of my alert duties, I was on with Boxcar. The weather was really "stinko"! It was blowing snow almost horizontally *across* the runway, with the ceiling obscured and the visibility ¼ mile. The runway was ice and snow covered, although most of the snow had been plowed leaving a runway of sheet ice. Snow was piled along the runway edges, burying the runway lights in snow. We were rather relaxed, thinking it would have to be an act of war to be scrambled in that weather.

Wrong! Suddenly the klaxon horn sounded and we jumped out of our skins. Boxcar and I were the two crews on five-minute alert. So it was us with our ROs! A scramble in this weather had to be for a very serious unknown aircraft (bogey) in or approaching the air defense area. This scramble would have taken a higher authority than normal to order the scramble. Boxcar was the first out of the hangar with me right behind. Taxiing to the runway, Boxcar and I quickly do our condensed check-list, as the fighters are set up for a scramble by the aircrew upon arriving for alert duty. The ROs copy the scramble instructions from the tower. The takeoff clearance is automatic for an active air defense scramble, except for emergency landings. We kept thinking surely they will cancel the scramble before takeoff. Not so! We reached the runway and no cancellation: Press on! Unlike Tactical Air Command fighters, ADC rarely did formation takeoffs. In ADC the lead would release brakes, and number two would release brakes five seconds later. This permitted a three-mile in-trail formation position, with the RO maintaining position on the lead with his radar. The identification was made by the lead pilot; while the wingman remained high and back in an attack position, should such action be necessary.

About 15 minutes after takeoff, our ground radar controller advised that the bogey had been identified and we were to RTB (return to base). The weather was still obscure with an indefinite ceiling and ¼ mile visibility in blowing snow. Obscure meant fog-like visibility obscuration; and indefinite meant a ragged ceiling, not clearly defined. I have stated previously what a stable instrument flying airplane the F-89 was. It was sure appreciated on that day. We were on instruments from takeoff. If we couldn't land, then we would likely divert to an air base in Maine. I don't recall, but Harmon AFB was probably as bad as the Goose, making it an unacceptable alternate.

Boxcar made the first approach. He was unable to land so he executed a missed approach. Now it was my turn. Instrument flying is 100% concentration. An instrument approach into conditions like these demands *150% concentration*. Our approach was a ground controlled approach (GCA); meaning that a ground controller would transmit directions to the pilot, in order to maintain the runway centerline and glide path. The pilot controlled the airspeed, descent rate, and heading, based on those ground controller instructions. The legal instrument approach weather minimums for such an approach were a 200 foot ceiling, and ¼ mile visibility. I always suspected - based on Boxcar's missed approach, and on my approach and landing - that the actual weather was slightly below regulation minimums, but fudged to get us home. It was a white-out condition! Upon reaching the authorized minimums I prepared to initiate a go-around, when I spotted the dim glow of the runway lights which were glowing through the snow piled along the edges of the runway. The runway surface was not visible even after touchdown due to being ice and snow covered. The landing was made without incident, with a very cautious roll-out and taxi back to the alert hangar. Boxcar landed soon thereafter. I think the bogey turned out to be an airliner, well off-course and schedule. Air defense and air traffic controllers probably worked out a coordinated identification prior to our intercept.

Additional Duty – Security Officer

It was not all fun (flying) and games. All officers were assigned additional duties to fill those necessary functions in any organization, i.e. Administrative Officer; Supply Officer; Operations Officer; and a host of other duties. Therefore, for most aircrews, when not flying, their time was spent taking care of those additional duties. When scheduled to fly, it took a large chunk out of the day. Also, there were the other required squares to fill: Night flying, alert duty, cross-countries and exercises. Additional duties usually meant extra hours.

My additional duty was Security Officer. Foremost, this meant a laborious and time-consuming inventory of all classified documents and items, prior to assuming the inherent custodial responsibility. This, of course, would be repeated for the new Security Officer once my tour of duty at the Goose was completed. Woe to the Security Officer who could not account for a classified document or item on his transfer of inventory. Periodically, classified documents of no further value were gathered, documented and destroyed – by burning. This detailed list of documents and items destroyed had to be certified by the destroying officer and a witness. Another responsibility was the issuing, monitoring for proper use, and accounting of all Restricted Area security badges. These were laminated badges with clips attached to the outer garment while in secure areas: Squadron, flight line, and in the alert hangars. They had a specific format that included a photo of the individual, and color codes for entry into various areas.

The badges provided a quick and visible means to determine one's authorization to be in an area. Persons without the badge or with questionable badges were to be apprehended and turned over to the Security Police. It was forbidden to wear the badge off the flight line and off base; the point being to prevent compromise of the badge format, photo, and information included thereon by any unauthorized person, and specifically by enemy agents. Loss of a badge was a serious offense. Remember, we were on a Strategic Air Command base (the American side). SAC was notorious for its strict security regulations. And tenants had to comply with the host command (SAC) regulations. With their nuclear bombers, tankers, and alert facilities, the regulations were not without just cause. SAC had frequent security exercises, in which they would have simulated penetrators and infiltrators attempt to compromise the area; particularly the alert facilities. And, of course, as a tenant the 59th was deeply involved in these exercises. Fortunately none of those *penetrators* or *infiltrators* were ever killed or injured by an extremely nervous or trigger-happy security guard.

As is the case with most organizations, there are those individuals (few thankfully) that just have to test or resist the organization's rules and regulations (non-conformists). There was one aircrew (pilot and RO) that just seemed to delight in being a thorn-in-my-side regarding compliance with the strict security rules and regulations. Most personnel seemed to recognize the seriousness of our mission and protection of the weapons we worked with – and accepted the necessary inconveniences. Fortunately I had a very good sergeant (NCO) who manned the office, controlled the classified documents, and kept up the routine stuff. Most importantly – he kept me out of trouble. Thank goodness for good NCOs. It has been said that a good organization is run by good NCOs. True!

There was only one incident that could have had disastrous results. We flew with classified encoding and authentication tables. These were used to verify the authenticity of serious or suspicious orders. They were drawn and signed for prior to a mission, or upon assuming alert duty. Once the mission or alert duty terminated, they were of course returned to the issuing agency for security in a safe or vault. Following one particular flight, the aircrew could not produce their authentication codes. A check of flight suits, clothing, lockers, and retracing steps to the aircraft did not produce the codes. This was a serious breach of security; possibly a court-marshal offense. And as squadron security officer, I might have been involved in such a court martial, as the officer-in-charge of maintaining security of all classified documents. The military hierarchy works that way you know. I asked and got permission of the squadron commander to muster a detail of squadron personnel to scour the snow-covered ramp and flight line. So I formed a sort of line-abreast detail to scour the area. Fortunately, the codes were discovered in the snow intact, still sealed, and untampered-with. This was satisfactory in squelching any concerns regarding compromise of the codes. Apparently they had fallen out of the individual's clothing or gear undetected while on the way to the mission debriefing – and not discovered on the initial retracing of his path from the aircraft.

Mid-Tour Leave

If possible, personnel on the Goose without family (unaccompanied) were granted a very short leave at some time during the tour. My turn came. I really can't recall the time or travel arrangements, but I got home for a few days in April of 1959. It was such a short time, maybe it became just a blur in my mind. I know it was a joy seeing Pat, her Mom, Norris and Robert; and my Mom and Dad. Robert did remember me! But it was all over too soon. I do know that I got to take a T-33 to the States while at the Goose, and later an F-89 to the overhaul depot for updating and inspection. It may have been that I had a courier flight to the States with a T-33. I do remember that I landed at Dobbins AFB, just northwest of Atlanta, about 45 minutes to an hour from home, and from Pat and her Mom with Norris and Robert. As I mentioned above, I don't remember anything of the time with my families except: On my departure day, Dad and Mom drove me to Dobbins and watched me do my flight planning for departure in the T-33.

They walked with me to my T-33 and watched while I did the aircraft walk-around pre-flight. I felt ten-feet tall knowing that Mom and Dad were finally going to get to watch their jet-pilot son takeoff in his jet. Mom was probably wrought with apprehension and fear, as she was about to witness her son take to the air in his *dangerous jet air-machine*. Dad was probably more curiously interested than anything else. Pat was probably at work, but she and Norris had seen me fly before. Robert was too young to remember, and his young ears would have been too susceptible to the noise levels.

After saying our goodbyes, I climbed the ladder to the cockpit and crammed my still *ten-foot- tall* body into the cockpit. After strapping in with the transient aircraft crew chief's assistance, I gave the start signal; flicked the start switch to "START"; waited for the 10% RPM windup; ignition switch "ON" and throttle to the "IDLE" position. There was the normal "BLOOP" as the fuel ignited, followed by a sometimes two to three foot flame from the tail pipe, until the increasing RPM caught up with the fuel flow. Poor Mom! I forgot to brief them. I probably attempted to signal them that all was OK. Also, the crew chief was calm and unconcerned so I'm sure they assumed all was OK. After the engine start-up, cockpit check and the OK from the crew chief following his external check, I signaled for chocks out; waved to Mom and Dad; throttled up (it takes a good bit of power to get the T-33 moving) and started my taxi to the runway. I had briefed Mom and Dad where to stand so that they didn't get blown over with the jet exhaust. I had told them which runway I would be using; and that, if the tower permitted, I would double back for a low altitude fly-by down the runway. I don't remember a high-speed, low-level fly-by so the tower must not have approved. And I was not about to jeopardize my wings for an unauthorized maneuver. After the climb out to altitude, I deflated my ten-foot frame to its normal five-foot nine inches.

Goose Tour Shortened

My assignment to the Goose from Hamilton AFB was for 18 month as an unaccompanied officer, with reporting on January 13, 1959. The Goose Bay tour was increased from 12 to 18 months just a couple of months or so before receiving my Goose Bay orders at Hamilton. At the Goose I received orders in June 1959 (as did every unaccompanied person), changing my end-tour date from 12 July 1960 to 12 April 1960, shortening my 18 month tour by three months, to 15 months. Oh happy day! Most unaccompanied overseas tours were 12 months. But those were reserved for the extremely remote and/or hardship assignments. I gladly took my shortened tour. Really, though, except for the restricted travel opportunities – especially winter time, Goose was not a terrible tour. There were plenty of activities on base to keep one occupied.

Aircraft Delivery to Depot Maintenance
On October 26, 1959 another 59th pilot, two ROs, and I were ordered to deliver two squadron F-89s to the maintenance depot at Brookley AFB, Mobile, Alabama. Periodically Air Force aircraft were sent to the manufacture's depot for inspection, repair and updating as necessary. There, all systems were gone over with company personnel and updated as applicable. One more trip back to the States! But this time there would be no detour to see my family. Each crew signed for their F-89, all accessory equipment, all documents and manuals; then we were on our way. After delivery and transfer of the aircraft, if other squadron aircraft were ready for pickup we would sign for and deliver them to the 59th. I don't remember returning an F-89 so we likely returned by commercial or military airlift. It was nice to be back in the States, if ever so briefly.

New Assignment – Ground Radar Controller: Inevitable
On March 7th 1960, I received my orders assigning me back to the States. It was a well-established fact that pilots could expect some type of ground assignment approximately four years out of pilot training. Then after that four-year ground assignment, they are usually returned to a flying job. Well it finally happened. My assignment was to be a ground-control intercept (GCI) controller, the same guys who had been directing us to bombers or unidentified aircraft. The assignment however, would be cross-command to the Tactical Air Command's (TAC's) 728th Aircraft Control and Warning (AC&W) Squadron, Shaw AFB, Sumter, South Carolina. My duty location would be the Squadron's Detachment #2, Fort Gordon, Augusta, Georgia. I would be going TDY en route to the 3625th Combat Crew Training Group (Air Training Command – ATC), Tyndall AFB, Florida for the ten weeks, training course number 174100, Class 61-B-1C. I was to report to the air terminal traffic coordinator at the Goose on April 10th for transportation to the States, with a report date of May 21, 1960 to Tyndall. My orders included an authorized 37 days leave en route, to spend with my family. Pat, Norris and Robert would then accompany me to Tyndall. I flew my last F-89 flight, with 468 total hours, at Goose Bay on April 5th 1960, in a 59th Fighter Interceptor Squadron F-89J.

A Few Memorable Goose Moments
Winter Time: The north woods in deep, snow-covered splendor (picture post card style).

Summer Time: Endless green forests, blue skies, blue lakes and rivers.

White-Outs: Total blindness created by a "white-out" caused by snow cover everywhere.

Ice Fog: Fog formed by ice crystals created by the jet exhaust of the aircraft ahead of you.

Northern Lights: Heavenly lights dancing around the heavens from horizon to horizon (aurora borealis).

Midnight Sun: Seeing the sun set just barely below the horizon; then watch it move slowly to the left along the horizon for a few minutes; then sun rise!

Powdered Snow: Snow so dry it blows like dust back into your face, trying to throw a snowball.

Indoor Pistol Range: My first! Fun! But it's like using a hospital bed pan: you know it's OK, but it just doesn't feel right – shooting indoors, and *"going"* in bed.

Flight Picnic on Lake Hamilton: Guys turning blue in frigid water, acting tough and unfazed.

Night-time Scramble Horn: Jumping out of your skin; doing a Three Stooges act; then piling up on each other at the bottom of the fire pole.

Minimum Ceiling and Visibility Approach: Obscure and indefinite ceiling; blowing snow in a crosswind with ¼ mile visibility.

Home on Leave Mid-Tour: Just seeing my family again!

Goodbye Goose!

 Departure day came. I had *stuffed*, boxed, bagged, packed and *stuffed* my *stuff* for shipping, after *stuffing* my duffel bag with all the *stuff* that I could *stuff* and drag to the terminal; a chore that would be repeated many times over during my career. So long Goose! Hello, family, Tyndall, and beautiful beaches!

****

CHAPTER ELEVEN
NEW JOB: MOBILE TACTICAL GROUND RADAR CONTROLLER
Tyndall AFB, Florida; Fort Gordon, Georgia; Shaw AFB, South Caroline;
T-33, L-19 (1960-1964)

Job Rotation
The dreaded nemesis for most pilots is being taken out of a primary flying position and assigned to a ground job. This usually occurred near the four-year point in a pilot's career and lasted for about four years; at the end of which rotation back to a flying position could be expected. However, a number of pilots were fortunate enough to avoid these non-flying breaks in their career. But if career progression was to continue, the pilot would at some point, of necessity, be taken from a flying assignment and placed in a promotion-enhancing staff job or career-enhancing position. Some pilots with extreme flying skills (and maybe having developed some influential connection along the way) could be fortunate enough to remain in operational flying positions throughout their careers. However this was not my good fortune.

Thus, the ground radar controller assignment was my fate upon completion of my Goose Bay fifteen-month tour. The assignment as radar controller could be expected to last the usual four-year tour. As mentioned in the previous chapter, this assignment was cross-command to the Tactical Air Command (TAC) as a tactical mobile ground radar controller. Tactical mobile radar meant combat theater/battlefield radar, usually co-located with army units and capable of being packed, loaded and moved on short notice; as fluid battle fields or maneuvering army units required. It was used to control and direct tactical fighter aircraft against targets behind enemy lines (interdiction), or watching the backs of friendly aircraft over the battlefield.

Assignment to a different major air command was not the norm but they did occur, especially between stateside and overseas assignments. Being assigned to TAC meant that the odds of an assignment to fighters would be greater at the end of my four-year radar controller tour. After all, TAC was the fighter command; ADC the air defense command (interceptors and missiles); SAC the strategic bomber command plus Intercontinental Ballistic Missiles (ICBMs) and MAC the military airlift command. Since my turn at a ground job had arrived, I felt fortunate in having been transferred to TAC. Of course, TAC units were subjected to frequent nationwide and worldwide deployments – either for training, or for real conflicts. This meant that I would often be deployed away from home. I had no clue at this time just how frequently I would be deployed for days and months at a time. These frequent deployments were a real millstone about the necks of many military families. Family life would be disrupted occasionally – even in the dead of night. Children would wake up one morning and Dad would be gone; Mom distraught, and the household routine disrupted. Sometimes no one knew for how long. *Family glue* is what held the family together during these frequent and long separations. Unfortunately a few families came apart because of these pressures and uncertainty. Thank the Lord that Pat and I had the super-glue that held together during these times. We had discussions about just such potential situations even before we married. On a few occasions Pat had to console and counsel her friends whose husbands were away for these long periods. That was Pat. She had a shoulder that many of her military-wife friends liked to lean on or cry on. Military wives are a close-knit group, supporting each other during long deployment separations and common trials and tribulations.

Proficiency Flying

Although not in a primary flying job, I would still be required to maintain flying proficiency through what was called the "Flying Proficiency Program". This meant that I would be required to fly 100 to 120 hours per year. Since flying would not be my primary job, I would have to accumulate the 100-120 hours mostly during other than normal duty hours, i.e. nights and week-ends. Flying would be in the front or rear cockpit of a T-33 and shared with another proficiency-flying pilot. Normal flying requirements such as night, instrument, cross-country (X-C), landings, etc., would have to be accomplished during other than normal duty hours; although an understanding supervisor would sometimes allow you time out of the office to *go fly*. The flying time would be split with the other pilot by trading seats on out-and-back cross-countries. Out-and-back meant a cross-country flight, out and back on the same day/night, without an RON (remain-over-night). Scheduling was always a problem: getting the time off and finding another pilot who was available at the same time. This was a real hassle in addition to your normal duty. Many times pilots would have to scramble to get the necessary "square filling" done as the end of the year approached and several "squares" were yet to be filled. With day/night out-and-back X-Cs on nights and weekends, and the frequent training exercises/deployments, family time was at a premium. If you can believe it, I saw many times where I was so busy I wished that I didn't have to fly. Never thought I would see that day when I didn't want to fly! And to qualify for the authorized flight pay, you had to fly at least four hours each month.

Tactical Radar Controller Training – Tyndall AFB, FL – May 1960

After a 37 day leave with my family in Georgia and Pat's family in Florida, I took Pat, Norris and Robert to Tyndall AFB at Panama City, Florida, where my radar controller training would take place. Although I would be busy learning a new skill; flying; and hitting the books, *they had a ball!*

My Goose Bay 59th Fighter Interceptor Squadron orders (A-73 dated 7 Mar 1960) assigned me to the 728th Aircraft Control and Warning Squadron (AC&W

Squadron) at Shaw AFB, Sumter, South Carolina. However, my duty station would be the squadron's Detachment 2 on the Army post at Fort Gordon, Augusta, Georgia. But first I would proceed to Tyndall Air Force Base, Panama City, Florida for temporary duty (TDY) radar controller training, with the 3625th Combat Crew Training Group. Training would begin on May 21, 1960. This would be a 10-week radar controller (Weapons Controller) training course. My 15 months of family separation behind me, my family and I arrived at Tyndall where I would be assigned to the 3525th Technical Training Group for Course 174100. I remember nothing spectacular about my training – other than the fact that I was chagrined at being taken out of a primary flying position for this ground radar controller job. But I had my family with me again, and with high hopes of being around for a while as husband and father.

I found a small duplex on Ivey Road in Parker, Florida, a few miles west of Tyndall and got Pat, Norris and Robert settled in. The duplex was located on a dead-end dirt road, nestled among beautiful pines with a nice grassy playing area and a nearby bay. There were a few neighbor children around about Norris and Robert's ages. Norris would turn nine years old while we were there. Robert was two years and nine months. Pat was...........Oh well! They had an enjoyable time and I was home again.

"On the Road Again" (Sorry, Willie)
My training completed, we departed Parker and Tyndall on July 15, 1960. On July 17th we arrived at Fort Gordon, Augusta, GA, the location of Detachment 2, 728th AC&W Squadron. This would be my first assignment on an Army installation, and a taste of Army life; which underscored why I didn't join the army! However, many times hence I would feel as though I was a real Army "grunt".

Weapons Controller (Tactical) – Fort Gordon, GA – July 1960
I reported to the 728th AC&W Squadron's Detachment 2 at Fort Gordon, and was given the usual time to find a home and get my family situated. The military service is very understanding in this regard; although I have experienced times when this courtesy was not possible, due to the urgency of the situation in progress upon my arrival – such as preparations for deployment or, as in some cases, critical real-world alert conditions. We had many of those back during the Cold War with the Soviet Union and China, which began almost immediately following World War Two.

The detachment had a great commander. He was a "Gung-Ho" Air Force Major who acted as though he thought he was an Army grunt. And he tried to make us into the same. He was a small man with thin, balding gray hair; a large gray mustache; and walked with a limp, supported by a cane. He was a dedicated career officer and believed in regimented group physical conditioning. He often would have the officers and enlisted men form up to do physical training (PT): Calisthenics and/or jogging around the site for half an hour or so, always in our combat boots, and sometimes with our field gear. He reminded me of the character Colonel Nicholson, played by Alec Guinness in the 1957 movie: The Bridge on the River Kwai. Due to the nature of the dirty work and the frequent PT sessions, we wore our green fatigue work uniforms daily. Being on an Army post, you would frequently see the grunts out in formation doing PT, or jogging around the post. Although our detachment commander was a physical fitness nut, I felt that a part of his enthusiasm was to show the army grunts that we Air Force types were physical training nuts *too,* not just patsies – and to save face as tenants on an Army post.

The detachment had eight officers plus a number of enlisted personnel. The officers were: The commander; administrative; operations; maintenance; and four weapons directors; two of whom were active flying pilots: another lieutenant, and myself. All officers, except for the maintenance officer, were radar weapons controllers, qualified on the radar scopes, with an enlisted technician assisting. Then there were the usual enlisted surveillance scope operators; plotters; radio operators; and the Senior NCO, assisting the Senior Director. We were operational on a daily basis; although our actual radar weapons controller duties were limited, due to non-availability of aircraft to work with. So the main activity was tracking and plotting live aircraft transiting the area. Occasionally we would get a couple of T-33s from Shaw AFB to practice intercepts with us. For our required flying time, the other pilot in the detachment and I were authorized to travel to Shaw AFB to fly their T-33s, in order to maintain our pilot proficiency.

There happened to be an Army aviation unit located at Augusta's civilian airport: Bush Field. They flew the single-engine, high wing, propeller-driven, tail wheel, Cessna-made, Army L-19; later designated the O-1. They were also short of pilots, which was a blessing for me. A request was made to their commander and to the Shaw AFB flight Operations Officer to permit our two pilots to fly the Army's L-19s at Bush Field, in addition to the T-33s at Shaw. Everyone was a winner! The Army was delighted, because it increased their pilot roster to show more utilization of their aircraft. Flight Operations at Shaw was delighted, because it relieved them of having to provide some of the flying support to our two detachment pilots. We were delighted, because it afforded L-19 transportation between Shaw and Fort Gordon – rather than the two hour drive; and it was fun flying the L-19 around and on Augusta airports, and Fort Gordon's reservation with its short, sod, unimproved air strips. This flying experience would be very beneficial in a few short years, when flying the O-1 in Vietnam.

The primary mission of our Detachment 2 was to keep our equipment and vehicles ready for immediate deployment – either for exercises, actual alerts, or deployment to worldwide hot spots. Being a mobility-orientated unit we had to have a mobility officer, of course. Guess who was tagged *"it"?!* Yours truly! Everything from the large radar antennas; vehicles; office furniture; every piece of equipment; to the smallest of items; pencils, paper clips, etc. plus other incidentals had to be "pre-deployment" identified, marked and designated to a special packing crate for loading onto a designated vehicle. Large uncrated items had to be weighed, cubed and the center of gravity determined. This information was then stenciled onto the item; likewise for packing crates. External and internal packing list of contents were required on all crates and equipment. Upon deploying, the radars would have to be disassembled and prepared for airlift. When loaded, the airlift-ready vehicles would be formed up to convoy to the deployed site, or to Shaw AFB for deployment airlift (C-130s). Personnel were required to maintain worldwide immunization; keep their personal emergency file and personnel records up-to-date; and a packed "bug-out bag" for no-notice deployments. Wives would be suddenly thrust into assuming all the family support and duties that the husband/father had been providing.

Woe be to the unit that failed operational readiness inspections (ORIs) initiated by higher headquarters; or more seriously, encountered major deficiencies in actual deployments. As the mobility officer in this unit, I re-learned the reality of "24/7". Many hours and weekends were spent going over and over equipment and deployment plans to assure that all was in order. Then there was the frequent practice recall of personnel – even during the late evening or wee morning hours. It was not uncommon to be awakened during the night by the alert siren and/or a personnel recall-plan phone call. After completing my portion of the personnel recall-plan, it was a "no shave or shower" dash to the detachment. It was possible that you may not see your family for two to three days; maybe more if it happened to be a real-world crisis. There were established maximum times from initiation of the alert for all personnel to be present or accounted for. In those years, 1950-60s, the Tactical Air Command units operated with what was called a Composite Air Strike Force (CASF). When a worldwide hot-spot developed – which was usually in the Middle East, even today – Army, Navy, Air Force and Marine combat units would be deployed under existing plans to a designated location – or country – and join forces under a Joint Task Force commander. The duration of the deployment could be short term - as in the case of an exercise - or months, as in the case of real-world conflicts. In the case of real-world conflicts, it was often to "show-the-flag". We had a nearby abandoned airport where we often did practice deployments for a few days. It was North Field, approximately 30 miles south of Columbia, SC.

With the frequent separations, and the many others that would occur during the remaining years of my Air Force career, Pat was left unassisted to keep everything going at home. She did an amazing job and particularly so with our sons Norris and Robert. Later, as they grew older, Norris and Robert were a great comfort and aid to her during my absences.

Squadron Officer School (SOS) – April 1961

There are several military professional schools for officers and enlisted men. Enrollment is by in-residence or by correspondence. You cannot apply for in-residence enrollment; one is "selected". Enrollment by correspondence is available to all. It is generally accepted that resident attendance is more likely to result in promotions. Each progression in Professional Military Education (PME) school attendance is designed to enhance the officer's potential for leadership, staff, and command positions. The first on the officer career ladder is Squadron Officer School (SOS), which was then (and still) located at Maxwell AFB, Montgomery, Alabama. Some of the higher level schools are the Air Command and Staff College, Air War College (both at Maxwell), and the National War College in Washington, DC. Thus it was that I was selected to attend SOS class 61-B, reporting on April 19th 1961 for 106 days; and upon completion, return to Detachment 2, 728th AC&W Squadron, at Fort Gordon. Another family separation, but necessary in the professional officer career development. The class was made up of several seminars, with tons of outside reading and research, culminating in a thesis of the officer's choice. Maxwell AFB, the home of The Air University, has the Air Force Historical Center and Research Division. It also contains the Air University's multi-storied Library of countless classified and unclassified documents for study and research. My thesis was on the mobility and deployment of tactical radars. Physical fitness, in the form of super-competitive athletics between the seminar teams, was a major agenda item.

I had bought an old Desoto (about 1950 model I think) for my transportation from Fort Gordon and to get around Maxwell, and left our 1955 Ford for Pat to use. Sometime later – near the SOS July 28th graduation, I think it was - I invited Pat, Norris and Robert over. It was about a six hour drive. On their way over the Ford's generator quit, a few miles after crossing the Alabama/Georgia state line. I received a call from Pat. She was near a service station, and a nearby family had befriended them. I told her to remain there and I would be over. After making arrangements for repairs and pick up on our return trip from Maxwell, we proceeded to Maxwell. On our way back after graduation, we picked up the Ford and proceeded to Fort Gordon without further incident. Home again!

On September 6th I, along with a few other Detachment 2 and 728th personnel, was ordered to Pope AFB, NC for airlift to Whidbey Island NAS, Oak Harbor,

Washington for a couple of weeks to participate in "Operation Sea Wall" an operational mission – not an exercise! I was amazed at the rugged coast line of our northwestern-most state in and around Neah Bay. Returning home, there was no reprieve from deployments.

Vietnam #1 – September 1961

Detachment 2 received orders to pack up and deploy our radars and personnel to Shaw AFB on September 25th, for further deployment to a classified location for 179 days TDY; which soon was known to be Saigon, Vietnam: Another long-term deployment! They never end! We would travel to Shaw AFB and join with a contingent from our squadron (728th AC&W), and from our group headquarters, the 507th Communications and Control Group at Shaw. Personnel would travel via military contract civilian aircraft, and the equipment would be deployed via military airlift. Our equipment would be accompanied by designated custodial personnel. There was hardly time to unpack from the Whidbey Island deployment before we were to be on our way to Saigon. At that time the deployment was classified, so the destination on our orders was blank. We knew where we were going however. But we were admonished not to mention our mission or destination to anyone under the strictest of penalties for security violations. Once again we were jumping through hoops in readying for another real-world deployment. As Pat helped me pack additional items and prepare for the deployment, it was extremely difficult not to share with her what was happening. She always complained that I never talked to her about what I did at work. I had told her long before that I purposely didn't talk much about my work because much of it was classified and I didn't want to slip and tell her things I shouldn't. And if I didn't tell her, then she couldn't slip and tell someone who shouldn't know. But she seemed to always find out what was happening and "brief" me on what was going on. I would never confirm nor deny what she said. What an "intelligence network" those military wives have!

Pat knew I was on my way to somewhere for a very long time. I simply told her to read the newspapers. Vietnam was hot in the news. The South Vietnamese government supposedly had asked for United States assistance in their war with North Vietnam and the Communist Viet Cong gorillas forces (Viet Minh commonly referred to as VC) operating in the south. Identified as a "conflict" by the United States, we would provide military advisory assistance to the South Vietnamese. It always amazed me that we were admonished not to talk about things that we could read in the headlines and in the newsprint. Before leaving I was trying to make sure Pat was briefed on things that needed to be done, that I had not gotten around to. This was one of the times that I had always warned her that would happen someday. Suddenly she would be thrust into the do-it-all-single-handedly role. Over the years and many deployments, she never broke down. She held up beautifully. I know she did it as much for me as for herself and the boys. Military wives have a strong support group among themselves. The time came: Goodbye for now! This one was for a real combat theater. I know I'm not the Lone Ranger, but on this and subsequent deployments I had thoughts that I may never see my family again on this earth. However, I tried not to dwell on such thoughts.

War or "Conflict?"

For reasons that Washington chose not to tell us, we were instructed to travel in civilian clothes. Of course it was to enhance the secrecy of the military movement. After arriving at Travis AFB, California for more briefing and processing, we were soon on our way via C-121 (Constellation) to Saigon, Vietnam. Along the way we crossed the international dateline. As I recall we lost a day (date) on the calendar never to be recovered. However, on the way back we would repeat a day so I'm still even. Having subsequently crossed the pond (Pacific Ocean) several times, I can't remember particular stops for each crossing but they were islands where scenes of horrific Pacific battles took place during World War Two. The islands that I remember were Wake Island, Midway, Guam and Okinawa! Whenever we made brief stops at these islands I would walk the beaches to see the WW II relics, and think on the battles that took place there and the cost in American lives (and Japanese). There were the gun emplacements and mangled hunks of military hardware. On one island (I can't remember which) the bow of a sunken Japanese freighter still stood at about 45 degrees out of the water and 50 feet or so above the surface; the Japanese insignia faded and barely discernable. The story was that the Japanese captain was trying to run the freighter aground before it sank. He was about a hundred yards short.

Our deployment commander was from our squadron at Shaw. Later he would be tagged "Little Buddha" by the Vietnamese people because of his likeness. He was short, rotund, bull-necked, cheeky, and had a stomach that would make Buddha jealous. "Little Buddha" was very descriptive of him but he was in great physical condition, as we would discover later.

We arrived at Saigon's Tan Son Nhut Air Base in our civilian clothes, and were hurried into more briefings and processing. On duty we would be in our Air Force fatigues, but off-duty we were to wear only civilian clothing. Theoretically we were supposed to be invisible to the enemy, I guess. Actually, we were only invisible to our families. Who did we think we were kidding? - unloading an aircraft full of Americans in civilian clothing and rush them into military briefings, and then assigned billeting in Saigon's Majestic Hotel. The Majestic was located on the waterfront along a loop of the Mekong River. Ship, boat and sampan activity was always present. Our job, as it turned out to be, was to erect our radar at the Tan Son Nhut Air Base and teach the Vietnamese to operate and maintain it. Once they had achieved proficiency, we would turn the equipment over to them and then depart for the US. They would *win the "war"* (or "conflict"?) with only token US Advisory support. We now know how that strategy worked out! Operationally we were initially assigned to the 2nd ADVON (Advanced Echelon) of the 7th Air Force at Tan Son Nhut Air Base.

There's a "War" out There!

A few weeks after arriving, we were told we could find our own billets in Saigon. My friend from Detachment 2 and I found a two-bedroom apartment in a newly constructed high rise apartment at 145, Vo Than Street in Saigon. We hired a female Chinese housekeeper/cook by the name of Wan, as I recall. She arrived early in the morning and left about sundown each day. I think we gave her Sunday off. She was a nice lady, and what a marvelous cook! She cleaned the apartment, hand-laundered and ironed our clothes, and did the grocery shopping. We gave her the money and free-rein for grocery shopping. Having visited the Saigon open-air market, we never asked her what we were eating. But it was fabulous! *What a way to fight a war!*

Transportation was usually by military bus to and from work. Military bus transportation was available at designated pickup points throughout the city. The buses had steel grids over the windows to prevent grenades from being thrown into the bus. For odd-hour schedules we could take a taxi (usually Volkswagen Beetles) or the ever present Asian rickshaws. Traffic was a nail-biting experience. Vehicles and pedestrians were a mixing bowl in the streets, sometimes on the sidewalks and in every direction, wall-to-wall: pedestrians; bicycles; motor scooters; large and small private vehicles; taxies galore; and all sorts and sizes of military vehicles, both Vietnamese and American. Right-of-way was usually *taken* by the larger vehicle. Never make eye contact; if you did, you just gave up your right-or-way to the other driver. The size of the load and the number of people that the Asian can transport on a bicycle or motor scooter has to be seen to be believed. Imagine a husband, wife and two to four kids, and maybe a pig or chicken or two on one bicycle or motor scooter; or one frail-looking old man, or small youngster, peddling a bicycle with a load of chicken crates stacked about five feet high; or four or five bushels of rice. How about a butchered hog strapped to the back of a bicycle! I have said many times, following our politically orchestrated defeat in Vietnam, that it was the North Vietnamese transportation system – *the bicycle laden with supplies* on the Ho Chi Minh Trail from Hanoi to Saigon – that defeated us, along with the "hand-tying" rules-of-engagement issued from our government in Washington, DC!

It was not all peaceful in Saigon. There were frequent bombings in and around the city and on the outskirts. When not on duty, we could sit on the balcony of our apartment – day or night – and see or hear air strikes and artillery bombardments taking place around the city and in the nearby country side. Two more times in the years to come I would be deployed to Vietnam. It was so frustrating and heartbreaking to see the same air strikes and artillery bombardments occurring in the same places over the years; only the *new* technology and hardware; the *improved* art of killing people; the *heightened* intensity of the battles, and the *numbers* of American units committed had increased horrifically. It was always the same opposing forces; casualties multiplying many times over! The United States always seemed to be playing catch-up and our politicians could never seem to get it right.

At night on duty at the radar scopes we would direct Vietnamese aircraft to assist friendly outposts under attack, or control flare aircraft on patrol and on-call to illuminate enemy forces attacking isolated outposts. On Tan Son Nhut Airport, our radar site was located in an isolated area guarded by Vietnamese guards (Army of the Republic of Vietnam – ARVN). This didn't make us feel too secure but that was what we had. It was customary for the Vietnamese people to take a siesta from about noon until about two or three o'clock in the afternoon. This included the military also. Often you could find the military guard sleeping during siesta with his rifle leaning against the opposite corner of the guard shack. There was nothing we could do about it. It was a national custom. At night you felt even less secure. Our operations shelter was a Quonset-like inflatable shelter that was held up by air pressure pumped into the building. Maintenance and ancillary buildings were of similar design which made for more mobility in a fluid battlefield situation. The noise of the pumps, generators and electronics was terrific. There was certainly no hiding our location on the air field. The hours got torturously long on the radar scope – especially at night. If nothing was happening, the controller was allowed to sleep. That tight GI canvas cot felt like a luxurious feather bed; even fully dressed and armed. One nighttime routine that would assure you were fully awake and alert was a visit to our hole-in-the-ground latrine facility about 20 yards from the operations shelter. On occasions a cobra was spotted around the area. So you know that walking that 20 yards through the weeds to the latrine at night in near blacked out conditions was a "pucker" factor.

Our daytime duties sometimes included classroom instruction for Vietnamese Air Force radar controllers on use of the scopes and operational procedures. Most of the Vietnamese controllers spoke varying degrees of English from very proficient to undistinguishable. With Vietnam having been colonized by the French after World War Two, most Vietnamese spoke very good French – but I didn't. Still it was difficult conveying the information to them. You never knew how much they understood. And the Asian mindset would never allow them to admit to not understanding.

Orders, Orders and More Orders!

On November 28th, our 507th Communications and Control Group at Shaw AFB published orders assigning our Fort Gordon Detachment 2, 728th AC&W (which was then in Saigon) to Shaw AFB upon our return; reporting April 30, 1962.

This meant we would be returning to Fort Gordon at the end of our TDY only to immediately pack up and move our families to Shaw. On December 27th Detachment 8, APO San Francisco Special Order Number A-1 was published assigning us for duty to Detachment 2, 5th Tactical Control Group (PACAF – Pacific Air Forces) at Tan Son Nhut AB, Vietnam for the duration of our TDY.

Pearl of the Orient!

Saigon was known as the "Pearl of the Orient," so I was informed. In my mind I am at a loss to justify that "honor". I did enjoy my off duty time however, and did a lot of shopping for Pat, Norris and Robert. Prices were so inexpensive. The postal service between Saigon and the states probably felt that they knew me personally. Except for the occasional bombings by Viet Cong elements, Saigon was reasonably safe in the well-established tourist areas. I wasn't all that comfortable at night however. Occasionally I would go into Saigon at night with a few guys but not often. They would usually find their way into a bar somewhere and I would go with them rather make it back alone at night in the city. Since I didn't drink I would have sodas until I could hold no more, then bide my time until late in the evening (or early morning) when they decided they had had enough.

During the day or night you would be accosted by beggars, or by small children wanting to sell you pornographic pictures or rent you their sister "...for a good time, GI"! Kids would come up to you and ram their hands into your pocket to get any loose piasters (money), or anything else you might be unfortunate enough to be carrying in your pockets. Hang on to your watch! Anything to make a living and stay alive! Those Vietnam kids learned GI English very quickly; especially the English you would never take to church – or to Mama. In America an assignment of a rating is usually number one to ten; number ten being the best and number one being the worst. In the Asian culture the ratings are reversed; number ten being the worst possible; even bordering on the profane. When a GI would refuse a handout for a beggar or street kid, he would usually get the middle finger and a: "You 'numba' ten, GI!" They learn fast!

I had never before witness such human poverty. I saw little old ladies much smaller than me carrying huge loads that I would have buckled under. Living conditions in more impoverished areas of the city were bamboo and paper shacks on stilts over the water's edge. The whole world (streets and sidewalks) was their toilet. Kids, some naked, would "go" whenever and wherever they felt the urge; adults too, especially the men. One day I was walking down the sidewalk a few feet behind a Vietnamese woman in the traditional black pajamas and conical-shaped 'coolie' hat. Suddenly without warning or checking around her, she stopped and pulled down her pajamas, squatted and did her thing. Then just as quickly stood up, pulled up the pajamas and preceded merrily (relieved) on her way. Beetle Nut juice covered the sidewalks and streets where old men and women spat it out. A beetle-nut smile is something to behold: black gums and black snaggled-teeth; those that are still there, that is.

The merchants in the tourist-frequented shops were usually very clean and polite. Some shops and malls would rival those in the states. You could round a corner and be in a totally different world: Night and day; impoverished and affluent. Many Vietnamese spoke French as a holdover from French colonization. They seemed to understand some English whether they spoke it or not. Thus communications was not a real problem. Much of the Vietnamese population was a mix of Vietnamese and French. This made for some of the most beautiful girls I have ever seen. I told Pat this but it was probably a mistake since I had bought her some of the skimpy lingerie from the European styled stores in the malls and sent it to her. She may have wondered how I got it – especially since I had gotten her the wrong size.

Baptist Mission and Catholic Orphanage
On the occasions that I had Sunday off, I and a few of the other officers visited the Baptist Mission in Saigon. I got to know the missionary pastor and his wife very well. Unfortunately I have forgotten their names. Although it was largely a Vietnamese congregation – as it should be – I enjoyed attending for the Christian fellowship and its touch of home. It was heartening to see the Vietnamese so absorbed in the service. As I recall, the pastor spoke in Vietnamese but that was no problem. The Bible and similarity of the service were all comfortably familiar. I often wonder what the fate of our missionaries in Vietnam was upon the fall of South Vietnam to North Vietnam in 1975.

One of our officers had been visiting a local orphanage. He saw the poor condition of the children and the state of the orphanage and organized a charity among our deployed troops on their behalf. We donated money and asked our families to send items to donate. He arranged for us to visit the orphanage to meet the Catholic Sisters and see the deplorable condition of the children – although the Sisters were doing a remarkable job with their meager support. It was a heart wrenching sight: Bed babies and small children in various states of health, diseases and birth defects. Insects were very much undeterred in their access to the facility. You can imagine the gratitude offered in response to our modest charity efforts. A number of visits were made to the orphanage by some of the guys to take money, food and clothes.

So Long Saigon!
February 1962 saw the completion our commitment at Tan Son Nhut and the turnover of our radar to the South Vietnamese Air Force. We boarded an Air Force C-121 and headed for the states. "California here we come, right back where we started from!" I was longing to see my family again. You never got

used to these frequent and emotional good-byes. The hellos took no adjusting. Homesickness would usually last for three to four weeks. But the busy routine didn't give you much time to dwell on it. I came to understand the GI lament and indescribable pain in the song: "No Letter Today". I worried constantly about my family as I know Pat did for me. Although I knew that several days transpired between mailing a letter and actual receipt, a missed letter only heightened the anxiety about my family. TDY to Saigon would be repeated two more times in my career. On the way home we stopped at the Philippines. I would see the Philippines two more times in my career; Japan twice, Korea twice, Taiwan two or three times and Thailand once.

New Home: Shaw AFB, SC April 1962

As mentioned above, while we were away our Detachment 2 was permanently assigned to Shaw AFB, home of our 728th AC&W Squadron and the 507th Communications and Control Group – our higher headquarters. However, we were returned to Fort Gordon to get reacquainted with our families again and await the reporting date of April 30th to the 728th AC&W Squadron at Shaw. On April 30th I left Fort Gordon for Shaw AFB leaving my family behind until I could get settled and a place for them to stay. The Group decided that since we were tactical radar controllers who moved and worked with the Army, we should at least try to emulate them. So the Group designed a "Ground Combat School" for all group personnel to attend: About a 10 day course to make us effective in assisting in base defense should we ever be called upon to do so. The course included some judo instruction provided by a civilian judo instructor – just enough to get ourselves killed should we ever try it on someone.

Back to Saigon!

Wham! On May 20th 1962, I along with a large contingent of 507th personnel was ordered back to Saigon. However we were instructed to delay at Clark AB, Philippines to await further orders to Saigon! I did not know the exact mission of this deployment although it was fairly well surmised that we would be augmenting the radar control mission of the South Vietnamese Air Force. Our deployed commander again was "Little Buddha" from our first Saigon deployment. While awaiting further orders at Clark for continued deployment to Saigon, he had us out in fatigues and combat boots daily for a half hour or more of jogging around the area. He would be out front leading the formation demonstrating his great physical condition. I don't recall how long we had been at Clark, but I think about a month after arriving, he informed me that he had a message from the American Red Cross (ARC) urging that I be released for an emergency return home immediately: Pat was in the hospital in Augusta, GA.

Emergency Return – Emergency Leave!

I had briefed Pat repeatedly that if I was ever needed at home for a serious family emergency while I was away, she should first call the ARC rather than me. They would start the emergency leave process through my commanders to get me home. If she called me, I could do nothing because an emergency leave authorization required that commanders have ARC verification of an actual emergency and the need for me to come home. Of course upon ARC notification to my commander, the process was already underway when I got the message. My "worry barometer" (that I got from my Mom) immediately elevated off the scale. Pat was home with only Norris and Robert. Norris would turn twelve in June and Robert was four years old. Fortunately Pat's best friend and her family lived only three doors down and our very good Army neighbor and family were next door to us on the other side. Upon arriving home, I discovered that Pat's friend had been taking care of her for about two weeks. She also was looking after Norris and Robert along with her four early teen and pre-teen daughters. She had an older daughter but I think she was either working or at college. However, at 12 years old, Norris was very capable of caring for himself and Robert. Norris was very good at "supervising" younger neighborhood kids wherever we were assigned. He seemed to relish his older "Mother Hen" role and neighbor children seemed to flock (no pun) to him. Later he and Robert would develop an affinity for older senior citizens. (Got it from their mother.)

As it happened, a week or so after I left Fort Gordon for the Philippines, Pat had become sick – very sick. Her friend took her to the clinic at Fort Gordon where she was seen by an Army physician. He diagnosed her condition as something like flu or virus and sent her home after treating those symptoms. Pat got sicker and sicker; weaker and weaker. Another week or so went by and her friend took her back to the Fort Gordon clinic. Another doctor saw her and essentially offered the same diagnosis. By now Pat was seriously sick. She wasn't eating, was vomiting regularly and needed assistance for everything she tried to do. Try as she may, her friend was not able to help her. It had now been two or more weeks since Pat was able to eat. Everything she tried came up. For the third time her friend took her back to the Fort Gordon clinic. While in the waiting room, Pat was so sick and weak that she could no longer stand or sit and just lay down on the floor. A doctor was called and he took one quick look at her and said: "Hepatitis!" She was immediately admitted and quarantined on June 3rd. Here is where the ARC got involved to get me home – after about three weeks of Pat's not eating, her relentless vomiting and total helplessness.

Pat's Life-Threatening Illness – Hepatitis
After arriving home, I was filled in by Pat's friend on all that had been happening. Thanks you Lord for best friends! I went to the Fort Gordon hospital to see Pat. They would only allow me to see her if I wore a gown and mask. The doctor told me she would not have lasted much longer without medical attention, and that she was still not "out of the woods". Norris, Robert and I were required to get gamma globulin shots – the biggest needles I had ever seen! So did Pat's friend and her family. Visits for Pat were highly

discouraged – especially for non-family. That night after I got home I did some powerful praying. So did our church: The Hillcrest Baptist Church, Augusta, GA. After not seeing much improvement in Pat I called her doctor in a couple of days. He was not very encouraging with his prognosis; in fact he indicated that she was in a very critical emergency state – the outcome of which was not certain. He said that everything that could be done for her had been done. After the obvious fear and panic in my voice and breaking down on the phone, he chided me and told me to buckle up; that it was largely up to the family now to force her to eat until she absolutely couldn't eat another bite. She was placed on an extremely high protein diet and was to eat at least four times a day forcefully stuffing herself until she could eat no more. Norris had his school during the day and Pat's friend would keep Robert whenever I went to visit Pat until her discharge on July the 11th. Everyone should have a best friend like Pat's! Over the years we lost contact with her friend and family, but I do hope she fared well. I know that she acquired many stars in her Heavenly crown because of her attending to Pat; and that it was her prayers, those of our friends, and church (Hillcrest Baptist Church) and medical personnel that saved Pat's life.

Pat's friend and her daughters attended Hillcrest Baptist Church also. But her husband would not attend church with them. Try as she did to get him to go with them, he had no interest in doing so. On several occasions I also invited him to attend church with me; and encouraged him to do so for the sake of his family if for no other reason. He was an avid golfer and Sundays were his golf days. Just as he had no interest in church, I had no interest in golf. So for several weeks we traded invitations: he inviting me to golf with him on Sundays; I inviting him to attend church with me. I had never played a game of golf in my life. One day I told him we should make a deal. I would take a Sunday and go golfing with him if he would then in-turn, go to church with me. We agreed. I advised him several times that I had never hit a golf ball. No problem! He said I could learn.

Sunday came. I went to the golf course with him. He met a partner there and we got underway. Or least he and his partner did. I had no idea he had invited a friend to join us. I assumed that his knowing that I knew nothing of the game that it would be just him and me with him providing the necessary instruction. With absolutely no mercy or instructions they had me tee-off first. After a couple of missed swings and a tap with a dribble for a couple of feet, I finally connected. The ball went 90 degrees left into the woods. I'm not sure if I heard muffled snickering or stifled disgust. I told them to go ahead and I would follow. After a couple more failed attempts at getting down-range (in pilot jargon) or down the fairway, I gave up; picked up my clubs and followed them the entire course. Not much was said during the (their) game. He never invited me to golf with him again – and he has yet to attend church with me. I hope for his family's

189

sake, he did later begin to attend with them. He had such a nice family! Sad! I haven't attempted a golf game since – and haven't missed it.

My squadron at Shaw gave me all the necessary emergency leave time (which is not charged against authorized normal leave) to take care of matters at Fort Gordon until Pat was well enough to move to Shaw. Pat was to remain bedridden for about six months except for very brief bathroom visits, etc. She was to have her meals in bed, do no lifting except for fork-to-mouth and eat, eat, eat!

I cannot recall all that transpired in the next couple of weeks or so. But as soon as Pat was well enough to move to Shaw, I moved her, Norris and Robert into military quarters that I had been assigned. I must have arranged for getting our household goods moved but I don't recall one thing about it. Norris, now 12 years old, was out of school for the summer and a great help for his Mom. Norris was like that – both he and Robert as Robert too grew up. Robert was now five years old. Pat was assigned an Air Force doctor in the Shaw AFB hospital. He seemed very capable and very interested in Pat's case. However, he reiterated much of what the doctors at Fort Gordon had said: Bed rest, high protein meals four times a day, eat, eat and eat! He said that after one year we would know if the "treatment" worked – or didn't! I needed to find someone to take care of Pat during the day and to see to Norris and Robert. She and I prayed for her successful recovery and to send someone to care for her. "The Lord provides!"

Enter Mrs. Harris!

I don't recall how Mrs. Harris came to us. It was probably an ad in the local newspaper – either hers or ours. But she was God-sent! My family and I loved her! The following manner in which I describe Mrs. Harris is with endearing terms and thanks to the Lord!

Mrs. Harris was a great Christian lady; extremely friendly with a matching smile, black and huge – as in "Aunt Jemima" of maple syrup "huge". She was as kind and gentle as a Christian person should be; and claimed Norris and Robert as "her boys" – and Pat as her charge. She took charge in a firm manner and it was hard to refuse her determined insistence on our behalf. We all loved her immediately and thanked the Lord for her. She supervised Pat to see that she ate her required four large meals a day. Pat was "Miss Pat" and I was "Capt'n Potteridge". (That's how many southern country folk pronounce the name of the bird: partridge, and thus my name). Although southern whites usually addressed blacks in the South by their first names, Pat and I address her as "Mrs. Harris. We insisted that Norris and Robert do likewise. We taught them that all persons are due respect unless their actions dictate otherwise; no matter their color or background. I felt totally relieved to have Mrs. Harris

190

caring for Pat, Norris and Robert anytime I was away. She either didn't drive or had no car; so her husband or daughters brought her in the mornings and I took her home at night. They had a farm about five miles from Shaw and had three daughters in their early and late teens: a very nice family. Her whole family were very nice people.

From the time Robert was a small child he hated to be kissed. It would embarrass him greatly. Sometimes in his sleep Pat would look in on him and sneak a kiss. He, in his sleep, would automatically wipe the kiss away with his hand or arm. If she kissed him during the day, he would do the same thing – wipe it away. I never kissed him. I had a thing about fathers kissing their sons. Right or wrong – I didn't do it. So, it was quite hilarious when Mrs. Harris sometimes would suddenly swoop down – or while sitting in a rocker – grab Robert up and smother him in her overly abundant bosom. She would dance around or rock him while he was held "captive and immobile". He was so embarrassed – or at least he pretended to be so. But I think he really enjoyed it.

A few months later when Pat could ride for short trips, we would often visit the Harris' farm. On one such visit Mr. Harris had just pulled his mule-team and wagon loaded with corn up to the corn crib, and proceeded to unload it by hand pitching the corn through an open window into the crib. Norris and Robert were both fascinated by the operation – and of course tried to help (but mostly got in the way). Mr. Harris was very patient with them however and allowed them to play farm-hand. On the way home Robert surprised us by exclaiming: "I wish I was black!" When we asked why, he said: "So I could be a farmer!" Such is the wisdom of a five-year old.

Healed! Praise the Lord!

It was about a year later (1963) that Pat's doctor said that he could find no evidence that she had ever had hepatitis – other than her remaining extremely weak which lasted for years afterwards. What bothered Pat most was that she had put on so much weight with those mega-meals and high protein diet. She claimed that she was as big as Mr. Harris. It took several years for her to trim down again and to regain most of her strength and stamina. Even after Pat was pronounced healed a year or so later we continued to drop by the Harris' occasionally for a short visit. After leaving Shaw we continued to correspond on special occasions. A few years later one of her daughters wrote to inform us that Mrs. Harris had died. We knew that she was enjoying a well-deserved rest in the "Bosom of Jesus"!

We found us a small church about three miles from Shaw: Long Branch Baptist Church. It was in the small community of Dalzell; a mixed community of black, white and Turkish ancestry. Pat's best civilian-friend here also attended Long Branch Church. Her best military-wife friend, who had been her best military-wife friend at Ft Gordon, was also now at Shaw. Her husband was transferred to Shaw along with all Detachment 2 personnel and became the Chief of the base command post (507th Communications and Control Group). He later became my mentor regarding my career plans.

728th AC&W Squadron Operations

Having been the Detachment 2 Mobility Officer at Fort Gordon, it naturally became my lot to be assigned the additional duty as the squadron mobility officer for the 728th at Shaw. More 24/7 to assure that the squadron equipment and personnel were maintained in a high mobility deployment ready status. It seemed that practice deployments, base exercises, higher headquarters operational readiness inspections (ORIs) or real world crises always started in the middle of the night; and usually Friday nights! Unless we were on authorized leave, we were required to be near a telephone at all times in case of a recall for these purposes. If we left our homes for more than an hour or so, we had to let the person who normally notified us on the telephone recall plan know where we would be and provide an alternate phone number. It got to the point that I would cringe at the sound of the telephone at home in the evenings. For hours, possibly days, the base would be an endless and relentless roar of arriving and departing C-130 aircraft; all hours of the day or night. C-130s were the aircraft used to airlift our personnel and equipment for exercises and deployments. Ear plugs were a necessary safety factor working around them. You would not believe the noise level inside those machines. For years later the sound of the C-130 (a very distinct sound) would conjure up memories of those long exhausting hours and days. Even today some 52 years later, the sound of the C-130 often brings back memories of those 24/7 days and family separations.

Our squadron commander was a very nice guy. He had a serious back problem and was in constant pain. It always made me feel great empathy for him as he would constantly shift in his chair to relieve the pain as he talked. But there was never a complaint or expression of pain – just the slight frequent shifting in his chair. Years later when experiencing my own back problems I would know personally what he was likely enduring.

Our Operations Officer, my boss, was a short guy; an extremely sharp and highly intelligent officer who always dressed impeccably – but I thought he acted like a little Napoleon (except for the hand in the coat) perfectionist! He was a perfectionist in everything and every sense of the word and expected it in others; but still a fair and reasonable supervisor. He also flew the T-33, as I did, to maintain flying proficiency. We flew together occasionally on out-and-back cross-country flights. Most of the squadron personnel knew that Pat and I didn't drink – even at our casual or formal squadron events. On one out-and-back cross-country flight as we were returning to Shaw, he told me that Pat and

I should partake of the drinks that abounded at squadron and group parties – in order to be more "sociable". In other words, be one-of-the gang. He wasn't angry or condescending. I think he thought he was giving me some fatherly (career) advice. It was not that we didn't participate in squadron events and festivities. We did, and enjoyed them very much. I told him that we did not drink alcoholic beverages. It was a religious thing for us; and for me, memories as a child with an alcoholic uncle that tried to stab my father while drunk. He never had anything further to say about the matter and never made an issue of it. Upon his reassignment, he gave me a very good efficiency report – reports that are required annually and every time an officer's efficiency-reporting official changes. There was usually a small group of guys and wives in every unit that didn't drink. It was always an issue with us that squadron and group functions had a no-pay open-bar. All personnel had to pay a prorated share of the cost of alcohol beverages consumed at these parties – essentially subsidizing other members' drinking habits. And some had big habits! It was years later that that units began to excluded such charges for those who did not drink – and eventually went to a *pay-as-you-drink* bar. Maybe our "squawking" began to be heard.

The successor to the operations officer position, who in turn became my boss, was a gruff and a no-nonsense supervisor, and a bit older. He was also a pilot but did not fly for reasons unknown to me. He wore thick glasses that when he looked at you, he appeared to be looking through magnifying glasses – not quite the coke bottle variety though. When discussing a subject, or problem, he would stare at you intently as though he was trying to see into your innermost thoughts regarding the subject at hand. We had many squadron mobility exercises and practice deployments during his tenure as Operations Officer. He was very complimentary of my work as Mobility Officer. However "very complimentary" would not get you senior-lever officer promotions. It would be about four years later that he would figure very prominently in my future career assignments. Competition in the officer effective report and promotion system was extremely keen. Our personnel records contained an 8x10 black and white head and shoulders photo. For promotion consideration tie-breakers on Air Force officer promotion boards it was not uncommon for board members to consider the photo's currency, the freshness of a haircut, whether awards and decorations were worn in the correct order and even whether the photographer had smoothed out all the folds and wrinkles from your uniform.

One of my friends at Shaw was a former photo reconnaissance pilot in the photo reconnaissance squadron, who also flew the T-33 for maintaining flying proficiency. We flew together often on our proficiency flights. He was tall, lean and lanky – quite a character; comical and fun loving. He would also figure very prominently in my later career assignments.

The 728th also had a Detachment at Pope AFB (Detachment 1). A friend from Goose AB was the Mobility Officer for that detachment. While I was the mobility officer for Detachment 2 at Fort Gordon, he and I often exchanged operational information on relevant issues. We were occasionally deployed on the same exercises. After I left Shaw I had a chance meeting with him at Luke AFB, AZ (1966 I think) when he was on his way to Thailand to fly the F-105 on missions over North Vietnam. He was shot down after a few missions over North Vietnam and spent about six years as a POW in Hanoi. The next time I saw him was upon our POWs' release from Hanoi and their arrival at Clark AB in the Philippines on March 4, 1973. (More about this in a later chapter).

Cuban Missile Crisis! (Cold War –Nuclear Threat)

For most of my life and the lives of my family, we have lived under the continual threat of nuclear warfare; which began with Atomic Bombs being dropped on Japan thereby ending World War Two. Notwithstanding the current threat from terrorist and nuclear powers worldwide as I write this (2016), probably the closest nuclear confrontation to date came during the Cuban Missile Crisis of 1962 between the United States and the Soviet Union; President John F. Kennedy and Premier Nikita Khrushchev respectively. It started January 1, 1959 when the Cuban dictator President Batista was overthrown by Fidel Castro, with US sanction, under the guise of freeing the Cuban people from a harsh dictator. He soon embraced the Soviet Union and began receiving economic and military aid causing great concern within the US. Something had to be done about this growing Communist menace just a few miles off the southern tip of Florida.

In April 1961 a small force of Florida-based Cuban exiles launched and invasion of Cuba with promised US air support. When President Kennedy did not provide the alleged promised air support for the full-scale invasion of Cuba, the invasion attempt failed. This was known as the Bay of Pigs invasion. The Cold War was escalating almost minute by minute. Castro and the Soviet Union embolden by the seemingly weak resolve by the US, began to increase their mutual ties to each other to include the clandestine shipment and basing of intermediate range nuclear-capable ballistic missiles in Cuba. The threat of nuclear war became very real to the American people. Nuclear weapons were now located just 90 miles off the southern tip of Florida and could strike well inland of the United States. Nuclear fall-out shelters, nuclear war safety precautions, stocking of emergency food and clothing and family briefings on the "what-if's" of a nuclear attack became the order of the day. With the growing confrontation between the US and the Soviet Union, I felt nuclear war was practically immanent. The US was having a difficult time convincing the world of the Soviet Union's positioning of nuclear missiles just 90 miles away from the US and poised to launch at our heartland; thus justifying a strike against the Soviet ships and missile bases in Cuba.

During this time the US was overflying Cuba with high flying U-2 reconnaissance aircraft; and low altitude Air Force, Navy and Marine photo reconnaissance flights. Shaw AFB had an RB-66 photo reconnaissance squadron which flew frequent low level flights over Cuba. They would return to Shaw and have the films immediately processed for delivery to the joint task force headquarters (established by the Pentagon) at Homestead AFB, Florida near Miami. At Shaw our T-33s were used as courier aircraft to fly these films from Shaw to Homestead. I had occasions to fly several of these T-33 photo courier service flights.

Following the photo evidence of Soviet nuclear missiles in Cuba, and subsequently showing them to the world, President Kennedy established a naval blockade around Cuba. There were some confrontations at the sea. A U-2 was shot down and the pilot killed in the crash. One Navy photo reconnaissance aircraft was damaged by ground fire. With the indisputable proof of Soviet missiles in Cuba and the increasing threat of US attacks, Khrushchev withdrew his missiles and a nuclear war was averted. It was a time of very uncomfortable and intense nuclear war uncertainty and close-call. This confrontation became known as the Cuban Missile Crisis.

(NOTE: Above Cuban Crisis dates and information are paraphrased from the Naval Air Station Pensacola, Florida newspaper Gosport, Vol. 75, No 31 August 5, 2011).

Shaw AFB Aero Club

Shaw had an aero club which it maintained at the Sumter, South Carolina airport. I checked out in their Navion which I truly loved. It was made by North American, manufacturer of the most famous World War Two fighter, the P-51 Mustang. In fact the Navion had similar wing and tail designs as that of the P-51, and also included a similar P-51 roll-back canopy. I think that is why I liked it so well – it reminded me so much of the P-51. It was also a four-place aircraft so I could fly my family home for visits. Among other aircraft, the club had an Ercoupe which was heralded as one of the simplest airplanes to fly because of its coordinated aileron and rudder control system – thus requiring little to no rudder input while flying. In fact it had no rudder pedals. I hated it! But it was cheap flying – in those days. It was hailed as the airplane Grandma could fly.

I decided to fly my family to Norcross, Georgia for a fun flight and to visit my family for a weekend. According to notes in Pat's calendar, this was February 27-29, 1964. I also thought it would be time to introduce Robert to the thrill of flying. Norris had flown with me on occasions at the aero club when we were at Hamilton AFB, California and seemed to enjoy it. After we had gotten airborne and settled in for the flight, I looked back to the right rear seat where Robert was *fast asleep.* So much for the thrill of flight! We had encountered light rain nearing the Peachtree-DeKalb Airport for landing (former Atlanta Naval Air Station) which coated the leading edge of the wings with light thin ice. No problem, although icing conditions should never be taken lightly (no pun intended). It brought back memories of the light snow when I took Pat flying at the Atlanta Fulton County Airport soon after getting my Private Pilot Certificate at Wilmington, Delaware. After spending three days with family – we had an uneventful flight back to Shaw.

On one occasion we decided to drive over to Norcross for several days leave time with my Mom and Dad. We did not tell them that we were coming over. It was to be a surprise. Upon pulling into the drive, my sister Oreese came running out of the house to the car before we had gotten out. She said in an excited voice that my squadron had called and that I was to call them back as soon as I arrived. They had called about an hour earlier and left a message for me to get right back to Shaw. I called and was told that there was a base wide alert and recall of all personnel; but for what cause, I don't remember. So much for our surprise leave-time with my Mom and Dad. After wolfing down a quick lunch we headed back. Such was the life of Tactical Air Command combat crew personnel. It reminded me of the time that Mom and Dad came to visit us in California. (The first vacation that I ever remember Dad taking). We had been placed on alert for a Middle-East crisis and not allowed to wander far from the base. We did manage to show them a little bit of San Francisco.

Losing Dad!

Dad never really had a serious health problem that slowed him up until late in his life. Then his back began to bother him a lot. He had injured it lifting a wagon in occupied Germany following World War One. He had also been gassed with mustard gas during the war. That plus his chain smoking is probably what hastened his emphysema which eventually took his life at age 69. He was in the Tucker, Georgia hospital and I was called home because of his serious condition. We drove over. At the hospital he was having serious breathing difficulty. I was by his bedside holding his hand and he was struggling to sit up. I urged him to lie back down and take it easy. He looked at me and told me not to be so difficult with him – words to that effect. He lay back down and in a moment took his last earthly breath while I was holding his hand. His next breath was in Heaven!

Operation Bootstrap

Operation Bootstrap was a six-month program whereby you could complete a bachelor's degree at the University of Omaha, Omaha, Nebraska (later to be designated Omaha University). Acceptance for the program was contingent upon having enough college and military academic credits to enable completion of the degree within the allowed six month period. In the late 1950s and subsequent, the Air Force began to really push for its personnel, especially officers, to have or acquire a bachelor's degree. This was considered essential to be competitive for promotions. Having only two years of college which I had obtained to enter Aviation Cadet Pilot Training, I applied for Operation Bootstrap. After evaluating my formal and military educational credits, the university accepted my application. This would be a "permissive TDY" which meant the Air Force would give me the six-month leave of absence to attend the program, but at no expense to the government. Normal pay would continue but travel, housing, curriculum, tuition and all connected expenses would by mine. I would still have to maintain the minimum of four flying hours per month. This was accomplished through "hitching" local flights out of Base Operations at Offut AFB, Omaha. Offut was headquarters for the Strategic Air Command (SAC); the bomber command. I never wanted to get close to that place but now I would be 'bumming flights" from their Base Operations. *I hoped SAC would never learn that I was there.*

Since my family would be traveling with me, I had to vacate the base quarters I had at Shaw and reapply upon returning. We stored most of our "stuff," hitched up a rental trailer, loaded up, saddled up and headed for Omaha at the end of June 1963 – in our 1955 Ford. Norris was 13 and Robert was five. After finding a nice two-story wood-frame house in Omaha, I got the family settled in and off to the academic grind. I choose the Military Science degree; thinking that would be more to my advantage; less of a struggle academically. However, the courses had nothing to do directly with military education. Some of the courses I recall: Business Law, Surveying, Economics, History and other generic courses. There was an option to choose two elective courses. I chose Mechanical Drawing and Photography. Those were chosen because I have some drawing talent and always had a passing interest in photography. I had no experience with either mechanical drawing or photography but, with my drawing talent and photography interest I figured they would be "crip" courses; simple and easy. Wrong! Wrong! They turned out to be two of my most time-consuming and tedious courses. Mechanical drawing was so tedious in its required perfection, details and the complicated subjects. Photography turned out to require hours and hours in the dark room and searching for assignment subjects.

Omaha would be our second hard winter climate assignment (New Castle, Delaware being the first). Robert would enter the first grade here. I think Norris would be entering the seventh. I seem to think that they attended different schools. Norris could ride the school bus to his, but Robert had to walk 10 blocks to his school; rain, sleet, snow – all of it! The school bus route was about a block from our house but he was not allowed to ride due to the route location/authorization – or whatever the reason was. He complained about having to walk in the deep snow and freezing cold. But of course I told him of the time as a small child I had to walk to school in all kinds of weather; barefoot and uphill both ways; which was a stretch of course with tongue-in-cheek. There was a bully at Robert's school which seemed to naturally deter his interest in attending. I talked with him and told him that if it continued, picking up a stick to defend himself was acceptable. I think the issue was resolved. His teacher seemed to think he was doing well; except for his sometimes drawing and talking rather than attention to the subject matter at hand. But he got that naturally. I did much of the same in school – especially drawing when I should have been listening. With a grandmother talented in oil paintings and a dad that had some drawing skill, it wasn't his fault. Norris and Robert were very good students. They both loved reading. Norris applied himself to very serious study and in his adult years he would develop an extensive library; particularly religious work following his entry into the ministry. As a young adult and later, he loved teaching and discussing deep-thought subjects; especially theological matters. Pat and I considered ourselves extremely bless with our two boys. While in Omaha we attended the First Southern Baptist Church. Meanwhile, the war raged on in Vietnam!

Ngo Dinh Diem – President, South Vietnam – Saigon 1963

For nine years the autocratic and nepotistic family rule of South Vietnam was headed by their president, Ngo Dinh. American discontent with Diem's regime had been growing with accusations of corruption and religious discrimination (The Diem family were Catholics). Mass Buddhist protest resulted in the shooting of protesters defying the government's persecution. In protest of the Diem regime, a Buddhist Monk burned himself to death sitting cross-legged Buddha style in the middle of a Saigon street after drenching himself in gasoline.

A coup by the South Vietnamese Army of the Republic of Vietnam (ARVN) led by General Duong Van Minh, allegedly with CIA backing and President Kennedy's approval, overthrew Diem's regime at the Saigon Presidential Palace on November 2, 1963. General Minh, known as "Big Minh" because of his physical stature – even for a westerner – supposedly had promised President Kennedy that Diem would be exiled and not harmed. However, "Big Minh" had Diem and his brother executed that evening thus establishing military control over the South Vietnamese government and greatly upsetting President Kennedy. Control of the government changed hands at least a couple of times during the remaining twelve years of the war.

(NOTE: Above details on the South Vietnamese coup and Diem assassination obtained from various sources to include Wikipedia, the free encyclopedia and the Pacific Stars and Stripes Vol. 19, No. 306 and 307; Nov. 3 and 4, 1963 respectively).

President John F. Kennedy

November 22, 1963. I was at home in Omaha engrossed in my homework when – I forget who – loudly and excitedly exclaimed that President Kennedy had just been shot! We, along with the nation – and world – were shocked. Pat, Norris and Robert took it extremely hard – I think Norris mostly. They really loved President Kennedy. Needless to say, there was very little studying done in our household the rest of the night.

A Bachelor I *Are*! – Degree, That is

At the University of Omaha, January 1964, I graduated with my Bachelor's Degree in Military Science. A few years later I would learn that this was not enough. The Air Force would be clamoring for their officers to have a Master's Degree and to attend all the Professional Military Education (PME) schools they could. Squadron Officer School (SOS) mentioned previously was my first PME step. The next step in PME progression was the Air Command and Staff College (ACSC) also at Maxwell AFB. I enrolled and completed the course by correspondence. Promotion allocations by Air Force headquarters in Washington were getting tighter and more competitive. You just wouldn't make it unless you had the graduate, post graduate and PME squares filled. Normally after three pass-overs for promotion by the officer promotion board, an officer would be separated from the service. Likewise, at specified points in their career, if an officer had not achieved a certain rank, they would also be separated from service. Of course if the officer had accumulated the minimum of 20 years of service, retirement would be the option; otherwise they would be separated without retirement.

Now back to Shaw AFB. We returned to Shaw near the end of January 1964. I had to reapply for base housing. Temporary base housing was available while awaiting permanent housing which was granted near the end of February. My friend who was the Chief of the base command post had been influential in my applying for Bootstrap. He and I had many discussions on the necessity for advanced civilian and military education. I resisted because I wanted to return to the cockpit and remain in operational flying. I argued that the Air Force should have career pilot assignments whereby one could remain in a flying position for most of their career. I was realistic enough however, to believe this would not likely happen. It didn't! This good fortune only befell a small number of pilots. Others either move up or were moved out! He of course had much more foresight and finally had encouraged me to apply for Bootstrap – for which I am grateful. We had become good friends. Once back at Shaw, he asked that I be assigned to the command post as a duty controller. I would be on a rotating shift but that would be no problem. It did mean that he would become my supervisor and reporting official.

Dog Bite!

The backyard of our base house merged into a large grassy area which then bordered the backyards of our neighbors across the way. The neighborhood kids used this area for a community playground. One neighbor had a German Shepherd dog named "Sheba". They usually kept Sheba tied in their backyard as the children played in the area. She wasn't vicious but was excitable as the kids ran about laughing and shouting. Most of the kids were small, about six to twelve years of age. Robert would have been five or six years old. One day there must have been about 15 kids running around and playing loudly in the area. Sheba could take it no longer. She worked herself loose and struck out into the group of kids – straight for Robert – for some unknown reason. Maybe he was the closest "victim". I think she was more or less entering the fray in an excited and playful mode. Nevertheless she bit Robert on his leg and left a deep puncture wound behind the knee. Of course you would have thought Robert had his leg torn off. Sheba's owners were very upset an apologetic of course and put Sheba up for the required observation for rabies. Robert's leg took a couple of stitches, as I recall; otherwise he was OK but always kept a wary eye thereafter on Sheba whenever she was tied out.

F-100 Assignment!

Nearing completion of four years in the radar controller field (mid 1964), thoughts of returning to the cockpit in fighters was foremost in my mind. The 507th Communications Group commander had promised his radar controllers that following four years of a job well done, he would assist us in returning to the cockpit of our choice. True to his word, one day he asked me what assignment I would like. Without hesitation I replied: "F-100s, Sir!" The F-100 and F-86 (of Korean War fame) were the first line fighters of that day. I would have loved flying either one. But remembering the F-100 assignment I passed up on graduating from pilot training for the assignment to my old unit at New Castle, Delaware in F-94Cs, I choose the F-100. Fortunately there was an assignment available for F-100s at Cannon AFB, Clovis, New Mexico: Dust storms, sage brush, tumbling tumble weeds, cactus, sidewinders and scorpions, all 5000 feet high upon an expansive desert plateau; where the deer and the antelope play! I was excited! Pat? I think so – for me. I was like a kid anticipating Christmas.

*****

CHAPTER TWELVE
FINALLY A *REAL* FIGHTER! Cannon AFB, Clovis, New Mexico – F-100
(1964-1966)

"Route 66" 1964

Sometime in June 1964, we were on our way to Clovis, New Mexico and Cannon Air Force Base. The 1955 Ford Fairlane was loaded wall-to-wall, floor–to-ceiling plus Pat, Norris, Robert and me. Robert had not yet acquired his cat or he would have been along with us also. I don't remember but I'm sure we spent several days with my family and Pat's mother knowing that, barring an emergency, we would not be back that way for some time. It was summertime so we traveled the "northern" route – Route 66. I remember that narrow two-lane highway and its miles of short steep hills and deep quick draws, not seeing over the hills until cresting them. Then there were miles – I mean miles – of straight, flat, no-nothing desert for mile after mile in which one barely had to touch the steering wheel. I remember one such situation when miles down the road you could see this small speck of an object, and as you approached it, it was a small *shack* of a service station. Gas, a soda and pack of stale crackers were the "services" offered. Of course no one in their right mind would pass up the opportunity to take advantage of the services offered in this desolate part of our country. Being stranded with vehicle problems in that environment would be a *real* emergency. Emergency situations during the hot summer and cold winter seasons could become a life threatening situation here.

In spite of the long desolate miles of desert driving, I was fascinated. I imagined what it would have been like in a pioneer covered wagon traversing those wastelands in life-or-death summer or winter extremes. Those had to be tough people. We took many pictures along the way with my 35mm camera. They would have made a real travelogue. (Here I am nearly some 50 years later trying to catalogue those slides into trays and transfer them to DVDs – another career).

Settling In

Arriving at Cannon AFB and getting settled was pretty much routine, if settling into a new assignment can be routine. Seeing those squadrons of F-100s on the flight was like dangling honey before a honey bear. I was charged up – just like when I was a kid sitting for hours by the runways at the nearby Atlanta Naval Air Station and watching those Navy fighters' takeoff and landings. I would drive out to the Cannon AFB perimeter and watch the F-100s' takeoffs and landings. Sometimes Pat Norris and Robert would go with me, but they didn't last as long as I did.

I was assigned base quarters next door to a colonel, the Deputy for Operations of the 832nd Air Division. Both he and his wife were wonderful neighbors; a gentleman and lady in every respect; no airs, and very unassuming. It made no difference that I was only a lowly captain and Pat a lowly captain's wife. Pat, as I've stated before, was comfortable with anyone of any status in life; and they soon learned that she was real; no fake, no put on, - a true friend to everyone. Pat and the colonel's wife became good friends and so did their son and our son, Norris. It was not until 29 years later (1993) while living near Maxwell AFB, Alabama that I learned that my colonel neighbor was a World War Two fighter pilot ace. He had flown with the Royal Air Force in Spitfires. Not once while at Cannon AFB did I hear him mention his fighter pilot ace fame. That's the kind of person he was.

Years later when I was assigned to Maxwell AFB, Montgomery, Alabama, the colonel and his wife along with other aviation personalities, were invited to Maxwell's annual "Gathering of Eagles". The Gathering of Eagles is a Maxwell AFB Air Command and Staff College (ACSC) Aviation Historical Foundation's event. The Eagles would address the ACSC students and faculty regaling their aviation exploits, sign autograph and lithographs, attend luncheons and other events. I generally made a nuisance of myself with the Foundation's staff by attempting to wrangle admission (*or admit myself*), to the lectures by the aces. Afterwards, I would meet as many as I could to obtain their autographs in my copy of the 1979 "Fighter Aces of the U.S.A" book by Toliver and Constable. My boyhood fighter ace hero, Brigadier General Robert L. Scott of Flying Tiger fame and author of "God is my Copilot", was an occasional guest Eagle and autographed my book. When I learned that my former Cannon AFB neighbor was an Eagle invitee – I doubled my efforts to get to the Gathering and a chance to see him and his wife again. Pat and I were able to make contact with his Maxwell escort and arrange a meeting with them. He also autographed my book. Now I had the autographs of my boyhood fighter ace hero, General Scott; and also that of my next door Cannon AFB neighbor, both of whom Pat and Robert had met. As a member of the Maxwell Aero Club I offered to take the Colonel on a local flight. He readily accepted. Although no longer actively flying, he seemed to really enjoy the flight. Pat had met General Scott twice: Once as the graduation speaker for my Pilot Training Class 56-V, Bryan AFB, Texas September 1956; and years later when I took her and Robert to meet him when, at the age of about 93, he was Public Affairs Director for the Aviation Museum, Robbins AFB, Macon, Georgia.

Back to settling in at Cannon: Pat usually took care of the routine stuff like making a house a home; and things like getting Norris and Robert registered for school and other wife/mother activities around the base – with one big exception: Getting Robert his required shots for school! Giving Robert a shot was like dealing with a cornered tiger. He was terrified of shots, but he got it naturally. His grandmother Vennie (Pat's Mom) was terrified of them also. When receiving a shot he would double his fist, tighten the muscles in his arm, tighten his jaws and grit his teeth. I had tried many times to get him to relax his arm so the needle would not have to penetrate flexed muscle with the resulting soreness. He just couldn't do it. It was not until he was about 10 or so that he could take a shot without stark fear. I had taught him to rotate his arm like a windmill for a several seconds following a shot. This was in order to get the serum dissipated throughout the muscle and arm rather than have it remain at the injection site making it more painful. Massaging the injection site also helped. I still do this today after receiving a shot.

I don't remember if it was at Cannon, or earlier – it could have been Omaha, Nebraska when he would have been six and had to get the preschool shots. Pat and I had Norris and Robert at an Air Force clinic for the shots. Robert stood in line as the line slowly advanced toward several white-clad medics administering the shots. When Robert was about number two from the medics, he could stand it no longer. "POW!" Like he was shot from a cannon, he bolted from the line and ran. After chasing him all around the area, we finally trapped him. (Reminded me of the time I bolted from my classroom on my very first day of school and had the teachers chasing me all around the school grounds). We took him back to the medics and it took three of them to hold him down (arms, legs and body) a fourth administered the shots.   Pat and I felt so terrible for him. It hurt us to see him so full of absolute fear. One medic made sort of an under-his-breath comment about not bringing him in again. We laugh now but it was certainly no laughing matter then.

1964 Oldsmobile Starfire

Before we left Shaw AFB, South Carolina, I had seen the new Oldsmobile Starfire Delta 88: Big engine, sporty bucket seats, gear shift in a center console between the seats and beautifully designed. It was the prettiest car that I had ever seen and I still think so today. I was determined to get one: Fire engine red with white leather interior. However, try as I might, I was unable to find the Starfire that I wanted before we left for Cannon AFB, New Mexico.   At my first opportunity I visited the Clovis Oldsmobile dealer to continue my quest. He too did not have the Starfire that I wanted; however, he took my order and began searching. In a few days he called to tell me that he found the exact Starfire that I wanted. But it was at a dealer 100 miles away in Lubbock, Texas (or maybe it was Amarillo).   Clovis was a 100 miles from anywhere. I told him I would take it! Very soon I had my Starfire – exactly as I wanted it. I loved it! It had a passing-gear that felt like an aircraft afterburner, and would really "squat-and-get" when you stomped down on the accelerator! You could almost see the fuel gage going down. Seat belts were just coming on the scene at that time and totally optional. I had five belts installed; one for each of the five seats. And I insisted that the family use them and they did – and still do. I kept it until years later when I received a two-year overseas assignment to the Philippines (1971). I then gave the Starfire to Norris when I left. Never have I had – nor seen – a prettier car, before nor since.

Wind and dust storms were native to Cannon on that desert plateau. And so were tumbleweeds. "Tumbling Tumbleweeds" was one of my favorite songs sung by another of my boyhood heroes: Hollywood's singing cowboy, Gene Autry. But I had never before witnessed tumbleweeds in action. But here you would frequently see them endlessly "rolling along" as the song goes; the wind never giving them a pause for a breather. I never failed to think of the song and Gene Autry whenever I saw them. One morning after waking up I noticed the front windows all darkened with something pressing against them. I went out the back way and around to the front having to fight my way through mountains of tumbleweeds. During the night the wind had piled the tumbleweeds against the house several feet thick and up onto the roof. The front of the house was practically obscured with tumbleweeds. The song "Tumbling Tumbleweeds" now took on a whole different meaning for me.

Base Operations Casual Status

Since I had no prior F-100 aircraft time, myself along with three or four other newly assigned pilots with no F-100 time were assigned duty as Airdrome Officer (AO) at base operations while awaiting an F-100 class at Luke AFB near Phoenix, Arizona. We were also awaiting an assignment to one of the Tactical Fighter Squadrons at Cannon. Among many other base operations details, AO duty involved checking ramps, taxiways and runways for FOD (foreign object damage): debris that could cut tires or be sucked up into jet engines). Runway and airfield lighting had to be check for proper operation at night; and runway condition and braking when water, snow or ice was present. It also included keeping tabs on current and forecast weather for appropriate action; and checking, clearing and signing flight plans as approving authority for transit and local pilots initiating their flight plans at base operations. The fighter squadrons had their own flight plan filing and clearing authority. Pilots with the required experience level and instrument rating were authorized to sign and clear their own flight plans.

One day when I was on AO duty, a transit Navy aircrew completed their flight plan and the pilot signed as his clearance authorization since he had the credentials to do so. Besides, what Navy pilot worth his seawater would allow an Air Force pilot to *authorize* his flight plan? Cannon had a 10,000 foot runway and was at 5,000 feet above sea level. All pilots know that the higher the elevation and the higher the temperature (both contributing to thinner air), the more runway required to get airborne. And on a hot summer day at Cannon, most of that 10,000 foot runway was necessary. Across the departure end of our runway there was a steel cable and net barrier rigged and erected about three feet high – earlier carrier style. It was there in order to trap any aircraft that had a takeoff or landing emergency that would otherwise send it off the end of the runway into a desert cloud of dust. It was manually erected and lowered which took about 15 minutes as I recall. As he filed his flight plan, I informed the Navy pilot of the barrier and asked if he wanted it lowered. Considering the elevation and temperature, he thought for a few moments then answered in the affirmative. The barrier crew was advised and I jumped into the Base Operations pickup truck and headed for the barrier to be sure that it got lowered. I watched his takeoff and he was still rolling as he rolled over the *lowered* barrier on the departure end of the runway. He got airborne a few feet into the runway overrun in a cloud of dust, staggering out just above the desert probably interrupting a few jack rabbit routines – whatever jack rabbits do routinely – and angering a few sidewinders. He had used all 10,000 feet of the runway plus a few extra feet. I can only imagine what transpired in that cockpit on those last few feet of remaining runway!

The Base Operations pickup was assigned for the Base Operations Officer and AO to use in their duties. Thus, I was in the pickup checking the runway one day when I spotted an object (FOD) down the runway a short distance. Being a diligent AO as I was, I was going to apprehend that FOD as being unauthorized on *my* runway. As I approached the FOD, I noticed that it was squirming across the runway in an odd manner. *A sidewinder!* My first ever encounter with a real live sidewinder! Sidewinders, you know, crawl by looping a part of their body forward then thrusting another loop forward to loop again, thereby creating the distinct and unmistakable track in the desert sand. Anyway, I decided that I would dispatch this "FOD" by rolling over it with the left front tire of the pickup. The sidewinder was only about two and a half feet in length but I felt a very slight bump as I rolled over it. I stopped and backed up, rolling over it again. I got out of the pickup to scoop up the sidewinder and take it to the side of the runway. All I had done was make an angry sidewinder angrier. It was about five feet in front of the pickup and heading for the offending left front tire. It was going to attack that tire that had just rolled over it! I hastily acceded this round to the sidewinder and retreated into the pickup. Next round! I backed up to keep the sidewinder in sight and make sure it didn't crawl up into the underside of the pickup. I then accelerated forward applying the brakes hard as I rolled over it again. Game over! *FOD* removed!

For maintaining flying proficiency while assigned to Base Operation awaiting the Luke class, we flew the T-33 locally for training, instruments, cross-countries, delivery of parts and transport personnel. The T-33! I think it was the longest lasting single engine Air Force jet aircraft in the inventory dating back to 1948 for 50 plus years. Some countries still operate the T-33.

The high-altitude thin air at Cannon and my generally out-of-shape physical condition made me realize that I was going to have to get serious about getting and staying in good condition. It was becoming a feat for me to climb the side of the T-33 to the cockpit and especially the higher cockpit of the F-100. I began a serious running and exercise program which I continued until years later after retirement when back problems curtailed the running.

Tactical Air Command (TAC) Sea Survival School

In September I received orders to report to The TAC Sea Survival School at Langley AFB, Norfolk, Virginia; the class to begin on the 20th for 5 ½ days. Not being a swimmer, I was a little apprehensive although I knew it was necessary since I expected to be flying the F-100 over the Pacific sometime in the future. After arriving at Langley and doing the required classroom academics, we were taken onboard the school's boat and out into the Chesapeake Bay for a little practical application. The boat was equipped with a 15 foot high platform on the back of the boat. We would launch ourselves off the platform in a parachute harness (minus canopy) that was attached to the boat with long web straps called risers. The risers simulated the risers normally attaching the harness to a parachute canopy. The jump off the tower simulated an open water landing in a parachute and the boat's speed simulated being drug through the water with an inflated canopy and a wind of 10 to 15 miles per hour. In a parachute water landing, a stiff breeze could cause your canopy to remain inflated and drag you at an uncontrolled and rapid rate through the water. To combat this, the harness had a quick release on each shoulder to release the risers (and canopy) from the parachute harness. Releasing both risers would separate you from the canopy completely. Releasing only one riser would deflate the canopy while retaining it for other survival purposes.

Our instructions were to inflate our life vest and jump from the tower into the water with an inflated dinghy attached to us by a long lanyard. The boat would immediately start towing you through the water. While you were being drug through the water you were to roll onto your back and spread your legs (spread eagle style) which would stabilization you. When the instructor was satisfied that you had mastered the procedure, he blew a whistle signifying that you were to release one riser. This simulated deflating the canopy whereby he would stop the boat. You would climb aboard your dinghy and release the second riser.

Next *victim* – me! When I jumped off the tower on the way to the water, one of the risers attached to the boat somehow got twisted to the other side of my harness when I hit the water. The boat started dragging me with both risers on the same side thus pulling my head under and acted like a plow trying to pull me deeper. I couldn't get spread eagled on my back. Had I had the presence of mind I probably could have released one of the risers. But I was under water being towed and all I could think of was getting my head up out of the water – which I couldn't do. The instructor finally stopped the boat after giving me ample opportunity to untangle myself, and realizing that I was going to continue making like a submarine. I then proceeded with the rest of the procedure and settled into my one-man raft.

The final event was to take us out of the Chesapeake Bay into Atlantic and drop us off individually alone in our dinghy – barely in sight of land and out of sight of anyone and everything else – for about three hours. We could fish, paddle around, put up our dinghy shelter, apply sunburn lotion, read or whatever. (The survival manual made great reading – if you had nothing else to read). I spent most of my time looking for sharks and listening for leaks in my raft. We had a mirror, colored smoke and flares for signaling plus a leak-repair kit. Once we spotted the boat making it rounds to retrieve us we were to use our signal devices to simulate completing the "rescue at sea".

Back at Cannon, whenever my schedule would permit, I would drive out to the gunnery range and watch the F-100s work. Once when driving the desert trail to the range I came upon another sidewinder which I dispatched with my tire and brakes as before. I also had the opportunity to see an occasional coyote and a roadrunner; reminiscent of the old "Roadrunner and Wiley Coyote" cartoons. Also there was the occasional antelope "playing". The range tower was about 50 feet high and contained the range control officer. His duty was to spot and score each pilot's hits, inform pilots of their scores and pass the flight's results back to their Squadron operations at Cannon. He supervised all range activities and if a pilot violated the established minimum safe parameters for weapons deliveries, he would issue warnings or eject the pilot from the range, depending upon the severity of the safety violation. I enjoyed watching the flights work from really close up and could hardly wait until it was my turn.

Luke AFB, Glendale, Arizona – F-100 Checkout!
Very soon I had orders to report to Luke AFB, Arizona on October 4, 1964 for the 4510th Combat Crew Training Wing's (CCTW) F-100 transition class 65D.

The class would commence on October 5th for scheduled completion on January 29, 1965. In the meantime orders had been issued designating me as a Senior Pilot which is routinely awarded based on years of service and total flying hours. It meant that I would have a star over my Air Force pilot wings; no promotion, no pay increase – just a visual indication of having achieved a milestone in my flying career.

Arrival and clearing in at Luke went routinely and soon I was into ground school for the F-100. I was really anxious to get going. The course was popularly known as the "short-course" because it was designed only for familiarization with the F-100 and to achieve minimum qualification in the various ground and air attack missions; 50 hours of flying time which barely scratched the surface for qualifying in the F-100. I would not get the full-blown F-100 check-out and gunnery course. Transition went well but I really had to work at ground attack and air-to-air combat. It was all new to me because in the Air Defense Command fighters about all that was required was flying a radar scope in straight and level attack, or at best a snap-up maneuver before the rockets were fired electronically. The training syllabus for the F-100 training course included such things as:

> F-100 checkout
> Formation
> Ground Attack
> Nuclear Weapons
> Air to Air Combat
> Air Refueling
> Low Level Navigation
> Instruments

All of the above were fun things. I really enjoyed the F-100 and the variety of missions and tactics that it employed. Our gunnery work would be done on the Gila Bend Gunnery Ranges. Gila Bend was a small town about 40 miles south of Luke and the ranges were south of the east-west highway through Gila Bend. Air-to-air gunnery would be done on a much larger range further south and west.

Aircraft checkout, formation flying, navigation and instruments were very much common to all aircraft. New to me were the ground and air attack, nuclear delivery, air refueling and low-level navigation missions. The F-100D and F models had a final approach speed of 140 knots (165 mph). The F-100C had no flaps so it approached at 182 knots (210 mph). What impressed me most on entering the F-100 cockpit was that it had a *real gun sight!* I finally felt like I was flying a real fighter. It looked like a fighter, felt like a fighter, smelled like a fighter and could do so many various missions. Transition, formation and instruments went very well with no problems. Aerial refueling, ground and air attack was a bit difficult for me in that it was my first experience at such things. Fun, but required a lot of book learning and practical application. All bombs, rockets and ammo were of the practice variety with small spotting charges or colored rounds for marking impact points.

Ground Attack: For conventional weapons: Low level bombing was done at 50 feet, 400 knots (460 mph). Strafing was done at 15 degrees, 400 knots and a quick burst at the optimum range of 1200 feet from the target with a pull out of four to six "Gs" at 50 feet above ground. Dive bombing and rockets attacks were done from a thirty degree dive and 400 knots entered at 7000 feet with bomb release or rocket firing at 3000 feet and a dive recovery altitude of 1000 feet.

Nuclear Weapons Delivery: There were three types of nuclear bomb deliveries, all entered at 350 feet and 450 knots. They were: A 350 foot straight and level delivery, or a 350 foot level approach with a 4G pull up to a 45 degree climb and toss the bomb to the target, or a 350 foot approach with a 4G pull up slightly past vertical then toss the bomb over your shoulder. Only the 350 foot level delivery and the 45 degree climb-toss procedures were practiced while I was at Luke. A distinct escape maneuver was performed for each type of delivery with the primary goal of putting as many miles as possible between you and the nuclear blast. To assist in this escape maneuver, each bomb had a built-in timer with a time-delay bomb denotation, a parachute deployed to slow the bomb's flight and trajectory and a long spike on the nose to stick it into the surface upon impact to keep it from skipping along the ground. All of these features were designed to maximize the distance between the fighter and the bomb's detonation. For the low straight and level delivery, escape was straight ahead with the afterburner for maximum speed. For the 45 degree toss delivery, the bomb was released then aircraft rolled inverted, pull the nose down to the horizon, light the afterburner, roll upright and continue the dive for the deck with maximum speed. For the over-the-shoulder toss, it was a continuous pull-up past inverted to release the bomb then over the top and rolling upright and dive for the deck with afterburner and maximum speed.

Air to Air Combat: An F-100 was used as a target tow aircraft pulling a target in the shape of an elongated dart in a racetrack pattern. Firing was done on the target in the turn at each end of the track. Learning to track the target in the gun sight and fire at the optimum range (1200 feet) was a very tricky. The sight was very sensitive to the slightest aircraft movement. Sort of like trying to balance a tennis ball on a pencil eraser. Sure made me appreciate fighter aces more. But it was great sport! I did manage to "scare" the dart on a couple of occasions. Once I shot the cable off the dart dropping it into the desert about 16,000 feet below – which happened occasionally during air-to-air work. Of course all of our work was done in designated ranges marked as restricted areas on aeronautical charts.

Air Refueling: Our air refueling was done at about 20,000 feet near Flagstaff, Arizona on KC-135 tankers – which were the military version of the civilian 707. The refueling probe was on the right wing leading edge of the F-100 near the fuselage and barely visible in the pilot's peripheral vision when looking straight ahead. The tanker's refueling boom was about 20 feet long with about a 10 foot hose trailing the end of the boom. At the end of the hose was a round basket shaped drogue which the fighter probe was flown into for the fuel transfer. The drogue was called the "basket" and danced around in the slip stream. It took great pilot concentration to contact the basket with the fighter's probe. You had to fly very close formation under and aft of the tanker and work with tanker's boom operator to complete the refueling procedure. This is very intense work and generally I came back looking like I had stepped out of the shower in my flight suit. Nothing significant about the training except on one mission, the instructor had me do several dry (no fuel in the hose) practice hook-ups with the drogue – just stick the basket, back off, stick it again. The hose was drained of fuel and flimsy like a ribbon rather that rigid with fuel pressure from the tanker like a water hose with water pressure and the nozzle closed. The instructor was satisfied with my performance and said to do one more and we would head for Luke. I stuck the basket dead center as you're supposed to, but before I could move off-center to prevent a flailing hose, it took one quick flip, like the ribbon it now was, and snapped the boom off the F-100. The boom had a designed break point for just such a situation. Of course that is no emergency unless you're short of fuel and no recovery base available – like in the middle of the Pacific. But in the middle of the Pacific you wouldn't be practicing dry sticks with an empty hose on the tanker. I'm sure that probe falling into the desert shook up a pair of jack rabbits, a sidewinder or coyote; maybe an antelope or two. Night refueling was intensified significantly.

Low Level Navigation: This was one of my favorites. It was low-level, radar avoiding, 300 feet terrain-hugging at 360 knots for 250 to 350 miles or so, simulating a nuclear weapons delivery with a practice bomb on a gunnery range target. At 360 knots we covered six nautical miles a minute (approximately seven miles). We made mission folders containing a strip map of our route which we folded accordion style into short, cramped-cockpit manageable segments. Then we glued one edge of each folded segment into a flip-chart type booklet. This made it convenient to flip the map pages as we progress with minimum head-in-the-cockpit time. At 300 feet and 360 knots there was no time to fold/unfold and orient maps. Besides, it was unsafe to divert your attention to such chores at such a low level. At this altitude above the ground, visual identification range of ground objects was limited to one or two miles. Checkpoints had to be easily recognizable since they flashed by almost as quickly as they were spotted. If a turn was required at a checkpoint, the actual turn radius was calculated and plotted on the map. Distances between checkpoints were marked in minutes and seconds with progressive accumulated hours, minutes and seconds. Seeing barns, windmills, desolate crossroads, forest towers, waterfalls, bends in small streams, even Indian mud huts flash by on time and realize that you were on course and on time was an exhilarating feeling. Livestock were often startled as you passed overhead; amusing, although I doubt that farmers and ranchers were amused. Missing your TOT (time on target) by more than three seconds was considered unacceptable. Fun work, but somebody had to do it! After all, I was the sound of freedom; defending our country and taking the war to the "enemy".

One very dramatic and beautiful event occurred on one of my low-level missions. My route crossed the Grand Canyon. Flying along at 300 feet, looking for check points, I was suddenly over the rim of the canyon. Instantly I was a thousand feet or more above ground looking into a great multicolored chasm and a stunning view – breath taking! Another of the limitless beauties and God given blessings of this great country of ours! It was almost disorienting for a moment.

As much fun and enjoyment as it was, this was serious business. In the not too distant future I would be sitting alert in the Far East with a live "nuke" shackled to the bomb rack of my F-100; a real mission folder and an actual designated enemy target. Sobering thoughts!

New Squadron – 523rd Tactical Fighter Squadron (TFS), Cannon AFB
In November while at Luke, orders were published at Cannon assigning me to the 523TFS which I would join upon my return. On January 20, 1965 the F-100 course completed, I was on my way back home to Cannon with approximately 55 hours F-100 time behind me. Back at Cannon, I reported into the 523rd and met my Squadron commander, "Woody". "Woody's Warriors" as the squadron was known. The squadron had a great bunch of guys and great camaraderie. I was soon flying the missions I had been introduced to at Luke. It was sort of "on-the-job-training" here at Cannon but great fun.

Our gunnery range was located about 20 miles west of Cannon and ten miles south of the small town of Melrose located on Highway 60. A small dusty trail led from Melrose to the range. In addition to the usual daily training missions on the range, occasionally we would be tasked to provide "close air support" to some army "grunts" playing war games on their own ranges. Fun! Legalized buzzing! I would think to myself how great it was to be up here and not down there playing "grunt" games – totally unaware that in just a few months, I would be down there with the grunts in a real shooting war!

While I was at Cannon the base had an annual fire-power demonstration at Melrose Range to demonstrate the massive capabilities of various Air Force weapons. The event was for the benefit of Air Force and local civilian

211

dignitaries. Cannon personnel were invited to the full dress rehearsal on the day prior to the event. Our squadrons would demonstrate live ordnance deliveries on simulated enemy targets before a viewing area that was located on a nearby hillside. The viewing area was a safe distance, yet being close enough for good viewing, feeling the heat and experience the blasts. I took Pat, Norris and Robert. It was a treat, a thrill and an eye opener regarding the destructiveness of those weapons.

On the home front things were very much routine. Robert was a Cub Scout and attending Ranchvale Elementary School in Clovis. Norris's school was in Clovis also. Pat was very busy in the Officers' Wives Club and our church: the Central Baptist Church of Clovis; Dr. Carl Scott, pastor. Central Baptist was in revival with visiting evangelist preacher, Reverend Baker. One Sunday morning February 7th 1965, Robert gave Pat and me a memorable pleasant surprise. After his sermon, Reverend Baker invited anyone wishing to make their public profession of faith in Jesus Christ as Savior to come forward and do so. Suddenly without any previous indication, persuasion or discussions of his intention to do so, Robert – who was six years old at this time – left the pew and went down the aisle alone to meet Reverend Baker. He made his public profession of faith before the church. On February the 21st Robert was baptized into the Church – a day after Pat's birthday. What a birthday present for Pat! We were so pleased and praising God. Our family was now complete in Christ! Dr. Scott would later play a significant role in my life.

Robert had surgery on one of his legs and was on crutches for a while. Norris also had his time on crutches with a broken leg (or ankle) but I don't recall where it was. I think maybe it was Shaw AFB, South Carolina. My family and I had made great friends with a couple of other Air Force families at Cannon. We would maintain contact with them and their families over the years. Although Pat died years later, I still maintain contact with these friends.

523rd Deployment to Misawa, Japan

A month and a half after I returned from Luke, the 523rd received deployment orders to Misawa Air Base, Japan. All TAC squadrons had a designated overseas deployment base to which they rotated from the US; either Europe or the Far East. This was done on a recurring basis in order to maintain deployment ready status and mission training. They then further rotated elements of the squadron to a forward base from which they conducted immediate response alert status as a deterrent against our Cold War enemies: China and Russia.

Some of the pilots flew our F-100s across the Pacific to Misawa – island hopping along the way accompanied by KC-135s air refueling tankers. On Mar 24th the remaining 523rd personnel (me included) would board military airlift aircraft bound for Misawa. We did refueling stops at the Pacific islands along the way. I crossed the Pacific a few times during my career but I don't recall the specific stops made on each trip. On each trip I took advantage of the stops– within the brief time we had – to visit World War Two battle sights, war relics and memorials. On the itineraries for the many trips were island stops such as: Hawaii, Midway, Guam, Wake Island and Okinawa. Misawa is located about 400 miles north of Tokyo and experiences extreme winters which begin to taper off near the end of March.

Upon arrival we set about flying local area orientation flights and routine practice missions. I was soon sent to Kunsan Air Base, Korea where I would be sitting nuclear alert to strike our Cold War targets in the event war broke out. Kunsan is located on the west coast of central South Korea. Just as in our training missions; mission folders were prepared and details were committed to memory along with target intelligence. Prior to being designated alert qualified, you had to undergo an evaluation board interview. At this interview you were required to describe, without reference to your mission folder, minute details of your route to include checkpoints, times, headings, target identification, intelligence and other target strike times on or near you and your time-on-target (TOT). You had to be able to fly the mission by memory without the aid of a map if necessary. This was one mission you hoped never to have to fly. The mission folder contained recovery bases and emergency bailout procedures. However, it was unlikely that you would return – even if there should miraculously be a place to return to. You knew there would be other weapons launched at, or near, your target via bombers, intercontinental and submarine launched missiles. With Russia and China simultaneously launching their weapons, it would truly be a Hollywood style "Doomsday".

After a few days alert duty you had opportunities to descend upon the local populace; sample the food, shop for souvenirs and make like a tourist before resuming daily training missions until your next alert tour. In downtown Kunsan I bought one of those tall, black, flat-brimmed, tapered crown hats worn by the Korean Papa Sans (old Korean men). I also learned to like fried rice – or as the locals pronounced it" "Flied Lice". Many Asians have difficulty with the letter "R" which they pronounced as "L".

"You want *Massagie*, GI?"
Kunsan AB had a fitness center containing a massage parlor which some of the guys used when coming off alert in order to "unlax". Some would use it on a frequent basis just for the tension relieving benefits. I never considered it for at least three reasons: One, I had never had a massage before and really thought them unnecessary. Two, I just didn't relish the idea of someone doing a rubdown on me in a near naked condition – me nearly naked that it. Third, the masseurs were local females. This made me extra reluctant. Naivety? Maybe so. There were a couple of friends that frequently took advantage of the

massage and urged me to do so; regaling the benefits thereof. I continued to resist. One day after some persistent urging, I agreed. I think they were more interested in getting my reaction to the female masseurs than they were the massage benefits for me.

Anyway, I went into the fitness center's massage parlor and was ushered into a room by a Korean female. We were immediately joined by another female with a couple of large towels which she handed to me. I stood there looking at the two of them. They stood there looking at me. After a seemingly long uneasy moment, one of them told me to get undressed. I continued to stand there waiting for them to leave the room. They didn't! They said again to get undressed. Still I didn't move. I finally said: "Now?" They sort of begin to giggle between themselves realizing they had a newbie here, then slowly turned and left the room. I placed one towel on the massage table, undressed and lay face down on the towel. I then strategically placed the other towel over me and waited. They soon returned and proceeded with the rubdown. Following the massage was the sauna and steam bath. My friends were right. It was a great relaxing feeling and you really did feel like a refreshed person. However, I never went back for another massage. It's just something that I'm not inclined toward. I did do the steam bath occasionally. Sometime later after our squadron returned to Cannon I told Pat about the message. Nothing happened! Her reaction was neutral – I think. Another interesting experience was public co-ed restrooms. It's attention getting to be in the restroom doing what men normally do in a restroom, and in walks a Japanese lady who proceeds to do what ladies normally do in restroom – whatever that is. Maybe it's co-ed because of the always long line of ladies to use public female-only restrooms.

Mission Incomplete: *Walking Home!*

Local training flights continued on Kunsan AB after alert duty. We had a practice bombing range on a tiny island off the west coast about 70 miles north of Kunsan. The bombs were small practice bombs that were designed, upon release, to provide the trajectory of a nuclear bomb with its drag chute deployed. Another gunnery practice range was located inland about 30 miles. Our routine was to takeoff, climb to altitude and proceed to the first bombing range on the coast to do our practice; then proceed to the inland gunnery range and complete our range work there (rockets, bombs and guns). We would then climb toward Kunsan (about 60 miles or so south) and contact Kunsan Approach Control for a practice instrument approach and landing at Kunsan. This was routine day-in and day-out stuff.

It was late May 1965 that I was scheduled to fly just such an early morning mission in a flight of two F-100s out of Kunsan and return. At this time I had accumulated about 150 hours in the F-100. I was designated flight leader for our flight of two. My wingman was an "old head" F-100 pilot with a thousand hours or more in the F-100. I guess the squadron scheduler was giving me an opportunity for flight lead experience. The weather check revealed unsuitable low clouds for our mission. We needed better weather for the planned mission on the ranges. Thus our flight was put on hold until the weather improved as it was forecast to do. About noon the weather had improved to 2500 foot scattered clouds and 10 miles visibility. Great visual flying weather! It was forecast to remain that way for the remainder of the day. A "no sweat," "piece-of-cake" weather situation!

I briefed the flight and did a final check of the weather; still no change. The weather briefer did indicate however, that there was low-level scud deck off the coast about 10 to 12 miles west; not unusual for coastal areas. He requested that we give him a "pilot report" on the condition as we proceeded north to the range. I agreed as this would only require a short detour in distance and time to the range. All flights used what was called "bingo" fuel meaning the absolute minimum amount of fuel required to recover to home base and have the required fuel reserve. I briefed my wingman that we would increase our "bingo" fuel by 500 pounds above the normal 2500 pounds in the event the weather went "sour" on us. (Jet fuel quantity and rate per hour is indicated in pounds of fuel rather than gallons of fuel. One gallon of jet fuel weighs six pounds).

We had a normal takeoff and departure. I took us out over the low scud for the forecaster's requested pilot report as we climbed out to the north for the practice range. The scud was so thin that you could see the ocean through it and looked to be about two hundred feet off the deck and 10 miles off the coast. I reported this to base weather forecaster on their pilot-to-weather radio channel; got an acknowledgement and thanks, then proceeded to the bomb range. A pretty ho-hum mission thus far! Standard procedure called for the flight leader to determine periodic fuel-states of aircraft in the flight. Early in the flight my wingman's fuel-state was running slightly less than my own; which is normal for formation flights where wingmen are jockeying to maintain their position on the leader. After completing our work on the bomb range we proceeded inland to the gunnery range. A few miles inland, I decided to call Kunsan weather to get an update on the scud off the coast – still harboring a suspicion that that stuff might decide to thicken up and move inland. Unable to get Kunsan on the radio, I established an orbit and contacted nearby Osan Air Base. I requested that they call Kunsan on the land line and inquire about the scud off the coast, and their forecast for the next couple of hours.

After about five minutes or more, Osan came back on the radio and said that Kunsan was 2500 foot scattered, 10 miles visibility and forecast to remain so the rest of the day. No change. It was the same as we had received during our flight briefing. Great! I sensed a slight relief and proceed to the gunnery range.

215

On the gunnery range our attack tactics required the use of the afterburner as you pulled off the target and climbed back to altitude for another attack. Therefore we did repeated attacks with repeated use of the afterburner which consumes fuel at an astronomical rate. After a few attacks I requested another fuel-state from my wingman and noted that I was running slightly *lower* on fuel. *This was not normal!* Everything else was going routinely well as briefed so I had no real concern. I reminded him of the briefed 3000 pounds "bingo" fuel although the Osan weather forecaster had confirmed the no-sweat weather and forecast for Kunsan. Weather-wise everything was looking good – just as it had been briefed for our flight. Still I could not shake the visual image in my mind of that scud off the coast of Kunsan. Thus I decided to remain with the 3000 pounds "bingo" fuel rather than our normal 2500 pounds.

Upon completing our range work, we climbed to 16,000 feet for our recovery at Kunsan which would normally terminate in a practice visual instrument approach and landing under control of a GCA controller. (GCA – ground controlled approach). As is standard practice after leaving the range, I called for a fuel state and I had considerably lower fuel than my wingman – an abnormal condition for the flight leader. Normally wingmen use slightly more fuel that the leader because of the throttle jockeying to maintain position. About 35 to 40 miles from Kunsan I switched my flight to Kunsan Approach Control. I was cleared to begin our descent for the initial approach to landing.

It was then that I noticed a very low solid under cast of clouds ahead extending from the ocean over Kunsan and for a few miles inland. This was quite unexpected since I had been told a few minutes earlier that Kunsan was 2500 feet scattered and 10 miles visibility. I asked Kunsan Approach Control for their current weather. They came back immediately that they were 2500 feet scattered and 10 miles visibility. Someone must have been reading from an old teletype report. I told them that I could see a low solid under cast over Kunsan and to reconfirm their current weather. They came back shortly with 400 feet overcast and 10 miles visibility. Although this meant that I was now operating under instrument flight rules regulations requiring a fuel reserve that I was well below, the 400 foot ceiling and 10 miles visibility at Kunsan would be a piece-of-cake. Osan was about 50 to 55 miles north of our position at this time and was clear with 10 miles plus visibility. However, we were only 15 to 20 miles north of Kunsan and I felt that landing at Kunsan would be no problem; Osan likely being "iffy" at the rate I was burning fuel.

Kunsan AB being on the west coast was at sea level elevation. Air Force minimum altitude and visibility for a GCA approach and landing was 200 feet and ¼ mile visibility. Minimum altitude and visibility is the criteria at which *if* you don't have the runway in sigh, you are to make a missed approach and try again – or proceed to an alternate airport. A solid overcast at 400 feet with 10 miles visibility underneath is a true "piece of cake" that you could do all-day-long with one arm tied behind your back. But higher headquarters had arbitrarily established our instrument approach minimums as 300 feet and ½ mile visibility. Still, a 400 foot solid ceiling and 10 miles visibility above those minimums – would be a no-sweat situation. This would give me an opportunity to break out of the overcast at 100 feet above the regulated minimum altitude of 300 feet; and with 10 miles of visibility. With what I now believed to be the current weather situation, we began our descent to the approach for Kunsan. After being turned over to the GCA final controller, we entered the under cast at about 1000 feet in our descent on final approach, landing to the north.

About this time my minimum fuel light, indicating 800 pounds of fuel remaining, came on and I attempted to advise the final controller. I'm not sure he heard me. When under final approach control, the pilot makes no further transmissions (except for emergencies). It's a one-way conversation with the controller transmitting continuously with minor heading and rate-of-descent changes to maintain you on the extended centerline and glide path to the runway. If the controller's instructions cease for 5 seconds, the pilot is to immediately execute a missed approach – since the controller's instructions are what keeps the pilot on centerline and on glide path. The pilot's responsibility is to maintain proper airspeed and to execute the final controller's commands in a smooth and timely manner. In the event a missed approach is necessary at minimum altitude, the controller issues instructions to execute the missed approach if the runway is not in sight. However, he continues to issue heading corrections to keep you on the centerline until established in the missed approach. There was a slight left sea breeze which required the controller to issue frequent heading corrections. Even with the red minimum fuel light illuminated I was not concerned because of the reported 400 foot ceiling and 10 miles visibility.

At 400 feet where I should have broken out of the overcast, I was still in solid clouds. I continued the approach with the controller issuing instructions. The controller had been constantly correcting me to the left a degree or two. Then 300 feet – *the headquarters directed mandatory minimums*! Still in solid clouds – no runway, no visual contact with the ground! The controller issued a missed approach command stating that I was "...right of the centerline". If I had been visual at this time, as I should have been based on the weather given me, I could still have landed with no problem as my wingman was on my left wing which would place me right of the runway centerline. However, I was at the missed approach altitude but probably descended to the Air Force minimum of 200 feet looking for the runway – which was still not in sight. I gave the visual signal to my wingman for the missed approach. Once I got the "miss" established I looked around for my wingman and he *wasn't there!* I gave him a call and he said he lost me in the clouds on the missed approach. (He later confessed that he was also looking for the ground and missed my hand signal for the missed approach). Now there were two of us milling around in the clouds for approach to deal with rather than one flight. Since he had the required fuel, I told him to proceed to Osan where we had just been and knew it was clear. I would try another *last* approach.

As I started my turn out over the coast to do another approach I realized that: Presently I did not know the actual cloud ceiling – it could have been down to the ground as far as I knew. Neither did I know the actual visibility. All I knew was that it was not the 400 feet and 10 miles that approach control was telling me; it was not the 300 feet and ½ mile headquarters minimums and it was not the 200 feet and ¼ mile Air Force minimum. Secondly, I remembered that the approach to the runway has two hills just before the threshold of the runway, one each side as you approach the threshold. One hill was about 50 feet and the other was about 75 feet high. With these two thoughts in mind and knowing that my fuel state would likely press me into continuing my second approach attempt to the absolute lowest altitude (i.e., the ground), I did a quick mental calculation of the little fuel I had left and the distance to Osan. Osan had clear weather and I made a "thumb-nail" estimated that I may barely make it by climbing to 17,000 feet; even if it meant a flame-out landing I would at least be in the clear. I preferred a possible visual flame-out landing in the clear over another unknown instrument approach situation which would assure insufficient fuel to reach Osan if I was unable to land.

Having initiated my missed approach I was by this time over the coast which is normally wall-to-wall sampans and fishing boats. I was carrying external practice bomb and rocket racks under my wings and thought of the few extra miles I would gain from jettisoning them into the ocean to reduce the drag. But, I was in the clouds and would not jettison them for fear of hitting the fishermen below. Once inland, I would not jettison them for fear of hitting someone on the ground.

I was on my way toward Osan AB hoping and praying for the best. But the best was not to be. In my climb I was soon out of the clouds and in a few more miles I was clear of the undercast below. It was clear all the way to Osan. I was handed-off to Osan Approach Control who had already been briefed on my predicament. They advised me that my wingman had landed safely. (Later I would learn that he landed with questionably enough fuel for a go-around). At about 17,000 feet and 25 miles south of Osan I flamed-out – a really eerie feeling; Quiet and no throttle response. I advised approach control and prepared for the eventual ejection. The F-100 flight manual recommended against a flameout landing – especially on unprepared surfaces – and recommended ejection above 2000 feet as an extra safety precaution. Ejection survival decreases significantly below 2000 feet and much less so with lower ejection altitudes. The Korean country side is dotted with small villages, homes and fields. There was a runway capable of handling jet aircraft about 15 miles south of Osan. I spotted the runway immediately after my flameout and told approach that I would attempt a flameout landing there. They came back with a "Negative" that there were men and equipment on the runway for repairs; and that they had no means of alerting them to vacate the runway. I was too far from Osan. I realized that I was now going to have to "walk home". I advised approach that I would stay with my aircraft until "fifteen hundred feet" attempting to assure the safety of people on the ground. I made one last quick check of my ejection preparations – double checking that my "Zero-delay lanyard" was attached to my parachute "D" ring (ripcord), which I'll explain later. Constantly looking for a clear area in which to eject, I saw what seemed to be the best area around that I could reach. Foremost in my mind was safety of people on the ground, and secondly was *having to face an accident investigation board!* I guess thirdly would be having to face my squadron commander and the guys in the squadron. Concern over the ejection was well down on my list; otherwise I would have ejected a few thousand feet higher for the enhanced safety aspect of an ejection. At 1500 feet I advised approach that I was "out'a here"! This was about fifteen miles south of Osan: Close but not close enough! By the time I ejected I was probably about 1200 to1300 feet above ground.

Eject! Making like a Paratrooper

I breathed a quick prayer and took one last look to assure that there was no village below me – only farm land with scattered homes. I raised the right arm rest on my seat which jettisoned the canopy (either arm rest would do the job). Surprisingly there was no noticeable explosion from the charge or noise from the loss of the canopy. Raising the right arm rest also exposes and arms the ejection trigger, which is in the right hand grip only. I squeezed the trigger. Wham! I was outta there! There was no jolt as there would have been in an explosive charge. Our seats had been modified with a rocket charge for seat ejection providing a softer ejection – which saved many a crushed disc in the spine. (Years later I would be told by an Air Force orthopedic surgeon that I had upper-back compressed discs, which probably occurred upon this ejection). There was no sensation of being ejected from the cockpit. Rather, the sensation was of my being suspended in space as I found myself looking down into the cockpit of this F-100 slowly falling away from me – no canopy, no seat, *no pilot!* Surreal! This sight will remain indelibly etched in my mind as long as I have my memory. Everything that transpired from squeezing the seat ejection trigger until my parachute was deployed required approximately two to three seconds. Describing it will take a *little longer.*

As I was ejected, a cable attached between the cockpit floor and my seat fired a charge that, through a system of hoses, released my seatbelt buckle and shoulder harness. The cable also fired a charge activating a reel at the upper back of my seat. That reel is attached to straps running down behind and under me, then forward to and attached at the front edge of the seat. The reel is instantly retracted which causes the straps under me to kicks me out of the seat. (Ejection fatalities have been recorded whereby the pilot was wedged in the seat by his parachute and the paraphernalia he was wearing). Everything described in the ejection sequence above is automatic and designed to provide the quickest chute deployment possible; and provide safe pilot and aircraft separation on ejection. Of course everything could be done manually from bailout to chute deployment, but would require crucial time and altitude. My ejection and chute deployment were text-book perfect. However, my pre-ejection positioning and parachute landing were less so. I did not get myself in the proper back-straight, head-up and feet-retracted into the seat stirrups before ejection. This would cause me some back problems years later.

Remember the "Zero-Delay lanyard" that I mentioned hooking to my parachute harness "D" ring (ripcord) above? In addition to being attached by cable to the parachute pack to open it and deploy the canopy, the "D" ring was now also attached by this lanyard to another cable connected to the seatbelt. When I was kicked out of the seat by the "seat-kicker," the cable attached to the seatbelt pulled the "D" ring and deployed the parachute. The next indelible memory I recall is being spread-eagle, face down looking at the terra firma about a 1000 feet below with nothing, *repeat nothing,* between me and a hard place except the Lord God! I was silently repeating over and over: "Lord, please let the chute open!" I didn't know how many times one could repeat that phrase in the couple of seconds that it took for the canopy to deploy; but I was trying to establish a record.

"POP!" With a very loud pop, the canopy inflated and popped open. The opening shock was terrific. One moment I was spread-eagle face down; then the next I was snapped upright with my feet seemingly going above my head. Then I was swinging wildly in the canopy. The oscillations were so severe that I felt like I was oscillating through a 180 degree arc. At the end of each upswing, the lower edge of the canopy would flap violently as though it might collapse. I was now only a few feet above the ground and if I didn't get that oscillation stopped, it would either collapse the canopy or slam me sideways into the ground at the extreme end of the cycle. There is a procedure for stabilizing an oscillating canopy. By pulling down on the upper risers as the canopy reaches it maximum up swing for two or three oscillation, the oscillations will dampen out and stabilize. This procedure worked as advertised. Once stabilized, I looked around to see if I could spot my F-100. I saw it a couple of seconds before it impacted. It was in a perfectly level attitude and hit in a wheat field. The impact caused the wheat to lay over in a pattern radiating out from around the aircraft as if an invisible wind had blown it over. The engine separated and went tumbling across the field toward a farm house. I was holding my breath and praying that it would not hit the house. It stopped a matter of a few yards short in the backyard. In another few seconds I was on the ground – a wheat field. I was uninjured! Thank you, Lord! In the brief time of my parachute descent, with the oscillations and many other thoughts running through my mind, I had forgotten to deploy my survival kit which was attached by quick releases to my parachute harness seat-sling. When released, the kit hangs on a 10 foot lanyard during the descent to avoid possible injury by landing on it, or pulling you under in the event of a water landing. Upon my landing, I immediately went down on my rear end sitting back on my survival kit. I was fortunate indeed because some such landings have popped knees as the pilot sat back with the kit caught between the thigh and calf of the leg. The normal parachute landing fall (PLF) is to land with feet together, knees slightly bent, and on impact roll to one side in a shock-absorbing procedure. My PLF would have brought the toughest paratrooper jump master to tears of shame and disgust. But at least I was safe and seemly uninjured! Years later I would be found to have upper back compressed discs typical of an aircraft ejection incident.

I stood up and shed my parachute harness knowing that Osan would be sending someone for me soon. A small group of Korean civilians began to gather around but maintained a short distance away. I had indicated that I was OK. In a matter of about five minutes, an Army helicopter having heard the calls on the emergency radio frequency, landed to pick me up. A crewman retrieved my parachute and I climbed aboard. They delivered me to nearby Osan AB where I was met by the Air Force Flight Surgeon and medical crew for the required physical exam following such incidents. In a couple of days I was back at Kunsan, having to explain everything to my squadron commander and every other safety and investigating official. It was in very short order that I was before the accident investigation board. Of course all my flight records, medical records and training records were reviewed as a matter of routine. The finding was – as expected – pilot error in that I did not divert to Osan once I was told the weather to be 400 feet and 10 miles visibility. Weather did get a "contributing factor" statement in the final report.

The finding was a correct one since I knew my fuel condition required flight under instrument rules; rather than the visual rules my flight was operating under. Instrument flight rules require much more fuel reserve that visual rules. At that point in my flight when instrument weather was a certainty, I was already below reserve fuel required for instrument flight. I could have gone directly to Osan which was under visual conditions. But "get-home-itis" has jumped up to bite many a pilot. I thought the pilots on the accident review board felt that they would have done exactly as I did, but of course they could not voice those thoughts; nor reach any other conclusion. Several squadron pilots told me that they too would have done exactly as I did with the conditions reported to me. I had to undergo the usual written and flight evaluation to be recertified as a matter of standard procedure in such accident cases. We were required to be evaluated on a semi-annual basis anyway. Soon I was back flying and sitting alert and flying routine training missions with the squadron.

I called Cannon to talk with Pat to tell her the events and to assure her that I was OK. I knew the word would get back quickly. In fact I made the news. My brother later sent me a clipping form his Atlanta newspaper that had a two inch column about my accident. But thank the Lord I was OK apparently except for the not yet discovered compressed disc in my back. Years later when I was seeing an orthopedic surgeon for severe back, leg and foot pains he asked me if I had ever ejected from an aircraft. Not having discussed my ejection with him I told him yes and then the details. He then said he thought so because, what he saw was typical of aircraft ejection injuries.

Contributing Factors

As I stated above, the accident board finding was: primary cause "pilot error" with weather as a contributing factor. "Weather" inherently can never be declared a "prime or major" cause of an aircraft accident. The theory being that it can always be avoided in some way. About two weeks following my accident, the Tactical Air Command Headquarters at Langley AFB, Virginia, issued a command-wide priority message to all tactical fighter wings and squadrons warning of possible F-100 afterburner "eyelid" malfunction. The message stated that the "eyelids" could fail to *close* properly if the afterburner is cycled on-and-off in repeated and frequent succession. This is exactly what my flight had been doing on the gunnery range. The "eyelids" are located on the aft end of the engine tailpipe/afterburner and function to increase or decrease the area of the tailpipe opening to accommodate the additional thrust generated by use of the afterburner. They look like eyelids, thus the name; and function like the iris of the eye – opening and closing to admit more or less light. In the case of the afterburner eyelids, they open during afterburner use to allow for the additional thrust, and close to a smaller diameter to accommodate the lesser thrust required for normal non-afterburner operation.

The message went on to say that the repeated use of the afterburner has been found, in some cases, to cause the eyelids to only partially close after afterburner use; thus requiring more power (and fuel) to maintain normal non-afterburner thrust. This sounds exactly like a scenario that could have caused me to use fuel at a more rapid rate that normal; and why I was using more fuel than my wingman which is also an abnormal situation.

I submitted a request to the accident board that they amend their finding to include this phenomenon (unknown at the time) as an additional contributing factor, the sum of which ultimately ended in my having to eject from my F-100. They refused to do so.

Redeployment Home to Cannon

Near the end of June we were scheduled to redeploy to Cannon. On the first leg from Misawa I flew the front seat of an F-100F (the tandem two-seat, version of the single-seat F-100D model). The squadron operations officer flew in the back seat. I guess he wanted to monitor me for a couple of air refueling before we landed at Okinawa (I think it was). He was satisfied so I continued the trip in a single-seat F100D across the Pacific to Cannon. We flew in flights of two as a cell with one KC-135 tanker. There were several such cells taking our squadron back to Cannon. I think we made at least a couple of air refueling on this leg to Wake Island I think it was. At each RON base (remain overnight) we turned in early and were given "no-go" pills to be sure we slept undisturbed and were sufficiently rested for the early wake up and morning brief for the next long haul across the Pacific.

Each morning we were awaken well before first light, given a "go-pill" to keep us awake and alert during the next several-hour leg, then herded off for a full breakfast – only solid foods, no greasy stuff, no coffee and limited liquids. For the flights, we were provided bottled water, which we carried in our flight suit, and a sandwich cut into small bite sizes and stowed on the floor by the seat. If I remember correctly, we stopped at Guam (Johnson AFB) next; then on to Hawaii (Hickam AFB), then to Cannon.

There is no bathroom facility in the F-100 cockpit – except for the funnel stowed by the seat for #1 relief. The funnel was plumbed over-boarded for just such a purpose. But using it was tricky and carried a caution for it use. The funnel had a little thumb-operated valve on the bottom where it joined the tube. Cockpits were pressurized which kept the valve closed and prevented loss of cockpit pressure. Once you found your #1 apparatus through a myriad of hoses and cords, seatbelt, parachute harness and your flight suit – all the time maintaining control of the aircraft (most autopilots didn't work) – then you filled the funnel, removed your apparatus, pressed the thumb lever to open the valve and let the cockpit pressure dump overboard. If you forgot and pressed the thumb lever valve before you extracted your apparatus, you would not forget – ever again! I've heard of one such situation. *It wasn't me!*

Conducting an in-flight #2 operation was much more involved. Generally with the diet we were provided for these long over the water flights and the preparations we made, this was not usually a problem. However, I did hear a story of one pilot who just had to go on one such long overwater flight. The story went something like this. He had to do #2 really bad and he was two to three hours away from landing and still over the big pond (ocean). He moved out to a loose spread formation from the lead F-100 for some maneuver room. Then he trimmed-up the aircraft for mostly hands-off flying, unbuckled his seatbelt and shoulder harness, removed his parachute harness, unzipped his flying suit and came out of the upper portion, climbed into and squatted in seat, grabbed his helmet bag and completed the job; all the while continuing to maintain aircraft control; no small task. A contortionist would have been proud. *It wasn't me!*

The last leg from Hawaii to Cannon was the longest. It was a great sight to see the "Gold Coast" and the Golden Gate Bridge go under the wing. We had departed the tankers after our last air refueling with a full fuel load sufficient to reach Cannon then formed up in squadron formation. Weather was clear all the way. Cannon Approach Control and the tower had been informed of our arrival time. The base and especially our families were out in *force*. The fight formed up in close formation and the leader started a long descent from around 20,000 feet and 100 miles out. We accelerated slowly in the descent and when Cannon was in sight the leader tightened up the formation and powered-up to arrive over the base with a show of speed and a sharp peel-off for our landings. Quite a show for the home folks! Their "Knights" on their silver F-100 charges had returned! (F-100s still wore their shiny factory silver then before they were later painted in Vietnam war-paint – camouflaged jungle green and tan).

Our families were permitted to greet us on the flight line at our aircraft as we taxied to parking and shut down. It was a great reunion as we dismounted from our "steeds" *sweaty and smelly* into the arms of our families. The frequent and long TDYs or deployments always made for happy homecomings. Pat once remarked to a friend that she enjoyed her "assignment to Cannon" and only wished that I had been assigned there too.

The next chapter will cover my second, TDY deployment to Vietnam.
*****

CHAPTER THIRTEEN
VIETNAM AGAIN AND FORWARD AIR CONTROLLING; Cannon AFB, Clovis, New Mexico – F-100, O-1 Bird Dog (1964-1966)

"Home on the Range!"

It was indeed great being home again; especially having recently ejected from an F-100 and lived to tell about it. My apologies had already been made to the crew chief for losing his aircraft. Having been a crew chief, I could appreciate his loss. Now I needed to do something for the parachute rigger who had successfully packed my parachute. Normally one would most likely present the appreciated personality with a bottle of Champagne. Being a non-alcohol Baptist person, I chose to invite him home for a dinner in his honor, along with a friend of his choice. Pat was in wholehearted agreement with my plan. He and his friend seemed to appreciate the gesture of gratitude. I only wish I had recorded his name. It would be nice to be able to occasionally remind him of my thankfulness.

In July 1965 I had returned from a three-month deployment to Japan and Korea. I was really enjoying my assignment at Cannon, even though Pat thought I was assigned elsewhere – because of my numerous TDYs away from home. About 30 days later near the end of July, hardly having completed unpacking my bags, I would be packing up again and on my way for a six-month TDY; this time to Fort Riley, Kansas and then to Vietnam for my second TDY there!

In the meantime, I was enjoying "home on the range," – Melrose Gunner Range, that is. Guns (20mm cannons), bombs, and rockets: what fun! Although they were all practice munitions, it was great sport. My family and I enjoyed week-end drives into the desert. I loved seeing all the various plant life, especially the cacti; and the many other interesting things (secrets) of the desert. I never knew there were so many different species of cacti; or that some could "jump up" and 'bite' you. You learn fast! Jumping cactus it's called. It has tiny balls with barb like needles that actually grab your clothing as you walk by. The balls break off and by hanging on to your clothing giving the appearance of having "jumped" on you. Of course you don't realize they're there until the barbs work through you clothing into *you*. Great squadron and flying buddies, great neighbors, great family, great church, great life! Great flying; it was simply too great to last. *It didn't!* Read on:

In 1965 Vietnam was rapidly becoming a very HOT topic and U.S. involvement was rapidly building. As a career Air Force Officer (and gentleman according to Congress), a Captain and F-100 pilot of the 523rd Tactical Fighter Squadron, Cannon Air Force Base, Clovis, New Mexico these facts were foremost on my mind. But I was comfortable in my knowledge that if I ever went to war it would be as a fighter pilot – my life-long dream. Becoming a fighter pilot was my dream as a very serious college student doing the two years required (at that time) to become an Aviation Cadet. It was my dream as a young Georgia plowboy trudging barefoot in the cool plowed sod behind an old Georgia mule – while watching fighter planes from the nearby air base doing their thing over my Dad's farm. I day dreamed of what it would be like to be one of those pilots up there in the "blue" – climbing, diving, rolling and looping – mixing it up with a make believe "enemy". It was my dream as I walked, hitchhiked, or biked many miles to a small airport so I could spend every dime of my allowance on an all-too-brief flying lesson. It was my dream as a pre-teenster building model planes in every spare moment at the expense of my homework. It was my dream, undoubtedly confirmed even as a small boy of about seven years old, when I begged my dad to buy my first airplane ride at Chandler Field (now Hartsfield International Airport, Atlanta, Georgia). I can barely recall that moment, but the scene from the air is still imprinted very clearly in my mind. I cannot remember a moment in my life (except for a few months after my wife died) that I was not intensely interested in flying. I feel as though I was born wanting to fly!

Too young for World War Two, I devoured newspaper and newsreel accounts of our fighter aces. With her oldest son at war half way around the world in the Pacific Theater, I now realize how much it must have torn at my mother's heart each time I would tell her that I wished I was "old enough to be in the war flying fighters". Every Fighter pilot believes in his heart that if given the chance to fly combat, he will soon become an ace – no doubt about it! At Cannon AFB in 1965 as an F-100 pilot my dilemma was that F-100s were not being used in air-to-air combat in Vietnam; although I seem to recall a rare story where an F-100 pilot shot down a Mig over North Vietnam. Rather, F-100s were relegated mainly to ground attack in support of friendly forces in contact with the enemy, or to bombing enemy supplies, equipment and communication routes. *How does one become a fighter ace by attacking ground targets?*

Fighter pilots also know that they are always subject to that dreaded nemesis of all fighter pilots: assignment to an army unit as an Air Force Forward Air Controller (FAC) to control air strikes against enemy troops. I must be quick to add however, that in Vietnam FAC-ing again became a "respected occupation" as it had in World War Two and in the Korean War. If I remember my history correctly, *"FACs"* were used in balloons as early as the Civil War – and probably were known only as observers.

So, imagine my chagrin (and surprise) when in July 1965 at the Cannon AFB Officers' Club, I met a fellow pilot friend from another base who was visiting

Cannon AFB with carte blanch authority to select fighter pilots to become FACs and Air Liaison Officers (ALOs). They would be assigned to the U.S. Army's First Infantry Division – the "Big Red One" – at Fort Riley, Kansas. The First Infantry Division was scheduled for a September air and troopship deployment to Vietnam. Needless to say that after this surprise meeting, greeting, and exchange of "old flying stories" with my friend, I made myself as *"un-visible"* as possible. This friend would become the ALO for the First Infantry Division. He selected Cannon F-100 pilots to fill FAC and ALO positions with the Division's nine infantry battalions and three infantry brigades. Pilots throughout the Air Force would later be selected to fill liaison airlift and reconnaissance functions operating under command of the ALO.

My friend selected me to become one of his nine battalion FACs; notwithstanding my pleading that I had just returned from 90 days in Japan and Korea. He wasn't having any of it! "Sidewinder" would be the call sign for our FACs and ALOs assigned to the First Infantry Division. He was also selecting enlisted men and Non Commissioned Officers (NCOs) to fill other positions in the Air Force Tactical Air Control Parties (TACPs) assigned to the Division's units.

After arriving at Fort Riley on 21 August 1965, I was assigned as the battalion FAC for the 2nd Battalion, 2nd Infantry Regiment of the 3rd Brigade. The division's three brigades were assigned three battalions each which were given numerical designations of former historic army battalions and regiments. Thus, 2nd Battalion, 2nd Infantry Regiment, normally stated as "2nd of the 2nd," and written in brevity as "2/2" or "2/2 Infantry," was one of the 3rd Brigade's three battalions and in no way indicated a numerical position within the brigade. My assigned call sign would be: "Sidewinder 35".

Each battalion was assigned an Air Force FAC and enlisted ROMAD, which constituted a two-man battalion TACP. "ROMAD" was the Air Force acronym for radio operator, maintenance and driver for the Air Force FAC MRC-108 TACP communications jeep. (MRC–108 is pronounced as "Mark 108"). These ROMADs were selected from combat control units that precede units into combat to set up tactical control functions. They were usually parachute jump-trained and qualified. Combat Controllers hated the term "ROMAD". They felt that it did not describe their specialty training and in fact viewed the term as a putdown. I feel their "pain."

Airman Second Class (E-3) Keith L. Fabian of Rochester, Minnesota and a Combat Controller from the 3rd Aerial Port Squadron, Pope AFB, North Carolina, was assigned as the ROMAD for the 2/2's TACP. I was very fortunate to be paired up with Keith. He was a great guy and an outstanding ROMAD, very adventurous and always busy at something. After some intensive "grunt" training to include simulated ambushes and counter attacks, jungle warfare,

M-16 (automatic rifle) qualification and intensified tactical air control training, we were released to return to our homes for one week to say goodbye to our families. Those from other bases were likewise given short passes. Leaving my wife, Pat, and our sons, Norris and Robert, was always a heart rending experience for me regardless of the countless times we had gone through the "drill" before. I know it was for Pat too. But, if there ever was a real "trooper," she was one! Neither of us permitted our feelings to show.

Vietnam #2 – September 1965

Back at Fort Riley, we departed by contract air carrier for Oakland, California on 20 September 1965. The next day we sailed from the Navy Support Center, Oakland, California on the troopship, USS GENERAL W.A. MANN, for an "all-expense paid cruise and tour" to the beautiful port city of Vung Tau (Rhymes with "hung cow'), Vietnam and *beautiful resort areas* and points of interest further inland. On this second visit to Vietnam I would not have the opportunity to visit Saigon, the "Pearl of the Orient"! Sailing under the Golden Gate Bridge brought some serious reflecting. When, or will I ever see it again? I always had similar thoughts regarding my family whenever I was deployed away from home. Sailing under the Golden Gate also brought some reflective thoughts about my Dad and the thoughts he must have had as he sailed from New York Harbor (and the Statue of Liberty) bound for "The Great War," on 20 June 1918 aboard the HMS EURIPIDES. We sailed in the light of day with hardly a concern for our security and none for enemy submarines. Dad departed in the middle of the night under blacked-out conditions, maximum security, and subject to surprise submarine attacks.

On board the USS MANN, officers were assigned one-man quarters (barely larger than the bunk we slept in) while our enlisted troops were quartered below in three or four tiered hammocks with barely enough room to navigate through the area. Of course in your bunk you were up against the bottom of the bunk above you. Really close quarters. However, the chow was great! (I recalled the great Navy chow I had at the Atlanta Naval Air Station Mess when I was a Marine Air Reserve private). There were movies, chapel services and the usual amenities to keep the troops *happy* aboard ship. I would spend hours up on deck at the rail (never got seasick – only homesick) looking out over the sea. The weather was great for our sailing. Upon entering the South China Sea, the ocean surface was glass smooth. You could see flying fish leap out of the water and sail for a short distance. Sometimes they would just come up to the surface and flutter along for several feet seemingly trying to match the speed and direction of the USS MANN. Their wake would leave ripples for great distances that would seem to linger forever on the glass-flat surface. The sun setting over the horizon on that glassy sea was a beautiful sight: blue, red yellow and orange; all reflecting off the undisturbed surface. At night in my bunk lying against the steel hull of the ship, the gentle and slow roll in one direction seemed as it would never stop. When it seemed that the ship would surely capsize, it would slowly reverse and seem to roll wanting to capsize in the other direction. I knew better of course, but after an hour or so listening for the "abandon ship" signal, I would finally drop off to sleep. During the daytime, jogging on the upper deck was a favorite pastime of the "grunts". I tried it a few times. Jogging on a rolling, pitching "track" was interesting.

We arrived at Vung Tau, Vietnam on 9 October. The next day we were airlifted by Marine CH-43 helicopters to Bien Hoa Air Base (pronounced "Ben Wah") a few miles northeast of Saigon. Although not overly fond of helicopters as a means of transportation, for this segment of our trip, I considered them to be a blessing for we had been told that the road from Vung Tau to Bien Hoa was not secure. On 21 October, we were moved to a nearby "secure" staging area for in-country indoctrination and more "grunt" training. Our 3rd Brigade formed up on 25 October to convoy to our new home away from home: Lai Khe (pronounced "Lie Kay"), a rubber tree plantation with a deteriorating, short, dirt (laterite) airstrip just east northeast of the village of Ben Cat (pronounced like it's spelled). Ben Cat is 30-35 miles north of Saigon on National Highway 13. Keith and I, in our FAC jeep, moved into our assigned convoy position with our battalion. As the convoy was clearing the city limits of Saigon one mortar round was lobbed at the convoy several vehicles ahead of Keith and me. Soon afterwards, some light and sporadic sniping occurred. Needless to say this impeded the convoy somewhat. The mortar round (some say it was a land mine) destroyed a civilian bus and wounded a South Vietnamese soldier and several civilians. As we passed the destroyed bus I noted that it was nothing but twisted, grotesque junk. I was one very much "puckered" FAC for the remainder of the trip to Lai Khe. But I suspect some others were too.

The Brigade established its headquarters in an old French rubber plantation building on the north side of Highway 13 across from the airstrip. The 2nd of the 2nd Battalion made its headquarters deeper into the rubber trees on the south side of Highway 13 away from the airstrip and Brigade headquarters. Establishing a base camp at Lai Khe was an interesting experience. The battalion troops seemed constantly amused (with some snickering) at seeing the two Air Force types feverishly digging their "FAC hole" (Air Force for fox-hole). Keith and I filled sand bags, prepared our "fortified" dugout, and erecting our teepee-styled FAC tent over our new home. Our dugout was barely large enough for two GI cots each side of the radios and small table located in the center. Much of our gear and equipment was stored in the jeep's trailer. At night I sleep with my M-16 by my side (loaded); and of course my loaded 38 cal. revolver. Word was going around that Air Force FACs were a Viet Cong (VC) priority target because of the havoc FACs could bring down on them from the sky. We were not hard to find! We definitely stood out among the army grunts. Everything about us was notably different. Our FAC jeep bristled like a porcupine with its multiple antennae and it was the only jeep around with a canvas top. Our tent was easily singled out by its round teepee-style as opposed to the rectangular army general-purpose type tents. Our fatigues were brilliantly "decorated" with the regulation blue nametag, aeronautical badge, and rank insignia. *Great for combat!* Not the subdued style that the army used. Eventually (much later) we were authorized the subdued style accruements. Our Division Air Force ALO was later able to obtained authorization, through Air Force channels, for TACP personnel to wear the "boonie" hat (Australian style) much to the chagrin of the army brass and personnel – after all it "wasn't regulation!" As I was saying, the Army grunts were amused at Keith's and my "preparations for war". That is – until one night we received a few mortar rounds in the camp and began to receive sniper fire. The next day's activities found the 'grunts" digging deeper foxholes, and piling additional sand bags around bunkers. The enemy had gotten their attention!

Except for the occasional mortar rounds and some sniping, things were routinely quite around the base camp for about three weeks until 12 Nov 1965. Things were not the same following that fateful day! My eagle-eyed hindsight tells me I should have kept a diary – which was really forbidden "for security reason". The following events are told only as I remember them (with a few notes) plus a bit of memory jogging courtesy of some reports, written articles, military orders, my FAC friends and my Combat Controller (ROMAD) friend Keith.

"Bau Bang Bust!"

NOTE: My following story appeared in the 2008 Forward Air Controllers Association, Inc. book "Cleared Hot – Forward Air Controller Stories from the Vietnam War" Page 88. (I've done some editing to this version for "My Story..."). grp

Ap Bau Bang, South Vietnam, 10-12 November 1965: Recollections from my experience as an F-100 Pilot of the 523rd Tactical Fighter Squadron (TFS), Cannon AFB, NM; temporarily assigned as a U.S. Air Force Forward Air Controller (FAC) to the 2nd Battalion, 2nd Infantry, 3rd Brigade, US First Infantry Division, South Vietnam, September 1965 – February 1966).

The 2/2 Infantry Task Force – consisting of two of the battalion's companies and augmented by a few cavalry tracked APCs (armored personnel carriers) with a top-mounted 50 caliber machine gun, and a few field artillery 105 millimeter Howitzers – would conduct a three-day, two-night road clearing and securing operation. The operation would extend north from our base camp at Lai Khe along Highway 13 for about five to six miles though the village of Ap Bau Bang (pronounced as it's spelled). This was to be the battalion's contribution toward making Highway 13 safe for a unit of the Fifth ARVN

Division (Army of the Republic of Vietnam) moving north through our area on November 12th. The 2/2 battalion commander would command the Task Force. The tasks were: clearing the highway of likely ambush sites, removing or destroying mines, sweeping and clearing the area a few hundred yards along each side of the highway. According to an article I read years later in a veterans publication, it had the battalion command post with the battalion commander and his operations officer moving with Company A. Company B would be the advance company north and ahead of the battalion command post. Airman Fabian and I with our FAC jeep would move with the command element. The Battalion Commander had already made it very clear that he wanted "his FAC" by his side. (NOTE: My recollection has Company A as the advanced force just north of Ap Bau Bang and Company C containing the battalion command post element, to which Keith and I were assigned, just southwest of Ap Bau Bang.. My comments will address these units thusly with Keith and my involvement *as I remember them*).

November 10th would be our first day out. The morning came! In his usual thorough manner and adventurous spirit, Keith had everything prepared early and in order. We assumed our position in the convoy near the task force commander; then soon left the "security" of our base camp and ventured out into acknowledged "enemy territory" – especially during the hours of darkness. The enemy was out there! Where? How many? Who, among the Vietnamese people we encountered, were the enemy? We were soon to find out. The "enemy" would choose to contest this daytime excursion and territorial intrusion. It would prove to be the 2/2's first "really big" firefight since arriving in Vietnam; thus, the first major engagement with the enemy for the 3rd Brigade in its AO (Area of Operations). As we headed out onto Highway 13 and east into the boonies, my mind raced with thoughts related to this, *my first combat experience.* What am I doing here!? I'm a fighter pilot! How would I perform in hand-to-hand combat against a fanatic VC? Will my M-16 fail at a crucial time? (They had been known to fail in combat). Would I meet the challenge? I was out of my element – the comfortable, familiar cockpit of the F-100. I was a fish out of water; a Partridge out of his pear tree! Such thoughts permeated my mind as we ventured out that November morning. Highway 13! I am not superstitious...I am not...am not!

Since working with the "grunts" of the Big Red One, my esteem for the front line, bayonet charging, grenade-tossing, mud-slogging soldier has escalated off the scale. I think that I should add here for the un-informed, that the term "grunt" is not a derogatory term. It is used almost reverently in recognition of the rough, tough, close-quarter fighting, miserable conditions and personal hardships relegated to the infantryman. As for "personal" and "close," it doesn't get much more personal and close than hand-to-hand combat. My experience with The Big Red One and my research into my father's World War One service as an infantry rifleman in the trenches of France with the 38th Infantry Regiment, Third Division, have heightened my admiration for the "grunt, dogface, gravel cruncher, yank, doughboy," or whatever label you choose to apply.

The road clearing continued along the route and in the bush. Wherever the battalion commander went, he wanted *"his"* Air Force FAC and ROMAD with him. Keith was in constant contact with the Division's 3rd Brigade ALO at our base camp and the III Corps Direct Air Support Center (DASC) at Bien Hoa Air Base in case we needed instant air support. (The DASC is a joint Air Force and Army facility where air support request are coordinated between the Air Force and Army staff to determine if and or what resources would be committed against the requests from the field commanders). No sweat! We would have instant air support for the colonel if he (we) should need it. (III Corps – pronounced "Three Corps" – was one of four Army Corps areas in South Vietnam. It contained Saigon and extended south toward the delta and IV Corps; and north toward the mountains and plains and II Corps, and finally I Corps (pronounced "eye" corps) bordering North Vietnam and the DMZ).

Day number one and night one, November 10th came and went. No sweat, except for the tropical heat...and the constant 100% alert for the enemy. The next bush, the next curve, the next bridge, or the next moment may explode with hordes of Viet Cong (VC) and North Vietnamese Army (NVA) soldiers... bent on cutting me to pieces with their machine guns, rifle fire, grenades, mines and booby traps. "Ambush – the dreaded word! Not today, not November 10th. No sweat, yet!

November 11th came. It was very much a carbon copy of the previous day. Third Brigade medics and good-will civic-action teams spent those two days in Ap Bau Bang treating the villagers' illnesses and injuries, providing food and clothing, and caring for their other needs. We were now located roughly a thousand yards southwest of Ap Bau Bang in an old rubber tree plantation as nighttime approached. The trees had been cut down but the scrub brush had grown to about shoulder high. Company A was a few miles to the north. Night time approached. It was time to "circle the wagons" for the night.

Each element of the task force moved off the road to the west about 200 yards and was ordered to dig in. A few of the APCs with their 50 caliber machine guns mounted on top, and the 105 Howitzer cannons were positioned around our perimeter with their business-ends oriented outbound to repel any attack. Patrols moved outside the camp to provide security and early warning in the event of an attack. The camp perimeter was about 250 to 300 yards in diameter and probably contained about 500 personnel. Keith positioned our FAC jeep within 10 yards of the command element foxhole which was located near the center of the bivouac area. We dug shallow trenches under the rear of our jeep in order to be handy to the radios located back there. We also needed to be ready to roll if the army instantly decided to move out – which experience had taught us that they were inclined to do without so much as a thought of "consulting" with Keith or me. *How dare they!* Positioning ourselves under our jeep was not a great idea that I came to realize later. The jeep actually offered no protection and was in fact a desired and readily identifiable target as already indicted. A real "magnet" as we would soon discover. If the jeep had been blown up by a direct hit, so would have been Keith and me. The VC and NVA were well aware of what the FAC O-1 Bird Dog aircraft, FAC jeep, FACs and ROMADs meant for them: guns, bombs, rockets, and napalm via "special delivery" from the sky! Thursday night the 11th of November was hardly different from the previous night. One ear listened to the radios, our link to the outside world (base camp and the DASC); the other ear listened for strange noises; one eye open to catch the first sight of a VC or NVA infiltrator; and the other eye tried to get a little sleep. I thought the night would never end!

Daylight! Friday 12 November 1965, about 0600 hours (6:00 a.m.), Ap Bau Bang, Vietnam! "Made it through another night," I was thinking to myself. But I was very soon to have some serious doubts about the day! We had just begun to stir in preparation for the third day's road clearing activities. I was looking forward to getting back to base camp again; to a clean "comfortable" canvas GI cot; cold shower from a 55 gallon drum; cold shave from my helmet; and the relatively tame harassment of an occasional sniper or mortar round. "Crack!" Was that rifle fire? Another! Then one over there; and a few more in the other direction. Soon rifle fire was rapidly increasing in intensity as the sounds encircled the camp. Then the unmistakable sound of the "fifties" on the APCs. The sound of continuous rifle, machine-gun, and artillery fire was deafening. A large Fourth of July fireworks finale pales in comparison.

There was no doubt that we were going to have a different kind of day! It was determined later that we had become surrounded during the night by what the intelligence folks estimated to be at least a regiment of 1200 or more NVA regulars plus hard core VC – for an estimated total enemy force of about 2000. Not favorable odds for our augmented company of 500 or so troops. I understand that the enemy was initially discovered and engaged by one of our night patrols that had been posted beyond our perimeter for just such a purpose – to prevent an enemy surprise attack on the camp. I believe the patrol was able to return to our perimeter although overwhelmingly out numbered. I immediately proceeded to the battalion commander's position, ready to call for air support if he so requested. He was a no-nonsense commander, and a great tactical air advocate. I remember that he had a favorite nickname, which he used for most everyone: "Buster"! And he frequently addressed his FAC (me) as such. Our base camp at Lai Khe had already been informed. Keith was immediately on our radio talking with the TACP at 3rd Brigade Headquarters.

The intensity of the enemy attack continued to increase. (I once told my son, Robert, when we were watching a July 4th fireworks display finale close-up, that it was a token of what Bau Bang sounded like).

The battalion commander wanted tactical air support. That was Keith's and my cue! When our request was transmitted, we were informed that we would have fighters immediately; and that the Brigade FAC, Lieutenant Kent Owen (Sidewinder 32) along the 2/28 Battalion FAC Captain Robert (Bob "Herk") Herculson, were airborne and on the way in our only O-1 Bird Dog. We were receiving constant reports of the enemy assaults around the perimeter. They were using mortars, rockets, and direct frontal assaults. Our APC 50 cal. Gunners and 105 Howitzers were firing point-blank into the enemy in some cases. Of course the cannoneers had to lower their cannon muzzles down as low as possible. The enemy shifted their main thrust indiscriminately around our perimeter to keep us off balance and/or probe for a point in which to breach our defensive perimeter. The shoulder-high scrub brush made observation of the perimeter and the immediate area extremely difficult. In order for a FAC to direct air strikes against an enemy, he must be able to see precisely where the enemy or the target is located. I was constantly crawling between the battalion commander's foxhole and our FAC jeep where Keith was dug in monitoring all four radios. The only way I could observe any portion of the perimeter was to stand up on the hood of our FAC jeep. Even then observation was minimal at best. I did this a few times then realized what a fool thing it was. One could get *lead poisoning* that way! The air was full of flying, whizzing lead. The enemy continued to search for a point to breach the perimeter.

FAC-ing can be done most effectively from the air. No doubt about it! Although our FACs and ALOs had been trying to convince army commanders that FAC-ing from the air would be more effective and provide better support, many like my Battalion Commander, wanted their FAC on the ground within arm's reach. Kent and Herk soon arrived over our position. What a great feeling to have an airborne FAC over us who could see the situation from the air. Fighter aircraft were on the way! Kent was a superb FAC and seemed to have a masterful talent for the job. As the Battalion Commander would inform me of the heaviest concentration of enemy fire, I would relay the info to Kent. He would quickly identify the enemy positions, and dispense fighters on the target forthwith.

The attack seemed to intensify during the first two hours then remained steady and heavy for the remainder of the fight – which lasted until about noon (six hours). Shortly after the attack began, it was apparent that this was much more than a small VC harassment action. Our requests for immediate air support were quickly approved and fighters dispatched. We were informed that due to the intensity of the attack and overwhelming odds against us, that we would have all available tactical air diverted to us that morning. Tactical air strikes were scrambled or diverted almost continuously until the ground attack began to abate shortly after 11:00 a.m. Reinforcements from our 3rd Brigade Base camp at Lai Khe were unable to come to our aid. Company A that was north of Ap Bau Bang was unable to assist. I can tell you unequivocally to a man, that on the morning of 12 November 1965, those Air Force, Navy, Marine and Vietnamese pilots were the heroes of the day. But I want to quickly add: The troops on the perimeter, the APC and 105 Howitzer crews saved the day initially as they absorbed the brunt of the attacks around our perimeter. They too are well deserving of heroes' accolades. In my book, the planners who included those APCs and howitzers in the task force have my gratitude forever. Chances are that they were never acknowledged, or thanked, for their foresight. I wish I had been able to do personally.

Sometime during peak activity, Kent discovered an enemy position firing rockets at us from inside the southwest corner of a berm around Ap Bau Bang. The rocket launcher and crew were protected by the berm around the village. I advised the battalion commander. He was naturally reluctant to attack or fire on the position because of the certain destruction of the village. This was the very village where our medics and civic action teams were treating the villagers and handing out food, candy, and clothing the two previous days! Of course the NVA and VC had probably threatened the villagers if they assisted the Americans or disclosed their plans and positions to us. Before long the villagers began to evacuate Ap Bau Bang to the north and south along Highway 13. With the NVA and VC using their village as a fortification to launch rocket and mortar attacks against us, it was not difficult for the villagers to forecast their eventual fate. Unfortunately, as the villagers (now refugees) crowded the highway to the north and south, they were traversing ground to the east of our perimeter that was hotly contested at that moment. I'm sure that the NVA and VC used those refugees to great advantage.

During one moment when Keith and I were in our foxholes behind and partially under our jeep talking to the airborne FAC (Kent), there was a muffled explosion immediately in front of us. We were instantly covered with a cloud of dust and dirt. The shock and concussion of the explosion left us momentarily bewildered. As the dust cleared, I noticed a twisted hunk of metal like a peeled banana peeling lying about a foot in front of my face. I tossed it over my head into our jeep in order to have it checked out later. I also noticed that the ground was disturbed about 15-20 feet in front of Keith and me. Keith discovered shortly thereafter that two of our four radios were not working. Then we noticed a half-inch deep dent in the steel body of our jeep only about four to six inches over my head. A dent that I would have been wearing on my forehead had it been six inches lower. There were seven holes in the canvas top to the jeep. It was immediately after this incident that Sidewinder 32 (Kent) told us that "they" were launching rockets at us from the southwest corner of Ap Bau Bang. Our FAC jeep stood out like the proverbial "sore thumb". With its canvas covered top on three sides and the antennae for the four radios erected, it was easily distinguished from all the other vehicles in the melee. Sometime during the battle I had received a small abrasion one inch below my left eye from an unknown source – like a grazed wound from a rifle round. One mortar round knocked the set out of Keith's ring! Too close! Thank you Lord!

NOTE: About 40 years later when Keith was visiting in my home we talked about the battle. He told me that he and I were unconscious for about five minutes after that rocket hit our position. *I had never known this.* He said it was confirmed by some Army guys he was talking with after the battle. All I remember was the explosion, the dust clearing and seeing the hunk of metal in front of my face. Keith said that the Army guys thought we were dead because we were not moving and were unresponsive.

Later back at base camp I would have the Intelligence Section (S-2 in Army parlance) check out the twisted metal object that I tossed into the FAC jeep following the explosion in our faces. They determined it to be the rocket motor housing from a rocket-propelled grenade (RPG). This particular rocket had an armor-piercing warhead. I jokingly, but somewhat seriously, commented that it had all of my initials, "GRP," but out of proper sequence; otherwise it might have *connected.* The forward directed "shaped" charge of the armor piercing round had dug into the ground when it detonated. If it had been an anti-personnel warhead, it would have hurled shrapnel in every direction and I'm sure I would not be telling this story. Thank you again, Lord!

In the heat of the battle, Keith was a very busy ROMAD. In addition to our tasks with the air strikes, he also found time to assist the battalion Forward Observer (artillery) with communications and target coordinates. We also needed "Dust-off" (call sign of medical evacuation helicopters) to evacuate the wounded. Keith assisted in coordinating the requests for Dustoff helicopters. The NVA and VC loved the Dustoffs and the "Jolly Greens" (Air Force rescue helicopters for downed pilots). They were sitting ducks; extremely vulnerable targets when low, slow, hovering, or on the ground picking up the dead, wounded or survivors. The Red Cross markings on the unarmed Dustoffs were a dead (no pun intended) give away for the NVA and VC gunners. A Dust-off helicopter arrived but was driven off with heavy enemy ground fire several times before being able to get inside of our perimeter. In my book, those Dustoff and Jolly Green crews are another group of professionals who never receive the just rewards for their heroic deeds – except for the satisfaction of a job well done; and a life saved. The Dustoff eventually made it through the ground fire to a pickup point about 40-50 yards or so from our FAC position. Keith, with full knowledge of the Dustoff's magnetic attraction for heavy ground fire, retrieved several wounded soldiers and placed them aboard the Dustoff helicopter. Eyewitnesses to his deeds stated that he performed with no regard for his own safety. I recommended Keith for a Silver Star for his actions on that day. It was eventually awarded to him.

That rocket launcher from Ap Bau Bang had been tearing us up. Other prime targets were our APCs with their 50 caliber machine guns and the 105mm Howitzers. The NVA and VC were so close and numerous that the APC gunners and Howitzers were forced to fire point blank into the advancing enemy. I witness the destruction of one of our APCs. It was a few yards west of my FAC position and I happened to be looking at it the instant it was hit by an enemy rocket. The blast and inferno it created are indescribable. The top hatch blew off and went spiraling straight up in a flat spin for about 30 feet, then as though attached by a bungee rope, spiraled right back down onto the APC. I could see directly into the APC. It was a furnace – white hot! It burned for 45 minutes or so. I believed that the driver and gunner could not have survived the inferno. However, years later I learned that they did survive.

The battalion commander decided that it was time to take out that rocket launcher and mortars; Ap Bau Bang notwithstanding. The village's fate was sealed either with or without the villagers' collusion. It was them or us! He obtained the authorization and gave the word which I relayed to Kent and "Herk" overhead in our O-1 Bird Dog. You could almost detect the sound of relief (maybe glee) in Kent's voice when I told him the battalion commander wanted that rocket launcher taken out. As I said before, the villagers knew it was only a matter of time before we would have to strike the village. The battalion commander had delayed as long as he dared in order to give the villagers as much time as possible to evacuate.

Within minutes Kent had a flight of F-100s over Ap Bau Bang – and the rocket launcher. Air strikes were not normally flown over the heads of, or toward, friendly forces in order to minimize the chance of friendly fire incidents. This air strike would have to be flown over the village toward our position to the southwest because of the protection afforded the rocket launcher and crew by the berm – if attacked from any other direction. And a "long bomb" would send the bomb over the berm sailing toward our position. Kent identified the launcher position to the F-100 flight and received their acknowledgement of the location. After being "cleared in hot" by Kent, the lead F-100 pilot smartly rolled in and splattered a napalm bomb squarely on top of that rocket launcher and crew. I suspect the launcher crew suffered more than just a splitting headache. Kent then went to work on the mortar positions and enemy troops in the village. It seemed pretty much downhill for the enemy from that point on. It was a "screwy" war. The NVA and VC knew they had a sanctuary in that village – even if only for a short time – due to our reluctance to destroy a village.

Willing or unwilling villager assistance to the NVA and VC smacks in the face of U.S. Army troops in the village the previous day providing medical and civil action aid to the elderly, ill, lame and children.

At one time about mid-morning – the enemy almost breached our perimeter. I expected to see swarms of charging NVA and VC overrunning our position at any moment. And me with no bayonet training although I had an M-16 bayonet, a Japanese copy that I had purchased sometime before because I was not issued one. Anyway, what does an F-100 pilot need with a bayonet? Why, I might cut myself! I mentioned earlier that our APCs were out near our perimeter. Suddenly I was surprised to see an APC backing through the brush from the southwest toward Keith's and my foxhole. The gunner was still firing away. I'm sure he was probably firing near point blank range although I could see very little because of the brush. Keith and I scrambled out of our foxhole to avoid permanent APC track marks on our fatigues. We figured our jeep was a goner! Fortunately, the APC began to move forward again toward the perimeter, still firing away. Due to the high brush I was unable to see any distance at all. For all I know, the NVA and VC could have been just beyond the brush. Of course the gunner and driver of the APC could see them. I'm sure they had to back-track to keep the enemy at bay and from getting behind them; which was Keith's, my, and the battalion command element's positions at that time.

Kent did an outstanding job of controlling those air strikes around our perimeter. There were no more beautiful sights that morning than seeing those fighters unloading their guns, bomb, napalm, and rockets around the perimeter. I believe, and the task force troops believe (they said so), that without tactical air we would have been easily overrun that morning. Kent was one of our best FACs; quick witted, very adept at making order out of chaos; and constantly on the radio. His constant dialogue maintaining control and making order of the fiasco quickly earned him the affectionate title: "Motor-mouth!" It was a comfort and delight hearing him on the radio working those fighters. Eventually Kent had to return to Lai Khe to refuel his O-1. He transmitted to me that he would see me back at base camp. I guess things were not all that certain yet and I made the comment: "If I get back". He chided me for the remark and I realized how defeatist it must have sounded. It was an uncomfortable feeling without Sidewinder 32 overhead even if only for a brief time. Our base camp at Lai Khe was only about 5-7 miles away so Kent was soon back overhead. Shortly after 1100 hours (11:00am) the action began to diminish and by 1200 hours it was over!

The last round had been fired. Everything was now quiet. The enemy's numerous assaults had been repelled and the battle damage was being assessed. We still had work to do – the road clearing. I suddenly realized that I was a little queasy. I sat down by a bush for a few moment and remembered that I had not so much a breathed a prayer during the whole battle – in fact I had no time to be really frightened until now! Now in this moment of quietness, I offered prayers of praise and thanks to God for Keith's and my safety, the safety of the task force, and for the victory. In the immediate area there were 198 enemy dead and six captured. Aircraft over the area reported many more enemy dead around and beyond the perimeter. I either read or heard later that enemy casualties were estimated to be 500 plus. We had 16 friendlies killed and 38 wounded. A later report put our total wounded at about 100. While discussing post battle matters with the battalion operations officer (S-3 in army talk) at his foxhole, he looked at me and said that I needed to see the medic. My right ear was bleeding. It turned out to be only a scratch on my ear but blood was in and around my ear and on my neck. The next day and for several days afterward, my ear and neck were black and blue. Apparently shrapnel from that RPG had been closer than I thought.

After cleaning up our area and breaking camp (of what was left to break), Keith and I prepared to assume our position in the convoy for return to base camp. We moved out toward Highway 13 but had to hold up to allow Fifth ARVN Division units to pass through north bound. Memory has faded a bit but it seems they were an hour or two passing through. I do not know if they knew what they had just missed; but they surely did when they passed through the smoldering remnants of the village of Ap Bau Bang. Intelligence reports a few days later (probably from prisoner interrogation) stated that the NVA thought they were attacking a much smaller ARVN unit rather that the larger and heavier armed US Army units.

It was almost dark before we were finally formed in convoy on Highway 13 for the trip back to Lai Khe. Concern was expressed that we would be caught out after dark on the highway prior to reaching base camp. Not a recommended predicament! It was road clearing all over again; but this time we were clearing our own way and not for the ARVN. Anti-ambush patrols had to be sent ahead. Nighttime caught us but we didn't stop. No circling the wagons tonight. We pressed on painstakingly slow. The convoy halted many times for what seemed an eternity while potential ambush sites and possible mine were neutralized. The jungle was so close to the highway in places that when we stopped, branches hung over into our jeep. If an NVA or VC soldier had sprung out of the jungle he would have been in our jeep before I saw him. We were hoping that they were all holed up somewhere licking very serious wounds with no time or stomach for a counter attack. We arrived at Lai Khe around midnight without incident. Needless to say the late night arrival was a glorious relief and event. My wife, Pat, was back at our home on Cannon AFB, Clovis, New Mexico with our two boys, Norris and Robert. Knowing that the story of Ap Bau Bang would get back to her, I wrote her a little of the details and tried to assure her that I had indeed only received a very minor "scratch" from the encounter. I was afraid that if word reached her from other sources it would have me critically wounded and near death.

About the time I was writing her she was writing me. Each of us was unaware of the other's letter. Our letters crossed in transit (probably somewhere over the Pacific or South China Sea). Her letter stated that during last Wednesday night's church service (10 Nov '65, Central Baptist Church, Clovis, New Mexico) our pastor, Dr. Carl Scott, suddenly stop his presentation almost in mid-sentence and said something to the effect: "You all know that we have one of our very own in Vietnam: Captain Partridge. We have no idea what danger he may be in at this very moment. But I have a definite feeling that we should have special prayer for his safety right now!" It is not so startling or out of character to have special prayers for congregational members away in service or for others with special needs. But consider this. Dr. Scott felt this special need on my behalf at that moment and interrupted his presentation to offer an intercessory prayer for me. The time would have been about 6:30 p.m. Clovis time on Wednesday evening 10 November 1965. Vietnam is 13 hours ahead of Clovis, New Mexico. That would have put Dr. Scott's prayer for me at about 7:30 a.m. the morning of 11 November Ap Bau Bang time.........right in the middle of our operation and less than 24 hours before the Ap Bau Bang battle. Reflect on the close proximity of the RPG rocket explosion and the brief unconsciousness, the scratch on my ear, the grazing on my cheek and the dent in the jeep's steel body just over my head. Consider Dr. Scott not having offered up that special prayer for me at Central Baptist Church! Thank you God, Dr. Scott, and Central Baptist Church!

The Battalion Commander recommended me for, and I was awarded, the Silver Star and Purple Heart for the Ap Bau Bang Operation. Other FAC events: To the best of my knowledge, only one of our Cannon AFB FACs was later killed in Vietnam; shot down by enemy ground fire. One of our ROMADs (not from Cannon AFB) was killed in a night mortar attack on their base camp. One of our FACs from Cannon who was with him received multiple superficial shrapnel wounds that covered most of his body. There were many other close calls. The VC night ambushed our 1/16 Battalion when they were caught mired in the mud on a night convoy return to Lai Khe after a several-day search-and-destroy operation. Captain Loren "Al" Doddroe, the Air Force FAC assigned to the 1/16 was in the ambush with them. "Herk" and I in an O-1 controlled the air strikes and flare aircraft for their extraction. There were reports of hand-to-hand combat during the ambush. (See "Night Convoy Ambush!" below).

On a later mission "Herk" shot a hole in the wing of his O-1 with his M-16 while firing at targets on the ground. He was promptly awarded the dubious title of "Rifleman" after the popular TV series by that name and that era. Another of our FACs received a 30 caliber round through the floor and seat of his O-1 that lodged in his rear-end. Not serious; very lucky! Many FACs began sitting on their flak vest rather than wearing them after that incident. Another Sidewinder received a 50 caliber round in a similar manner but did not fare so well. The round went through the floor and seat of his O-1 and continued up through his body destroying bone, tissue, and organs stopping just short of his heart. He was conscious long enough to land at a nearby US Army airstrip where there just happened to be an army field hospital with a surgeon specializing in internal wounds. It was touch-and-go for days before he was declared stable enough to be relocated to a rear area hospital. He survived but with a seriously crippling wound. One Sidewinder FAC had a fuel line in his O-1 cockpit shot out that began dumping raw fuel down his back. At first he thought he had been shot and that the fuel running down his back was blood. After realizing the situation, he used his flight glove to plug the rapidly leaking fuel line and landed without further incident. These stories and others I'm sure, are stories unto themselves better left to be told by those FACs themselves.

"Night Convoy Ambush!"

My following story with some editing appears in the 2009 Forward Air Controllers Association, Inc. book "Cleared Hot – Forward Air Controller Stories from the Vietnam War" Book Two, page 110. Also the Distinguished Flying Cross Society books published by the Turner Publishing Company, 2000 edition and the 2004 second edition, pages 36 and 38 respectively.

Chon Thanh (pronounced Chon Tahn), South Vietnam 20 November 1965; a Night Convoy Ambush: It was an action-filled early evening on 20 November 1965 that would assure a sleepless remainder of the night. A Fellow FAC, Captain Robert J. "Herk" Herculson, Jr., of our 2/28 Battalion and I were flying an O-1 Bird Dog covering a late afternoon convoy extraction of First Infantry Division units. They were returning to base camp over a rough and muddy trail after days in the field for a search and destroy operation. I was flying front seat; "Herk" was following closely "in trail" in the rear cockpit. The Division's operation had been in the jungle several miles north of Ben Cat/Lai Khe, and west of the small village of Chon Thanh located on Highway 13 a few miles north of Ap Bau Bang. One of our FACs, Captain Loren A. Al Doddroe, was with his 1/16 Battalion during this operation and was now with them in the returning convoy. "Herk" and I were maintaining radio contact with Al as we "S-ed" above, and up and down the convoy as they worked their way back over a very rain soaked and muddy trail toward Chon Thanh; then they would proceed south down Highway 13 to Lai Khe, the base camp of the Third Brigade. However, things were not progressing smoothly in the convoy. Recent rains had created muddy bogs on the trail necessitating delays to extricate vehicles from the muck. As I recall, "Herk" and I had done a couple of hours of local visual reconnaissance (VR) prior to covering the convoy. Nothing of note was observed during the VR. It looked as if it would be an uneventful extraction to base camp except for the miserable, unrelenting mud. Nighttime was approaching though, and the convoy was anxious to reach base camp before nightfall. Night time was VC time!

The prospect of a night convoy was rapidly becoming a reality. There were abundant ambush sites along the trail. Still things didn't look too bad. The convoy was only two to three miles from Chon Thanh and Highway 13. However, there were many hutches along both sides of the trail which could mean trouble for the convoy as they moved through the village. Because of the convoy's delay in completing the extraction, "Herk" and I were spending more time over them than had been planned. Darkness would dictate a recovery at Bien Hoa Air Base forty miles away since the Lai Khe airstrip at brigade had no lights, and would be blacked out along with the rest of the camp. Nighttime had fallen; we could no longer see the convoy nor ground objects clearly. However we stayed a while longer "just in case" and to give our FAC and his grunts a little more peace of mind and moral support. Finally, it was necessary to depart in order to make Bien Hoa with our remaining fuel. We said so long to Al and told him we would see him at base camp tomorrow to compare notes and trade war stories.

About five minutes after we left the convoy, we got an urgent call that they were under attack; a night ambush! There was only one thing to do – a "no-brainer" – return to the convoy. "Herk" got on the brigade ALO (Air Liaison Officer) net, briefed them on the situation and requested air support with flare aircraft. Of course the brigade FAC, Kent W. Owen, was fully aware of the situation from monitoring the FAC radio net and had already initiated requests for air support. He also was in contact with Al in the convoy. The ambush started as the convoy approached the hutches lining both sides of the trail. The hutches apparently were either VC or they had routed and/or captured the occupants well in advance of the approaching convoy. It was total dark! Severe dark! Moonless! No existing light from any source except from ground fire. First to arrive were Army helicopter gunships. "Herk" and I had four marking rockets with which we were able to identify the targets for the gunships. While I concentrated on maintaining right-side-up maneuvering in the dark, firing the rockets and staying out of the way of the gunships that went lights-out on their attacks, "Herk" continued receiving target info from Al which he relayed to the gunships. Ground fire was coming from the hutches. Soon they were ablaze from the gunship attacks.

By now the fighters and flare ship had arrived. They went to work on the ambush with "Herk" and Al coordinating their efforts. Dodging gunships, fighters, flares, and flare ships in the dark made for a "dicey" sport. The flares really do a great job of turning night into day for a few moments. The flare ship was kicking out a near endless supply of parachute flares that seemed almost motionless as they slowly descended to burn out well before reaching the ground. However, the burning hutches were providing excellent lighting in the immediate target area and made great references for identifying targets to the fighters and gunships. More than once I would suddenly find a flare igniting directly in front of the O-1 and 'staring' me right in the face. I don't know the candlepower of those flares, but suffice it to say that a momentary eyeball-to-eyeball contact with one leaves you very much "blinded" and "feeling" your way around the sky for a few moments. I'm happy to report that we were always right side up after regaining my vision. Also, a couple of times we had near mid-air collisions with burned out flares floating across my windshield and barely visible for an instant in the light of the other flares. Other dark shadows were darting about the target area. Of course I made sure we were lighted with our navigation lights and rotating beacon. It was the better of two situations. Take our chances with ground fire or being run over by the fighters. For a while the outcome of the ambush seemed in serious doubt. Al reported that there was some very close fighting, firing at point blank range in some cases; and some hand-to-hand combat with VC who jumped upon convoy vehicles.

After flying more than an hour beyond the time we intended to stay, we had used up our Bien Hoa recovery fuel. "Herk" and I agreed that fuel remaining was now a critical factor. Bien Hoa was out of the question. Figuring only a few minutes of fuel remaining, Lai Khe was the only choice. I made Kent at brigade aware and asked that he have the brigade mortars fire flare rounds without delay to provide a quick "DF Steer" to the camp. ("DF" – direction finding). For some reason the Army never got those flare rounds off! After a little dead reckoning navigation I figured we were near the base camp. Base camp was totally blacked out for security reasons and there was nothing but total dark below me on a dark moonless night. Nothing was distinguishable. I finally spotted a pinpoint of light below me which luckily turned out to be the camp. Shortly afterwards I spotted Kent positioning his jeep at the approach end of the airstrip. I proceeded to make the first blacked-out night landing at Lai Khe for any of our FACs. Thanks to Kent it was a very uneventful blacked-out landing.

As the O-1 was being refueled, Kent climbed into the front cockpit and said that he would relieve me; and that "Herk" could brief him on the way back to the ambush site. They would then continue the convoy coverage. However, they were back at base camp shortly stating that the division units had broken the ambush and some elements were continuing their recovery now on Highway 13. Some elements of the returning convoy, and our FAC friend Al had to spend the night on the trail. It was a sleepless night! "Herk" and I each were awarded the Distinguished Flying Cross for this operation. Back at base camp and battalion, things very much resumed routine day and night operations.

3rd Brigade Base Camp

Flashback: In September when we arrived in-country, our FACs only had our MRC-108 jeeps. Therefore, we were relegated to ground FAC-ing. At Bien Hoa AB, the 19th Tactical Air Support Squadron (TASS), had a few FAC aircraft but in limited numbers. They were the Cessna O-1 Bird Dog used for FAC missions, in-country, O-1 check-outs and airborne FAC orientation. The 19th TASS would be the Air Force logistical and administrative support unit for all Air Force FAC and Air Liaison personnel assigned to the Army's First Division.

Previously on October 16th I was flying an O-1 FAC mission out of Bien Hoa on a preplanned strike against some "suspected" VC bunkers and trenches. It also doubled as my Airborne FAC evaluation mission before being declared in-country Airborne FAC qualified. Our Air Force Air Liaison Officer (ALO) to the First Division was in the rear cockpit as my evaluator. The strike flight was a Vietnamese flight of two F-5s. The strike went well and there was no enemy activity observed. I gave the flight leader the strike report and cleared them off our radio frequency. The final portion of our mission would be to land at the short clay and laterite Lai Khe airstrip to evaluate the runway condition and suitability for fixed-wing aircraft. The Army engineers had just finished renovating the airstrip after years of deterioration. Lai Khe would be the future home of the Division's 3rd Brigade and its three battalions; one of which Keith and I would be the battalion's Air Force TACP (the 2nd Battalion, 2nd Infantry Regiment). Thus, I became the first fixed-wing pilot to land on the newly renovated Lai Khe airstrip. No big deal, just another routine landing at an airstrip, about 1500 feet, carved out of a rubber tree plantation. But the Army engineers were there, along with their photographer, to greet us and celebrate the completion of their work.

On October 25 the 3rd Brigade had convoyed to Lai Khe. It was from Lai Khe that my two stories above originated. However, at that time we had no O-1 aircraft. They would arrive later in early November when each of the Division's three brigade TACPs got one O-1 aircraft each. The O-1 would be shared by the brigade's TACP ALO and FAC; and the FAC for each of the brigade's three battalions. At that time we would begin airborne VR (visual reconnaissance) of the Brigade's AO (area of operations) which included a portion of the infamous "Iron Triangle". I believe it got it name because of the amount of "iron" (bombs) that were dropped in the area. We would control preplanned air strikes for the brigade and battalion commanders planned ground operations; and immediate air strikes should our ground troops experience a TIC (troops-in-contact with the enemy).

Around the base camp at night the darkness would sometimes light up with tracers traversing the sky. Sometimes at night when enemy activity was suspected around the perimeter, or sniper fire intensified, the battalion commander would request me to order a flare-ship – usually a World War Two vintage C-47, call sign "Spooky". Spooky would orbit the area and drop flares until things quieted down. It's readily apparent why the flare-ship is called "Spooky". With those parachute flares hanging in the sky slowly drifting to the ground and oscillating in their chutes, ground shadows would sway back and forth with the oscillation. "Spooky!" Many a shadow has "bit the dust" at the hands of a nervous "grunt" on the perimeter. When a ground commander would be conducting a night operation, he could request gunship support to quiet a trouble spot or discourage an enemy attack. Gunship support was used regularly for outpost support at night. The gunship was also a C-47 known as "Puff the Magic Dragon". It was equipped with side-firing mini-guns (multi-barreled machine guns) and 40 millimeter cannon grenades. The pilot aimed and fired the guns electronically. They produced an unbroken stream of steel that was absolutely devastating; an awesome sight particularly at night where the tracers produced a long fiery-like tongue, thus the name "Puff the Magic Dragon". I never had the occasion to control "Puff," but have seen them in operation through photos, videos and heard their stories. They were absolutely loved by ground commanders.

On other occasions, the artillery would strike up their H & I (harassment and interdiction artillery firing into known enemy areas). It was supposed to "harass" the enemy and keep them from getting adequate rest. But I can tell you it "harassed" me as much as it was supposed to harass the enemy. I remembered my Dad telling me that he could hear and see artillery rounds as they passed overhead when he was in the trenches of France during World War One. It true! You can see them. On one occasion I remained overnight night at Brigade Headquarter. Just outside of the window where I was sleeping there was an eight-inch cannon mounted on tracks (that's an eight inch-diameter artillery round). Sometime during the night that cannon was fired-off! I think I came straight up horizontally about two feet out of that bunk! Never before had, never since have, I witnessed such an explosion and concussion!

Every year the US forces would be ordered to unilaterally cease fire for the New Year holidays in the hope that it would lead to reciprocation by the enemy. There were always violations by the enemy and the cease fire never held. January 1966, the Army artillery troops invited us FACs to come up to the firing line where they had their 105 millimeter Howitzers to fire the first rounds ending the cease fire. I got to fire off the first round from one of the Howitzers. The resumption of the war was *entirely my fault!*

One day Keith came back to our FAC tent with a small dog. Against my better judgment, I let him keep it. After all, it was a diversion from the daily threat that we lived with. I think he got it from a local Vietnamese in Ben Cat; probably from one of the venders at the daily open air market along Highway 13. Not long afterwards the dog bit him and he had to undergo the series of painful rabies injections. The dog was never seen around the camp again. Our Brigade TACP senior NCO also acted as a quasi "First Sergeant" for all of our TACP enlisted troops. He had bought a small monkey. You would find that monkey sitting on his shoulder as he went about his duties around camp. As far as I know the monkey never caused any trouble. But I didn't then and still don't care for monkeys. I have no idea what he did with it when we returned to the US. He was a true "scrounger-in-chief" as are most senior NCOs. They can generally come up with anything you need, may need – or not need. "Midnight requisitions" are quite often a favored means of "shopping".

The Battalion Commander decided to order a helicopter to do a VR over an area of his battalion responsibility. He wanted his artillery forward observer (FO) and me to accompany him in the helicopter. We lifted off and after a few minutes of VR-ing from about 500 feet, we heard a single "pop". The pilot announced that we had taken a hit from small arms ground fire. He searched for a clearing away from the area and landed for a safety check. After checking over the helicopter, he said there was a small caliber hole in the underside but no other damage. We always flew with the sides door open for better VR-ing. If we had been in a turn, that round could very easily have come through the open door.

Another time I was alone VR-ing an area south of our base camp in our O-1. We normally flew our AOs alone as we didn't have the manpower for two-FAC VR except on special occasions. Our instructions were to do VR at 1500 feet. However, we did most of our VR-ing at 1000 feet for better possibility of detecting disturbances in the jungle environment or enemy troop activity; sometimes going down to 500 feet. A few FACs would go even lower briefly. For example, on this particular VR I noticed a small stream hardly more than three feet wide running through a grassy clearing for about two miles. There was about 30 yards – more or less – each side of the stream to the edge of the jungle. Nothing seemed unusual but after VR-ing the jungle area and seeing nothing (remember it's usually a three-tiered canopy jungle), I decided to go down and skim the grass along the stream for the length of the clearing. This would give me a better look into the jungle. It's generally easier to see through the jungle under the trees rather than down through the triple canopy. Before I went down, I called the Brigade TACP with my position and informed them that I was doing down for some close VR work. I called just in case I was a no-show later, or needed some help and was unable to get them on the radio. We flew with our side windows open in order to better hear ground fire, should we be fired at. As I was skimming along the grass looking left and right into the jungle, I heard the tell-tale "crack" of a single rifle shot. I continued briefly to get away from the area, then pull up and did a 180 degree turn back to toward where I heard the shot – descending to the weeds but this time at full throttle – maybe

130 mph. Doubling back over such a target is not recommended; but I was hoping to better pinpoint the source of the ground fire. Nothing! I pulled up and circled briefly; noted the area on my map and reported it to our Brigade TACP upon landing.

After my encounter at Ap Bau Bang, I had seen enough to reinforce my elation at having never been drafted to be a "grunt". There was a FAC at the Division Headquarters, Di An ("Z-Ahn") just north of Saigon. He did not get along well with our Division ALO. He was eager to get into the "field" away from his boss and also had a very good friend in the 3rd Brigade TACP. He asked me if I would be willing to swap assignments with him. After Ap Bau Bang I was very willing. The ALO agreed; probably delighted to get the thorn out of his side. The swap occurred sometime in early January of 1966 as I recall. I was now the Fighter Duty Officer at the USAF TACP located with the First Division Headquarters.

Air Force Liaison – Division Headquarters, Di An

There were two major events that I recall during my First Infantry Division Headquarters ALO-Fighter Duty Officer tour. One resulted in a tragic loss of an F-100 pilot shot down a few miles north of Saigon while supporting friendly ground troops in a firefight. He ejected after enemy ground fire had disabled his aircraft. It happened that he landed in a river nearby over which numerous Army helicopters were operating. The story was told that one helicopter crew observed his descent into the river and attempted to rescue him. The pilot was observed in the water appearing to struggle, either with his parachute or in an attempt to stay afloat. As the helicopter was hovering a few feet over him he went under. A short time later he resurfaced still struggling. This was not a rescue helicopter; rather, it was one of the Army's gunship or support helicopters and therefore did not have normal rescue equipment onboard. The helicopter descended low enough for a crewman hanging onto helicopter's skids to grab the pilot's pistol belt. As the helicopter started for the shore, the pistol belt broke. The pilot fell back into the river and the crewman jumped in after him. But the pilot disappeared under the water; never to be seen again. The river was extremely muddy and visibility in the water was severely limited. It is not known if the pilot was injured. He was not wearing the GI issue type of web pistol belt, but a locally made-to-order, poor grade "leather" western style holster and belt. Most of us FACs and many Air Force aircrews had them personally made and wore them into combat.

Another event had a much happier ending. This one was one of many, sometimes daily, troops-in-contact situations, but it occurred a few miles northeast of Di An (Division Headquarters). Enemy anti-aircraft fire brought down another F-100. Word was that it was a Quad-Fifty anti-aircraft gun that was really giving the F-100s supporting the friendlies a bad time. The Quad-Fifty would be a 360 degree revolving, swivel-mounted, anti-aircraft gun containing four 50 caliber machine guns fired simultaneously by one gunner. The 50 caliber round is about ½ inch in diameter, and the Quad-Fifty throwing up four streams of 50 caliber steel containing tracers and armor piercing explosive heads, presents quite a formidable barrage – something to be avoided as a serious health hazard. Sometimes you encounter a good gunner – or one who gets lucky – in spite of the pilot's "jinking" to avoid the ground fire. This day the F-100 pilot encountered one of those gunners. Fortunately, he ejected near our troops and they were able to get to him before the bad guys did. He received no serious injuries. During the course of the battle, our troops captured the Quad-Fifty that shot him down. A few days later, the troops presented the Quad-Fifty to the pilot's squadron as a jester of their appreciation for the air support the squadron provided on that day.

Our portion of III Corps was relatively safe at that time – "relatively safe" – meaning *relative!* As the war years continued, so did increasing VC and NVA antiaircraft capability. Remember I was there September 1965 to February 1966 for the initial massive buildup of US troop in the war. All Corps areas became increasingly "hotter" as the war continued, with some FAC stories in North and South Vietnam, Laos and Cambodia that would curl your hair and whiten your knuckles. The 58,000 plus names on the "Wall" in Washington DC can attest to the eventual cost. I was one of the more fortunate participants! PTL!

"Home Again, Home Again – Jiggidy, Jiggidy Jog!"
Along about mid-February 1966, our TDY nearing completion, we began our return to Cannon. My last ever military flight as pilot of the O-1/L-19 Bird Dog was on February 18th, 1966 with 220 total hours. These hours included my 56 combat missions, which qualified me for the Air Medal plus one Oak Leaf Cluster (25 missions required for each award). Many FACs acquired hundreds of missions. The First Infantry Division would award me, along with other members of our TACP, the Bronze Star for the time served with the Division. They would also award the Army Valorous Unit Award to all serving with the Division during this period. The Republic of Vietnam (South) would award all of us the Vietnamese Cross of Gallantry and the Civil Actions Honor Medal. Everyone serving in Vietnam was awarded the Vietnam Service Medal and the Vietnam Campaign Medal. A sad commentary on the Vietnam Campaign Medal: the pendant is adorned with a small metal scroll inscribed with the beginning year of the war, 1960, a dash then a blank space. The blank space was intended for the ending year of the war to be embossed in the blank space – which would have occurred had we won the war. *We could have won it!* It is not my intent to be coy or humble, but there are those who received the same awards as I did and who did much more remarkable and heroic feats. I am grateful.

Transportation back to the States was by commercial air and I had another chance to briefly visit some of the Pacific islands along the way. I can't begin to describe for you the elation at being reunited with my family again. Many times while in Vietnam with the First Infantry Division, I thought of my Dad with the Third Division, 1918, in the trenches of France. He endured much more miserable conditions plus air, artillery and enemy troop attacks. Yet he came home having been exposed to mustard gas and with only two medals to the best of my knowledge: The Victory Medal and the Occupation Medal. *He won his war!* I came home having worked in an Agent Orange environment and with a handful of medals but without a win! Ironic!

While the nine of us FACs from the 523rd TFS at Cannon were away in Vietnam, the 523rd was reassigned to Clark AB, Philippines to rotate to Vietnam; or possibly be assigned to a base in Vietnam. I don't recall the actual disposition of the 523rd. They may have been deactivated. Meanwhile, back at Cannon, pilots of our Vietnam US First Infantry Division TACPs were assigned to the 524th TFS in absentia, effective November 19th 1965, as more or less a temporary in-place move until we returned to Cannon. Upon my return to Cannon, I resumed flying the F-100 and T-33 awaiting further assignment to Luke AFB, Arizona. My friend Al Doddroe and I would be assigned to Luke in May and our friend, "Ken" McDaniel would be assigned to Vietnam flying the F-100. Once more my family and I would soon be on the road again – to Arizona. On this move we would traveled by Oldsmobile "Starfire". Norris was now 15 and Robert 8 years old. So long Cannon!

*****

CHAPTER FOURTEEN
LUKE AFB, Glendale, Arizona; The Valley of the Sun – F-100
(1966-1968)

"My Best Assignment Ever!"

Headquarters 832nd Combat Support Group orders A-515 dated April 19, 1966 Cannon AFB assigned me to the 4517th Combat Crew Training Squadron (CCTS) Luke AFB, Phoenix, Arizona with a reporting date of May 23, 1966.

The trip to Luke Air Force Base from Cannon was uneventful as I recall – except for driving this absolutely beautiful country of ours; God Blessed America! My two years of flying at Luke, about 15 miles west of Phoenix, Arizona were unremarkable except for my love of flying and the F-100. It was fantastic flying: no accidents and no incidents to speak of; except for one very close call! More on that later in this chapter.

Pat developed an interest in cactus (or is it cacti) and rocks. She, Norris, Robert and I also discovered the thrill of desert exploration among the cacti, rocks, dry creek beds, mountains and Indian ruins. We all became "rock hounds;" me to a lesser degree. The desert is a beautiful, intriguing and dangerous place. It is especially beautiful when the sage is in bloom – purple! Reminds me of that old classic western song: "....When its roundup time in Texas and the bloom is on the sage...". Here in the Arizona desert Norris developed a budding interest in girls – especially one by the name of Gwenda (Gwen), who would later become his wife, life soul mate – and a great daughter-in-law! Gwen's Dad was also in the F-100 business; he was in aircraft maintenance and crash evaluation. Norris would graduate from Dysart High School at El Mirage, Arizona a few miles north of Luke on May 23rd 1968 and Gwen the following year. Robert would "enlist" in the Cub Scouts, his first *uniformed service*. He seemed to really enjoy his Cub activities, projects and outings. We attended the First Southern Baptist Church of Glendale where Norris announced his intention to be a Minister of the Gospel at the Sunday morning church service on August 28th 1966. Pat and I were very proud of him. Norris was very devout in his Christian faith. As a youth leader in church, he occasionally sang and did mini-sermons in the churches we joined. His first sermon was on December 25th 1966. He had a beautiful voice which, years later, he would pass on to his daughter, Tessa. I don't know where Norris got his amazing voice and piano talents, but I do know where his daughter, Tessa, got hers. Their voices were definitely professional quality and very pleasing to hear. Norris was also very athletic and years later his son, (also Robert – "Robert A"), would exhibit that talent as a pitcher on his high school baseball team; winning several awards – and pitching at least one no-hitter. Norris named his son Robert after his brother Robert.

Pat would become a "Gray Lady", a volunteer organization of wives who helped in the base hospital visiting patients; reading, writing, doing errands and other small tasks for them. "Puff" would become a member of the Partridge family here at Luke. He was born August 12, 1967, a solid black half-Siamese kitten (except for a small white tuff on his chest); one in a litter born to our across-the-back-yard neighbor's cat. Robert and his neighborhood friends had watched Puff and his siblings from their very beginning; each choosing their favorite. One day I was sleeping when I was awakened by this tiny black thing sort of wobbling around on my chest. Its eyes were barely open trying to focus on that monster of a thing that it was crawling around on. Robert was begging to keep it; and he had some help from his Mom and Norris. What was a Dad to say against such overpowering forces? So Puff went back to its mom to grow a bit more before being adopted into the Partridge family. After adopting Puff into our family our doctor neighbor was put-upon to identify Puff as a *him* or *her*; after all a doctor should know. Right? *Wrong!* Soon thereafter Puff would definitely identify himself as a *him*. "Puff Partridge" we would shout at him when he misbehaved. His brother, Sam, with true Siamese markings, was adopted by our next door neighbors. Puff and Sam grew up next door to each other and were an endless source of fun and entertainment as we watched them scuffle, chase each other around our yards and up and down the trees; mostly up. I don't think I have known a cat that could get down out of a tree unassisted. He would usually slip and grab a limb dangling by his front paws and yelling for someone to get him down. Why is it that a cat can climb a tree or pole but can never get down? One of life's great mysteries! We made sure Puff became a house-cat and he seemed well pleased. A more pampered cat could not be imagined. He was a member of the family – literally – and went where we went. In my next life, I want to be a "Puff" in a Partridge family. Norris and Robert would occasionally announce that Pat and I treated Puff better than we treated them. Puff would endure his pampered, kingly and *independent* life in the "family" for 20 years before he gave up the last of his nine lives on August 23rd 1987.

For the first time in my Air Force Career my family had a stay-at-home husband and father: no alerts, no extended TDYs and deployments away from home, usually home for dinner each night and home to enjoy the weekends together. There were, of course, the occasional night flights and cross-countries. One more thing of note was our befriending a Middle-Eastern Air Force officer who was assigned to Luke on a foreign exchange program. His name and country will go unmentioned obviously to protect all parties, especially him and his family. I will simply refer to him as Major "H". All of these things were to become cherished times and memories together.

I acquired a Volkswagen "Beetle" after arriving at Luke. Whenever our time would permit, Pat, Norris, Robert and I would pile into our red "Beetle" and

251

drive off into the desert for exploring God's beautiful (and potentially deadly) desert artistry – always making sure we had food, water and signaling devices. (At that time cell phones were things of science fiction movies). The Beetle was great for that exploring. It had no radiator to worry about; was high off the ground to accommodate large rocks, ruts and sand; had a manual transmission and was very rugged. It did not overheat in the desert, accommodated dry river beds easily, climbed steep grades and bounced over large rocks. We enjoyed it immensely. I was introduced to a variety of cacti in numerous unintentionally close and personal encounters on their "turf"! *They usually made their point!* Pat and I often discussed our likely retiring in Arizona. (Never happened!)

On one or two occasions we took Major "H" with us into the desert for cactus hunting. When we found a small cactus, or cactus skeleton, that Pat wanted for her cactus garden we loaded it into the Volkswagen. She was a member of a local garden club where one of her favorite activities was doing dried flower arrangements. So scouring the desert for "accessories" for her arrangements was one of her enjoyments. She did some beautiful arrangements with dried flowers, cactus skeletons, rocks and driftwood that won her many awards. After we would finished the exploring and hunting, Pat and I, with either Norris or Robert (whoever happened to be along) and Major "H," packed ourselves very carefully into that "Beetle" among the cacti and I carefully (very carefully) drove home. Major "H," although accustomed to deserts of the Middle-East, often had a *"pointed"* introduction to the Arizona desert of the southwestern United States. However, he seemed to really enjoy his time with my family and us with him. Although of the Islamic faith he surprisingly accepted our invitation to attend church with us a couple of times. He was very polite and attentive. He and I discussed and compared our religious practices and beliefs: Christianity and Islam. Today I would not likely be permitted to do that: Not politically correct; proselytizing! How grievously our government has ruined this country with political correctness! Major "H" said to me one day following one of our discussions, that if I were in his country we could not be friends; that he would probably have to kill me! He showed us pictures of his wife and two small children. His wife was beautiful and so were his children, about three to five years old. One day Major "H" announced that he wanted to prepare one of his favorite native meals for us in our home. He was very insistent that he do this; and insisted that he was an excellent chef. A day was set. On the appointed day he brought in all the necessary ingredients *then invited Pat out of the kitchen.* He neither wanted nor needed any help he said. I forget what he prepared but it took him a couple of hours or so. It was fabulously delicious! We talked of his culinary skill many times following that stupendous meal.

After he returned to his country, I occasionally sent him a friendly note and an asthma inhaler for one of his children, which he had asked for. I was concerned that our correspondence might be intercepted and he would be severely punished – maybe executed. In a year or two our corresponding ceased. I never received any further communications from him. His country was in typical Middle East tribal turmoil and political strife – as so many of them are, even today. I often wondered if he had been imprisoned, killed in combat or executed.

"Home of the Fighter Pilot!"

I was absolutely overjoyed at being at Luke. As a youngster growing up on Dad's Georgia farm I would read of the pilot training at Luke, hoping that someday I would train there to be a fighter pilot: *"And here I am!"* (It was some years earlier growing up that I decided I wanted to be a Marine Fighter Pilot – but it was not to be). As a youngster I read an article that said during World War Two Luke was known as the "Home of the Fighter Pilot," and was the largest fighter training base in the Army Air Forces. Many well-known personalities trained there: my boyhood cowboy hero, Gene Autry, enlisted in the Army Air Corps, trained and flew there as a flying Sargent during World War Two. The article went on to say that Luke Field was originally located in Hawaii and named after Second Lieutenant Frank Luke, America's number two fighter ace of World War One behind Eddie Rickenbacker. Lieutenant Luke, born in Phoenix, Arizona was awarded the Medal of Honor posthumously. About mid 1941 the name "Luke Field" was assigned to an airfield 15 miles west of Phoenix. It was deactivated in 1946 following World War Two, and would be reactivated as Luke Air Force Base in February 1951, a few months after the beginning of the Korean War. It remains a fighter pilot training base today – 2017.

Awards, Decorations and Veterans Day Parade

On July 3rd and August 31st 1966 the 4510 CCTW at Luke conducted awards and decorations presentation ceremonies at the base headquarters – by the flag pole. There were a number of Vietnam veterans at Luke and they were summoned to be presented; I included. There were numerous presentations with base, local and media personnel invited to attend. The Vietnam War was well underway and our government was anxious to capitalize on favorable publicity. I was presented the Silver Star, Bronze Star, Distinguished Flying Cross, Air Medal, Purple Heart and other awards. My friend Al Doddroe, from the night convoy ambush in Vietnam, plus the rescued F-100 pilot shot down by the quad 50 anti-aircraft gun, along with several other recipients were also presented with several medals on that day. On Veterans Day, Nov 11th, the city of Phoenix, Arizona had a huge parade and celebration. Al, I and the F-100 pilot were honored to be Grand Marshals of the parade.

F-100F Instrument Instructor

Upon reporting to Luke AFB in May 1966 I was assigned to "A" Flight of the 4517th Combat Crew Training Squadron (CCTS) as an F-100F instrument instructor. The F model was a two-seater with an instrument flying hood in the rear cockpit. "A" Flight was the instrument training flight for the squadron. All other 4517th flights were gunnery training flights. Pilots with low time in the F-100 or day fighters, as was my case, were usually assigned as instrument instructors for one year to acquire additional F-100 time before upgrading to the cherished gunnery instructor status. Known for its acclaim as a day fighter, the F-100 was also a fine instrument aircraft. After completing my instrument instructor training, flying under the hood was a piece of cake – and I actually enjoyed it. On August 4th I was designated as an Instrument Instructor Pilot for the F-100F. On December 13th I was designated as a Standardization and Evaluation Instrument check pilot for students. Later, after the reassignment of the "A" Flight commander, I would be appointed Flight Commander as the senior ranking instructor in the flight.

Vietnam was still boiling over, becoming ever increasingly hotter! Pilots were continually rotating through Luke on their way to Vietnam. Many were destined to be Forward Air Controllers (fighter pilots) assigned to Vietnamese or American Army units. Based on the Air Force's doctrine that only fighter pilots would be assigned to US Army units as Forward Air Controllers (FACs), Luke had instituted an F-100 short-course for non-fighter pilots bound for Vietnam as FACs – thus anointing them as *fighter pilots*. Many of these pilots would distinguish themselves time and time again in combat. Pilots without fighter time would be assigned as air strike controllers for enemy targets where friendly ground forces were not involved. One of our squadron instructors, on a later assignment to Vietnam, would be shot down and interned in Hanoi as a POW for few months before the POW release in 1973.

One Very Close Call!

There were several CCTSs on Luke and as you might imagine, traffic was extremely heavy: departing and returning traffic to and from the multiple gunnery ranges to the south near Gila Bend, Arizona; instrument training traffic to the north and west; normal maintenance flight tests, routine administrative flights and arriving or departing transit aircraft. Glendale and Phoenix were to the east and Litchfield Park to the immediate south, so air traffic over those areas was prohibited thereby squeezing the local traffic to the west, south and north.

Luke had two parallel runways. To accommodate the traffic saturation, one runway would be used for takeoffs and the other for landings. A small mobile control tower was located between the runways at the approach end of the landing runway to relieve the control tower of some of the workload. This mobile controller was an F-100 instructor assigned the duty on a rotational basis and was called "the SOF" (Supervisor of Flying). One day on an instrument training mission with a student in the rear cockpit, I was taxiing in an F-100F to the departure runway. The SOF suddenly announced in the clear on the traffic control frequency to all traffic, that he was reversing the direction of landings and takeoffs due to a significant shift in the wind direction. This meant of course that the previous landing direction *was now the takeoff direction; and visa versa.* All traffic was required to obtain clearance from the SOF prior to entering the traffic pattern or taking the departure runway for takeoff. One of the many F-100s was returning from the Gila Bend gunnery ranges. The pilot had called for, and received, landing directions prior the runway reversals. However he had missed the SOF's subsequent transmission announcing the switch in the runways' traffic directions. I had now changed my taxiing to the new departure runway which, as I said, was the previous landing direction.

After receiving takeoff clearance and upon liftoff, I told my student to go under the hood and take control of the aircraft – which was normal procedure for instrument training flights. He continued climbing the runway heading – again standard procedure – until we would clear the traffic area. Today's fighters are so fast and super-powerful that even in a climb, the aircraft's flight path is straight ahead as seen by the pilot through the windshield – the pilot's line of sight. However in F-100 era fighters, the speed and power was not so startling. In fact in the climb attitude the nose was significantly above the actual climbing flight path of the aircraft such that the pilot's visibility toward the actual direction of flight was restricted by the nose-high attitude. Remember that I had just departed in the opposite direction of the previous landing traffic. Suddenly the underside of an F-100 *flashed* over my nose and canopy going in the opposite direction. It filled most of my field-of-vision and was *on initial approach for the now wrong runway.* I know that had I been a blink of an eye earlier in my climb we would have come to a meeting of the minds – literally – and scattered ourselves and F-100 parts over the Arizona desert. I never told my student in the rear cockpit. There was no need to alarm him; he was under the hood flying instruments anyway. It was over and we had missed! Thank you Lord! As the cliché goes; "A mid-air will ruin your day"! I think the pilot of the other F-100 was totally unaware of the close call until I told him later. I just don't know how we could have gotten any closer without bending metal or scratching paint.

F-100C/D/F Gunnery Instructor

Having done my year as an instrument instructor, I began my upgrade training to become a gunnery instructor in the F-100C/D/F. The basic difference between the C and D models was that the C had no flaps. Both were single-seat fighters. The D model's final approach speed was 140 knots (160mph) and the C's, having no flaps, was 180 knots (210mph). A student's first few gunnery flights were in the two-seat F model with an instructor. Gunnery was great fun which I thoroughly enjoyed, although initially I found gunnery – both ground and air – very challenging. However, our instructors were really great and under their instruction I slowly improved beyond the barely qualifying scores. The gunnery upgrade included nuclear deliveries, bombs, rockets, missiles, guns and of course low level navigation and air refueling.

"Friends in High Places!"

It has been said that if you really want to learn to fly an airplane, become an instructor. This is very true! I found it to be the case as an F-100 instructor at Luke and later after retirement as a civilian general aviation flight instructor. I was beginning to really feel comfortable in the F-100 and enjoying it very much, especially the gunnery phase of flying and instructing. Then "WHAM!" On December 14, 1967 the squadron received a message from Headquarters Air Force in Washington D.C. alerting me for an assignment to the Pentagon to report on March 31, 1968. What a "bummer"! The Pentagon was often referred to as the "Puzzle Palace," or "Disneyland East"! My apology to Mr. Disney. (There was no Disneyworld then.) I was devastated. I was so looking forward to January when I would complete the gunnery instructor upgrade. Why would I suddenly be assigned to the Pentagon? What had I done to deserve this? After a phone call to the Pentagon to discuss my assignment duties and office of assignment, I discovered that I was requested by name from my former supervisor in the mobile tactical radar squadron, to which I was assigned, at Shaw AFB in 1962-64; the 728th AC&W Squadron. He was then a Major and the squadron Operations Officer. Now he was a Lieutenant Colonel and Chief of the Tactical Air Control Branch, Command and Control Division, Directorate of Plans and Operations, Headquarters USAF, Washington, D.C. He was having none of my objections to the Pentagon assignment and taking me away from the best assignment I ever had. As you can imagine, I was furious but I managed to keep my cool. This also meant that I would miss Norris's high school graduation. I never got used to all the missed events during Norris's and Robert's growing up; our family Christmases, Easters and anniversaries.

After being earlier designated as a gunnery instructor, in January 1968 I was then designated a Range Officer and Dart Tow Target Pilot. This meant that as Range Officer I could open/close the range, score targets and evict pilots demonstrating unsafe operations. To an un-indoctrinated observer watching gunnery practice on the range, it would all probably appear unsafe! As a Dart Tow Pilot for air-to-air gunnery, I would fly to the range, reel out the Dart on the 1500 foot cable and clear the shooters to fire. Following the air-to-air mission, the Dart would be towed to a designated drop point and released for scoring.

High Score!

My squadron had allowed me to complete the gunnery upgrade and continue as a gunnery instructor until my departure date for the Pentagon; to report March 31st 1968. As I said above, if you really want to learn to fly, become an instructor. It seems that throughout most of my flying career, I was always struggling to be as good as my fellow-pilots; never quite catching them. I was flying in the company of great "stick and rudder" fighter pilots. But any fighter pilot will identify himself as the "World's Greatest Fighter Pilot"! If you had any doubts, all you had to do was ask him. (Before you female fighter pilots get all tweaked-up, I'm using "him/he" in the classic generic sense as including both genders: Not politically-correct of course). Remember, this is my story and I'm not necessarily politically correct. Anyway, there were no female fighter pilots in my day.

My gunnery scores slowly improved. I really felt good and enjoyed the gunnery instructing. The mission to the range was always a contest between the instructor and the students as to who would bring back the best scores. The range officer would phone scores for each flight back to the respective squadrons for the mission debriefing. The high scorer would collect whatever nickel-dime bets were made by the flight members. Sometimes the bet would be a beer at the Officer Club "Happy Hour". Being a non-drinking fighter pilot my bet was always nickel-dime-quarters. It wasn't often that I collected. But like I said, I was improving. And yes, there are some outstanding *non-drinking* fighter pilots out there.

One day on a morning gunnery strafe mission I came back with an 80%+ score which beat my usual 35-40%. This was my highest gunnery score ever! I think the average range strafe scores usually ran around 60-70%. Minimum qualifying was 25%.

> Note: Guns on the F-100 were "sighted-in" periodically. The F-100 also had a normal tendency to yaw left and right slightly. This was particularly annoying when trying to track the gun sight to the target. To correct for this yawing tendency, North American had built into the F-100, a "yaw-damper" which didn't always work. When it did, it made gunnery much easier.

On this particular morning my F-100 had recently been sighted-in and the yaw damper was working perfectly. This of course assisted my high scoring significantly. Word got around like wild fire; "Partridge scored 80% on the range this morning!" That afternoon pilots were scrambling to get themselves scheduled in the F-100 that I had flown that morning. I believe this occurred on my last ever F-100 flight on March 15, 1968, after 861 hours. It was in the F-100D as a gunnery instructor with a flight of three students on my wing.

Leaving Luke and Family – 1968

While at Luke I joined the base aero club which was located at Litchfield Park, just south of Luke. The club had a T-34A, the same Air Force model that I flew in pilot training and in the Hamilton AFB aero club in California. They had one small dirt strip graded out in the desert. Fun! Norris was now 16 years old and we had some flying fun together; letting him try his hand at flying. He was very good and seemed to enjoy it. Robert was 9; a bit young to put in the rear cockpit of the T-34 out of my reach from the front cockpit.

On March 20th 1968, I loaded the Volkswagen, said goodbyes – for what seemed like the hundredth time – and left behind the best family a guy could have – and the best ever flying assignment! Once again Pat, Norris and Robert were faced with an absentee husband and father! I did not look forward to the Pentagon assignment. It is sort of a travesty and irony that, as a career Air Force officer, I would begrudge what should be the highlight of an Air Force career -- an assignment to Air Force Headquarters, Washington, D.C. At this point I was barely past the mid-point in my military career. If I had played my cards right I possibly could have retired as a General officer, rather than a Lieutenant Colonel. But, I was never good at cards. In fact, I rarely played cards at all. I know Pat was not looking forward to my departure any more than I. It meant that once again she was left alone to care for Norris and Robert, to run the household, care for the car, pay the bills, arrange for moving, supervise the movers and clear the base. Norris had graduated on May 23rd. Both he and Robert were a big help to Pat in the moving process.

On Jun 5th after saying their "so longs' to friends and the car loaded, Pat, with two kids and a cat, began the drive across the Arizona, New Mexico and Texas deserts toward Washington D.C. with the many "Are we there yet?" inquiries from the back seat. Again, great friends and friendships that would endure for the rest of our lives were left behind.

*****

Worst Assignment Ever!

Leaving Luke AFB and my family on March 20th 1968 and the subsequent drive across this great country of ours is lost in my mind. But I'm sure I took the red Volkswagen because it ended up with me in Springfield, Virginia. I have no explanation for my not being able to recall any portion of my drive across country, arrival in Washington D.C., house hunting nor checking in with my new job and boss. I was, of course, given the customary time to house-hunt and settle in.

In Springfield, Virginia just outside the southwest section of the Washington "Beltway," I found a very nice two-story home with a split level down to an attached garage. It had three-bedrooms, bath, fireplace, and huge grassy backyard with tall scattered pine and hardwood trees. It was a rental. The landlord next door was a very nice young couple with small children. After finalizing the rental, I moved in and setup "camp" with the minimum stuff I brought with me in the Volkswagen, and the limited baggage that military transportation shipped. I got the utilities and phone installation coordinated; called Pat to let her know how I was fairing, then reported for work on March 31, 1968.

What a "rat race"! I think it is a travesty that a Pentagon assignment, which should be the ultimate assignment in any military career, is such a pressure boiler of inter-service rivalry. I must admit that being upset over my assignment to Headquarters, U. S. Air Force was largely due to my disappointment at being "yanked" out of my Luke AFB "best-assignment" ever; having just achieved F-100 Gunnery Instructor upgrade status. The meeting with my former boss and now my boss again who tagged me for the Pentagon assignment, was rather cordial. I reiterated my chagrin at his pulling me from my recently acquired best assignment ever. You know what? It didn't seem to faze him at all. He just gave me a sort of half-grin with a comment something like: "Why should you have all that fun?" He obviously knew I was upset but I tried to never let my disgust over the assignment interfere with doing my best on the job. But, I'm afraid it must have shown.

All military personnel are told in no uncertain terms upon entering the service that their job is 24/7; that sleep and time-off is at the pleasure of the government. This is understandable given the nature of the military mission. I was soon to learn it again – as in previous assignments at Fort Gordon and Shaw AFB. I enlisted in the Air Force. No one coerced me so I have no justification for complaining – just disgusted that I was assigned out of the F-100 with so little time in it. The inter-service rivalry in the Pentagon was my biggest disappointment. Of course it was all about "the money" and which service got what share of the defense budget *pie*! The Vietnam War was really "hot" at this time – 1968. Yet in the Pentagon it seemed at times that the other services were the real enemy.

Action Officers

I was assigned to the Air/Ground Tactical Control Branch of the Tactical Control Division under the Operations Directorate – a Two-star position as I recall. My boss and I had worked in the Tactical Command and Control system at Shaw AFB. I had recently completed five months as a Forward Air Controller (FAC) in Vietnam with the U.S. Army's First Infantry Division. So, my assignment to this position was a logical one; even though I despised it. Nights when I worked into the late hours I would just fall into bed when I got home. I never hated anything so much in my life as getting up in the mornings after a few hours of sleep to go back into that "rat race" at the Pentagon. The traffic didn't help matters either.

Officers at my level in the Pentagon hierarchy – which was about the lowest level in the organizational structure – were known as "Action Officers". The Action Officer was the person who prepared response documents for the colonels who forwarded them to generals who had asked the questions, requested the information or wanted recommendations on specified topics. Some requests were generated by the Chief of Staff or even the Joint Chiefs. On rare occasions an Action Officer might be ordered to accompany a general officer who was testifying before a congressional committee. I was never involved in such a situation.

It was the Action Officer's job to prepare background data, talking-papers, answers, possible solutions and recommendations to the problems or situations presented. The response package constructed by the Action Officer, as I recall, was something like this: On top was a document stating the question or topic with talking points on the subject. Following this talking-paper would be a synopsis with the Action Officer's recommendation on the subject. Next would be a prepared final response ready for the general's signature should he accept the paper. (They rarely accepted the first few cuts). The final portion was the background on the subject that would be identified by tab numbers in the text; tabs that were attached to various supporting documents with which the reader could quickly find the Action Officer's rationale for a particular recommendation. Finally, any extraneous material, i.e., photos, sketches, maps etc. that the Action Officer felt might be beneficial to the general signing the prepared document. Prior to the package going to the requesting general, every intermediate and lateral office with any interest in the subject had to coordinate on the package to indicate agreement; or disagreement; including cross-service coordination if necessary.

Disagreement had to be supported with appropriate rationale. This coordination is where it really got sticky – sometimes downright mean. *How often do you find any two individuals who agree on anything?* And if cross-service implication was involved, coordination and agreement were especially dicey. Talk about real rivalry, especially if one service thought the other was trying to pull a fast one involving budgets or mission propriety. These packages could vary in thickness from a quarter inch to an inch or two; sometimes more. Completion of the package sometimes require a few days for completion – depending on the opposition encountered in the coordination process. The hallways were always filled with the hustle and bustle of high level activity. Action officers could often be identified because of their hurried pace – sometimes jogging – through the maze of the hallways and corridors.

It never seemed to fail, that about mid-afternoon on Friday a request would come down from a general officer requesting specific information or recommendation on a topic; and requiring the answer to be on his desk when he arrived for work the next day – or on Monday. Usually this meant working late into the night and early morning hours – even weekends when the usual secretarial and necessary office personnel for coordination were unavailable. Sometimes calling out secretarial help or other agency support was necessary. Every response to a general's enquiry usually meant building a response package. Administrative work was never my forte and I begin immediately to work on a plan to get out of the Pentagon; often referred to as the "Puzzle Palace."

Needed: New Forward Air Control (FAC) Aircraft!

The Air Force doctrine and missions manuals specified that the Air Force would attach (loan) fighter pilots to the Army as FACs to provide liaison and to control tactical air support that the Air Force provided to army ground commanders. This FAC support could be ground and/or airborne. Since FACs must be able to locate and identify ground targets for fast-mover jet fighters, they must operate on the ground in jeeps with the ground commander or be overhead with radio contact in slow and low (vulnerable) FAC aircraft. At this time Air Force FACs were using multiple-radio jeeps called MRC-108s and the O-1 Bird Dog aircraft – previously designated L-19. The O-1 was slow and vulnerable, had no armor protection and carried only four white phosphorous smoke rockets to mark targets for fighters. Built by Cessna, it was a single-engine propeller, high-wing, tail-wheel aircraft. Its high-wing, slow speed (100mph) and endurance made it an excellent platform for searching for enemy ground targets; but not very survivable in a high threat environment. I often said that the O-1 could zoom 200 feet – if it first dived off 300 feet. As the battlefield survivability of such aircraft decreased with enemy air defense capability increased, the Air Force realized the need for a more survivable FAC aircraft.

Part of my function in Tactical Air Control at the Pentagon was to work with other appropriate staff agencies in finding the ultimate FAC aircraft which we called the FAC-X. I regret to say we never found the ultimate FAC-X aircraft; and I think they're still looking. In America's Civil War (I know, it wasn't technically a civil war) balloons were used. In World War One, balloons were also used along with small fragile aircraft. In World War Two, small observation aircraft such as Piper Cub J-3s known as L-5s called Grasshoppers were used. In Korea, the T-6 Texan (a World War Two trainer) was used. In Vietnam FACs used the O-1 Bird Dog and their MRC-108 jeep. Later the civilian Cessna 337 Skymaster was "drafted" into service as a FAC aircraft and designated the O-2; which was later followed by newly designed North American OV-10 Bronco. Both the O-2 and OV-10 were twin-engine; the OV-10 having turbo-props.

Although the Research and Development Directorate (R & D) was principally responsible for acquiring the FAC-X, the Operations Directorate was a major player as the ultimate "user" of the FAC-X. With my having recently completed a FAC assignment in Vietnam with the First Infantry Division, the general (one-star) in charge of the Command and Control Division referred to me as his "FAC expert". I worked very closely with my counterpart in the R & D Directorate. They were the people who went out to contractors with requirements and were the final R & D authorities.

On the Operations side, I was tasked to brief a conference of representatives from tactical commands worldwide who possessed the tactical air expertise to assist in establishing operational requirements for a new FAC-X aircraft. Representatives were from: Tactical Air Command Langley AFB, Virginia; Pacific Air Forces Hawaii; Air Forces in Europe and I think Southern Command from Central America. Naturally everyone had their own ideas of the ultimate FAC-X. As I recall, the conference lasted about a week. Vietnam was hot and getting hotter! Part of the tasking was to find a suitable civilian aircraft that could be converted to an immediate interim FAC aircraft. Aircraft manufactures presented, and conducted demonstration flights, in their aircraft as the answer. I received demonstration flights in the Cessna 337 Sky Master and the OV-10 Bronco. R & D chose the Cessna 337 as the most suitably available airframe that could be immediately modified to perform the interim FAC aircraft role. It was designated as the O-2. It had a front and rear engine with side by side seating. Windows were installed in the lower part of the doors and fuselage for additional ground surveillance. A rocket pod was hung under each wing to provide for target marking. I don't recall, but I think each pod carried seven rockets – a definite advantage over the O-1's four rockets. However the side-by-side seating was less than optimum for FAC-ing. Its combat configuration exceeded its civilian gross weight. On take-off if the rear engine failed it could not sustain flight. It was not a very suitable FAC aircraft but that's what we could get our hands on immediately. After the OV-10 became available in quantity it eventually became the FAC aircraft. It was a really maneuverable aircraft and had a huge bubble canopy which sort of spilled over the side of the fuselage. Great for surveillance over the side; great visibility all around! It also had the addition of two small caliber machine guns. Just what fighter-pilot FACs wanted. The Marines bought it for FAC-ing and also used the guns to help the Marine "grunts" in contact with the enemy until the fighters arrived. But, wouldn't you know! The Air Force said "No Dice" on their FACs using the guns. Rationale varied but I heard that they were afraid their FACs would want to play "fighter pilot" rather than tend to their FAC-ing job – thereby making them more vulnerable to enemy ground fire. I don't know of a FAC or ground troops engaged with the enemy that would not want guns on the FAC aircraft to help suppress enemy ground fire while awaiting the fighters to arrive. Of course if the FAC was shot down he could be of no use to the ground commander and the fighters. In the task of finding the suitable aircraft for the FAC mission, I was assigned to attend a few conferences at bases throughout the country.

Proficiency Flying

Once again my flying was relegated to "proficiency flying" in the T-33 at Andrews AFB, Maryland: 100 to 120 hours a year, barely enough to be proficient. Minimum requirements for all pilots, i.e. instruments, instrument approaches, night flying and landings had to be accomplished including the two mandatory annual flight checks: Instruments and proficiency. The annual hours would require an average of four or five flight each month, most of which had to be done at night or on week-ends. With the hectic pace in the Pentagon, getting out of the office to fly was difficult. I never thought I would hate having to go fly; but with the hours and pressure, sometimes I truly wished I didn't have to do so. There isn't much to tell regarding my flying while at the Pentagon: no emergencies, no incidents to speak of.

Family Travel: Luke AFB to Springfield, Virginia

Meanwhile back at Luke AFB in Arizona, Pat, Norris and Robert (Puff too) were preparing to leave and drive to Washington, D.C. The household movers and house cleaners had done their thing by May 6th (1968). Norris graduated from Dysart High School on May the 23rd – another family event that I missed. Robert's school was out for the summer. On May the 27th Pat began to get the final things together and ready to load the Starfire for the trip to Washington. Base Housing inspectors OK'd the house and completed the departure clearance. After a few days saying goodbyes to friends, they left Luke AFB on June 5th.

I was greatly concerned about Pat, Norris and Robert traveling alone; particularly across the wide expanse of desert they had to traverse. They made it OK arriving in Springfield, Virginia on June 9th. However there was one incident on their trip that upset me and could have been very serious.

Sometime after they started the trip, Pat stopped for gas. I don't recall where nor the station's petroleum brand. But they were facing a long drive in the desert. The loaded car and out of state tag indicated that she was not a local resident. The station mechanic checking under the hood (they used to do that you know) told her that she needed a new alternator – a very expensive item. When she asked why, he said because the battery terminals were corroded. Of course she didn't know better and with miles and miles of desert ahead and with Norris, Robert and Puff aboard, she didn't want to take any chances. She had the new alternator installed.

It was a day or two after they arrived in Springfield that I was under the hood of the Starfire for some reason. I noticed this large two-inch bolt lying in the bottom of the engine compartment. Looking around I found that the mounting bracket of the alternator was missing a bolt. In essence, only one bolt was holding the alternator and mounting bracket to the engine. Had it fallen on the belt en route, either the belt would have been broken or one of the engine accessories damaged. When I mentioned the bolt to Pat, she told me of the alternator replacement. I was very upset with that service station and that mechanic in particular. I inquired of a couple of mechanic friends if in fact that battery terminal corrosion is an indicator of a bad alternator. Each said no.

I wrote the petroleum company operating the service station with my anger at their mechanic knowing that a female driver with kids about to face the long desert trip, could likely be intimidated with the suggested need for an alternator replacement. The company was very apologetic of course, and reimbursed me the cost of the alternator. I was still upset over the mechanic's scam and the shoddy work in which he either didn't tighten the bolt or left it out altogether. There was no massive interstate highway network as there is today. What makes me most angry is that they could have been stranded in the desert (June) on a lonely stretch of two-lane highway.

The movers arrived in Springfield, Virginia on June 10th, so they didn't have much time to settle in before it was two days of movers and unpacking. Everyone – including Puff – seemed to like their new home and surroundings. Not long after their arrival, I had an opportunity to show them around the Pentagon, and my desk (one of several) in the large open office that was the Tactical Air Control Branch in the basement – often referred to as the dungeon.

Except for my brief encounter in Los Angeles (1958) this was my first experience with high-density commuting traffic. Between Springfield and the Pentagon was a converging eight lanes of traffic – called the mixing bowl – where I had to navigate across eight lanes of traffic to get to an exit lane.

Puff's Friends

Up to this point, Puff's only friend was his "brother" next door at Luke. He was now about two years old and discovering that he was a "Tom". There were a few cats in the neighborhood that liked to "party" outside our bedroom window at night. Puff was a house cat. His friends couldn't understand why he couldn't come out and play at night. Neither could he. He let us know his displeasure by his Siamese meow throughout the night; and up and down on everything available, the higher the better – bed, dresser, chest-of-drawers, curtains, etc.

We decided it was time for a visit to the vet to convert him from a "he" to an "it". He had a great disposition and didn't mind traveling until he learned that traveling sometimes meant "vet". Still he traveled well until you neared the vet's office. I told the vet that I didn't want the procedure to destroy Puff's great disposition. He assured me that it would calm him down and even improve his disposition. It did! Puff became a great lap cat – which he sort of was before the procedure. Now he would jump into my lap and stay there until something disturbed him. He would stretch himself out on my leg draping his legs over my thigh and his chin over my knee. He was Robert's cat but I enjoyed him as much as anyone; especially his antics and playful moods. About the only things he would not tolerate were very small children and other cats. He would even tolerate dogs to a degree. In fact it used to bother Robert so much when he would hold Puff and Puff would start that Siamese meowing until I took him from Robert whereby he would quiet down. Another thing that would get him all cranked up and excited was squirrels in the yard. When outside we monitored him or had him on a leash. He actually learned to accommodate the leash to a fair degree considering his feline independence. We all loved him. Norris and Robert often complained that Pat and I loved Puff more than we did them. Not so of course, but I'm sure it seemed so to them.

Break-In and Robbery!

When we returned home from shopping and errands about 10:30am on the morning of February 4th 1969, I noticed that the front door knob was damaged and the door slightly ajar. We called the police and upon entering we found every drawer removed and the contents scattered on the floor. This was very scary and eerie to know that strangers had entered our home in the middle of the morning and did all this then left undetected. Our house was closely surrounded with neighborhood homes yet no one detected the robbery. The police asked for a list of missing items. No large expensive items were missing. According to Pat's notes, we were missing: One of her purses, two $2 bills, a rare oversized $1 bill, ten silver dollars (some of which her father had given her), ten to twelve 50 cent pieces, two mint sets plus miscellaneous stuff. None of the expensive china, silverware, tools, TVs, stereo etc. were taken. Nothing was ever recovered.

Moon Landing! Hurray USA!

July 20th 1969 Apollo 11 American Astronaut Neil Armstrong stepped on to the surface of the moon; a first and never to be forgotten event! I'm glad my family and I were TV viewer witnesses to that memorable event. The Apollo 11 crew: Neil Armstrong, Edwin Aldrin and Michael Collins returned to the earth on July 24th. It was a proud and happy day for the USA!

North Virginia Airport

In nearby Alexandria, Virginia (I think it was) there was a small airport nestled among businesses and homes: North Virginia Airport. It had a really difficult short runway to operate in and out of with the obstructions created by surrounding homes and businesses. In spite of my pressure cooker job at the Pentagon, I decided that I would go for a civilian flight instructor certificate and a multi-engine rating with an eye toward someday becoming a civilian certified flight instructor (CFI) after retirement. I had my commercial pilot certificate and instrument rating. The Federal Aviation Administration (FAA) would issue these certificates and ratings to any Air Force pilot training graduate upon their application and passing the written examination. I did this upon being assigned to New Castle County Airport, Wilmington, Delaware following the completion of my Air Force pilot training. After my CFI training at the North Virginia Airport I was certified on October 15th 1969. I went right into multi-engine training which I completed after having failed the first flight check. The examiner failed me and had me do an immediate hour of extra training with an instructor; whereupon the examiner flew with me again and certified me for a multi-engine rating.

Norris to College

Norris chose and was accepted by Richmond College, University of Richmond, Richmond, Virginia to enter in the Fall of 1968. It was a Baptist college and was in keeping with his goal to complete his degree in theology and become a Baptist Minister. In July we went to Richmond to find him a place to stay. I don't recall what we found but I think it was a room in a boarding house owned by an elderly lady needing financial support from the rent. Pat was busy getting Norris ready for college at Richmond and Robert ready for his new school year – at Poe Elementary, I think it was. We did find time to take 12 days in August to visit our families in Georgia and a "Partridge Reunion". On August 27th Robert got his school physical at Fort Belvoir, Virginia. Norris was off for Richmond College in the red Volkswagen on September 14th. Then on September 27th I bought a yellow Volkswagen "Beetle" to replace the one I gave Norris. On October 19th we visited Norris at Richmond for parents' day open house. November 11th we visited Robert's class for parents' day. Norris and Gwen continued their romantic relationship by correspondence while her family was now, or would soon be, at MacDill AFB, Tampa, Florida.

"On the Street Where You Live"

Our church was the First Baptist Church of Springfield. They only got to know Norris briefly before he was off to Richmond. But they recognized the fine young man that he was. He began to work closely with the youth programs and the following summer, 1969, the church made him an assistant minister for the church youth. And of course, recognizing his work toward a theology degree at Richmond, was given occasional opportunities to practice his preaching – although it wasn't practicing for him, it was sincere preaching.

Norris was a nice looking guy with a super-fabulous voice and often did solo numbers in church programs. I'm not sure of the particular event – likely the church youths' Valentine Day Sweetheart Banquet – that Norris was asked to sing a solo as a major feature of the program. Everyone was gathered at their tables throughout the fellowship hall. The young ladies and young men were in their finest Valentine's Day evening formal dress. Norris was in dark trousers, white coat and black bow tie. As he began to sing he strolled smiling among the tables carrying a single long-stemmed beautiful red rose in his right hand and held close to his heart. He would occasionally pause at a table and sing directly to one of the many beautiful young ladies in attendance. We were all wondering who of the lovely young ladies he would give the rose too. I was sitting with Robert at a table up front near the stage. Pat had chosen to sit on the edge of the stage facing the hall surveilling everything. Of course we were all enthralled with Norris's voice. You could just see the motherly-pride in Pat's face as Norris sang. She tried not to let her emotion and pride overwhelm her. The song Norris was singing was "On the Street Where You Live". As he sang the last lyrics he slowly approached his Mom while extending the red rose to her and ending with... "I want to be on the street where you live". Pat was visually and comely moved! Their love for each other showing on their faces was memorable. I was pretty choked-up too.

Years later after Norris married Gwen; they named their only daughter, Tessa. Tessa was gifted with an equally spell-binding beautiful voice like her Dad. She sent me a CD of her singing beautifully melodious songs. I sent a copy of her CD to my brother Richard, in Atlanta, who had never heard Norris or Tessa sing. He was surprised, amazed and impressed! He said he knew of a lounge/restaurant near his home that might need a live-entertainment singer. I then contacted Tessa to see if she was interested in moving from Idaho to accept the job. Tessa was grateful for the opportunity but was so dedicated to her severely handicapped mother's care that she declined the offer. I know Tessa would have been a tremendous hit! Her voice is so beautiful and reminds me so much of her Dad's. Sometimes I would tell Tessa that she was my *favorite* granddaughter. She would respond: "I'm your *only* granddaughter, granddaddy". Likewise, I have told Norris's son that he is my *favorite* grandson. He too is also my *only* grandson.

On August 3rd 1969, Gwen, Norris's fiancé flew into the Washington National Airport (Now the Ronald Reagan National Airport) to visit Norris, his Mom and me. (Mostly Norris, I think). Gwen and her family were then in Tampa, Florida (MacDill Air Force Base). On August 9th Pat's sister, Carrie and her sons, Morris and David, visited from Florida. Norris broke his leg on the 23rd and Pat's mother, Vennie, broke hers on the 30th. Great month for visits from family and friends – and for broken legs! Robert received his Pioneer Badge on October 1st from the Cub Scouts; or was it Royal Ambassadors (RAs) from church. Anyway, it was a Pioneer Badge.

Vietnam Volunteer

Meanwhile the Pentagon continued it usual hectic pace. I hated getting up for work. I decided that the only way I would keep my sanity was to get out of there. So, I submitted a letter July 8th 1969 requesting that my Pentagon tour be curtailed in order for me to volunteer to go back to Vietnam – in the F-100. Here I was just over a year in my tour. Pat was never one to let her disappointment show but I know she was hurt. I knew it wasn't career-smart to request an assignment out of the usual four-year Pentagon tour, and expected my request to be disapproved. Low and behold! On August 22th I received a letter authorizing curtailment of my Pentagon assignment for Vietnam effective March 15th 1970. I was elated although I knew I had probably shot myself in the foot career wise.

I enjoyed flying the F-100 so I was satisfied with the approval of my request although it meant leaving my family again – for a war zone. At that time the F-100 was the Air Force workhorse for the ground attack war in Vietnam. However, it was beginning to be replaced by the F-4. I could hardly wait to get out of the rat race. Don't get me wrong about my wanting out of the Pentagon. The work is interesting, never dull, and quite rewarding if done well. My problem with the Pentagon was the politics and rivalries. It was a daily confrontation to defend your work, idea or program against intra-department rivalry and inter-service jealousies. This was not my forte.

Vietnam, No! North Carolina, Yes!

We made some great lifetime friends in our church in Springfield; some of which I still casually correspond with today. Wherever we were, when we had to move, our friends would usually have a going away fellowship for us. I always told them it wasn't me that they hated to see go; rather it was Pat. True! She was amazing with her people personality.

On January 6th, 1970 I received a letter that my Vietnam volunteer tour in the F-100 was changed to the 19th Air Force at Seymour-Johnson AFB, North Carolina. It was one of those mixed-emotion situations. The F-100s in Vietnam were being rapidly replaced by the newer F-4 so they didn't need more F-100 pilots over there. I was still getting out of the Pentagon but I wouldn't be going back into the F-100 which I really wanted to do. And I wouldn't be leaving my family after all. Two days later I received orders assigning me to the 19th Air Force at Seymour-Johnson Air Force Base, North Carolina to report on March 31st 1970.

*****

"Bug-Out Bags!"

The 19th Air Force, located at Seymour-Johnson Air Force Base, Goldsboro, North Carolina, was known as the "Suitcase Air Force" and with very good reason. It was a nucleus around which deployed air forces formed as a task-force for contingencies, real or practiced. This task-force was referred to as a CASF. Pronounced as "cass-af," CASF was an acronym for Composite Air Strike Force(s). Thus for worldwide contingencies, 19th Air Force would deploy a headquarters component to form and command deployed CASF response forces – combat and all support elements. On occasions when joint service forces were involved, 19th Air Force may be charged with providing the joint command element. Additionally, the 19th Air Force was the planning force behind all those contingencies. In other words, write the plans for worldwide contingencies against any country that might – in the near or long term – initiate belligerent actions against the United States or their allies. Plans had to be written, updated and maintained in a current status at all times should a deployment be required. I would be a plans officer for the 19th Air Force; full title: Numbered Air Force Operations War Plans Officer. Each plans officer would be assigned a number of countries for which to prepare and/or maintain contingency plans. Of course we didn't prepare the plans in a vacuum; in addition to initial guide-lines, we had intelligence, logistics, communications, operations and other agencies which all had inputs to the plans. All personnel were required to maintain prepacked bags – termed "bug-out-bags" – in a ready-to-go state at all times; thus, "The Suitcase Air Force". Once again I would be in a frequent-deployment mode for short, long and no-notice deployments – world-wide.

Settling in to a New Job

March 1970: Two years from Luke AFB my family and I were again in the selecting, packing, moving mode. Been there, done that a few times in my career. Now: Washington, D.C. to Seymour-Johnson AFB, North Carolina. As frequently as we had moved it never became routine or without trauma; always a hassle. However, reporting in for duty and getting Pat and Robert settled (Norris was at the University of Richmond, Virginia) into base housing was rather normal – if such can be labeled "normal". In spite of our many moves, Robert and Norris adapted readily and after a day or two at their new schools, had new friends. Pat too; especially Pat. Thank the Lord for Pat. She had learned to handle household problem and emergencies quickly since I was away so often. Being the "people person" that she was, she was soon involved in base, church and community activities. Base housing had a ready vacancy so we were able to move right in without having to locate temporary quarters until base quarters became available. I had been to Seymour-Johnson once before on TDY (temporary duty) and stayed in their temporary quarters (BOQ) while there. The building was nestled among the pines and had a long hallway. My room was about half way down the hallway. It was summer and the building was very hot; doors open at each end of the hallway. I returned to my darkened room one evening and as I opened the door, light from the hallway dimly illuminated the floor. I thought I saw a crooked stick about a foot and half in length and in the middle of the floor. After turning on my light (which was also dim) I studied it for a moment and decided that it was a snake. SNAKE! It appeared very sluggish. I called the Air Police. They arrived and took it away. The consensus was that it was a "copperhead" – sometimes called highland moccasin. I stripped my bed and remade it; but you can be sure that I got very little sleep for the next few nights just listening or feeling for the slightest noise or movement.

No-Notice Recalls/Alerts for Duty/Deployments

As part of the CASF command element for contingency deployments, my job as plans officer was somewhat different from the deployments I experienced as mobility officer for my unit assignments at Fort Gordon, Georgia and Shaw AFB, South Carolina; although each had its own function as an element of a CASF when deployed. C-130 airlift aircraft were used as the cargo/passenger carriers. The C-130 has turboprop engines which have a very loud and distinct sound. During those years the turboprop was relatively new and I'll never forget the sound. Even to this day whenever I hear that sound it brings back memories of those "middle-of-the-night" recall alert phone calls for no-notice deployments to places unannounced. Or it could be a no-notice higher headquarters Operational Readiness Inspection (ORI). The base was like a beehive in a moment's notice. The better a unit performed on these ORIs, the less likely higher headquarters would bother you in the near future. And if the performance was very poor, the unit commander could be subjected to replacement along with other supervisory personnel – and the unit could expect frequent ORIs until performance improved significantly.

After completing my portion of the recall alert plan, bug-out-bags were grabbed, a quick kiss for Pat and a last look in on Robert and away I go! "Don't try to call me; I'll call you!" The noise from the ramp full of C-130s was deafening throughout the base.

Fun Things!

As for my plans officer job while at Seymour-Johnson, nothing spectacular occurred. My flying was again relegated to the T-33 and meeting annual proficiency flying requirements. I did have time for the base aero club. As always, I enjoyed flying small general aviation aircraft around the country side and on cross country flights. A local girl scout leader ask me to present a condensed pilot's ground school to her troop as one of their projects. It was fun and I hope stirred an aviation interest in the girls. They really seemed to enjoy their newly discovered knowledge. Norris and Robert seemed to harbor an interest in flying and I enjoyed teaching them aviation fundamentals whenever I had an opportunity. A few years later Robert would go on to get his private pilot certificate.

Robert also became an avid fisherman while at Seymour-Johnson. A good friend and father of Robert's two best friends there would often take the three boys fishing on a nearby lake or stream. Robert and I would occasionally go to a backwoods lake or stream to try our luck. Generally we ended our fishing excursion in a tie: Zero! Luckily our dinner table didn't depend on our fishing skills. Actually, Robert developed his fishing interest earlier with a friend and his father while we were at Shaw AFB, South Carolina.

My family and I joined the Calvary Baptist Church of Goldsboro; an independent Baptist church as I recall. Our pastor, Robert E. (Bob) Lee, was a "fire and brimstone" evangelistic preacher; similar to what I grew up with in Mom and Dad's church. I like that style of preaching occasionally. It gets you doing some serious thinking. The Pastor's wife and another friend's wife became a couple of Pat's best friends while we were there. Actually Pat always had many "best friends" – of all ages – wherever we were; very typical of her love for people.

The first air race I ever witnessed was at Wilson, North Carolina several miles north of Seymour-Johnson. I took Pat and Robert to the air race and we thoroughly enjoyed the experience – complete with a quilt picnic lunch on the grass, food venders, sky divers and static aircraft displays. And you could wander among the racing aircraft and talk with the pilots and ground crews. Gone are those days! *Thanks Bin Laden!* The main show was a race by North American T-6 "Texans," a World War Two advance trainer and later primary trainer in the middle 1950s. I stood amazed at the close proximity of the aircraft as they raced maximum airspeed and 80 to 90 degree banks around the course – often seemingly to overlap wing tips. The course was close enough that the aircraft were in sight throughout the circuit. There were other smaller home-built racing aircraft but it was the T-6s that "stole" the show. Although I enjoyed the race, I have never attended another, due largely to the fact that air racing is not really my "thing" and that I have never been in the vicinity of another one.

TDYs and More TDYs!
I was involved in several TDYs while at Seymour-Johnson; from a few days to a few months. Except for a three-day TDY to Shaw AFB, SC for the recurring three-year Physiological Training Course (Altitude Chamber) and the annual three-day Instrument Flying Refresher Course, other job related TDYs were:

Norfolk Naval Air Station, Virginia May 1970 for Exercise Exotic Dancer III briefing.

Langley AFB, Virginia July 1970 for Exercise Bold Shot 1-71.

Nellis AFB, Nevada August 1970 for a Tactical Fighter Commander Course.

MacDill AFB, Florida August 1970 to attend US Strike Command planning conference.

Homestead and MacDill AFBs September 1970 for a planning conference and communications facility survey.

Little Creek, Virginia October 1970 for air operations planning and joint task force contingency operations plans.

Fort Bragg, North Carolina and MacDill AFB November 1970 to Attend coordinated operations plans briefings.

Hdq Tactical Air Command (TAC), Langley AFB November 1970 for team briefing to the TAC staff.

Hdq TAC December 1970 to attend a Guantanamo NAS, Cuba briefing.

Detailed to Commander Air Forces Headquarters (at Seymour-Johnson) January 1971 for 8-day Exercise Bold Shot 4-71.

Hdq TAC March 1971 to coordinate operations plan.

Air Force Headquarters, Atlantic Exercise (Seymour-Johnson), 18 days April/May 1971.

Fort Hood, Kileen, Texas Jun-Sep 1971 to participate in new tactics evaluation for Air/ground operations: PROJECT MASSTER.

Note: PROJECT MASSTER was a Mobile Army Sensor Systems Test and Evaluation Review.

A friend and I were sent TDY (June 2nd to September 5th 1971) to Fort Hood, Kileen, Texas to join the joint Army/Air Force PROJECT MASSTER evaluation already in progress. The evaluation was designed to test a new concept in sensor intelligence gathering with air and ground combined operations, particularly air support of mechanized armor (tanks); foretelling Desert Storm – Iraq/Kuwait – in 1991.

The TDY was expected to evolve into a PCS (permanent change of station). Pat and Robert would join me later if the PCS became a reality. While at Ft Hood I checked out in the O-2 FAC aircraft and managed to accumulate about 40 hours. As it was to be, after about three months my friend and I were ordered back to Seymour-Johnson. The TDY was terminated. All during my time at Fort Hood Pat kept telling me that our Pastor's wife was praying that my TDY would be terminated and I would return to Goldsboro. She didn't want us leaving Seymour-Johnson. (Make that: She didn't want her good friend, Pat to leave). Upon my return I told The Pastor's wife that her prayers worked – as General MacArthur had said he would return – so had I returned. But within a couple weeks I had orders for a two-year tour to Clark Air Base, Philippine Islands. I told the Pastor's wife that her prayers were not specific enough. True, I returned to Seymour but it didn't stick. She should have prayed that I would return to and remain at Seymour-Johnson.

Norris and Gwen's Wedding!

There was one great event that occurred shortly before I had to leave for the Philippines: Norris and Gwen's wedding, September 11th 1971! Gwen was a lovely bride! I was glad they planned the wedding for a date before I had to leave. The wedding was in the MacDill AFB Chapel with the reception following in the home of one of Gwen's friend. Norris's friend was to do their wedding pictures with his new camera. Unfortunately the film did not roll; therefore none of his pictures were made. Fortunately I had taken a few pictures with my 35mm camera. Those plus a few by friends are the only wedding pictures they have.

They were soon back in Richmond, Virginia for Norris's senior year at the University of Richmond; graduating in 1972 with a degree in history. They acquired a small kitten which they named: "Trouble" and was the exact replica of Puff in his infancy. Unfortunately "Trouble" went missing when Norris and Gwen were preparing to move to Fort Worth, Texas where Norris would enter the Southwestern Baptist Theological Seminary. Suspicion is that his Trouble's cat-curiosity took him on board the moving van and he was shipped off to a new and hopefully, good home.

Orders for Clark Air Base, Philippines

I had a reporting date of November 8th 1971 to the Military Airlift Command (MAC) Passenger Terminal, Travis AFB, California for transportation to Clark AB, Philippines. Clark AB had no vacant military housing available so Pat, Robert (and Puff) would be remaining behind until I could find adequate off-base civilian housing and obtain authorized travel for them. Since Pat and

Robert would not be permitted to remain in Seymour's military housing after I left, I would take 30 days leave between Seymour and Travis to get off-base housing; visit family and friends and generally enjoy my family before leaving them for an unknown period of time. We found a nice rental house on Acorn Road in Goldsboro. The house was located on a large beautiful lot with an in-ground septic tank in the front yard. (Remember this; it will be critical at a later time).

November: Time came for me to say good-bye to Pat and Robert and report to Travis AFB, California for transportation to Clark. Upon arrival at Clark I was immediately placed on the base military housing waiting list. Once I had found off-base civilian rental housing or was assigned base housing (whichever came first), the Air Force would publish orders for Pat and Robert to proceed to Clark on contract military airlift aircraft. They had long since obtained travel documents, passports, visas, etc. (except for orders). The wait was expected to be a month or two. However, soon after I arrived at Clark AB the Philippine President, Ferdinand Marcos, declared martial law and practically declared a dictatorship. The US government suspended all military dependent travel to the Philippines. The Philippine government constantly had to deal with the "Huks," a Communist guerilla insurgency group operating throughout the country. The Communist Party of the Philippines (CPP) had a military arm called the New People's Army (NPA) and often conducted assassinations, highway roadblocks and ambushes of government forces; plus the frequent attacks on government forces by Moslem radicals in the southern island of Mindanao. There were frequent armed confrontations between the Moslem and Christian groups in the southern islands. A couple of American servicemen were killed off-base around Clark. I don't know the circumstance of those murders.

The Philippine government was accused of corruption. There was also the criminal element for black marketing, thievery, highway banditry and road blocks/check points to collect "taxes". Some well-known and perpetual stories linger about "infamous" thievery of US government and personal property on Clark AB. I was apprehensive about Pat and Robert coming over into such an environment, yet hoping for an early travel authorization for them. With marshal law declared, I had no idea when, or if, Pat and Robert would be permitted to join me at Clark AB. I might be doing the entire two-year tour alone. Soon however families were permitted to join their spouses and I found off-base housing in Angeles City just outside the main gate about five minutes from my office. However, marshal law remained in the Philippines until about 1981.

Moving! Oops, Who Put That Septic Tank There?!
Air Force orders were issued for Pat and Robert's March 1972 travel to Clark AB. Once again Pat would have to handle the move and overseas travel alone.

Most of the household goods would go into storage for the duration of my Philippine assignment. It generally took movers two to two and a half days to pack and move us. Terminating the rental agreement was no problem due to the military clause stating that it would be terminated upon proper government reassignment orders. On March 17th Pat and Robert picked up their passports and visas.

March 21st, moving day arrived. The driver of the 18-wheeler moving van backed his rig into the front yard to the front entrance. Pat told him that he was parked over a septic tank. He sort of pooh-poohed it as of no concern; after all, what did a woman know? When the truck had been partially loaded and while Pat was in the house, she heard a loud "crash". She ran to the front door and there sat the 18-wheeler with a set of its 18 wheels resting in the septic tank. Did that driver ever have egg on his face – or was it something else?

Travel day finally came. Puff had been put in his travel kennel earlier, March 4th, and taken to the airport to board Piedmont Airlines for his travel to the Philippines. Pat said they gave him to the baggage handlers and watched him on the baggage cart as they took him to the airplane. Although she couldn't hear him, she could see him meowing at the top of his voice. It broke her and Robert's hearts. Pets had to be sent to a veterinarian in Manila where they would be examined, papers check and observed for a few days before they would be allowed official entry into the country. Puff would be delivered to me at Clark by the vet several days later and a few days before Pat and Robert arrived.

*****

CHAPTER SEVENTEEN
CLARK AIR BASE, PHILIPPINE ISLANDS – T-33 (1971-1973)

405th Fighter Wing Plans

After arriving at Clark Air Base, about 50 miles north of Manila, and doing the necessary customs processing, I reported into the 405th Fighter Wing Headquarters. The parent unit was the Thirteenth Air Force also located on Clark. Following base in-processing, I reported to my boss, the 405th Fighter Wing Plans Officer. I would be his Assistant Plans Officer in a three-person office: The Plans Officer, myself and a secretary. Our secretary was an outstanding secretary, office manager and "gopher". The Wing had F-4 aircraft crewed with a pilot in the front cockpit and in the rear cockpit, a Weapons System Officer (WSO) who was also a pilot but not front cockpit qualified. He operated the onboard electronic systems and was popularly called "Wiss-0" for the acronym WSO. The Wing rotated aircrews and aircraft to South Vietnam and Thailand for the Southeast Asian War (Vietnam, Laos and Cambodia) on a temporary duty (TDY) basis.

I had two good friends in the 405th who, like me, were not F-4 qualified. We were relegated to flying the T-33 for proficiency flying. One friend was the Wing Intelligence Officer so he and I worked very closely together due to the nature of the plans and intelligence functions. The other friend worked in Wing operations. I maintained my contact with them for years after leaving Clark AB.

Nora!

Since Pat and Robert were not yet allowed to accompany me to the Philippines, I was assigned to the Bachelor Officers Quarters (BOQ). During off-duty time I had a chance to explore Clark. The base is beautiful, as you would expect a tropical paradise to be. Even the surrounding jungle is beautiful (and deadly!). Clark abounded with beautiful flowers, immaculate landscaping and gardening. Most buildings, except those of modern structure, have no glass windows. Rather, they are open-air and screened all around from about chest high and above. Clark AB played a very prominent role during World War Two, as well as historical roles in earlier wars. Some of the buildings still remain. I enjoyed exploring the many historical sites. There is a beautifully kept national cemetery along the main road on the base just inside the main gate.

Having arrived in early November 1971 without my family, we would again be facing another Christmas and New Year apart – almost on opposite sides of the *planet*. Winter in the Philippines – if there is such a thing as winter in the Philippines! The only way you knew it was winter was by observing the calendar. The New Year, 1972, arrived. Surprise! Although marshal law hung on to sometime in 1981, about the end of 1971 military dependent families were once again authorized travel to join their spouse sponsors in the

Philippines. I called Pat and told her the good news and to start preparing for the move to the Philippines. She and Robert received orders dated January 10, 1972 authorizing their travel to Clark AB. There was no on-base housing available for me. However, I applied for family housing and was placed on a long waiting list. In the meantime off-base civilian housing was authorized until base housing became available. I found a small rental house a short distance outside the Clark AB main gate in the adjacent town of Angeles City. I moved into what would soon become our new home. It was a nicely furnished place with window air conditioning. Most Americans bought or rented houses that had window air conditioning units already installed.

As was the practice of American families assigned to Clark AB I began looking for a *house-girl* and *yard-boy*. I found a nice Filipino lady by the name of Nora to be my house-girl. She was not a live-in house-girl, although Pat was not very pleased with the arrangement when I called her – especially since she wasn't there to *keep an eye on me*. I'm joking of course – I think. Don't misunderstand. Pat knew she could trust me completely and I likewise her. I think maybe she didn't trust Nora. But I can understand her concern. She did not know Nora although I tried to assure her that I considered Nora completely trustworthy. Pat would soon come to love her once she met Nora. I moved from the BOQ into the rental house and Nora started to work. She would eventually become a great friend of Pat and me. She and Robert would become more like brother and sister frequently teasing and jokingly picking at each other. But it would be about a month before Pat and Robert would arrive.

In the meantime, Puff arrived from Manila via veterinarian courier. I was at our Angeles City home. I expected to see him hungry, dirty, scruffy, emaciated, confused and disorientated. Boy was I ever wrong. The vet brought Puff in and set his pet-carrier in the middle of the floor and opened its door. Puff casually strolled out and in typical feline independency, strolled about checking out everything in sight, barely acknowledging me. He looked great! I was quite relieved but also quite miffed that he seemed to purposely ignore me. His black fur was clean and shiny. He looked well fed and seemed fully cognizant. I had been quite concerned due to his long journey alone in the care of strangers – and not the least of which was the knowledge that some Filipinos ate cats on a routine basis. Not to worry. Puff made himself at home. He and Nora became good friends and I made sure that Nora understood that he was a *member of my family and was not a menu item*.

Nora was prompt each day and meticulous with her housework; and a great cook. I was attending the Clark Field Southern Baptist Church located immediately outside the Clark AB main gate on 1st Street, New Balibago, Angeles City. I always left my Bible on the front room coffee table. One day I discovered Nora reading my Bible. We began to discuss the Bible and our beliefs. She attended a local Catholic church in Angeles City. The Philippines Islands have a predominantly Catholic population especially in villages, town and large cities largely due to the Spanish influence through the years. There is significant Muslim influence in the southern islands, and particularly Mindanao. I invited Nora to attend the Clark Field Baptist Church with me; the congregation of which was about 50% Filipino. She accepted my invitation and soon began attending on her own initiative. Later discussions with her revealed that she was not Saved; had not accepted Jesus Christ as her Savior. She soon had some of her friends and relatives attending with her.

Pat and Robert Arrive!

I don't remember Pat and Robert's actual arrival date but it was likely in March 1972. It was sure a great sight when I spotted them in the customs and immigration line at the Clark AB terminal. Although tired and weary, they still looked great. Of course the Wing gave me a few days to get them settled in and processed onto the base. And they were delighted to get reacquainted with Puff – and me too, I hope. One of the first priorities was to get Robert enrolled in the on-base Wagner High School to finish the school year. After the summer break he would return for the new school year beginning Aug 28, 1972 with an open-house for parents on October 11th. I had purchased a 1965 Volkswagen (I think it was) and later a 1950 Dodge (or was it a Desoto?) in order that Pat and I would both have transportation around the base; for work, shopping, errands and such. Most Americans did not drive off-base due to the nature of the traffic congestion and disadvantage in the event of an accident. We did likewise and restricted our driving to on-base. Vehicles and drivers were very inexpensive for off-base traveling. In fact the country is a poverty stricken nation and everything very inexpensive – by American standards. Filipinos viewed all Americans as millionaires and by their standard of living and income, we probably were. (As a side note here, on March 29th 1972 I reached the 20 year milestone in my active duty military career. No bump that I noticed anyway.)

Pat was a little cool to Nora initially but kind. She wasn't sure that she liked the idea of having a house-girl in the house and in her kitchen. She wanted to do everything herself as most American housewives wish to do in their own home. I told her that every American household on Clark employed a house-girl and yard-boy. It was an employment opportunity for them in an impoverished land; and that they would keep the house and yard immaculate. In fact the entire base was a beautiful and immaculately kept tropical paradise maintained by employed Filipino maintenance personnel and grounds keepers. This provided ample leisure time for the wives and jobs for the local Filipino populous. It wasn't long until Pat warmed up to Nora and decided she liked the house-girl/yard-boy idea with all the leisure time it provided her for shopping, travel, base events, Officers Wives Club and church activities. We joined the Clark Field Southern Baptist Church located immediately outside the base main gate and

279

soon Pat was busily involved there. On May 10th I was ordained into the church as a Baptist Deacon. As mentioned above, it was a mixed congregation; about half American and half Filipino. The pastor was an American Southern Baptist Missionary: Allen Smith and his wife, Frankie, who would become one of Pat's best friends while we were at Clark. They had two daughters. The assistant pastor was a Filipino by the name of Nordito and would become a great family friend of ours.

Nora kept the house neat and clean and she had a brother, Romey, that we hired as a yard-boy. Her husband, Ruben, would also do some yard work for us on occasion. I think Pat quickly came to enjoy our home in Angeles City in spite of the geckos on the ceiling and walls. The geckos had tiny suction-cups on their feet that enabled them to cling to walls and ceilings. It was very entertaining to see them suddenly dart across the ceiling or up the walls in pursuit of some tasty tidbit in the form of a pesky mosquito or other tropical pests. Jungle wild life was not a serious threat around Clark and in the villages; but, it was something to be aware of. There was always the occasional sighting of a snake of some tropical variety in the neighborhood. And of course, with the poisonous varieties in the tropics, they were not to be taken lightly. One evening just about dark I heard some kids yelling excitedly in the back yard. I stepped outside the back door in the dark and to this day I'm sure I felt something slither quickly across my foot. The kids said they thought they had seen a snake. We looked and looked but never found anything.

A short time later around May 10th 1972, I was authorized, and moved into, family quarters on Clark AB. It was a nice house at 301 19th Place in base housing. We packed up and settled in to our new home. Pat and Nora became great shopping buddies and companions. To do otherwise would have been grossly out-of-character for Pat. We gave Nora money to do grocery shopping off-base. She cooked delicious meals and knew American concerns for food preparations and potable water. Whenever Pat wanted to go off-base Nora would accompany her to the main gate where she would hail a Filipino Jitney for their shopping. (Jitney: Filipino taxi – World War Two Jeeps converted into colorful taxis. The Jitney drivers tried to outdo each other in their colorful decorations and painting of their Jitneys). Nora didn't want Pat to be cheated or scammed so she would not let her buy anything at the Filipinos' American prices. She would always make sure the vendor gave Pat the *Filipino prices.* This applied to everything: food, clothes, furniture, transportation, etc. Pat loved oriental furnishing and pictures. She took advantage of the unbelievably low prices to purchase furniture, pictures, wood carvings and brassware. I believe that Pat and Robert thoroughly enjoyed their Philippine tour. I did! In fact the three of us became very close with Nora, her friends and family. On June 25th Nora made her profession in Jesus Christ as her Savior and joined the Clark Field Baptist Church. We of course were overjoyed for her.

We were invited into Filipino friends' homes for dinners and to community festival events. It seemed that they could not do enough for the *Americanos.* I know it would have been rude of us and embarrassing for them if we declined their hospitality, but I always felt that with their impoverished conditions that we should have been treating them. I don't think I have ever ate more delicious meals than those in Filipino homes; although cooked on/in ancient utensils, on floor hearths and over coals. The Filipinos had a reputation for thievery. I had heard stories of American passengers in jitneys having their watch snatched from their wrist as they moved slowly along in heavy traffic with their arm overboard. There was the perpetual story about some Filipinos stealing a fire truck from the base fire station. The black market was evident in stores off base. You could find American goods that were also in the Base Exchange. We trusted Nora and her family explicitly and felt totally safe.

Norris: University of Richmond to the Southwestern Baptist Theological Seminary

Graduating from the University of Richmond on June 5th 1972, Norris would enter the Southwestern Baptist Theological Seminary, Fort Worth, Texas that Fall for a Doctorate in Theology. We would miss his University of Richmond graduation but was able to later attend his Seminary graduation.

Berserk Bat!

This story was told to me by Pat. I think I must have been away TDY to Vietnam. Pat said she was sitting in our bedroom one afternoon reading. Nora was in the middle of the floor in the front room reading with a blanket over her lap. Robert and Puff were also in the front room. Suddenly Pat heard Nora let out a blood-curdling scream and began hysterical screeching. She ran to the front room to find Nora doubled over in the floor with the blanket over her head and continuing to scream at the top of her voice. Robert had Puff by the tail trying to restrain him as he lunged about trying to get loose. Then she saw it! There was a huge bat flitting about the room from wall to wall and swooping down occasionally toward Nora. Each time the bat would ricochet off the wall or swoop down, Puff would lung at it while Robert held on to his tail for dear life – Puff's life actually. Pat retreated to the bedroom to call the base Air Police. By the time the Air Police arrived, Puff had been secured in another room and the Bat had lit in a small tree branch that Pat had mounted on a large board and hung on the front room wall as a three-dimensional "tree" decoration.

Two Air Policemen arrived and knocked on the front door. Robert answered the door and they asked about the problem. Apparently they had not been briefed by the desk sergeant taking Pat's call. Robert told them that there was a Bat in the tree. When they asked where the tree was, Robert said "In there" and pointed into the front room. The two Air Policemen looked at each other first with a puzzled glance then with an all-knowing smirk and rolling of their eyes.

281

One of the Air Policemen stuck his head in the door, then in a moment turned to his partner and said: "There is a bat in a tree in here!" They proceeded to *arrest* the bat but we never learned its sentence. The source of the bat's entry was never determined but squirrels would find their way into the attic from the roof eves. I suspect that the bat found the same route into the attic and then into the house – or maybe by an open door. It could have been on some fruit brought into the house.

Puff Lost!

We had decided early on in Puff's life to make him a house-cat, rather than let him be endangered by dogs and/or become a neighborhood nuisance. In the Philippines we had a third concern: Some Filipinos eat cats. So imagine our consternation one night when Puff – as cats will – darted pasted us into the dark of night while the door was ajar. Instantly Pat, Robert, Nora and I also darted after him but he disappeared into the dark; his being black didn't help. Up and down the street and around the neighborhood we went calling his name and flashing a flashlight about. Now how many cats do you know that when they are aware that they are being hunted, will come at the calling of their name, not to mention their feline independence. Foremost in my mind of course was that he will become someone's gourmet dinner. This search went on for half an hour or more with not a "meow" or response from Puff. Then I, for at least the third time, got down on all fours and flashed the light under our car by the curb in front of the house. There was a pair of glowing orange eyes staring back as me as if to say: "You looking for me?" "Of course, you silly cat!" Were we ever so relieved!

"Royalty"

One weekend, Nora and Romey, her brother, invited Pat, Robert and me to spend a weekend with her and her parents at their home on the shore of the Lingayen Gulf, about 100 to 150 miles north of Clark AB. It was in the Lingayen Gulf that an Allied amphibious operation headed up by the American 6th Army established a 20 mile beachhead to commence a January 6th, 1945 invasion – one of many such invasions – to take back the Philippines from the Japanese. Filipino resistance to the Japanese occurred throughout the Philippines. Clark AB was recaptured from the Japanese during the last week of January. Romey gave Robert a Japanese Navy steel helmet he picked up on the beaches of the Lingayen Gulf. Of course all the leather was long gone. It was identified as "Navy" by a faint anchor barely visible painted on the front of the helmet.

The gulf and beaches were beautiful. Nora and her family treated us like royalty and we ate better that kings in spite of their impoverished conditions. Cooking was done on an open hearth of fire and coals at one end of the room in their thatched roof home. The feast was fabulous with their family and friends – a room full of people. Most spoke English except for one of the grandmothers. You couldn't have asked for a better fellowship. We bonca-boated out into the gulf and swam in the clearest blue water I have ever seen – then and since. From a few feet down into the water when looking up at the boat above, the water was so clear that you could see clearly the blue sky and white puffy clouds. The boat seemed to be suspended in air. Later, as was the Filipino custom, I was invited to take a siesta in the afternoon. I was escorted into an open air room and shown a bamboo-slated bed; no bedding. I sleep well on that bare bamboo. We had no fear for our safety or of thievery.

Back at Clark when we would travel off base to or through a small village, there would be a crowd of school children that would press around the vehicle to get a glimpse of the Americans. They would be waving and shouting: "Americano, Americano!" I was concerned that the driver might run over one of them. But we had to move so slowly that they were able to push their way clear of the vehicle. They must have a fabulous intelligence/communication system because other schools' children would be ready for us and repeat the scene at the each village down the road. It seemed that each elementary school would turn out their students to see the "Americanos" pass by. For the most part Filipinos seemed to appreciate Americans. They hadn't forgotten The American GIs and Allies routing the Japanese from their islands in World War Two with the assistance of Filipino "gorilla" fighters. General MacArthur was their hero.

We would be invited to local community social events. Before Pat and Robert arrived, my friend from the 405th Wing and I had been invited to a festive occasion. You would have thought we were the honored guest. Sometime after Pat and Robert arrived, we were invited to a Valentine Ball, I think it was. Although I don't dance I shuffled around a bit on the dance floor with Pat. I was sitting at a table with Pat on the edge of the dance floor when suddenly a really cute little Filipino girl about five years old, came across the dance floor swinging her hips and right up to me and extending her hands. She wanted me to dance with her! I know someone had to have put her up to it. I turned all shades of red but I couldn't refuse. Anyway, I shuffled around a bit with her and was so delighted at her apparent joy of dancing with the "Americano". At one event, maybe this one, I was asked to speak. I briefly spoke of the friendliness of the Filipino people; and my appreciation for their hospitality toward my family and me.

Except for the Filipino civilians hired by the US government on Clark, local Filipinos were very poor and as mentioned previously, house girls and yard boys were paid typically cheap wages. Pat and I decided we were uncomfortable paying such low wages. So we paid just a bit more than the typical wage. Later we learned that Nora was not saving anything; in fact most of her wages went to her father for the family, as was common in many Filipino families. We also learned that she did not have and had never had a bank account. We convinced her to open a savings account in her name and we would increase her wages, again very slightly, if she would deposit the increase into her savings account – without telling her father! She agreed and for the first time in her life, she had a bank account. By the time my two-year tour was over, Nora had a modest savings account by Filipino standards. After we returned to the States, Pat and Nora continued to correspond for many years. We learned that Nora's father found out about her bank account and demanded that she turn it over to him. I don't remember if we ever learned how he found out.

Exploring the Philippines

After Pat and Robert arrived and got comfortable with their new surrounding and the Filipino culture, we set out to enjoy the adventure. On April 10th, Pat had her first trip by Jitney into Angeles City with Nora. Our first earth quake experience (tremor) was during the night of April 26th which we all slept through and then another tremor on May 22nd. They were getting their initiation early. All travel off-base would be with a hired Filipino driver and vehicle, or base provided transportation through the base recreational office. I didn't dare drive in that traffic spaghetti bowl! The main street in Angeles City was a narrow two-way two-lane street. However, there were no identified lane lines and all sorts of pedestrian and vehicular traffic used the street, all at the same time and in every direction: Foot traffic, bicycles, carts, Jitneys, small and large sedans, trucks and busses. All traffic mixed, going in every direction at the same time, weaving in and out among everything and everyone; a true traffic mixing bowl. You may find yourself on the left side of the street and the next moment on the right side; or even crosswise to the street. The horn was used instead of brakes. It meant that the driver was taking the right-of-way and you better yield. It was constant honking! If you looked a pedestrian or driver in the eye, you just yielded the right of way to them. So no one looked at anyone. As Americanos, if you had an accident, you were at the mercy of the Filipino court system – and they thought you were rich! Even if you were a passenger in a hired car with a Filipino driver you might be charged with the accident.

Pat, Robert and I attended a Clark Field Baptist Church organized retreat at the Southern Baptist Camp Grounds on the southern tip of The Bataan Peninsula. The island of Corregidor is an islet at the entrance to Manila Bay. Corregidor contains the World War Two remains of General MacArthur's Headquarters from where he was ordered by President Roosevelt to Australia to avoid immanent capture by the Japanese advance in 1942. The tunnels, gun emplacements and small dirt landing strip still remain. Quarters on the Bataan campground were barrack-styled and built with screened open-air windows from about chest high. The meeting place was an open pavilion with thatched roof. Pat and Robert had Filipino boatmen in bonca boats (hewed out log canoes with stabilizing outrigger floats) take them out onto Manila Bay – and I think across to Corregidor. My memory is sort of fuzzy of that event. Our route from Clark AB to the camp ground was the route of the infamous World War

Two Bataan Death March forced upon American, Filipino and other Allied captives after the fall of the Philippines. One could not help but think of the stories of horror that those captives endured at the hand of their Japanese captors. You can read about the horrors of "The Bataan Death March" on the internet. We also travelled to Camp O'Donnell, the POW camp just north of Clark AB where the march from Bataan ended and the prisoners were interned until shipped to Japan.

"Civilization!"

We met some great missionaries while in the Philippines. Pat was always involved with our church Women's Missionary Union (WMU) and foreign missions were her interest. Our church has an annual emphasis on both a "home" and "foreign" mission work and we always made annual donations to each. We met Howard and Marge Olive at Clark Field Baptist Church. They invited Pat and me to visit them and their Southern Baptist mission work in Manila, which we did for a couple of days in November. Howard was director of the Far East radio ministry and Marge was engrossed in helping Howard and in conducting other missionary duties throughout the Philippines. We also met Ken and Connie Glass, Southern Baptist missionaries in Davao, Mindanao, while they were visiting Clark Field Baptist Church. They too invited Pat, Robert and me to visit them in Mindanao. We arranged for a week's visit in December 1972 while Robert was on his school's Christmas Holidays.

We flew down to Davao, Mindanao on a Philippine airline with one en route stop at Cebu. It was a different world outside Clark AB and Manila. Passengers would "swamp" the ticket agent at the ticket window with everyone pushing, shoving and shouting all at the same time. The only way to assure that you got a ticket was to hold up a few extra Pesos for the ticket agent. American dollars would likely guarantee that you wouldn't be "bumped".

Ken met us at the Davao airport and transported us in his Southern Baptist Mission-provided Scout to their missionary home in M'lang, Mindanao. This was about a two to two and a half hour bouncing trip over dirt, mostly rutted, rough and occasionally rock strewn jungle road into the inter-island. Occasionally it seemed that I would be tossed out of the vehicle and that we would never get there. I thought of stories I had read and heard about American aircrews being shot down over the jungle during World War Two; stories that told of the aircrews being hidden from Japanese search parties by friendly natives whose villages had been visited by Christian missionaries long before.

About half way to M'lang, we came to a small settlement where an American agricultural missionary and his wife had a small farm. They taught the Filipinos proper farming and gardening to prevent erosion and how to grow healthy crops. Of course underlying all missionary assistance to the local populous was the teaching of Jesus Christ and Salvation. The island of Mindanao was a hot-bed of Muslim insurgence against the Philippine government. Skirmishes were common occurrences. This was foremost in my mind throughout our stay in Mindanao. Generally towns and villages were safe. It was the remote jungle areas that were the sites of these encounters. And of course we were in a remote jungle location. We came to another clearing about a hundred and fifty yards long and fifty yards wide: M'lang! There were just a few shacks on each side of the one-and-only dirt-street through the village. These were small businesses and a market place. The market place had a couple of Jitneys parked in front and appeared to be a "taxi" stand. Half way through the village on the right side of the dirt street in front of the market was an open shed (no doors) which function was immediately apparent. It was open to the street side and contained a *two-holed* accommodation: An outhouse! Ken said that it was the public co-ed restroom. Then I saw it: A red Coco-Cola truck parked by the outhouse – "Civilization" here in the middle of the jungle! *I had no more concerns.*

It was often that you would see young boys out and about ridding their caribou (water buffalo): plowing or pulling heavy laden two-wheeled carts. Nearby was a slow-moving muddy stream about 75 feet across and about a caribou's back deep. It was the local swimming hole, fish "pond," bathhouse and *carwash (caribou).* The boys would be scrubbing the caribou with brushes for its "Saturday night" bath and theirs too. It was a community gathering place for just about anything that had to do with water.

There was a huge two-story Southern Baptist church on the outskirts of the village and a long screened building which was a Southern Baptist mission operated school: The village school house. Of course Ken and Connie (with their two small daughters about five and eight years old), were the Christian focus in the village, church and school. We thoroughly enjoyed our visit with them. Their youngest daughter was a fair-skinned, yellow-haired blond. When she was in the village, young Filipino children would gather around her to stare at her yellow hair. Too soon it was over. Back into the Scout and on the road to Davao – (not "the road to Mandalay" of the Bob Hope and Bing Crosby movie) – for our return flight to Manila; then the vehicle trip back to Clark AB. I had always had an appreciation of Christian missionaries around the world. I came away from M'lang with an even more heightened appreciation for them.

Back at Clark AB

I joined the Clark AB Aero Club which was a small dirt strip on Clark AB parallel to the main runway. I flew Pat and Robert around the islands, over extinct and active volcanos, dense jungle and into and through mountain passes and valleys. There are thousands of rice paddies terraced on the mountain sides. We flew low along the river in the valley looking up at the near vertical walls of rice terraces high above us, and around miles of the western coast of Luzon and the Hundred Islands. Beautiful! I flew them to the mountain Baptist Seminary at Baguio about fifty miles or so north of Clark AB. We landed on their short mountain top airstrip with shear drop offs at each end of the runway. This was some of my most enjoyable aero club flying experience. We also visited the Baptist Seminary at Baguio sometime later to see some of our Filipino friends graduate. On another excursion we joined a group tour several miles east of Manila into the jungle to a small resort area. There we did a river canoe trip to a remote water fall area: Pagsanjan Falls. Beautiful! I kept looking for Tarzan; or more correctly, Jane!

All Play and no Work......

........Doesn't get the job done. I still had a job to do. Pat had more time to enjoy life in the Philippines than me; but, I was happy for her because she had had to handle so many moves and home front chores alone while I was away *defending America.*

My boss soon rotated back to the States ending his tour in the Philippines. He was an avid sail boat enthusiast and had a sailboat built which he sailed back to America with his family. Somewhere along the way he decided to send his family on ahead and finish the trip sailing alone. I think it was after his boat was robbed of some major equipment and some cash while in port. The robbery occurred at one of his ports-of-call; Hong Kong, I think I was. With his return to the States, I was now the Wing Plans Officer. It was the office secretary and me. She was a jewel! Not only was she great at typing, proofing, editing, spelling (my weakness), filing and steno graphing; she also gladly kept my coffee cup filled as needed – without whining that it was not in her job description – as I've known some staff secretaries to do.

Note: As I write this, I am saddened. I recently received a Christmas card (our annual correspondence) from her husband that she passed away about a year ago.

My T-33 flying got me out of the office occasionally. I flew often with my good friend from the operations section and my friend, the Intelligence Officer. I had two or three cross-country flights to Tainan, Taiwan; across the ocean between the Philippines north coast and Taiwan. The trips were over water and on occasion you could see the angry wind-blown waves white with froth between them – *and you would suddenly remember that you only have one engine.* These flights were courier flights between Clark and the Wing's detachment located at Tainan. One such flight was about March 9th, 1973. I recall that I had an opportunity to visit Tainan that night and make like a tourist. The Chinese people were great and I had absolutely no concern for my safety; even visiting the shops at night alone. I know I bought gifts for Pat and Robert but my memory fails me as to what the gifts were. Pat liked oriental furnishings.

Vietnam #3 – June 1972

A few months after Pat and Robert arrived; I was sent TDY to Tan Son Nhut AB, Saigon, Vietnam on June 11th 1972 to perform duty in the 7th Air Force Tactical Air Control Center (TACC) as Fighter Duty Officer. This was a three month TDY to augment the TACC when North Vietnam decided to invade South Vietnam after the United States had begun to draw-down our forces there. This should be a lesson for the US; but alas, we never seem to learn. Here I was for the third time in Vietnam (my second to Tan Son Nhut) since 1961 for a total of thirteen months in South Vietnam. Basically, nothing had changed in the war except for more sophisticated hardware; more proliferation and more lethal guns, planes, bombs and other tools of war. Battles raged in the same places but on a much larger scale. *The day belonged to us; the night still belonged to them!*

During my three months there the Philippines endured a terrible typhoon engulfing Clark with inundating rains and extremely high winds. Much damage was sustained although mostly debris and large tree limbs were downed around our home on Clark. Pat and Robert had endured a typhoon which I have never had the pleasure of experiencing.

While at Tan Son Nhut I had a chance to send many oriental gifts and souvenirs home to Pat and Robert at Clark. Among the largest items were ceramic elephants about two feet tall. These were the rage of Americans and I bought six (I think) for our home; and was enlisted to purchase several for friends at Clark. They must have weighed about 20 pounds and were very awkward to carry. I had to carry each one about a quarter of a mile to my "hooch" (BOQ) and then to the post office for mailing back to Clark AB. Years later these elephants in our home at Eglin AFB, Fort Walton Beach, Florida would generate an interesting and amusing event with some Vietnam refugee friends visiting in our home. (More on that later).

Duty shifts in the TACC were 12 hours: Four days on followed by four nights on then four days off – as I recall. As a Fighter Duty Officer I was a liaison between the TACC, the fighter wings and other duty officers regarding ordnance loads, Air refueling coordination and mission progress for in-country and out-country missions. Aircrews referred to missions over Hanoi as "Going down town"! I had a radio, phone and mission board access as tools-of-the-trade. The mission board was a huge wall-to-wall, floor-to-ceiling plotting board with plotters behind the board using grease pencils to track the progress of each mission. North Vietnam was divided into geographical mission sectors called "packages". Memory fades but some earlier geographical/packages/missions into North Vietnam were: Steel Tiger, Rolling Thunder, and Route Pack One. I'm sure the aircrews who flew them remember them well. Linebacker I (B-52 bombing) occurred while I was at Tan Son Nhut. Linebacker II occurred later. "Linebacker I and II" were joint Air Force/Navy bombing campaigns. Many times there would be a "Mayday" call, or the aircrew emergency beeper would go off. Everything immediately focused on rescuing the downed aircrew. Unfortunately some were unsuccessful. It was very saddening to hear that an aircrew member was captured or there was no possible way that he or they survived the crash. I renewed my running as a means of trying to stay in condition should I literally find myself running for my life. In 1964 at Cannon AFB when I was assigned to F-100s I established a running program for conditioning, and intensified my running each time I was assigned to a combat zone. Great motivation! Tan Son Nhut was no exception. For years later I continued a jogging program until my back just wouldn't cooperate anymore. After three months I was back at Clark AB and to my daily plans office routine.

Floods!

Being the tropical paradise it was, the Philippines Islands were occasionally flooded by heavy rains, especially during the monsoon season. Clark AB, however, was on slightly higher ground than the surrounding Angeles City and other villages and thus not generally affected by flooding during these heavy rains. At Clark I did see some of the heaviest rains ever experienced in my life: Rains so solid and heavy that you could not see 10 feet into them; literally they were a wall of water! Being out in the downpour was not really uncomfortable due to the warm temperature of the water. Sometimes a rain shower would be a bit cooling, but after each rain the sticky, muggy humidity would raise sharply – a real sauna!

One period of time we had unrelenting rains for days. The nearby river became a rampage of rapidly moving angry dirty water undercutting village homes and property and sweeping them away never to be seen again. Villages and rice paddies were flooded as far as you could see. Even from the air it looked as if the sea had overtaken the islands except for the higher mountains. Homes, schools and highways destroyed; many lives lost. Clark AB personnel pitched in to help with the disaster relief. We had a sergeant friend who volunteered his assistance. Robert asked us if he could accompany him. Robert was fifteen years old so Pat and I were very reluctant to let him go. The water was very high and rapidly moving. However, we finally relented, charging our friend to take care of him. They had the use of a base 2 ½ ton truck (commonly known as a "duce-and-a-half"). Stories they later told of the perilous situations they encountered caused Pat and me to wander what possessed us to grant Robert's participation in the first place. Robert said at times water was over the engine of the truck; which had intake and exhaust systems that enable it to ford lakes and streams. Other times they were on foot up to their necks in the water. They did a lot of sand-bagging for shoring up levies and homes, hauling people across raging waters and generally assisting wherever they could. We were proud of Robert and I think the participation made him feel good in that he had contributed significantly to helping save homes and lives.

Snake School!

Aircrew personnel assigned to Clark were required to attend the Air Force Jungle Survival School at Clark, more commonly referred to as "Snake School". My turn came on October 7th 1972. Following the days of classroom work that included jungle survival uses of the parachute, edible and poisonous plants and jungle wildlife, we were taken into the jungle and dropped off at individual locations away from other class members. Our provisions were the bare survival items: A portion of a parachute canopy, a couple of "C" rations, knife and a small bag of rice which we were instructed not to eat. We were instructed to set up our individual camp until daybreak. There were many unknown sounds throughout the jungle night; some very near my parachute shelter: Birds, man or beast? After a couple of days of onsite ground school our instructions were to break camp and proceed further into the jungle and hide as though trying to escape and evade capture from enemy troops after parachuting into the jungle.

The Survival School employed local Negrito tribesmen – expert trackers – to look for us. The Negritos are small indigenous, tribal, pigmy-like people who live deep in the jungle and are rarely seen in populated areas. Our mission was to hide and evade them for the day. The reward for us was simply knowing that we had evaded some of the best jungle trackers in the world. If we were found, we were to surrender the bag of rice to the Negrito finding us (his reward). We would then make our way back to the main camp while the Negrito went literally running off to find his next "captive".

I sat out to find my hiding place for the day. You would think that finding a hiding place in the jungle would be a snap. After some time looking, I found a place before the Negritos would be turned loose to look for us. I decided on a pile of jungle debris nestled against a large tree. I crawled under the dead limbs and trash until I thought I was thoroughly hidden and waited. While waiting, my mind played dirty tricks on me. I thought to myself, what am I doing under this pile of jungle debris with the possibility of finding myself none-to-nose with a cobra? They were around! I kept listening for sounds and movement. Fortunately none developed – until about fifteen minutes later – when I felt a tapping on the bottom of my boot. For a moment I wasn't sure what it was. Cautiously I looked around to see a beetle-nut stained, snaggle-toothed grin (that an orthodontist would love) staring at me under the pile of debris. The grin belonged to a small brown Negrito motioning for me to come out. I struggled out and there he stood, about four feet tall in bare feet and loin cloth, brown and wrinkled, not an ounce of fat and extending his hand for the bag of rice! As soon as he had his bag of rice he was gone in a flash back into the jungle to "capture" his next victim and receive his reward. Needless to say, had this been a real-life escape-and-evasion scenario, I would have been a POW. Lots of mind stimulating thoughts on this afterwards. I think one guy out of our class of about fifteen succeeded in avoiding capture. It was a great school and I'm sure saved many a downed airman's life in Vietnam. Fortunately, I never had to use the skills taught by the Clark Snake School (PTL). It would be nice if I could remember all that was taught. If so, I would probably compete for a spot, and a million dollars, on the popular TV reality show: "Survivor". I did learn that you can do most anything with a piece of bamboo – even build a fire with it while it's soaking wet.

The school kept a few pythons for demonstration purposes. One about eight feet long or so they used to demonstrate how a python could strike in the wink of an eye to capture its prey with its mouth, and almost simultaneously throw a couple of coils around the victim; then begin its increasing constriction depriving the victim of breathing capacity. I took Pat and Robert by the school to show them around. One of the instructors let Robert and me handle a six-foot python and drape it around our necks. Not a comfortable feeling. Pat held it in her lap. Never would I have thought Pat would do such a thing, but she did!

US POWs Return From Hanoi!

I don't remember the exact time when the United States began to pull-out of Vietnam indicating that the American will had wilted and our government was "taking their marbles and going home". Unfortunately we left many of our most valuable marbles in the Hanoi "Hilton" and other prison compounds as POWs of the North Vietnamese. Our billions of dollars of war-fighting equipment, airbases and construction projects were left in South Vietnam which soon fell to the North Vietnamese Communist. What a landfall we handed to the North Vietnamese! "Hanoi" Jane (Jane Fonda) and her North Vietnam sympathizers were influential in encouraging the North Vietnamese and duping the American people. Sadly, with her fame and celebrity status, she could have done so much for the American service man.

The American people and our government were slow to take up the cause of our POWs and MIAs (missing-in-action); except for the POW/MIA wives and families. There was a well-coordinated and oiled POW wives organization to get Hanoi to release our POWs. The wives organized meetings with government officials, held rallies, published pamphlets and documents detailing the plight of their loved ones. They met with North Vietnamese government officials at the 1973 Paris Peace Accords in France on behalf of their husbands and family POWs still held in Hanoi. The wives had bracelets manufactured containing their POW husbands' name and date of capture. They then organized nationwide distribution of the bracelets free of charge. While at Seymour-

Johnson AFB, Goldsboro, North Carolina before being permitted to travel to Clark AB, Pat became friends with the wife of a POW. She gave Pat a bracelet with her husband's name and his date of shoot-down. Most of those wearing the bracelet of a named POW/MIA expressed intention of wearing the bracelet until Hanoi released that particular POW. The POW wives' organizations are entitled to a lion's share of the accolades for getting our POWs released beginning in March 1973 following the 1973 Paris Peace Accords.

Pat, Robert and I had the extreme emotional fortune to be at Clark AB when the POW release began in March 1973. They were airlifted from Hanoi to Clark via US Air force C-141s converted to medical air evacuation aircraft. Words won't convey the emotion experienced at seeing the POWs emerge from those C-141s, salute the American flag and the throng of welcoming crowds; some struggle proudly unassisted down the stairs to meet the military dignitaries welcoming them. They then boarded an Air Force bus to be transported to the Clark AB hospital. Of course the emotions exhibited by the crowds (throngs of people) can only scratch the surface compared to the emotions experienced by those returning POWs – some whom had been imprisoned for up to eight years. In addition to Pat's friend's husband, I had two POW friends that would be returning. One had been a POW for six years or more and the other for six months. Two of these POWs would be on one of the earlier returning POW aircraft; February 12th 1973. And one later on March 29th since release was in order of the shoot-down date. The date, time and names of POWs on board each aircraft were published before the aircraft arrived. But the base psychiatrists warned the base personnel that they should not go to the flight line to welcome the returning POWs; because it would *upset them emotionally since they had been so long interned as prisoners of war.* NUTS! (No pun intended). Fortunately no one paid any attention to this nonsense. The flight line crowds were massive, cheering, whistling, waving American flags, etc. Later the POWs would confirm that those crowds were the most beautiful sight they had seen in many years; and put to rest their fears that they would not be welcomed back.

I had made a large sign about two feet square and in large letters naming Pat's friend's husband and my long-time friend welcoming them Home! When their plane arrived, Pat, Robert and I were in the middle of the throng of people. When the bus was loaded with the POWs and getting ready to leave for the hospital, I held the sign as high as I could reach. Suddenly, I heard a voice in the bus shout: "_____," there's your name!" I saw a head stick out the window as the bus drove by and it was my friend. He saw me and yelled: "Hey, George!" We were instructed not to attempt contact with any POW. If they wished contact with anyone, they would be the initiator. The second night that these POW friends were in the Clark hospital, our home phone rang. It was my friend! He sounded great. We talked a few minutes then he asked if we would like to come to the hospital for a visit. Of course I told him yes. Pat, Robert and I were excited as we drove to the hospital to meet him. It was great seeing him again. Pat and Robert knew him also. He told me when he saw my sign from the bus while at the flight line, he immediately recognized me – and that he would "...recognize that nose anywhere!" I can only imagine the joy he was experiencing at being free again. We had served together in 1959 to 1964 at Goose Bay, Labrador and Shaw AFB, South Carolina, although we were assigned to two different detachments of our squadron at Shaw AFB, SC; him at Pope AFB, NC and me at Fort Gordon, Georgia. I last saw him at Luke AFB, Arizona in 1965 while I was checking out in the F-100. He was on his way to Thailand to fly the F-105 and was there only a short time before his shoot-down.

We asked him if he knew Pat's friend's husband and showed him the bracelet on Pat's wrist. He said yes. Technically we still were forbidden from asking to see him, but my friend asked us if we would like to meet him. "We certainly would" we responded. In a couple of minutes he was back with this POW friend. It was an emotional meeting and particularly so when Pat showed him his bracelet on her wrist and explained that his wife had given it to her. Pat asked him if he would like to have the bracelet. He did of course and Pat let him remove the bracelet from her wrist. The POW wives had mass produced a wooden plaque about 10 inches square with a red, white and blue shield on front and the inscription: "POW MIAs, don't let them be forgotten!" We showed them our plaque and asked them to sign the back. They did, and then my friend asked if we would like him to take it through the hospital getting more autographs. "Yes"! Soon he was back with the back of the plaque completely filled with autographs. I still have the sign that I made which is autographed by our two friends; and the wives POW MIA plaque full of autographs. They only shared brief stories about their POW experiences – and of course we didn't ask. It was a great reunion and I can only imagine the great joy, relief and thankfulness those POWs were experiencing. On March 7th, they boarded a US Air Force C-141 to the United States. Thank the Lord it was over for them and their families. The emotional high for me is something I won't forget as long as God allows me to have my memory. Certainly it was the highlight of my tour at Clark. Since my tour at Clark AB, I have read many of the books authored by the former POWs and marvel at the courage, resistance and endurance they exhibited. I have told my friends it is a fortunate thing that I was never captured. With my low pain threshold, I would not have made it out alive.

Goodbye to Paradise!

I had additional TDYs while at Clark other than Tan Son Nhut and Tainan. They were: Osan AB, Korea; Hickam AFB, Honolulu, Hawaii; and Kadena AB, Okinawa, Japan.

Our Clark AB assignment was coming to an end. On April 26, 1973 I received orders assigning me to the 19th Tactical Air Support Squadron (TASS) at Osan

AB, Osan, Korea. This would be a consecutive overseas tour; however Korea would be unaccompanied – meaning that my family was not authorized to accompany me. The orders authorized 31 days of leave (delay en-route) which included five days delay in Tokyo. Pat was big into Japanese flower arranging and she was excited that she would be able to experience her hobby in Tokyo.

On May 22nd The Wing had a "Hail and Farewell" banquet for those of us leaving within a couple of months. Then June 15th I sold our vehicles with permission to use them until our departure. On June 16th our friend Nordito (assistant pastor) was married to his fiancée, Mila (Mee-la). They were married at Clark Field Baptist Church. Amidst all the preparations to return to the States, Pat found time to coordinate their wedding and make their wedding cake. On June 18th Puff was picked up by the Vet to be shipped back to the US (to Pat's mother). Our final base housing inspection was on June 25th with base out-processing on June 27th. June 28th was our port call at the air terminal for transportation to the US.

Our en route stop in Tokyo was a great five days where we sat on the floor to eat at Japanese restaurants. The waitresses were beautiful Japanese girls in kimonos. We tried the chopsticks which seemed the thing to do – since that's all we were given to eat with. Pat was having particular difficulty with her chopsticks and rice bowl. Then she noticed a Japanese gentleman at another table staring at her while holding his rice bowl up to his mouth and holding his chopsticks over the bowl. Once he had her attention, he extended his chopstick toward her slightly then began shoveling his rice into his mouth. He was showing her how the Japanese people do it; rather than trying to dig the rice out of the bowl on the table and bring the chopsticks up to the mouth. The Japanese people were extremely friendly and polite; even when boarding crowded bus and rail transportation. We boarded the "bullet" train, which is supposed to do well over a 100 miles per hour, to a tourist area about a 100 miles south of Tokyo. It was the first time in my life that I had ever traveled faster than 100 miles per hour in surface transportation. (That's my story and I'm sticking to it). We got to see a Japanese funeral procession (according to our bus driver) making its way on foot through town. They used the long dragon costume "snaking" its way through the streets. In Tokyo Pat got to visit the Japanese flower arranging school which was a real treat for her. It was a great fun time we had – but we had to end it and get on our way to the US. (Besides, Japan was expensive – even then in 1973). We also had a couple of days in Honolulu, Hawaii – I think. I had been to Honolulu a couple of times before and got to visit Waikiki Beach and the American National Cemetery. The national cemetery was very impressive and emotional. Then to Florida to find Pat and Robert a home and visit our families before I was to head back across the "Wide Missouri" and the Pacific to Osan, Korea.

My travel orders en route to Osan would take me to the US Air Force Basic Survival School at Fairchild AFB, Spokane, Washington; and to the US Air Force Air/Ground Operations School (FAC School) at Hurlburt Field, Florida. This was sort of a "cart-before-the-horse" situation since I had already been to Southeast Asia (Vietnam) as a FAC. I would have a few days with Pat, Robert and our families before reporting to Fairchild AFB; between Fairchild and Hurlburt; then between Hurlburt and Osan. My 1973 reporting dates were: Fairchild AFB July 8th; Hurlburt Field August 19th; and Osan AB September 30th. So long Clark AB!

I found a duplex for Pat and Robert while I would be in Korea. It was only a few blocks from her mother's home in Florida. I enjoyed our time with our families and our visits with friends. On one of these visits we would be away for a few days. A young lady friend of ours agreed to feed and check on Puff daily while we were away. As a kitten, when he wanted to go outside, we had taught him to jump into our hands which we would hold in front of us at hip high. He was now grown and about twelve pounds but still jumped to us to go outside, especially if we stood by the door. But we forgot to tell our lady friend. When we returned she told us of a day that Puff scared the daylight out of her when she turned to the door to leave. Suddenly she found this twelve pound black ball of fur climbing up her shoulders. She showed us the claw marks on her shoulders. I felt so bad for her and that we had forgotten to warn her. But she was laughing and good natured about it. One of the highlights of our time together before I left was a deep sea fishing trip with Pat's sister Carrie on their boat. I'm not much on fishing but it was fun. I even took her boys, Morris and David flying while there – or maybe it was on one of our previous visits. I recall that my son Norris and his family visited us at one time and I flew all of us to visit Carrie. That too may have been an earlier time. But all of this fun-time was soon over and on July 6th I was on my way to Fairchild AFB, Washington for Air Force Survival School. So many departures: Always difficult. So many homecomings: So great!

*****

CHAPTER EIGHTEEN
CAMP RED CLOUD; Uijongbu, Korea (1974)

U.S. Air Force Survival School

The time came for me to leave Pat and Robert for my reporting date of July 8th, 1973 to the Air Force's basic survival school at Fairchild AFB, Spokane, Washington. The school was scheduled for 14 days. I was glad it was the middle of the summer rather than the middle of winter. There would be a few days back with my family between survival school and my reporting date of August 19th to the USAF Air/Ground Operations School (AGOS pronounced A-GOS) at Hurlburt Field, Mary Esther, Florida. Hurlburt Field is on the Gulf Coast a few miles west of Fort Walton Beach and Eglin AFB. It was the center for Air Force Special Operations – formally Air Commando School – which included, among other secret things, C-130 and C-47 gunships; psychological air warfare aircraft; combat Air Rescue aircraft for all climate and geographical locations and AGOS. AGOS was the Air Force FAC School or "FAC-U" as it was commonly called ("FAC University"). As mentioned earlier, I had already been a FAC in Vietnam. I think this was the Air Force's way of giving me a few more days in the States with my family before they sent me overseas again on a consecutive overseas assignment, this one without my family.

"Thanks, Sarge"

Sign-in was swift and the survival school instructors were waiting for me (us, the students) with looks of glee and anticipation on their faces. There were about 30 in the class. We got right to work with a few days of classroom work then into the field where we were instructed in all kinds of survival gear and situations. In class and in the field we hit escape and evasion rather heavily as the Vietnam War and our POWs' treatment at the hands of the North Vietnamese was foremost in the news. We had lost many airmen to shoot downs, capture and internment in the Hanoi Hilton and other prisons in the Hanoi area.

Roasted snake on a stick over a small camp fire taste very good (*"like chicken"*) and there were other wild game for those fortunate enough to trap them. The game didn't seem to like my traps very well. We had to construct back packs, foot-gear, clothing and shelter from parachute packs, canopies, straps and hardware. It is amazing the things that can be done with a parachute. Terrain navigation (day and night) with only a map and compass was part of the practical application exercises. For these navigation exercises we were paired into two-man teams, given a map and compass and dropped off in the woods at a known location marked on our map. Our task was to terrain-navigate over heavily wooded hills and through meadows and marshland to a designated point about five miles away. We were to arrive by a specified time for a simulated rendezvous with rescue forces. Piece of cake, huh? Yeah! We would be carrying a 60 pound pack of survival gear. We had made the pack from parachute parts (to include sewing them together with a makeshift needle of wire and bone). The upper portion of the parachute harness would be our pack harness. The forest was largely devastated with many felled trees from seasons of apparent tornados and windstorms. The tree trunks were just low enough to prevent ducking or crawling under them carrying our 60 pound pack. So, most of the felled trees had to be climbed over (about a three to three and half foot high obstacles). Going around the trees would be too time-consuming, too much zigzagging and could possibly cause you to lose your navigation orientation. The route also contained a few marshy areas. You could possibly be upon a marshy area before you realized it. At this point in my life I thought I was in reasonably good condition for a thirty year old fighter pilot. (Of course all fighter pilots feel that they are the greatest!). My partner was a much older career Master Sergeant. I thought that he will never be able to keep up with me and we will miss our simulated rescue rendezvous time.

We started out with me doing the navigating. Very quickly I realized why this area was chosen as the terrain navigation problem. You could not see more that 40 to 50 yards ahead because of the forest. Navigation was by way by taking a bearing on the map, then transferring that same bearing over the terrain to a distant tree, geographical feature or object. You would then make your way to that point; then another bearing and so on. After a quarter of a mile or so of climbing over seemingly endless felled trees, I was thoroughly exhausted and *struggling to keep up with the sergeant.* So much for the great condition I was in and my rapidly dwindling physical esteem! The sergeant was pressing on! And as I write this, I'm hard pressed to remember a time that I felt more exhausted. Yes, for athletic events with timeouts; but there was no resting here. Theoretically the enemy was behind us and we had to make that pick-up point. Our rendezvous time gave us little time to spare – *and the sergeant wasn't slowing down!* I struggled on, exhausted – trying to keep up with the sergeant. Then we came to this open meadow with knee-high grass. We soon realized that it was a huge marshy area that we had to cross or circumnavigate. There was a very narrow foot path through the marsh. The marsh had the typical slimy green water about two feet deep with surface scum. The marsh on each side of the path was inundated with weeds and reeds. I started along the path, which seemed to be solid ground, with the sergeant about 15 yards behind me – luckily. I stopped, for what reason I don't recall, and turned to face the water then bent over to look at something. I had forgotten the 60 pound pack on my back. The momentum carried me over into the marsh, head first! I was head first upside down in the marsh and unable to push up because my hands only sank further into the muck. *I was about to drown!* Suddenly I felt something grab my belt and lift me straight up out of the water and stand me on the path. *The sergeant had saved my life!* This older guy that I thought wouldn't make it! We had designed quick-release cords from parachute shroud lines which would release the pack with a tug on the cord. I hope I would have had the presence of mind to have released the pack and recovered myself once I discovered I was unable to push up. But, I'm here. Thanks Sarge!

We made our rendezvous barely on time. There were a few teams that had already arrived; and a few arriving shortly after us. For training and reality, an HH-3 "Jolly Green Giant" helicopter of Vietnam War fame was used as the rescue helicopter. It arrived soon to lower a jungle-penetrator to individually hoist each one of us aboard. We were then returned to base camp for the next day's training session which would include a night terrain navigation problem. At least the night navigation was without the back pack and a much shorter distance around the camp. All we had was a small near blacked-out flash light and a luminous dial compass. No helicopter pick-up this time.

"Captured!"

One major feature of the survival school was the escape-and-evasion exercise with capture and POW internment. Without disclosing too much detail, the prison was made up like North Vietnamese POW camps with instructors playing the role of North Vietnam prison guards and interrogators – in North Vietnam army uniforms. I think they very much enjoyed this part of their instructor role. It was another night exercise where we were individually to play the role of a downed airman in enemy territory. We were to hide to avoid capture. Once captured, we were placed in replicated cells of North Vietnam POW prisons. We were then taken blind folded to an interrogation room with a uniformed interrogator sitting behind a desk. The blind fold was removed and the interrogator, in broken English with a fake oriental accent, attempted to get military and personal information from us (no physical torture.) Then we were subjected to psychological and propaganda warfare (lectures and loud speakers with irritating music). We were blindfolded and paraded about the camp in single file – hands on the belt of the "POW" in front of you. There were solitaire confinement cells and everything that could be used to make you feel that you were truly in a North Vietnam POW camp. With such realism, your imagination seemed to make it real – which was the intended training goal. Then, after a couple of days of this we were blindfolded again and led to a large room. After everyone was in we were told to remove our blindfolds. There in front of the room was a huge American Flag covering the entire wall. Everyone broke out in cheers. I'm not clear on this but I think the National Anthem was played over a PA system. I don't doubt that there was a tear or two. After a short lecture, it was all over.

After taking care of the administrative detail and clearing out, I was on my way back to Florida and my family for a few days before heading to Hurlburt Field for AGOS.

Air and Ground Operations School (AGOS)

My reporting date for AGOS was August 20th for seventeen days. This was very much an uneventful temporary duty assignment. The class was rather large, about thirty students, to include a few senior officers. There was the necessary classroom work and visits to special operations and counter insurgency units for briefings on their missions. We had a few days in the field (no overnighters) playing ground-FAC and practicing control of local aircraft simulating air strikes on ground targets. As I recall, T-33s and helicopters were used as strike aircraft. Emphasis was on identifying enemy targets and friendly position for the strike aircraft and conducting a standard formatted briefing. In addition to the radio, various signal devices were used: Signal mirror, colored smoke, colored panels and verbal descriptions, etc. Types of weapons for various types of targets were a major subject. It was soon over. Then back to my family for a few days and on to Korea for a year. Sometime around this time, I don't recall when, Norris and Gwen would move to Fort Worth, Texas for his entry into the Baptist Southwestern Theological Seminary. He would study for a Doctorate in Theology in preparation for his ministerial career.

I would purchase a 1974 Oldsmobile and leave it with Pat. Then leave on September 19th 1973 for Travis AFB, Sacramento, California and air transportation to Osan Air Base, Korea. My assignment would be to the 19th Tactical Air Support Squadron (TASS) where I would be further assigned to a Direct Air Support Center (DASC, pronounced "DASK). While I was away, Robert would take his PSAT exams and Pat would enroll in an "Old Testament" college course.

19th Tactical Air Support Squadron (TASS), Osan Air Base, Korea

I arrived at Osan Air Base September 21st 1973 for my year tour. Osan AB is located several miles south of the South Korean capital city of Seoul. After the customary in-country briefing and base clearance, I reported to the 19th Tactical Air Support Squadron. The TASS owned O-2s, a FAC aircraft of the Vietnam War. Although my job would be Operations Officer for the DASC at Camp Red Cloud, Uijongbu, Korea (We-Jong-Boo), it would be a non-flying position. Uijongbu is about twelve miles north of Seoul which is about 35 miles south of the DMZ (Demilitarized Zone), the line separating North and South Korea established at the 1953 Armistice halting the Korean War – which has never officially ended as of 2017. In fact the current North Korean President, Kim Jong-un, is frequently threatening preemptive nuclear attacks on the United States and just recently launched a test intercontinental ballistic missile.

Camp Red Cloud was the headquarters for the US Army's I Corps (First Corps) and the Military Assistance Command-Korea. An Air Force DASC is charged with providing tactical air support to the various Army units within a Corps. The 19th TASS DASC would support both US and ROK (Republic of Korea) forces in Korea. The Corps maintained a Tactical Operations Center (TOC) which is assigned forward with their combat units. As the DASC Operations Officer I was charged with assuring the necessary FACs and tactical combat personnel were assigned to simulated targets selected by joint TOC air and ground planners. Except for emergency "troops in contact" situations, all targets were pre-planned and orders issued the day/night prior to the TOT (Time on Target). Fighters would be assigned specified targets. FACs would be located with the ground commanders to control and brief the fighter aircraft and assure ground personnel were aware of the air strike's TOT, ordnance, etc. The DASC was an Air Force tactical mobile unit capable of moving with the Army Corps' TOC as the fluid battlefield scenario changed. Thus the DASC was a conglomerate of air-inflatable ("bubble") shelters for the various functions of operations, communications, maintenance, transportation, etc. In other words, the DASC was designed to be taken down and packed up to move on a moment's notice whenever the ground commander moved his TOC.

Korean Winter!

I did fifteen months in Goose Bay, Labrador so I know what cold is! However, I believe I never felt colder than during the Korean winter. I'm reminded how our American soldiers suffered during the Korean War because they were sent into that war without proper winter clothing and gear – into a winter colder than any on record for many years previous. One day I was standing by the side of a road shivering in my thermal underwear, winter clothing, GI sweater and a fur pile cap over my head and ears, winter field jacket with hood and a pair of "bunny boots" (lined, layered and insulated artic boots). Then I noticed a couple of elderly Korean ladies walking by in what appeared to be thin patterned calf-length dresses, sweaters, thin head scarves and slip-on shoes on otherwise bare feet. I can only imagine what they thought of the bundled and shivering American. Hardy people, those Koreans!

Korean Friends!

While at Camp Red Cloud, I attended the Post Chapel. There I met a Korean civilian who spoke good English. We became friends and he invited me to his home to enjoy a Korean dinner with his family. When I arrived I was greeted by his two very cute small daughters about four and six years old who did the traditional Korean welcome of bowing and escorting me into the dining room. In addition to his wife, he had a son of high school age an older daughter maybe early twenties. His son would often try to help me with the Korean language. (I was taking an on-post conversational Korean class – which I never mastered). Of course his entire family was interested in practicing their English on me – my help of which was questionable. They all were very delightful people – and Methodist. It was a very modest home and small. Dining was on the floor cross-legged; a very delicious meal, even the Korean kimchi. Of course they were aware of the American disdain for Korean kimchi and its horrific odor; but this was prepared differently and very delicious. Cooking and heating was by an open charcoal hearth. I had several memorable visits in their home.

Through my Methodist Korean friend, I met a few Methodist ministers and college professors at a nearby Methodist college/seminary. They invited me to their prayer breakfast at the college/school. Although I could not understand their language, I could almost guess the jest of the banter and conversation. During their group prayers I noticed that when one would finish his prayer, they would expel a whooshing sound. Later I asked my Methodist friend what that was all about. He explained that when a Korean prays he often emits such a sound as a testimony to the presence of the Holy Spirit.

Sometime later the ministers ask me to speak at one of their student rallies. I agreed. I designed my speech to be a combination religious testimonial, general encouragement to the students and my appreciation for the Korean peoples' friendship. (Imagine me giving a religious testimonial in todays politically correct, Jesus expunged, culture. It's a wonder that Jesus has not yet expunged us!) I think the student rally was a co-ed high school/college/seminary youth group. It was to be held on the open-air athletic field. Come the day of my speech, I was ushered to an elevated (dirt embankment) reviewing stand type of affair from which to conduct my speech. There were some school and ministry officials and myself; overlooking this huge parade/athletic field filled with uniformed students sitting cross-legged on the ground; perfectly aligned and squared off into two groups which were separated to form an aisle way directly in front of the speaker position. Their formation would make any military commander proud.

Again of course, I understood little of what was said by the speakers before me. When it came my time to speak I was provided with an interrupter. I kept my speech relatively short and tried a joke or two. When a couple of jokes went flat, I gave up on the joke thing. I don't know if it was my jokes or the interpreter's interpretation. I did note a great disparity between Korean discipline and discipline dispensed in the United States. The audience of students had about a dozen adult monitors wandering throughout the formation. Whenever a student would become restless of seemingly lose concentration, a monitor would kick them in the rear end. I don't know if that was a testimony to my speech or to Korean discipline. They are a disciplined people – especially the military and their physical conditioning. We, as Americans, should have our rear ends kicked, sit up and take note.

Fender Bender!

One day I happened to be driving off post in one of our jeeps. I pulled up behind a stopped ROK Army truck convoy. Suddenly the truck in front of me backed into my jeep bending the hood and smashing a light. No great damage.

Information was exchanged, ROK military police arrived and the matter was dispatched. I can only imagine the disciplinary action taken against that truck driver for the incident knowing the ROK Army's reputation for strict discipline and the oriental for saving-face; especially since the incident involved an American Officer and vehicle.

Interesting Events

While in Korea I had the occasion to participate in a few guided group tours. The events/tours that I recall were:

The Korean Air Force Military Academy.

Inchon Harbor: Where General MacArthur conducted an invasion to retake the Korean Peninsula during the Korean War.

The American carrier, USS Midway off the coast of Pusan.

Helicopter tour of the DMZ.

Goodbye, Korea! Hello, Florida – Again!

In July 1974 I got my assignment to the States following completion of my one year Korean tour. My orders were to report on November the 5th to the 602nd Tactical Control Group at Bergstrom AFB near Austin, Texas. However, about one month later the orders were changed to have me report to the Tactical Air Warfare Center at Eglin AFB near Valparaiso, Florida where I would be a branch Chief evaluating newly developed Command and Control equipment. Eglin was probably the better assignment (especially for my family) but I think I would have enjoyed being a Texan again.

It was either my departure from Korea for Eglin, or an earlier TDY to Osan Air Base that I encountered a K-9 airport security dog that seemed bent on seeing that I didn't leave Korea. At that point in time security was focused more on drugs and contraband – rather than preventing a terrorist act as it is today. To accomplish this, all passengers were required to pile their bags in the center of a room and move to the wall. An Air Force Security Policeman entered the room with a drug-sniffing dog on a leash. The dog was led to the pile of baggage and turned loose. It circled the pile of bags a couple of times sniffing vigorously at each bag as if desperately seeking something; it was: drugs! If it detected drugs it would begin pawing and biting the bag furiously. Suddenly the dog *attacked* my bag. I was terrified – thinking of all sorts of terrible scenarios: Like someone slipping drugs into my bag; like not seeing my family again; life in a Korean jail; a court martial and demotion; or all sorts of scenarios. The Air Policeman went over and pulled the dog off my bag and told everyone to claim their bags. I sort of sheepishly went to claim my bag but the Air Policeman said and did nothing. I asked him what it was with the drug-dog. He explained that the dogs will usually paw and bite a soft bag regardless of contents; and if there was something in it, he would have gone nuts trying to get into the bag. My bag was a soft canvas Air Force B-4 bag. Whew! I was soon on my way to the Good Ole USA – not looking back!

*****

CHAPTER NINETEEN
TACTICAL AIR WARFARE CENTER, EGLIN AFB; Valparaiso, Florida
(1974-1977)

Welcome to Eglin Air Force Base

After a year separation in Korea, it was great getting reacquainted with my family and our families. With my leave time evaporating all too quickly, we were soon packed and on our way to Eglin Air Force Base just north of Fort Walton Beach, Florida; reporting on November 5th 1974. The base was actually located at the small town of Valparaiso about ten miles north of Fort Walton Beach. Fort Walton Beach and the Gulf Coast along the Florida Panhandle have some of the prettiest white-sand beaches I've seen. The sand is snow white with the coastline and gulf view picture-post-card quality. Eglin AFB was not a spectacularly beautiful base. However, being a weapons and equipment test and evaluation base, I believe it had the second largest real-estate area of all Air Force bases in the States. The real-estate was necessary of course for the numerous weapons ranges for testing. Eglin was the location of the Air Force's Tactical Air Warfare Center (TAWC, pronounced "tawk") for operationally testing new air and ground weapons and equipment to include new aircraft. For the most part this was an eight-to-five Air Force assignment with occasional TDYs. The bad part was, although it was a pilot position, I would not be flying; my second such non-flying assignment; Korea being the first. My flying would have to be relegated to the Eglin Aero Club. I was assigned base quarters. It was a small home with a picturesque back yard having a large inlet to the Choctawhatchee Bay leading to the Gulf of Mexico. After base clearing-in and processing I was soon in my office as Chief of the Command and Control Branch. Pat received her base orientation and got Robert enrolled in Niceville High School for his senior year. Niceville was a small town on the bay between Fort Walton Beach and Valparaiso. With all settled in, we were "off and running" for our daily routine.

My job was basically a paper-work job which I utterly detested. Detesting paper work as I do, such jobs always seemed to be a magnet in my career progression. We had several projects going, each of which had a project officer assigned. The project officers worked for me as Branch Chief and me in-turn for the Command and Control Division Director. Fortunately I had great project officers who saved my rear end and kept me briefed on their projects. I had to force my interest in the job. I know that my project officers got exasperated with me on a few occasion because of my frequently repeated request for information and briefs on their progress. They quite literally "saved my beacon" as I attempted to keep the director informed. Testing and evaluating command and control equipment was not my thing. And as fate would have it, this turned out to be my longest stabilized assignment to date, just over three years at Eglin.

I wasn't too upset however, because my family was happy, Eglin was a great base in a great location, and it had a great aero club. Pat and I weren't too far from our families. In fact I flew Pat and Robert to visit our families in Georgia and Florida on a few occasions.

We would join the Valparaiso Baptist Church while at Eglin which was a short distance outside the North gate of Eglin. My boyhood friend from the farm-next-door where I grew up was the Director of Music Ministry there. It was great renewing an old friendship and reminiscing about growing-up on our adjacent farms. He was the most musically talented person I ever knew. He taught piano and had many award-winning student. His mastery of the piano was phenomenal. When we were kids on the farm and he was practicing piano I was building model airplanes. He couldn't understand why I spent my time building those "dumb" models and I couldn't understand why he spent his time practicing that "sissy" piano. When we visited him in Valparaiso I told him that I guess we now know which one of us was most successful with our careers: No one has ever flocked to watch me do my job; but they flocked to hear and applaud his recitals and concerts – and those of his students. Sadly, I learned recently that he had died of a long term illness.

Eglin Aero Club

I immediately joined the Eglin Aero Club. Robert and I had many fun flights together. I would give him pointers on aircraft control and aeronautical knowledge. He adapted to flying very quickly. I was proud of his flying aptitude. For his next birthday I enrolled him in the Aero Club and told him I would pay for his flying lessons through the Private Pilot Certification. Norris and I had also enjoyed many hours of flying together but I had never offered him flying lessons. For what reason, I don't really know. He did not seem to be quite as military and aviation orientated as Robert. After promising Robert to pay for his flying lessons as a birthday gift, I felt obligated to Norris for an equivalent sum to obtain a Private Pilot Certificate. However, due to poor eyesight and other interest, I think he chose to invest in his impressive theological library.

Although I had my flight instructor certificate, I chose not to teach Robert to fly – for the same reason that a surgeon would choose not to operate on a family member, or that a husband should not attempt to teach his wife to drive (or fly). I did buy Robert his first pilot log book, instructed, logged and signed off his first hour of flight instruction – just for the novelty of a proud father giving his son his first hour of flight instruction. He then was assigned an Aero Club Flight Instructor. I was very proud of him. It brought back many happy memories of my flight training days as a 16 year old high school student.

Robert's First Solo and Solo Cross-Country

On March 15th 1975 Robert was launched into the Wild Blue Yonder sans flight instructor – first solo. It was in a Cessna 152, N3206V. He came home with the back and tail of his shirt having been ceremoniously and traditionally cut off by congratulatory fellow flight students. I was a proud pilot-father!

On June 14th he would fly his first solo cross-country (X-C). I would be kidding myself and the reader also if I said I was not concerned. I remember my first solo X-C in which I didn't get lost but I couldn't find one of my destination grass-strip airports among the green fields and meadows. After orbiting the area for some time, I went on and completed my planned X-C. My flight instructor appeared skeptical that I had completed it, but he relented and signed off my solo X-C in my log book.

Pat didn't show it but I know she was concerned about Robert's solo X-C. It was summertime and almost like clockwork, the afternoon thunderstorms appeared. Robert's X-C was planned early enough for him to be back well before the "scheduled" afternoon storms. However, afternoon came. Then the middle of the afternoon and I could see the storms to the north in the direction of Robert's X-C. I was more than just a little bit concerned since we had not heard from him. I know Pat was too but she never visibly showed her emotions. Late afternoon came and I was a bundle of nerves inside but tried to hide it. Then the phone call that Robert had diverted to the small airport at Florala, Alabama (on the Florida/Alabama line). What a relief! *He was safe!*

At his first destination airport he had landed and gotten his logbook signed – certifying that he had indeed landed at that airport. As he taxied onto the runway for takeoff, one of those monster helicopter cranes landed right in the middle of the runway and remained there for an hour or so at least blocking Robert's departure. This was a non-tower airport so he could not inquire as to the helicopter's delay in moving off the runway. The helicopter finally lifted off but Robert was now very late on his schedule X-C. He decided to amend his route to go direct to Eglin and eliminate the second destination because of the late hour. Very ominous thunderstorms were now forming throughout the area. Dark thunderstorms with lightning and heavy rain showers lay in his flight path to Eglin. He spotted the Florela airport on the Florida/Alabama state line off to his left in the distance and diverted there; another smart move on his part. He radioed his plight to Eglin. A pilot transiting the area heard the transmissions and recognized that Robert was a student pilot on his first solo X-C. He landed at Florela to offer assistance and support until the storm dissipated. After it was apparent that the thunderstorm cells were moving away, the pilot departed. I'll be forever grateful to that pilot for landing to check on Robert as a student pilot. Pilots are like that: A fraternity of sorts.

As the storms moved away, Robert departed for Eglin. He arrived a couple of hours later than scheduled of course. His instructor seemed a bit miffed about the delay and diversion; but as a flight instructor, I know he was proud of Robert because he used proper judgment in handling a serious weather situation – and on his first solo X-C. I know I was. Pat and I were both overjoyed at the news that Robert was back safely at Eglin. I cannot convey the relief that I experienced. There had been a lot of prayers offered up for Robert's safe return by Pat and me. Robert went on to get his Private Pilot Certificate. I was very proud of him.

Mom's Art Lessons

My mom was a self-taught artist. It was her hobby along with short-story writing. But it was her life's dream to take art lessons. As a struggling farmer's wife and homemaker, she had no time or money for such a dream and leisure. And no one in the family seemed to have an interest in her hobby and dream. She often complained that no one was interested in her paintings or story writing. Pat and I had often begged Mom to come spend a few months with us at our various assignment locations. But she was reluctant to leave Dad then and her numerous chores. Dad had now been dead for several years. We continued to urge her to come stay with us for a few months. At Fort Walton Beach there were numerous art stores and studios; and my friend there was also an artist. He was very fond of my Mom – as everyone was – and Mom thought very highly of him and his family back on the farm when he and I were growing-up farm-kids. Pat and I used the "artist approach" to finally coerce Mom into coming to visit a few months. Promising to pay for her art lessons seemed to be the bait that worked. However there was another bait trick up Pat's and my sleeves: Robert's Niceville High School graduation. I don't think Mom would have turned down either bait trick: Robert's graduation or art lessons. Mom absolutely loved all of her grandchildren. So I know Robert's graduation would have gotten her to Eglin in any event.

Mom was in her heaven taking those art lessons. She always painted with oils. Here she was introduced to water colors and pastels. She mastered them extremely well and I think some of my favorites were paintings she did while at Eglin following her lessons.

High School: Robert Graduates (We Think!)

But, Mom was not to see Robert get his diploma. The graduation exercise was scheduled for June 1st 1975 and to be held in the football stadium because of its seating capacity. The high school graduation came. Mom, Pat and I were in the stand's upper level so we would be sure to see Robert when he walked across the stage for his diploma. Dark clouds began to form quickly. (Remember those late afternoon thunderstorms typical in the south during the summer?) Then almost without warning, a heavy down pour started. In the rush to get Mom under an overhanging roof to prevent her getting drenched (and pneumonia), and to avoid the crowd's panic, we missed seeing Robert receive his diploma. I think the graduating class and faculty endured the drenching. We were convinced that Robert got his diploma however, because he showed it to us later. He soon was accepted for enrollment in The University of Florida at Gainesville.

Vietnam Refugee Camp (Eglin AFB)

In February 1973, after more than 10 years in a controversial war, North Vietnam began releasing our POWs held in and around Hanoi due to heavy B-52 bombings raids on Hanoi; and in no small part to the nation-wide campaign by the POW wives. The United States had begun to extricate itself from a long and developing untenable/unpopular situation in South Vietnam due to the enemy's dedication to a cause; and lack of our government's resolve to win. A vocal but minority "anti-war" movement of marijuana-smoking, free-loving "peaceniks" and deserters got the attention of our government who acquiesced to them rather than to the majority of patriotic Americans. So we tucked-our-tails and began to run. The US began "Vietnamization" of the war – A President Nixon Administration term. This meant trying to save our face by extricating ourselves and turning over our equipment, our bases and the lead in the war to the South Vietnamese. "Peace with Honor" President Nixon called the plan. I have yet to discover the *"honor!"* We, the greatest and most powerful nation on earth, beaten by bicycle-riding, homemade-sandal shod, black-pajama clad, straw-cone-hatted peasants with more will and dedication for their cause than we had for ours! What was our cause? To keep South Vietnam with a pro-American dictator in Saigon. True, he was corrupt; but so are a lot of our politicians. At least he was friendly to the United States and was trying to keep South Vietnam from being overrun by North Vietnam who had an anti-American agenda with a Communist dictator in Hanoi. Results: Today we have a *united* Vietnam lead by an anti-American Communist dictator thanks to our tucking-tail and running; and to the likes of Jane Fonda, other well-known celebrities(?) and a like crowd who lead the "Anti-War" charge here at home in the United States.

Most American forces were out of South Vietnam by 1975 when North Vietnam began a mass and rapid reinvasion of the South thereby routing South Vietnam forces which created panic and chaos. I read somewhere that the last two Americans killed in the war occurred on April 29th 1975. On April 30th Saigon fell to the North Vietnam forces. *The war was over!* The United States air and sea-lift had begun evacuating the last remaining Americans, South Vietnam military personnel and pro-American Vietnamese civilians by the tens of thousands.

Meanwhile back at Eglin AFB there was Lieutenant Colonel George Partridge of the Tactical Air Warfare Center and his family watching the shocking news accounts of the events in Vietnam; as was the rest of the world! Little did I realize that I would soon be embroiled in those unfolding and terrifying event. America and other countries around the world began accepting these refugees and building refugee centers to receive, process, and assimilate them into their new hosts' cultures. The United States would receive 100,000 or more refugees. Eglin AFB was designated one of four Vietnam Refugee Centers in the United States and would eventually receive more than 10,000 refugees with the first increment arriving in May 1975.

Refugee Liaison Officer (RLO)

Eglin established a "tent-city" of hundreds of GI general-purpose tents to house the refugees. It was located a few miles from Eglin. Office space, personnel, supply and medical facilities were provided to accommodate the influx of refugees. A command and support organizational structure was established. I was assigned TDY to the refugee center as an RLO for supply and logistics. Great effort went into trying to maintain family integrity in tent assignments. With the unfamiliar Vietnamese names, their customs and less-than-sanitary practices which were "foreign" to Americans, it was extremely taxing for all US personnel. And of course these refugees were traumatized over what they had just gone through in escaping Vietnam with their lives and, in some cases, fragments of their families. Some had only the clothes on their backs. Now they were herded together in an unfamiliar culture and strange new world half-a-world away from their homeland. It must be acknowledged that in some cases, even in these undesirable living conditions, some refugees were better off than they were in their homeland. They just didn't realize it yet. Being in crowded conditions seething with humanity was, for the most part, not new to them. But, as could be expected, families got separated, wrong names were applied to documents due to unfamiliar spellings and pronunciations and arguments surfaced that American RLOs had to quell. Some families were separated because volunteering American sponsors could not, or would not, accept huge families. Many religious, civic and welfare organizations admirably volunteered to assist in helping find American homes and sponsors for the refugees.

My job as RLO for supply and logistics was extremely taxing for me. Supply and logistics were some of the many functions that I had always hoped to avoid in my Air Force Career. (Of course I always wanted to avoid anything except flying). My office was a small desk in a crowded open-bay Quonset hut. It was a constant buzz and the squelching of "fires," both large and small. There were two phones on my desk and I would, at times, have both of them to my ears at the same time. Pat, as did many of the Air Force and community wives, got involved as volunteers. I remember one day she and Robert walked into the hut and saw me with a phone on each ear. She seemed amused. But I think she finally realized why I was spending so much time at the refugee center. We all were working shifts of 12 hours or more. My civilian friend from my childhood even volunteered to sponsor a young Vietnamese man. He was able to get him a local job. My friend said his Vietnamese refugee would come home frustrated at the "lazy" Americans he had to work with. That says a lot doesn't it!? The Vietnam refugee eventually went on to a better job.

Most of the Vietnamese people were just like you and me: Human wants and needs. I met several fine Vietnamese people, both during my duties in Vietnam and here in the center. There were two families that Pat, Robert and I befriended while they were in the center and for many years following their sponsorship. One was a physician and I don't remember the occupation of the second. They were brothers. The doctor and his family were sponsored and employed by a large hospital in northwest Florida. The other brother and his family were sponsored by a longtime friend of Pat's who operated a dairy farm in central Florida. Before they were sponsored, we invited them into our home on Eglin for a large dinner and fellowship. The two families with teenagers and young adults and a grandmother seemed to really enjoy themselves. Most spoke and understood some English; the doctor was very proficient in English. However, the grandmother spoke and understood no English. She seemed very shy and even embarrassed at trying to communicate with us. All the others seemed to be very much at ease in our home and company.

Remember the ceramic elephants that I mentioned earlier in my story about sending them to Pat and a few friends at Clark Air Base from Vietnam? They were the rage for many Americans at Clark and in Vietnam. Well, Pat and I had about six of those elephant located throughout our home. They were about a foot and a half high and bright glossy green in color. While sitting around in the front room of our home, our Vietnam guest began smiling, laughing and giggling among themselves. They were obviously embarrassed and reluctant to tell us what they were so amused about. Finally one of the daughters told us that they were laughing at the elephants in our home because in Vietnam they are used in funeral homes as casket-bearers. The elephants had saddles with flat platforms on top which supported the casket; and they had long straight trunks that drooped to the floor. The daughter told us that in Vietnam an elephant with a drooping trunk is a "sad" elephant. A happy elephant has an upward curled trunk. They were all laughing at the crazy Americans who use funeral casket-bearers in their home as décor. The Vietnam merchants in Vietnam probably had a prosperous laughing good time at the Americans buying up the funeral casket-bearer elephants also.

I think the Doctor and family later moved to California. He seemed to be doing rather well. The other brother and his family eventually moved to Minnesota, I believe it was. We maintained occasional contact with them over the years until

Pat died. I informed them of her death but I just didn't maintain the correspondence. We did learn that the children were doing really well with their Americanization; one earning outstanding honors upon her high school graduation as valedictorian. We could learn a lot from our Asian friends! I often wonder how my Vietnamese friends have fared in America.

Meritorious Service Medals and Headquarters commendation letters with intermediate level commanders' endorsements were given the RLOs. Higher ranking medals were awarded to senior commanders.

Norris's Graduation: Southwestern Baptist Theological Seminary

In December 1975 Norris graduated with a Master's Degree in History from the Southwestern Baptist Theological Seminary in Fort Worth, Texas. Pat and I were able to get out for his graduation and short visit with him and Gwen. Norris had intended to study for a theology degree for his chosen career as a minister. However, he found some of his professors to be overly "liberal" and therefore switched to a history degree. I believe they then moved to California.

Family Fun Times!

While at Eglin and with the proximity of Pat's and my families, we had occasions to get together at their or our homes; especially on significant family orientated holidays. I remember one Christmas; I think that Carrie and her sons, Morris and David visited while Norris and his family were with us. It was a great Christmas! Norris and Gwen had brought with them our first grandchild: Tessa. I have already mentioned the great singing voice that Norris had. Tessa would grow up to have an equally great voice. So did my friend, along with his great musical and piano talent. Norris, Robert, Morris, David and my friend from our boyhood farm-neighbor days would gather around a piano and sing Christmas carols and hymns. It was great!

While Morris was visiting us at Eglin, he gave me a model of the F-100 with squadron markings on it. I still have it today. David gave me a khaki military-styled summer flying suit. I still have it today also. I think it was later that Carrie gave me a Danbury Mint set of World War Two aircraft; one at a time. She and Pat teased me by withholding my favorite, the F4U Corsair, until the very last. There were also occasions that I flew my family to visit our families at Zephyrhills and Jacksonville, Florida and to my sister in Lawrenceville, Georgia. While in Jacksonville I took Morris and David flying with me. The actual years and events I can't put into proper sequence but it was on some of the flights that I learned how really adapt Robert was at flying; and especially on actual instrument flight in real weather.

Amid all the fun, Robert had to have a not-so-fun major dental procedure during the summer 1976. But he was soon operating normally again.

311

Assignment New York!

Although I had had much more enjoyable jobs, my family and I were enjoying Eglin. Then one day I got another of one of those – out of the blue – new-assignment phone calls. I answered the phone and on the other end was an Air Force Colonel at McGuire AFB, New Jersey who identified himself as Commander of the Northeast Region for Air Force Liaison to the Civil Air Patrol (CAP). He wasted no time and asked me if I would like to move to New York City to be the Air Force Liaison Officer to the New York Civil Air Patrol Wing. I was stunned for an instant! New York City with all of its asphalt and concrete was one of those *never-to-visit* places. Who in New York would be interested in my going to New York City? "No Sir!" I replied. "I don't want to go to New York". "Well, you don't have a choice. You're going to New York. You'll be receiving orders soon," he said! And I did!

At that time there was a serial psychopath killer on the loose in New York City called "Son of Sam"! The newspapers were full of his several senseless random murders. He had killed several people because "Sam" or "God" had told him to do so. The police were baffled and seemed not close to solving the case. I did not want to take my family into that New York City scenario.

The CAP is a civilian Auxiliary of the Air Force. It is charged with air and ground search and rescue efforts in the 50 states under control of the Air Force Search and Rescue Coordination Center at Scott AFB, Illinois. Sea search and rescue is performed by the Coast Guard and Coast Guard Auxiliary. The CAP also conducts aerospace education for senior and cadet members of the CAP. They wear the Air Force uniform and are barely distinguishable from active Air Force personnel except for the small CAP insignia they wear. Washington DC and Puerto Rico also have CAP Wings for a total of 52.

The Colonel briefly explained that I would be the Air Force Liaison Officer to the New York Civil Air Patrol Wing. I learned that each of the 52 CAP wings had a two-man office – an Air Force officer and enlisted person – assigned to assist and monitor CAP wing activities. At that point I admit – shamefully – that I hardly knew that the CAP existed. My office would be on Mitchel Field in Garden City, New York just east of New York City on Long Island. Mitchel Field was an inactive base with only military housing and some support functions for military personnel of all services assigned in the New York City area.

I briefed Pat and told Robert, who was now enrolled in the University of Florida at Gainesville. Pat was aware of the "Son of Sam" stories. She didn't show enthusiasm nor disappointed. She had learned over the years that my assignment wishes didn't matter; "expediency of the service" always prevailed.

(Only twice in my career were my wishes considered in my assignments: my F-89 assignment to Hamilton AFB, California in 1958, and my F-100 assignment to Cannon AFB, New Mexico in 1964.)

Orders soon arrived for me to report on October 31st 1977. Three years on Eglin was my longest assignment to date. Base clearing, sorting, packing and moving was old stuff. It was all too familiar yet always stressful and traumatic as we said so long to friends and moved out. The nice part of moving was usually a brief visit with family as we relocated. "New York, New York!" I don't remember if Liza Minnelli's popular song of that title was on the charts then or not. I know it was popular while we were in New York. Good bye, Eglin!

*****

"New York, New York..."

"...if I can make it there, I'll make it anywhere!" – So the song goes. I'm not sure about that axiom but I managed to survive. I loved to hear Liza Minnelli sing that song. The song made the charts sometime around the time that I got my assignment to New York, or soon thereafter – I forget which. Anyway, Pat and I sort of took its success as an omen that we would fare well in New York. We did!

After arriving at Mitchel Field in October 1977 and checking in at the Navy Housing Office I was told that there was "...no room in the Inn". (No intent to be sacrilegious and Pat was not pregnant). So, I applied for military housing and was placed on the waiting list. In the meantime I would have to find a temporary place for us to stay until a house on Mitchel Field became available. The runways had long since been destroyed and the community had taken them over. Hofstra University sits in the middle of one of the old runways. Nassau Coliseum and Adelphi University are, I believe, on property that once used to be Mitchel AFB. Some of the old hangers were still there and one on them is used as an aviation museum, even today: The Cradle of Aviation Museum I believe it is called. Mitchel Field had become a Navy facility for all services military family housing. It had a small Navy exchange and a Commissary. The military family housing units were left from the Mitchel Field AFB era and were assigned to all services military personnel working in the New York City Metropolitan area.

I found an apartment out on Long Island at Long Beach. The apartment was in a state of disrepair without any attempt to repair it due to plans to totally renovate the apartment building. The apartment was far enough away from New York City and in a condition that made the rent affordable for a short period of time. And it was right on the beach. Our apartment overlooked the Atlantic – a beautiful sight. I mentioned to Pat that is the only time we will likely ever have a beach-front home. The sliding doors to the balcony overlooking the beach were in such a state of disrepair that the sea breezes howled in around them making the heavy curtains stand out into the room – *and it was cold!* With the cold air coming in almost unimpeded, heating was practically ineffective. Remember it was the last of October and winter was not far away. We saw some frightful and threating looking storms come ashore off the Atlantic. There were also some very beautiful island sunsets and cloud formations.

Meet the "Boss"!

Although my office, the Air Force Liaison office for the New York Civil Air Patrol Wing, would be on Mitchel Field, my "boss" would be located on McGuire AFB, New Jersey. He was Commander of the Air Force Northeast Liaison Region for the Northeast CAP Region to which the New York Wing belonged. The Civil Air Patrol's 52 wings are organized into eight regions. There is a CAP National Headquarters located at Maxwell AFB, Alabama. The Air Force provides liaison personnel at each of these organizational levels – wings, regions and National Headquarters. At Maxwell, the Air Force CAP Liaison Headquarters and the CAP National Headquarters were co-located and jointly manned. There, Air Force and civilian personnel jointly performed many of the functions of the CAP National Headquarters. Generally each wing was organized to conduct the main functions of operations, search and rescue (air and ground), aerospace education, cadet program and personnel. Wing squadrons were designated as Senior, Composite or Cadet Squadrons. Membership category was either Senior or Cadet. Anyone not a cadet was designated a senior member (age notwithstanding). Composite squadrons were composed of both senior and cadet members. Wings had the option of organizing their squadrons into groups.

My office had an authorized Air Force staff car and general aviation contract rental aircraft on Air Force contract at Republic Airport, Farmingdale, Long Island about 15 miles east of Mitchel Field. The aircraft were general aviation single-engine propeller Cessna, Piper and Beech aircraft. Soon after arriving I was taken to our New Jersey office by my liaison NCO, Master Sergeant Gordon Richardson, in order for me to meet our commander and do my personnel in-processing with the McGuire Air Force Base personnel office; which would be maintaining my personnel records. Sergeant Richardson was absolutely phenomenal; a better NCO would be hard (if not impossible) to find. He was popularly referred to as "Rich" by his CAP and Air Force friends. He and his wife, Ann (now deceased), became very good friends of Pat and me.

The Colonel was tall, slender and sharp looking. He was from northwestern Pennsylvania and retired a couple of years after I arrived – no connection to my arrival and his retirement, I think. Sergeant Richardson made the introductions and escorted me around McGuire as I did the necessary clearing-in. Later Colonel Win DePoorter reported in as the new Commander for the Northeast CAP Liaison Region. He is an outstanding pilot and a Vietnam War veteran with 657 A-1E combat missions flown in Laos, North and South Vietnam. His knowledge of airplanes, aerodynamics and flying regulations is generally unchallenged.

The Air Force charges the CAP (an official auxiliary of the Air Force) with search and rescue within the 50 states, Puerto Rico and Washington DC under the coordination and control of the Air Force Search and Rescue Center at Scott AFB, Illinois. CAP aircraft were purchased by the CAP with financial support from the Air Force. The next largest function was logistics. The CAP was authorized a priority acquisition of surplus military and government equipment. Sergeant Richardson did a superb job of acquisition assistance, monitoring and equipment distribution for the CAP. There had to be hundreds of thousands of dollars in surplus equipment that our liaison office acquired for the CAP. Once the equipment was transferred to the CAP, accountability was their responsibility with Air Force Liaison monitoring. It was a challenging and new experience. One of my favorite duties was that of visiting, inspecting and speaking to the CAP cadet squadrons. I challenge many of the active military units to match their enthusiasm, dedication, performance, appearance and drill precision. My responsibility was to periodically visit each squadron and group throughout the state of New York – an absolutely beautiful state once you got out of the "City". Usually Master Sergeant Richardson accompanied me for these inspection and assistance visits. In doing so, we flew or drove to each corner of the state and most places in between – plus all the boroughs in New York City – *another real experience!*

On one occasion our operations officer from the Air Force Liaison Region Office at McGuire AFB was visiting my New York office to accompany me on one of my many visits to a New York CAP unit. We were flying over beautiful upstate New York on a fabulous flying day when over the intercom he said: "Can you believe they pay us for this?" He used this inquiry quite often as a way of exclaiming the absolute joy of flying. I relied that he better stop saying that or someone is going to overhear him and ask why are they paying us for this.

Mitchel Field and the New York CAP Wing

Mitchel Field and the New York Wing CAP were located in Garden City on Long Island; just east of Flushing and Jamaica. After a couple of months or so I was assigned military family housing on Mitchel Field. It was about a five minute walk from home to my office on Mitchel Field; which was about a two minute drive to the CAP wing headquarters in Garden City. The house was a brick two-story three bedroom duplex with a basement and working fireplace. Each set of quarters had an assigned detached garage about 30 yards from the duplex. We had great neighbors. The houses were probably pre-WW II with old steam-heat radiators; you know, the ones that go "clank," "bang," "clunk" frequently; especially during the night. The windows were mostly painted shut from years of over-painting the wooden frames. But, the quarters were comfortable and well-constructed. A more convenient location to my work and the CAP wing would be hard to imagine.

Sergeant Richardson introduced me to the NY CAP Wing Commander, the Deputy Commander, and the Wing staff. I would learn that they all were dedicated volunteers for the CAP missions. All CAP members are unpaid civilian volunteers of the official Auxiliary of the Air Force, and wear the Air Force uniform and rank, but with distinctive CAP insignia. Many members, based upon their means, used their own funds to avail themselves for the CAP missions and tasks. The Air Force does reimburse CAP members and units for fuel, oil and fair wear and tear on equipment used in actual and exercise Search and Rescue operations. They do their duties out of dedication to the Air Force and their particularly assigned staff function; many using their own aircraft, vehicles and equipment. While I would mainly oversee their operations and training, Sergeant Richardson would oversee their equipment acquisition and accountability and personnel functions.

I think Sergeant Richardson and I were able to visit every CAP unit in the state – some multiple times. I would show Air Force training and historical films; discuss flying operations and flying safety and usually do a short motivational speech to the personnel about the CAP mission. Sergeant Richardson would review personnel and logistic documents. We flew to units upstate and drove to those in and around the New York City area. Visiting the CAP Cadet Squadrons was usually as motivational for me as it might have been for them. You would have thought Sergeant Richardson and I were visiting from Air Force Headquarters. The cadets usually were in sharp formation and crisp uniform whenever we arrived and expected us to do a personal inspection of their unit and personnel. All the squadrons and groups treated us like military "royalty".

"Don't Splatter!"

Once a year the Wing would hold emergency search and rescue training exercises at some designated location in the state. One summer the exercise was conducted in upper northeast New York near Plattsburgh Air Force Base. Air Force Bases were authorized to host CAP units for actual and exercise operations to include CAP personnel use of transit military billeting. We were assigned billeting on Plattsburgh AFB Base. When checking in at the desk I was behind one of the CAP Wing female officers. The Airman at the desk told her he had only two rooms left with a connecting commonly-shared bathroom (latrine, in Air Force parlance). He asked her if she would object to my having the adjoining room with the connecting bathroom. Without a blink of an eye she said: "Not if he doesn't splatter!" For an instant I was puzzled by her response, and then I realized what she was saying. I said of course I want "splatter". From that day on I realized that guys standing over the facility to relieve themselves splatter the bowl, seat and walls. It dawned on me what the dark stains on the walls were. Henceforth, I have taken to being seated to do number one in my and private homes; except for public facilities. I don't want my family and friends having to deal with my "splattering".

When I received the assignment to CAP liaison, I was grossly disappointed. I could envision a highly undesirable assignment associated with liaison and advisory to the CAP. But I soon found out that CAP liaison is one of the best kept secrets in the Air Force. I thoroughly enjoyed the five years that I spent with the New York Civil Air Patrol: Good people, good flying, generally unsupervised by higher headquarters. No over-the-shoulders meddling and I had possession of blanket orders authorizing travel (fly and/or drive) all over the state and the northeast region. It was the most enjoyable flying assignment I had in the Air Force after the F-100.

Br-r-r-r-r! (Winter!)

While at Eglin AFB, one of my project officer's parents lived on the east end of Long Island near the town of Montauk. I promised him that Pat and I would visit them after we got settled in on Mitchel Field. I voiced my concern over the winters on Long Island and ask him if he thought I should get a set of snow-tires. He assured me that the winters were mild on Long Island and snow-tires would not be required. After we moved into our quarters on Mitchel Field – and in January of 1978, New York City and Long Island experienced the worst snow storm in twenty years or more. Streets were practically non-negotiable. Snow was knee deep in most places and drifts much higher. Very carefully I was able to drive the short distance to and from the Wing Headquarters (sure could have used those snow-tires). I had not seen so much snow since Goose Bay, Labrador. Sometime later after Pat and I had visited my friend's parents on the end of Long Island, I called him to let him know how delightful his parents were. I forget his father's occupation; but his mother was a retired Metropolitan Opera singer. She looked the part: beautiful, regal and gracious. I told my friend of the *"mild"* Long Island winter and light snow which he promised I would find there. Of course he already knew of the hard winter that New York was experiencing. During my five years on Long Island I would see some serious winter weather in upper New York state: Buffalo, Niagara Falls, Plattsburg, and in between – driving and flying. I think Pat enjoyed the winter wonderland. I know she enjoyed the New York Theaters with the Mitchel Field recreational support provided.

New York State – A Great State to Visit

Pat enjoyed New York City, Broadway and *Macy's*! New York City was much more enjoyable after the capture of the Son of Sam! We were able to get into New York City to see a few of the great Broadway plays and performers; some in Westbury, New York. Memory fades, but I remember seeing Andy Williams on stage in Westbury and I think Mitzi Gaynor also. Our visit to the West Point Military Academy was fantastic. We got to visit some of the historic spots on the campus grounds and to view one of their cadet corps parade. Specular! Pat and I even got to Niagara Falls on vacation. I was awed by the vastness of the Falls. On one occasion we got to picnic in a park about a half mile above the Falls and on the bank of the river. Words fail me in trying to describe the roar, the foam and the speed of the rushing waters toward the Falls. One slip from the bank into the water and any hope of rescue would be useless. One has a chance to observe the Falls from an observation station right on the corner of the Falls where the water spills over the lip of the Falls. What a spectacular and heart-stopping close-up view! Even today on rare occasionally I have dreams of viewing the Falls close up and fears of slipping into the rushing water speeding toward the Falls. Fortunately I wake up before it happens!

Old Rhinebeck Aerodrome!

One of my favorite attractions was the Old Rhinebeck Aerodrome at Rhinebeck, New York about 60 to 70 miles north of New York City. It is located on the east side of the Hudson River across from Kingston, NY. When Robert visited us, we went to see Old Rhinebeck. Old Rhinebeck is a World War One (WW I) theme museum and air show. It is a comedy skit that takes place across the grass runway with two-dimensional Hollywood-movie styled buildings, a WW I tank, ambulance and vehicles. The "Allies" are to the left side of their make-shift guard shack with the "Germans" on the other side separated by their adjacent guard shack. The "war" ensues on and over the airstrip with air battles, troop battles, tanks, artillery, anti-aircraft guns and vehicles to include a WW I ambulance. "Gordy Goodfellow," the Allied hero pilot, and the "Black Baron," the German villain pilot vie for the affection of Trudy Truelove, the heroine. This love-trio make up the motivation for the air dual between Gordy and the Black Baron. Failing in his attempts to gain Trudy's favor, the Black Baron kidnaps her; and therein begins the air battle. A great show worth your time if you're ever in the area.

Flying New York!

Flying New York in small general aviation propeller-driven contract-rental aircraft was a fun – and occasionally tension filled – experience. The old adage that flying is hours of boredom broken only by occasional moments of start terror, is painfully true. I enjoyed most of it however! On occasions I experienced light to moderate icing, both day and night. Sometimes I flew in night weather with ice slowly accumulating on the wings, and with lightning crashing around me. On other occasions turbulence was so great that I was concerned for the plane's structural integrity. There were a few of those "What am I doing here?" moments. Some Liaison Officers wouldn't fly night single-engine and particularly night weather. I had many takeoffs and landings on snow and ice covered runways; but always very cautiously. Flying safety was of primary consideration of course. Some weather conditions of course just dictated that you didn't fly.

I think I saw every part of the state from the air and in most weather conditions. I remember one time having to pick my way through a mountain valley because the cloud base was forcing me lower and lower. But I made it! Beautiful country: Green fields, mountains and streams in the summer; beautiful snow covered terrain from snows off the Great Lakes; and a frozen Niagara Falls! A great experience!

On one occasion after a visit to a CAP Group at Niagara Falls, I had taken off under very low cloud ceiling and visibility to return to Republic Airport at Farmingdale. I broke out of the clouds about eight thousand feet into bright clear sunlight. Suddenly I noticed that my attitude indicator (that tells you the attitude of the airplane) was malfunctioning and showing a slowly increasing bank to the left. That meant had I not broken out of the clouds I would have soon been trying to follow the attitude indicator which would lead me into a diving right turn spiral – unless I noticed the error in time to prevent a very insidious malfunction leading to loss of control. The attitude indicator is gyro-stabilized which will give you your attitude indication in relation to the real horizon. Without it you only have airspeed, altitude and turn information: The very basic instrument flying; just like the early air-mail carriers of ole. Since I was in the clear and the clouds would dissipate about half way to Farmingdale, this was a "no sweat" situation.

On another occasion I was returning from a visit to a CAP unit upstate New York in my contract Piper PA-28 Arrow (T-tail) with the CAP Wing Deputy Commander in the right seat. We were in weather shortly after takeoff all the way to Republic Airport. About twenty minutes out from Republic Airport (my destination) my bladder was beginning to indicate an impending urgent need – *I had to go!* (No bathroom on board this small airplane and I had no relief bottle!). New York Approach Control cleared me to enter the holding pattern prior to my approach. So I figured I could "hold it" for a few minutes. We were still in the clouds. Weather at the airport was 500 feet overcast and three miles visibility. After my turn in the holding pattern and approaching the point to begin the approach for landing, Approach Control cleared me for the approach and landing. "No sweat!" I could "hold it" a little longer. I completed my checklist and lowered the landing gear. "Whoa!" The three green landing-gear-down indicator lights did not show the nose gear "down and locked!" I informed Approach Control and requested another turn in the holding pattern to work on getting my nose gear down. They cleared me for the holding. At my request the deputy CAP commander read the emergency procedure for landing gear malfunctions over and over to be sure I had done everything correctly. Nothing! I tried some porpoise maneuvers and other things without success. I switched the nose gear down and locked light bulb with one of the working main gear light bulbs in case it was only a burned-out bulb problem. No, the bulb was not the problem. I did not recycle the landing gear because if one gear does not come down and locked – you never retract the gear for the possibility that the other gears may not come down the next time. After a few more circuits in the holding pattern, I decided that I would make the approach and landing, hoping that the nose gear would lock down on landing. By now my *personal emergency* was competing with the nose gear emergency. It had now been about forty minutes since I first had the urge to go.

I informed Approach Control of my intentions and requested to fly-by the tower after I broke out of the clouds for them to do a visual check of my nose gear. They cleared the maneuver. After breaking out I got a visual "Looks down and locked" from the tower on my fly-by. I requested a closed traffic pattern and made sure they understood my situation (nose gear, not the other *situation*). Of course Approach Control had already informed them of my nose gear emergency. I came around for my landing and told the deputy commander that on short-final I would shut the engine down in case the nose gear collapsed on touch-down. (This would stop or slow the propeller to the point that "sudden stoppage" of the propeller would not damage the engine). Sudden stoppage is when the propeller of an operating engine is suddenly stopped by striking an object; i.e. ground. It automatically requires taking the engine apart to inspect for internal damage. I also told him to get his hand on the starter switch in case the propeller stopped vertical. If so then "bump" the starter to horizontally level the propeller in case the nose gear does collapse. Just before the overrun I shut the engine down and made the smoothest landing I had made in a long time – holding the nose gear off as long as the elevator would do so. But the propeller would not stop. However it ticked over very, very slowly – enough so that you could follow the blades around. After the nose came down, the nose gear contacted the runway and the roll out was normal – for a few seconds. Then the nose gear collapsed. We came to a skidding stop. The deputy commander was out immediately. I shut everything down and was out right behind him. My next move was to walk back under the tail and relieve myself. I told him that people would think that the incident "scared the pee out of me". Not so. I had now been holding it for about an hour – so long that I was afraid I going to injure myself.

There was not any real danger in the nose gear incident. Holding the nose off long enough to dissipate my speed reduced the nose skidding to just a few feet with no real threat of damage or fire. The only damage was to one propeller tips that was slightly bent and to the nose gear steering mechanism that acquired a few scrapes. The aircraft rental operator had the aircraft flying the very next day. They thanked me profusely for saving their engine which would have been thousands of dollars. That was the only potentially serious incident that I experienced during my five years flying CAP liaison missions.

War Bird and Aerobatics!

I became acquainted with a pilot who owned an SNJ – a World War Two – advanced trainer and the equivalent of the Army Air Corps T-6. He took Robert and me flying with him in his SNJ for some real fun flying. He also checked me out in his fully-aerobatic Decathlon. He let me fly his Decathlon and I took Robert flying for some fun aerobatics on a few occasions. Fun!

I personally rented an aircraft on a few occasions from the Republic Airport Operator. This gave me a chance to show off New York City from the air to Pat and Robert. (Robert was visiting us at the time). It was awesome flying low over the Hudson River and looking up at the skyscrapers above on each side of the river; and skimming over the numerous bridges crossing the Hudson. No, I didn't fly under them! The World Trade Center Towers were still there at that time and were near the Hudson in lower Manhattan. What a sight! We also flew low along the Long Island southern coast which was a beautiful costal flight.

College: Great Day Halleluiah; Robert Graduates!
A great day in the annals of the University of Florida's history at Gainesville: Robert graduated on June 14th 1980! Pat and I were extremely proud. My checkbook was overjoyed!

Before graduation, Robert had spent a few months with us and worked at a warehouse job near Garden City, as I recall, where he sprained his back. However, it didn't seem to cause him any great problem. His back would give him some back pains later in life. He would later go on to obtain a Master's Degree in Information Systems at Auburn University in Montgomery, Alabama.

In the summer of 1980 Pat and a good friend from New York City decided to indulge in a long time dream of theirs: To become artists. They discovered this elderly and charismatic gentlemen artist, Edgar Whitney there on Long Island. Mr. Whitney is a well-known watercolor artist. They engaged him as their art instructor for water color and both became quite good at it. Robert tried it and became quite good also. Pat also took lessons from a lady artist near Garden City whose name I can't recall. I can truly say that Pat enjoyed her New York adventure. If only she could have seen the parts of the state that I saw in my CAP liaison travel; she would have fallen in love with it.

Dining-In and Departure!
About once a year the CAP Wing would hold a formal dining-in patterned after those of the Air Force; though a little less rowdy. Quite often I would be asked to speak at their banquets; but it was generally the Wing Commander who held sway over the proceedings. Pat, in her usual way befriended everyone and had long since won the hearts of the CAP personnel. On the final dinning-in before we left for my next assignment, the Wing gave her a beautiful plaque showing their appreciation of her. They did likewise for Sergeant Richardson's wife, Ann.

In late 1981, Colonel DePoorter, was assigned to Maxwell AFB, Alabama as the Deputy Commander for the USAF-CAP Liaison to the CAP National Headquarters. He asked me to come to Maxwell to work as the Current Operations Chief. I really didn't want to go. Pat and I were enjoying our New York assignment; especially Pat, although we had hated the thought of coming to New York when I initially received the assignment. (Remember, Son of Sam the schizophrenic serial killer was still at large there at the time!) Nevertheless, the needs of the Air Force prevail. Very soon I had orders assigning me to the USAF-CAP Liaison Headquarters at Maxwell AFB; reporting not later than July 31st, 1982.

Two great historical events occurred before Pat and I left New York in 1982: Son Robert had graduated from the University of Florida. Then a few months later our second grandchild, also named Robert, was born to our son Norris and his wife Gwen. Two great *historical* 1980 events!

*****

CHAPTER TWENTY-ONE
MAXWELL AFB, Montgomery, Alabama (1982-1984)

CAP-USAF Headquarters

Upon arriving at Maxwell in late July 1982, I soon found a house in Prattville, Alabama about eleven miles north of Maxwell. There was no base housing available for me on Maxwell. After getting Pat settled into our home, it was time to report for duty. My job was the Current Operations Officer for the Director of Operations who was a super fine officer. I soon had an eager young Captain assigned to work for me. When he arrived, Pat and I put him up in our home free gratis until his family and household goods arrived. He offered to cut my lawn while he was with us. After about three weeks of yard work, I think he was glad to move out. I was also fortunate to have a good secretary. After good NCOs, office secretaries are the next major force that makes the Air Force work! The job was basically a paper-work job with occasional fun flying Air Force contracted civilian general aviation aircraft for our travel and flying proficiency. Most of the traveling was for CAP unit inspections and exercises; with occasional travel to planning and operational conferences. For large conferences, Air Force C-130s were used; an extremely noisy turbo-prop four-engine aircraft. And those web-strap seats along the sides and down the center of the interior fuselage: Ouch! Oh, my back and bottom! After about 30 minutes the rest of the flight was spent trying to find a comfortable position to ease your backside and bottom from the relentless torture of those web-strap seats.

CAP-USAF Headquarters is the National Headquarters for the Civil Air Patrol. It is staffed by civilian and active duty Air Force personnel jointly to perform all functions of a military organization for the CAP; although they have their own commander and staff (civilians all). Air Force personnel performed the liaison function to their counterpart CAP positions plus attending to their own assigned duties.

Large vs Small Plane Check-Out

As for the chores in the office (ugh!), it was very much routine: Writing memos, letters, revising regulations, policies, etc. The fun part was getting the opportunity to fly. Even the little airplanes (general aviation type) are fun. Fighters are the most fun of course. I'm so glad that I was never assigned to the "Big Multi-Engine Airplanes," B-52s, C-141, C-130 etc. Part of my job was to check out our newly assigned Air Force pilots. Many of the younger pilots had never flown a small civilian airplane or anything with a propeller. Our check-outs were done at small local airports, one of which was the Prattville Airport about seven miles northwest of Maxwell. The airport had a single-runway 3000 feet long and 100 feet wide. A few pilots who were used to operating from 10,000 foot plus runways that were 200 to 300 feet wide had to get psyched-up to operate on a *small* 3000 by 100 foot runway. Crosswinds and wind-gust that can create control problems on landing for small planes would likely never cause a ripple in the huge multi-engine airplanes. It did a number on their egos for a brief time before they mastered the techniques for small aircraft.

Old Age Reality Sets In!

Back at Eglin AFB between 1975 and 1977 I had a few days of upper back pain for which I was hospitalized about three days, but nothing other than bed rest was prescribed. Sometime about June of 1983 I began to have lower back pains again which got progressively more severe. Pat had noted in her garden club calendar that I had an orthopedic appointment with Maxwell orthopedics on June 12th. On June 22nd Norris, Gwen and family, flew down to visit us for a few days. I remember another time that granddaughter, Tessa (about 9 or 10 years old) flew down to visit a few weeks with Pat and me. But my back pains were so severe we could not go anywhere or show Tessa a good time. In fact I was very much immobilized with my back pain. I hated it terribly that I could not enjoy Tessa's visit.

The orthopedic surgery clinic at Maxwell X-rayed my back and told me that I had a "classic" herniated disc at the L4/L5 vertebra in the lower back. The orthopedic doctor asked me if I had ever ejected from an aircraft. This surprised me because I had never mentioned, nor discussed with him, my 1965 ejection in Korea. I told him about the Korean ejection event and he said that he suspected as much because I had an old injury, a crushed disc, which is typical of what he sees in ejection events. Never had I been told this before nor had I been informed that it may happen as a result of an ejection. In a few days my back pain was so severe that I had to literally roll out of bed in the mornings; crawl to the bathroom and shave on my knees while hanging over the sink. After shaving and breakfast, I was able to gingerly make my way to the car and drive to work. A few years earlier my boss had gone through the same back and discs problem; so he was well aware and sympathetic to my condition. My hip and right leg began to ache almost unbearably. I could walk only about 20 to 30 feet without stopping for a couple of minutes to allow the pain to subside slightly in order to continue for another 20 to 30 feet. Eventually, I developed "foot-drop" as the orthopedist called it. I had no control over my foot and when my heel hit the floor my foot would flop down with a "plop!" Nor could I stand back on my heels.

The doctor gave me a scare story about the potential for paralysis of my back and leg at some future unpredictable time and offered three options. One was to do nothing – which sounded like a non-option to me. The other two options were standard back surgery with about a six-inch scar and a few weeks bed rest and long-time recovery; or go to Wilford Hall, the Air Force Medical Center at San Antonio, Texas for micro-surgery with a half-inch scar and immediate relief. Guess which I opted for? Wilford Hall! I was air-evacuated, along with Pat, to Wilford Hall and the surgery was performed on August 6th. I had immediate relief and felt like I could lift the world. However, the doctor cautioned me that this would happen, but that I had to be extremely careful with my physical activities (especially lifting) for the next year or so to allow complete healing. Years later I would develop other back problems unrelated to this one. But for now, I was a new man!

After I was released from Wilford Hall, Pat and I were scheduled for air-evacuation back to Maxwell on the scheduled air-evacuation flight that made the rounds to southeast bases. Of course I was stretcher-bound for the flight. Upon landing at Maxwell, the aircraft taxied to and parked at base operations. I was then carried off by two medics. There on the ramp was my boss and his operations office staff to greet us. What a welcome sight. I was thoroughly humbled. Following a mandatory 30 day convalescent leave I would be returned to flying status 60 days following the surgery. I continued to improve, feeling like a new man.

Brooks AFB Hospital

In December I was scheduled for my annual flying physical. Every Air Force pilot gets an annual flight physical within 90 days prior to their birthday. Things were going rather routinely and my back was healing nicely except for an infection at the sight of the incision, which was dealt with promptly. During the EKG portion of my physical, the doctor noticed a slight variation from previous years' EKGs. After more EKGs and evaluations, on 14 May 1984 I was flown to San Antonio, Texas to Brooks AFB Aviation Medicine Center for evaluation. On May 16th I underwent my first ever heart catheterization. After the procedure, I was moved to the clinic with an Airman medic to monitor me. He cautioned me not to move or cough for a few hours in order for the incision site to close properly. After an hour of so I experienced a very mild involuntary cough, barely perceptible. Immediately I felt a warm sensation in my groin, the site of the incision. I was bleeding profusely. The medic was there immediately. He had heard the cough. He applied pressure and called out to the doctor, who was almost out the door for the day. Another 30 seconds and the doctor would have been out the door. The doctor came back and applied pressure (extreme pressure) for about 20 minutes. His hands had to have gotten tired. I felt like he was going to punch through me. He stopped the bleeding and stayed around for about another 45 minutes. He then issued some instructions to the medic and left. I was again to lie still for a few hours. It was the medic and me. I barely dared to breathe. The remainder of the night was uneventful but I was so tired of lying still; daring not to move even the slightest. I was afraid to go to sleep for popping the incision again and bleeding out.

The Air Force cardiologist discussed my situation and placed me on medication for which the Air Force would ground me. However, The Federal Aviation Administration (FAA) permitted civilian pilots to fly while on this medication. *For the first time in my Air Force Career I was permanently grounded from flying.* I felt somewhat reminiscent of the first time that I was rejected for aviation cadet flying training. That afternoon I was on the Air Evacuation aircraft back to Maxwell. But I was able to continue my civilian flying with FAA authorization.

Commander Retires

The Brigadier General Commander of the Air Force Liaison function would retire on May the 31st. He would be hired by a major airline for their training department and he told his staff that if he could ever be of assistance to them in seeking employment to let him know. My retirement would be later in October and he would be instrumental in assisting me in obtaining my first post retirement civilian job interview. Meantime, I too was preparing for my retirement and attending mandatory briefings. My retirement as a Lieutenant Colonel was involuntary and based on rank and years of service. Had I been promoted to full Colonel, I would have been able to remain another two years on active duty; with much better retirement benefits of course. Competition for promotion to full colonel was very keen and after a couple of pass-overs for the promotion, I knew I was out of the game. Pat attended briefings on what she could expect as the wife of a military retiree. *(The biggest warning she received was that she would now have a husband underfoot 24/7).* In September I would take what is called "terminal leave;" leave that had been accrued and would be lost if not taken before retirement. A side note: Pat's notes in her calendar indicate that Norris started at the Boise University in Boise, Idaho on the September 4th; but I don't remember what his course of study was.

My Retirement

I continued my current operations chief position but I missed Air Force flying immensely. On September 22nd my office arranged a retirement for me at a local park and recreation area. What a great time! My family and relatives from far and near were there, plus countless friends and coworkers. I was asked on a few occasions when did I begin to think about retirement. My response was always: "From my very first day of employment!" My official retirement ceremony was conducted at CAP-USAF Headquarters on the 25th. It seemed almost surreal. Was this really happening after 33 plus years? Of course Pat and Robert were there. Pat was given the usual certificate for enduring years of maintaining the home-front while I was deployed numerous times around the world and for her dedication to the Air Force by understanding and supporting various difficult missions – namely me!

Finally retirement day arrived: October 1, 1984: I became a *used and unemployed* Air Force pilot! What now, Coach??????????
*****

CHAPTER TWENTY-TWO
MOTH-BALLED! RETIRED! "NOW WHAT, COACH?" (1984-1998)

Mixed Emotions!

Now that retirement day had arrived – a day that I had anticipated for more than 33 plus years – I wished I had more active duty years to do. But it was a mandatory retirement as I mentioned in the previous chapter. I still had an FAA waver for civilian flying and wanted to stay active in flying. Since my arrival at Maxwell AFB in 1982, I had been a member of the Maxwell-Gunter Aero Club. I contracted with the aero club as a "self-employed" instructor. Colonel DePoorter was also an Aero Club instructor and the club's Chief Instructor Pilot. So, once again I was working for him now as an aero club flight instructor. I enjoyed introducing young potential pilots (and older) to the world of aviation. The club acquired an aerobatic Citabra on lease which I enjoyed immensely. Aerobatics had always been a delight for me. Some of my best flight memories are when my son, Robert, and I would fly together for a fun time of aerobatics. Years later, Robert would join an aero club in Florida and check-out in their Citabra. I remember puffing out my chest and being proud of him when he took me Citabra-flying in his club's Citabra. My last recorded flight as an instructor was on May 14th 1994 although I continued recreational flying for a few years afterwards with family and friends. Flight instructing did become a little routine after a few years. And when I quit instructing, I told everyone, jokingly, that it was because the guy/gal (still politically incorrect) in the seat next to me was always trying to kill me.

Confederate Air Force and the Texas State Trooper!

One of the things I had always wanted to do was see the Confederate Air Force (CAF) Air Show at Harlingen, Texas. It was one of the biggest and best air shows in the country and they were dedicated to maintaining the heritage of and flying World War II aircraft. They recreated great air battles of World War II complete with "Japanese and German aircraft". Their best was the recreation of the Japanese attack on Pearl Harbor. Years later the Confederate Air Force would change their name to "Commemorative Air Force" most likely to be politically correct and still maintain their acronym: "CAF". I hated to see them acquiesce to the political correct madness since the term "Confederate" was not racially inspired, but rather it was chosen because it started out with one old and rather worn-out dilapidated, ratty-looking looking World War II fighter: The P-51 Mustang. The story that I have read is that a guy interested in World War II aircraft purchased a military surplus P-51 which was obviously in much need of repair. One day someone thought it was so "ratty" looking that it looked as if it was from the "Confederate Air Force". Later the words "Confederate Air Force" mysteriously appeared scrawled on the side of the plane. *The Confederate Air Force was born*! How thin-skinned and super-sensitive we have become! World War II fighters have always been my dream to fly but it was never to be; my favorite all-time fighter being the Navy/Marine F4U Corsair. One day while Pat and I were attending an air show, I stood *drooling* over a Corsair on the flight line. I told her that the only competition she ever had to worry about was the F4U Corsair. *She understood.*

I had always told Pat that when I retired and before really getting into job hunting, I wanted to go see the Confederate Air Force Air Show at Harlingen, Texas while I had the time. I told her we would drive to Harlingen and do a little sight-seeing of this great land of ours on the way; about 1500 miles round trip. The show occurred annually the second week-end of October. Since I had just retired on October the 1st, the timing was great. We loaded up the second week of October and away we went in our small compact car. Before leaving, I had ordered AAA books and strip maps for the trip. We were enjoying the travel and sight-seeing.

About half way between Houston, Texas and Harlingen southbound in the right lane on a divided four-lane highway, I was happily anticipating the airshow the next two days, Saturday and Sunday. Travel had been relatively easy and presently there was no traffic in sight. Then I noticed a lone State Trooper car approaching from the opposite direction in the northbound lanes on the other side of the median. Instinctively I glanced at my speedometer (nobody else does that I know). I was doing 57 miles per hour. The speed limit was 55. I didn't even let up on the accelerator for those 2 miles per hour. As the Trooper approach abeam of me northbound, he suddenly wheeled across the median doing a 180 degree turn and pulled up next to me in the left lane matching my speed. I commented to Pat that he must have gotten a call for some place south of us. But he continued abeam of me matching my speed. I looked over at him and waved – a friendly acknowledgement kind of wave. Then he dropped back behind me practically on my rear bumper and turned on his flashing beacon. Again I commented to Pat that he must have gotten an emergency call and would probably exit at the exit we were approaching. Not so! He continued past the exit close on my tail.

I pulled over and stopped, totally mystified as to what was happening. I watched in my side view mirror as he emerged from his vehicle. I waited rather anxiously as he approached. He looked as tall as the Empire State Building from my small compact car. In fact as he stood by my window I was staring eye-ball to eye-ball with his humongous, shiny belt buckle. He stood straight and unsmiling in his neat uniform, holstered side arm and scowl on his face. He asked for the usual: Driver's license, registration and insurance. As I handed them to him, I thought that he's going to question why I have an Alabama license and Florida tag. Being a military retire, I had 30 days to change my tag to my state of residence. But he didn't ask. I assume that he saw my Maxwell AFB decal on the windshield and guessed the reason for the discrepancy between the two. I didn't say a word. I didn't know what to say so I only sat there. *Silence!* Finally he asked me what my hurry was. I replied that I didn't think I was in a hurry. He said that he "clocked" me at 78 miles per hour. Later Pat told me when he said he had clocked me at 78 mph, my jaw dropped open. Of course I sprinkled my comments with "Yes Sir," "No Sir". I didn't want to jeopardize my chances of getting to the air show. I told him that I was only doing 57 mile per hour. He then said that he had 78 miles per hour on the radar in his vehicle and invited me back to see it for myself. I told him that I didn't need to do that; if he had it on his radar there's nothing I could say or do about it.

At this point he said he was going to have to cite me for speeding. He said that he had a partner a few miles down the road and asked me what his partner would think of him if he let me go without issuing me a speeding ticket. Then, he leaned downed and got his face in my open window and asked me why I was jeopardizing my wife's safety by driving so fast; and with a sarcastic tone said: "If she is your wife!" Then the hammer! He said that he would have to take me in before the judge; but the judge would not be available until Monday. I begin to get a sickening feeling in my stomach. I had traveled over 700 miles to see the Confederate Air Force Air Show that I had wanted to see for years. Now I was going to spend the weekend in jail until Monday when the judge returned; having completely missed the air show. I was devastated. What would happen to Pat?" *Silence!* I continued to not protest, mostly from not knowing what to say. I knew that there was nothing I could say that would placate him. He was definitely not the type that would take any "lip". I just sat there silent and unmoving. I had the feeling he was just looking for an argument from me.

Finally, maybe because I wasn't taking the "bait," he said that he was only going to issue me a warning; but his partner down the road would be looking for me. With that warning he said something like: "I don't know how you folks drive back home, but out here we don't drive like that". "Yes Sir," I said and with that he gave me back my license, registration and insurance. "Whew!" Believe me I literally crept the rest of the way to Harlingen. Later I would check my AAA trip map for the location where we had been stopped. Right there on the map at the exact spot, AAA had stamped an arrow pointing to the location with the notation: "Speed trap!"

The Air Show was absolutely fabulous and well worth the trip and expense. Our return trip was uneventful but you can be assured that I pegged 50 miles per hour as we drove through that AAA identified speed-trap section of the highway. I highly recommend the CAF Air Show; but watch out for those *speed-traps.*

Back home, I continued flying with the Maxwell Aero Club. They had acquired a T-34 (1950s Air Force and Navy Primary Trainer like I had flown in primary flight training). This was the T-34B Navy model and I enjoyed it immensely. In fact I flew Norris, Robert, and my brother, Richard, in it when they visited. I had also flown my grandson Robert A. in the T-34 when he visited. Norris and Gwen visited us for about nine days in 1984. That's probably when I flew Norris. However, I don't remember flying Pat in it. It was in the Hamilton AFB, California aero club T-34 that I frightened her unintentionally during a 1958 flight off the coast of California. What to do? In order to continue to live in this manner in which I had become accustomed, I had to find a job.

Well, What Can You Do?

What can I do? Fly! That's all I ever really wanted to do. But who would hire a has-been, used up fighter pilot? I wanted to stay in the aviation career field in some capacity. For a brief time I worked as a flight instructor at the local Prattville airport (Grouby Airport). In the meantime I must have submitted what seemed to be a hundred plus job applications (before the internet).

I contacted my former commander, now working in the training department for a major airline, to see if he might follow through on his promise to assist any of his former staff in their quest for a post-retirement civilian job. He seemed more than delighted to help and arranged an interview for me with the company's operations department chief. The job interview was scheduled and the airline flew me to their headquarters for the meeting. I had been told to prepare a class-room styled presentation on any aircraft system that I chose. Knowing that the company flew large multi-engine passenger aircraft, I chose the hydraulic system for the B-52 bomber. Of course I knew nothing of the B-52 but had access to the hydraulic schematic and a description of the system and its operation. I prepared a couple of charts and practiced my presentation many times. Travel day came. Of course, as any job applicant would be I was rather anxious. After all this was to be an interview with a prestigious airline for a great job.

I arrived and went through the introduction and personal history formalities. The operations chief invited the personnel chief to sit in with him on my prepared presentation. After about five minutes (maybe less) the operations chief stopped me and said: "It's obvious you have done this type of thing before. Very good presentation! Go see the company doctor for your employment physical". I was elated. *I was hired!* I didn't anticipate any problem with the physical in spite of my recent back surgery and cardiovascular problems; after all this was for a simulator/classroom instructor position – not a flying position. Shortly into the physical and medical history portion, the doctor stopped me cold and said he was sorry but they couldn't hire me because of my medical history. I was shocked. When I reminded him the job was for simulator and classroom instructor only, not flying, he replied that it made no difference what position I was applying for; that it was company policy. I returned to the operations chief and told him everything. He said he was sorry and reiterated that it was company policy not to hire anyone with a medical history such as mine. I pleaded that if it was insurance concerns, not to worry because I had my own insurance and would take care of my medical expenses. That still didn't carry any weight; *it was company policy!* I was devastated. It was a great job to lose over what I considered to be a none-factor. I proceeded to inform my former commander of the rejection and reason. He too seemed disappointed, especially for me. But I was soon on my way home courtesy of the company airline. Of course Pat was disappointed for me also; but I don't think she was all that disappointed in not leaving Prattville. She had come to love Prattville and Prattville loved her.

Master's Degree

I decided that I needed to increase my educational credentials in order to make myself more employable. So I entered the Master of Science in Adult Education program through Troy State University (Montgomery campus). Since I had hopes of staying in the aviation field and instructing in some manner, I thought having an education degree would help. And I thought it would be less demanding than other programs of study. But it was no crip course! I graduated in December of 1986, in Montgomery. The Air Force had for years been pushing professional military and civilian education. A Master's degree (in anything) had become an almost necessity for promotion – even before I retired. It was a standing joke among the troops that a Master's degree in "basket weaving" would fill the promotion-essential-higher-degree "square". I should have gotten a "basket weaving" degree a few years before retiring. It may have (but not likely) gotten me one more promotion. I was about three years too late in obtaining a Master's Degree.

Robert would get the Master's degree jump on me though. He came home to spend a few months getting his Master of Information Systems degree at Auburn University (Montgomery campus), graduating in June 1986. While here, he worked as a crewman on the Montgomery River Boat and its Alabama River cruises. Following his return to Florida in July, he obtained a job with a large information systems company and bought a really nice house in a beautifully landscaped community; complete with ponds, ducks and peacocks!

Second Chance Job Offer

I applied for another ground school teaching job with a well-known company that conducted simulator/classroom pilot-refresher training. The aircraft simulator was a twin-engine turboprop executive type aircraft used in the military and civilian flight operations. I had no turboprop time but figured I could learn. My application was accepted and I was invited to a nearby regional training facility for a job interview and instructional presentation. My B-52 briefing worked so good for my previous interview I decided to stick with a proven "horse". The presentation and acceptance was almost a carbon copy of my first presentation for the major airline. I was hired and no physical was required. The job location would be at the home office training facility in a mid-western state. This time I loaded up and drove out after saying goodbye to Pat.

Upon arriving and after introductions were made, I was told that my training would be *by non-participation auditing of classroom presentations and monitoring flight simulator instructors conducting their training sessions.* I was given an aircraft manual and told where the film library was and that it would be basically a self-taught training program. There were a couple of other trainees there but they both had experience in the aircraft they would be simulator instructing in. Not so for me. In fact I found the turboprop system rather difficult. In the classroom instructor-trainees "auditing" the class were not permitted to join the class discussions or ask questions. That was reserved for the "paying" clientele. Occasionally I would be scheduled to *monitor* an hour of simulator instruction conducted by other instructors. For some reason I was not comfortable with this "training" method and was struggling with learning the systems and aircraft. The simulator time was mostly devoted to practice of all emergency procedures so the instructor had little time for helping me learn the simulator. This went on for three or four weeks and I spent the nights in my apartment studying the manual; particularly emergency procedure, still with little success. It was almost as if I had acquired a mental block for all things related to the aircraft and simulator. I couldn't understand why I could not master this "beast". I would be "instructing" pilots who had hundreds of hours in the aircraft and were here for refresher training. How was I, with no turboprop time, nor time in the type aircraft, going to "instruct" experienced pilots in the aircraft without some type of formal training in the aircraft simulator? It was obvious that the other instructor-trainees were more familiar and knowledgeable than I in the aircraft systems.

Eventually the chief instructor came on board one of the simulators in which I had managed to wrangle some familiarization time. He put me through a few emergency drills then abruptly terminated the session. I didn't do well! In an hour or so I was called to the front office and told that they couldn't use me and were letting me go. Of course I was emotionally devastated but understood that they had no choice. I just wasn't cutting it! I couldn't shake that mental block. I'm sure I was more disappointed and mystified than they were. As I look back on that terrible experience, I can see God's hand in it. I returned to Prattville, humiliated, and poured out my heart to Pat. She was very understanding but was probably again secretly delighted that we weren't leaving Prattville. As the years developed, so am I.

T-6 Check-Out!

Southeast of Montgomery a rancher had a grass air strip and hangar where he kept his vintage aircraft which included a T-6 Texan, PT-17 Stearman and Piper J-3 Cub. I had gotten to meet him at some of the local aviation events and he invited me out to his airport. He asked me to fly in the back seat of his T-6 to instruct him in commercial pilot flight maneuvers. He was preparing for the FAA Commercial Pilot flight test and written exams. I was delighted to do so and for the T-6 time. He also needed ground school refresher training that I was able to provide. The day came and he passed his commercial pilot flight test and written exam with no problems.

Annually he had a fly-in of his friends with their vintage "war-bird" aircraft for a day of fun flying and Bar-B-Qing. Generally they would have a formation briefing then go practice their formation skills. During the summer of 1986 or 1987 Robert and I were invited to sit in on their briefing and then fly with them (as passengers). One of the highlights of my experience with the guys was the ensuing mass "gaggle" 16-aircraft formation of T-6s in which Robert flew in the back seat with the rancher/owner as the leader; and I flew in the back seat of the number two T-6 with a retired Navy pilot/owner. That was quite a sight and experience. What fun! The ground-bound human will never experience such thrills! It was not a really close formation, and with the varied experience level of the mostly civilian pilots I was glad to see a rather loose formation of 16 T-6s.

One instructor pilot who owned a T-6 provided flight instruction for me in the front seat of his T-6 for a check-out. After about 15 hours he said I was qualified to go buy my own T-6 and fly it home. However, I never followed through with his suggestion. He could not let me solo his T-6 because of insurance restrictions. On one occasion I asked him if he would fly Pat for a few minutes. I wanted Pat to have the experience of a true military aircraft other than the T-34 (militarized civilian Beech aircraft) that I had flown her in. He readily agreed and Pat readily accepted. They took-off and immediately he went into about 20 minutes of low-level aerobatics right over the air strip between 50 to 800 feet. I was half-horrified and half-delighted and all jealous. I hadn't asked him to do aerobatics with her; only fly a few minutes of flight. I just knew Pat was heaving her insides all over that rear cockpit; but she did fine. After they landed she emerged all smiles and said she enjoyed it but would not do it again! No one could have been more surprise that me.

Pat Rejoins the Work Force

In August of 1987 our cat, Puff, died after living "independently" with us for 20 years. He was a great old cat and was sorely missed. Pat said she wanted to go to work. I don't think it was Puff's death, but more likely she wanted to live in the manner to which she was accustomed – before I retired. Just kidding! I really think she just wanted rejoin the workforce as she was before we married. She submitted a few job applications and one day, September 30th 1987, the editor/publisher of the local newspaper in Prattville interviewed her for a job as the paper's advertising representative. He hired her "on the spot" and would later say it was the best decision he ever made. Pat was a people person so this position in which she would have contact with all businesses in the area was a joy for her. She had already learned to love Prattville and its people so she knew many of the business owners. Prattville learned to love her. Quite often when I was out-and-about I would overhear someone say: "That's Pat's husband". I was quite pleased to be known as "Pat's husband". Someone once said that Pat should run for Mayor; she would be a shoo-in. I believe it!

She never ceased to amaze me at her energy. She worked day and nights. I was concerned for her health. After working all day on the job, usually with overtime, she would come home and spend hours of preparation for the next day's schedule – sometimes into the early morning hours. While maintaining her job, she found time to be deeply involved with other community and church activities. Some of the things in which she was involved were:

Sunday School teacher. She would visit absent and ill members on weekends.

Garden Club secretary.

Council of Blind Citizens secretary.

Board of Directors member for the Chamber of Commerce which was responsible for getting the world-class Robert Trent Jones golf course in Prattville.

Panel member/participant on the local paper mill Woodlands panel.

And certainly I shouldn't forget wife and homemaker.

Other activities, which escape me at the moment.

Pat would keep her job until her instant death from a massive heart attack on March 5th, 2001. She died on her job walking across the parking lot to her car; loving her job! The doctor said she was probably dead before she hit the ground. Her death came six months after our son, Norris's death; and two months after her Mother's death. I lost all three of them within six months!

In 1989 I would find a job at a local developmental center for the mentally disabled as a "Job Coordinator". This was job searching to find an employer who would hire our job-capable clients. Then I would hire a "job coach" to coach them until they mastered the job. This relieved the employer of the training and initial supervision responsibilities. The job was quite rewarding when I could get a client on the job and they would become a good employee. After 10 years (1999) I decided to "retire" again. Pat wanted to continue working. I tried unsuccessfully to get her to quit her job but she really loved it.

F-100 Pilot Seat!

Sometime around April or May of 1994 I begin to mull over in my mind how nice it would be to have a den chair fashioned from an F-100 seat. I had enjoyed the F-100 so much I could imagine myself relaxing in the seat, leaning back and losing myself in thought and memories of those long-gone unforgettable days. I had for a few years been collecting military memorabilia related to World War One and my Dad's service in the trenches of France. But I had not given much thought to my own memorabilia except for the handful of items I had. I began to think of collectables from "my war" eras: Korean War era, the Vietnam War and the Cold War. Weeks went by and I thought often of the F-100 seat den chair possibility. However I had never seen any such seats available from a multitude of military collectible catalogs and the many military collector shows that I attended. I didn't hold out much hope of finding one.

One day searching through some military surplus equipment catalogs lo-and-behold there was a dealer advertising not one but *four* F-100 seats. I immediately contacted him (in Missouri) and discussed the seats and my plan. *I told the dealer to send me the best of the four seats.* It is important to note here that I allowed the dealer to select the seat for me. The seat was complete with the seat's survival kit container (empty) and its attached seat cushion. Soon he had them loaded onto a truck and on the way to me.

I think it was about this time that I told Pat, Norris and Robert of my plans. I just knew that they would be delighted since they all were very close to my flying career: The F-94C, F-89, F-100, O-1 and O-2. (Robert would not remember my F-94C and F-89 times since they were during his infancy). The F-100 at Cannon and Luke AFBs would be my last operational fighter assignments. Pat, Norris and Robert had been with me throughout all of these assignments but Norris would soon be off to college.

Finally my seat arrived. I was very excited about the prospect of my F-100 seat den-chair. It arrived very dirty and grimy looking like it was straight from the "bone yard". Not what I expected from "the best of the four seats". I set about drawing sketches, taking photographs and planning how I was going to mount the seat as a den chair. I made a wooden prototype of my proposed mounting which would provide for reclining and 360 degrees of rotation. All of this paraphernalia I had laid out on the den floor, grimy seat and all, when one day

Pat's friend showed up. She looked at the dirty and grimy seat and the scattered display on the floor and asked Pat what all of this was about. When Pat told her I was making an F-100 den chair, Pat's friend told her she was crazy if she let me put that thing in the den!

After cleaning up the seat, survival kit and cushion they looked very nice; in fact I thought they looked very good! I took my mounting sketches and wooden prototype to a machine shop and explained my plans to the machinist. He made me 3/8 inch steel plates for the back and base and a steel rod with brackets to hinge the back and base plates together. I went to a local auto junk yard and found a front passenger seat reclining mechanism. A furniture dealer gave me free gratis a circular wooden base from an old lounge chair. Now all I needed was an F-100 seat; and I had one! Attach one F-100 seat and *"Voila"* an F-100 den chair that rotates 360 degrees and reclines 30 degrees! I installed the survival kit with seat cushion and the parachute from my F-100 ejection in 1965. Sitting in that seat brings back tons of memories. And I think my family was (and is) proud of it too. Pat would sometimes sit in it and do some of the work that she was always bringing home from the office. *That's not all; Read on!*

For a few weeks I would occasionally sit in my F-100 seat and the odds of my having flown in that seat would cross my mind. Finding the seat was a lucky break but of all the F-100s built what would be the odds that I had flown in this one. The seat was from the back seat of an F-100F a two-seat model that was used in F-100 training courses, for the annual back-seat-under-the-hood instrument flight checks for all pilots and the "Misty" FAC missions in Vietnam. Military aircraft have what is called a "tail number" which is a six-digit number combination of the contract year and manufacturing sequence. I had recorded in my pilot log book the last three digits of the F-100s that I flew.

One evening sitting in my F-100 seat I determined that I was going to try to end the suspense of having flown in the seat or not. The seat had stamped into its data plate the tail number of the aircraft that it came from. I went to my log book and there was the last three digits of this tail number recorded in my log book. "Wow!" But that wasn't proof. There could be others with the same last three digits. So I took the six-digit tail number to nearby Maxwell AFB and the Air Force Aircraft Historical Records Branch and asked for the unit and location of that particular F-100F on the date that was in my log book. The research technician soon came back with the exact same date, unit and location that were in my log book! *Not done yet.* Since it was an "F" model I could have been in either seat. Remember this was the *rear seat* that I had purchased. So I went back to my log book to find out what type of flight I flew in that F-100 on that date. It was an instrument flight for me which meant that I *was in the back seat* under the hood on that particular date in that F-100. The hair stood up on the back of my neck. Here I was sitting in an F-100 seat that I had flown in years ago with a parachute in which I had ejected from another F-100 before that! *And this was a seat that I let the dealer select for me from the four he had available.* "Wow, wow, wow!"

Norris's and Gwen's Health

Meanwhile, Norris, (in Boise, Idaho) had begun to have heart problems. On September 23rd 1987 he had a heart cauterization and on October 1st would have four-bypass open heart surgery. On October 21st Pat and I would fly out for about eight days to visit with him and his family. Unfortunately Norris's health would never really improve. He would die of heart failure on September 5th 2000; six months before his Mom and one month before he was to go to Salt Lake City to be evaluated for a heart transplant. Pat and I would again fly to Boise.

Later, Gwen's health would deteriorate as she developed Multiple Sclerosis (MS) and force her to give up her job as Chief Nurse on a VA hospital ward in Boise. She and her Mother are both in an assisted living facility in Boise. Both Tessa and Robert are helping care for their Mom. Tessa is the best caregiver ever and will have many stars in her Heavenly crown!

Pat's Mom

Pat's Mom was still living in Florida in 1992 and on some of our later visits her neighbors told us of a neighbor that was seen walking over to her house about mealtimes. They suspected that he (a young man) was going over to "mooch" meals off her. On our visits we had noticed that she would leave food out of the refrigerator, stove burners on, water running and have long overdue bills unpaid, etc. During one of our visits we talked to the young man in question and he said that he was going over at mealtimes to help her and to be sure that she would eat; which she also sometimes forgot to do. After discussions with Pat's sister, Carrie, who lived several hours away, it was decided that Pat and I would take their Mother in to live with us. We felt so "small" for our suspicion of the young man who was helping her and we wondered why her other "good-friend" neighbors didn't see her failing and warn us. "Dementia!" What a terrible thing! I pray that I never become that kind of burden on any of my family.

How to get Pat's Mom home with us? That would be a real problem. She was about 93 years old then and a more stubborn, proud and hard-headed woman you would not fine. She loved her independence! Except for the onset of dementia, she was in fine health. She took no medicines, vitamins or supplements; not even an aspirin. She had been widowed many years, lived alone and still drove her car wherever she wanted (locally or on trips). She even assisted her neighbors, the "old people" as she called them, with their grocery shopping and doctor visits. She also peddled a three-wheeled bicycle around town. She would never entertain the thought of moving from her home.

No amount of reasoning or encouraging would budge her. Finally, Pat and Carrie came up with a plan: Carrie would suggest to their Mom that she and Carrie come to visit Pat and me. Carrie would discretely pack a few of their Mom's things to bring along for her to move in with us. After a brief stay, Carrie returned home. Their Mom was very angry when she found out that Carrie left without her. She claimed that we "lied" to her – and I guess you could say that; also she claimed that she had been "kidnapped". There was no reasoning with her. Her almost constant theme was that she had to get home to take care of things: Check on her neighbors or, most of the time it was to do something that occurred in her childhood or early adult years, i.e., chopping cotton or some other field chores. She could remember events in her childhood and young adult life (although out of sequence), but couldn't remember what happened or was said 30 seconds ago. This caused much hassling and arguing for which I would feel remorse afterwards because of her condition. She constantly misplaced and lost things. One example was the fact that she would often take out her hearing aid and lose it. Then there would be an anxious search throughout the house.

One day her caregiver took her to the local senior center for lunch and games. I was home when they returned and I noted that Pat's Mom didn't have her hearing aid – she only wore one and for a short time only; but couldn't hear a word you said without it. Her caregiver had no clue as to where it was; only that she had it when they went to the senior center. I had previously noticed that Pat's Mom would occasionally remove her hearing aid and place it in her plate. A call to the center director was unsuccessful in turning up the hearing aid. I got permission from the director to come down and go through the lunchtime garbage to look for it. The center had three large garden sized trash bags of garbage. There was nothing to do but to roll up my sleeves and dig in.

After I had gotten to the bottom of the third bag, I heard a faint high-pitched whine. I scratched around a bit more and there it was; one hearing aid worth approximately $1000.00.

Pat's Mom would threaten to walk home. You couldn't make her understand the concept that it was 400 miles. She was going to walk anyway. By now walking without a walker or assistance was a rather unsteady chore for her. One day she walked out of the house after threatening to leave. I let her go and followed out of her sight to see just how far she would go. After walking out onto the drive way she stood for a couple of minutes looking up and down the street as if undecided on which way to go. Pathetic; heart wrenching! I finally took her and led her back into the house. Pat had hired a lady to be her caregiver so that I could have some of my time back. Of course Pat was at work and so was I for the most part until 1999 when I quit the developmental center.

This went on for the eight years she was with us until she died of a brain aneurysm three days before her 99th birthday. Four months earlier our son, Norris died of a heart attack. Two months after her mother died, Pat, would die of a massive heart attack at age 73. I lost the three of them within a six months period of time.

Fishing, Dumb Stunts, and Swamp "Things"!

Robert loved the water; especially canoeing and fishing. While growing up and into his young adult years, he was a fishing fan and had a tackle box full of store-bought and hand-made lures. They never improved his fishing luck beyond mine which was practically nil. But he enjoyed it and would take me fishing on occasions later in our lives. I enjoy the father/son time with him and just the lazy, relaxing time with a fishing pole in my hands. He didn't seem to have any better luck when he was a young boy than he did later when he became a young man. I think the fish caught on (no pun) to his attempts and shunned his store-bought lures.

One day when Robert was visiting, he and I shared some experiences in our lives which could only be described as "dumb". I told Robert of my explorations the North Georgia gold mines, as a North Georgia College student, crawling on my stomach through narrow tunnels and over collapsed ceiling rubble; a dumb-stunt I would never attempt again. He then confessed to some of his stories in the Florida alligator and snake infested swamps; things that he would never do again. It seems he and his cousins Morris and David would go baby alligator hunting in nearby swamps. He told me of his wading in swamps so deep that he had to lift his chin in order to keep his mouth and nose above water; and of occasionally feeling unknown things brush against his legs. Sometimes he would take his canoe out alone into those same swamp-critter infested swamps. I wonder how we ever grew up!

Pat's sister, Carrie, told her of coming home one day and her sons telling her not to go into the bathroom. Of course this is an invitation to a mom. Her sons had captured some small gators and snakes which they decided to keep in her bathroom. Opening the bathroom door she saw her bathroom literally crawling with snakes and baby gators; on the floor, in the tub and sink, on the commode, and hanging from the shower and towel bars. But she was accustomed to her sons' love of nature and all of God's critters; so she was not too shocked. She tells of her youngest son being "treed" by an irate mama gator and his having to spend the night in that tree. Ah, youth!

Tour of the World War One Western Front (WW I)

Sometime around mid-1988 I developed an almost overnight, interest in my Dad's World War One military service; especially his time in the trenches of

France as an infantry rifleman. After about three years of my best attempts at research for a manuscript of his service, I yearned to walk those battlefields of France where he fought; to travel his post-war march route to the Rhine River and to visit the occupied areas of Germany where he served during the occupation. I acquired copies of World War One army combat maps for his division and regiment and French highway maps to prepare an itinerary for a planned September 1991 tour. This would be a George Partridge self-guided tour for my wife Pat, my son Robert and me. After flights, hotels and a rental car were reserved, we were on our way from Atlanta, Georgia on September 16th. Pat would be the video photographer, Robert would be the driver and I would be the guide, narrator, navigator and map reader. French and German Phrase books were purchased which we all studied. Robert concentrated on French and me on German. To say that we mastered the phrases would be a wild stretch of the imagination; although Robert seemed to pick up the phrases rather readily.

I had studied the trench maps, order-of-battle maps, routes and legends in detail to include the exact location of trenches and hills on which Dad's units fought and occupied. A detailed itinerary was prepared. I didn't leave much tourist slack time although we managed to do some touristy stuff. The final portion of my itinerary was to visit the U.S. Army Third Division's Museum at Wurzburg, Germany to try to identify details of some photos of my Dad and his unit that were found in his trunk. Visiting those battlefields, trenches and hill sites was highly emotional for me as I stood on the very ground, maybe even the very spot, where my Dad fought, bivouacked and was billeted. Extremely emotional was the visits to several American military cemeteries throughout France that are maintained by the American Military Cemetery Commission. If one's patriotism ever wanes, you only need to visit these cemeteries and look over the seemingly endless field of white crosses to stiffen your patriotism and resolve. National cemeteries here in the United States will provide a similar feeling of gratitude for those who have fought for our freedoms.

We returned to Atlanta on September 28th from what was, for me, a highly-charged emotional and mission-accomplished tour. Pat had compiled a detailed daily diary, which I have, of our travels from day one to the day of our return. I compiled a narrative of the tour highlights; fun, emotions, sights and scares!

Grandson Robert Visits

Our grandson, Robert, arrived from Boise, ID to spend a few months with his GrandPat and me, summer of 1997 I think it was. He had been his high school baseball team's pitcher – and was quite good; pitching at least one no-hitter game. I think I probably flew him in the Maxwell Aero Club's T-34. I know that whenever Pat and I would visit Norris and his family in Boise, I would take them flying at a local airport – "… way beyond the hills of Idaho" as the song goes.

They showed us their mountains and resort areas. Beautiful country! There is also a nice Aviation Museum: The Warhawk Air Museum in Caldwell, Idaho which I enjoyed very much. Of course I'm always interested in aviation museums.

We got grandson Robert enrolled in the Prattville High School and I gave him the use of my 1982 Mazda. But he was soon homesick and returned to Boise.

Another Narrow Escape: T-34 Crash!

I continued to fly with the Maxwell Aero Club. My two favorite aircraft were the T-34 (military trainer) and the Citabra (aerobatic). Flying my family and friends in both aircraft was a delight; showing of the T-34; and demonstrating the thrill of aerobatics in the Citabra. One day I asked my newly certified private pilot friend Larry Bowdoin if he would like to fly with me in the T-34 to see what a real airplane is like, i.e. glass sliding canopy, control stick, retractable gear and constant speed propeller and military cockpit. Additionally, we would be flying off of a real-to-goodness Air Force base. He readily agreed. The day arrived: May 14th 1998. At the aero club the T-34 was ready. A friend had flown it a couple of hours earlier and said it was working great. After the aircraft preflight and necessary safety briefing for my friend, we strapped in. With taxi and takeoff clearance, I lined up on the runway centerline and inquired of Larry if he was ready. With an affirmative answer, we were on the roll, thinking to myself that he is going to really enjoy this. About liftoff I observed drops of what I thought was moisture running off the windshield and coming from what looked like condensation being spun off the prop tips. Larry saw it from the rear cockpit and asked me what it was. We had just gotten airborne when I realized that it wasn't water but oil. I told him it was oil and we were going back to land. After informing the tower that I had an oil problem and was returning to land, I pulled up into a left 180 degree climbing turn to go back to the landing end of the runway. They asked if I was declaring an emergency to which I affirmed that I was. The tower claimed never to have understood that emergency affirmation.

As I was completing my turn toward the other end of the runway, the engine failed at 300 feet above ground while still climbing for altitude. I was over the base and the only clear area was a 90 degree turn to the left toward the ramp. By this time the windshield and quarter side panels were completely oil covered obliterating any forward view. I informed the tower that I had engine failure and informed Larry. The standard guidance for emergency landings is that when you're down to 1000 feet above the ground, forget all attempts at restarts and emergency procedures and just concentrate full time on landing safely. At 300 feet above the ground with an approximately 500 feet per minute rate of descent my time to impact would be just over 30 seconds. Sometime after the accident a lady friend of mine commented that she bet I did a lot of praying. I told her: "No Ma'am. There was no time; but I was *pre-prayed!*"

During my turn toward the ramp I reached for the "Emergency Fuel Control". But at that moment my left wing dropped about 45 to 60 degrees and I thought I might hit wing tip first and cartwheel. So I forget the emergency fuel system and lowered my nose in case I was about to stall. I leveled the wings. It was one of the hardest things that I've ever done: Lowering my nose to preserve my airspeed in case I was on the verge of a stall, knowing I was about to hit the ground. With no forward visibility through the oil, I had no idea what was in front of me; but it was apparent now that I was not going to make the ramp. I got the wings level just before hitting the ground and felt a terrific shock to my seat. I felt two or three other shocks, one of which stopped me when I broadsided a van in the parking lot of a fast food restaurant on the base. It turns out that I had bounced off of a curb which was probably the first shock that I felt; then a tree which separated the left wing totally from the aircraft and a concrete stanchion at the entrance to the fast food drive-through which crumpled the outboard half of the right wing. The tail of the aircraft had totally separated. Although it was 5:00pm and the parking lot would normally be full, it was near empty and so was the van. Thank you Lord!

My aircraft and the van caught fire. The rear canopy of Larry's cockpit had separated from the T-34 on impact so he was out and clear immediately. His only injuries were bruises from the shoulder harness and a bit of singed hair. My canopy jammed and I could not open it more than a couple of inches. I could now see that both the T-34 and the van were burning. The heat didn't immediately seem severe but within a couple of minutes the windshield frame had heated up so severely that it would burn my fingers, hand and arms through the two-inch space between canopy and windshield. (Note: I often flew with a fire-resistant flight suit and gloves. That day because of the summer heat and shear disregard for safety I was in a short sleeve shirt and no gloves). The fire was now by my cockpit on the left side. I tried again and again to force the canopy open but couldn't budge it. In desperation, I thought that I would close and lock the canopy, unlock it and yank, hoping this would dislodge it. It worked! The canopy came open; I unbuckled my seat belt and started to climb out. *That is the way I remember it!* However, at that moment a couple of arms reached in and pulled me out of the cockpit onto the damaged right wing and then others joined the rescue and drug me onto the grass away from the aircraft. These were heroes that were in the immediate area who witnessed the crash and reacted disregarding their own safety. I was completely unaware of who was around me at the scene. Perhaps their actions and mine occurred simultaneously; but, for those people I will be forever grateful. They risked their lives climbing upon that burning aircraft and van; either of which could have exploded at any moment. Thank you men! Later there would be three hero awards presented for actions that occurred that day following my crash and rescue. I'm equally grateful for the emergency crews who immediately responded to the crash. I was then taken to the Maxwell hospital Emergency Room for stabilization; then to Baptist South Hospital in Montgomery for treatment. The oil problem resulted from an incorrect main oil seal installed in the engine. The cause of the engine failure was not determined. The oil problem should not have caused engine failure in such a short time. Larry and I both are thankful to the Lord for saving us that fateful day. I see him often in his local 'Laser Copy' faith-based printing business here in Prattville, Alabama.

Crash Injuries

I received second and third degree burns on my hands and arms. They were treated and bandaged. Additional treatments and surgeries continued during my three-week stay in the hospital. Burn treatment: I would not wish it on my worst enemy! However, during my three-week treatment, I complained about my back daily; more than about the burns. My back and shoulders felt as if they were weighted down; I was unable to stand erect. Several X-rays were done including consultation with an orthopedic surgeon. I was told that the X-rays showed nothing wrong and that everything seemed to be in place. Still I complained daily about my back and my inability to stand straight; but nothing was done about my back other than the X-rays.

After the three-week hospital stay, I was discharged on June 6th. My hands and arms were still bandaged and my hands were immobilized in casts to assure that they healed properly for therapy later. I was totally helpless; unable to use my hands at all. Norris flew down on May 27th for a month to help me as Pat was still working. He and Robert were God sends for both Pat and me. My complaints about my back continued with my burn doctor until I guess he got fed-up and sent me to a neurosurgeon. The neurosurgeon told me to bring the X-rays that were taken in the hospital. On the appointment day, which was eight weeks following my accident, the neurosurgeon took the X-rays and looked at them for about five seconds and announced that I had two or three fractured vertebra! *Eight weeks after the fractures and nothing had been done about them!* He said they had "anglicized" meaning that the vertebra had formed in wedge shapes at the fractures; thus causing my back to bend forward and preventing me from being able to stand up straight. My back now tires quickly and I have limited frontal lifting capability. His treatment was to put me in a back brace for three months. The brace helped when I would do yard work and other light chores; but anything other than light lifting was out of the question. Following this he referred me to an orthopedic surgeon for further evaluation. After a few visits I inquired of the orthopedic surgeon as to what could be done about correcting my back (spine). His reply was most depressing. He said: "Nothing!" My back had gone too far without correcting the spine which should have been done immediately following my accident. The fractured vertebras had healed in a wedge shape. He said as a surgeon he would love to operate on my back but that he could not correct the problem. So today I live with a weak back tiring often, using a back brace for some very light physical activities and still unable to straighten up. My neck has also bent forward. As the career military person I am, being unable to stand straight – bothers me terribly.

Obviously my flying was temporarily curtailed. However, on May 14th 1999, the one-year anniversary date of my crash I was flying again with my friend, Win DePoorter, to regain my flying currency. The front page of the Prattville Progress had a feature article and picture of the anniversary event. It was great to be in the air again. As my boyhood hero, Gene Autry, would have sung it: "Back in the Saddle Again!"

*****

CHAPTER TWENTY-THREE
MY STORY CONTINUES; NOW AND BEYOND.....

Community Events

Our town of Prattville holds an annual Veterans Day ceremony at the court house. In 1996 I began a "live" military uniforms presentation for all of America's wars at the ceremony as a tribute to our veterans of those wars. It also sufficed as a quasi "live history" in uniform for our young people who are no longer exposed to much of America's military history. I had purchased several military uniforms at military collector shows; and with the help of friends, family, military re-enactors and veterans, we did an impressive lineup of personnel in period uniforms for the local Veterans Day ceremony. Included in the formation were service, utility, fatigue, dress and combat uniforms with field gear and weapons. I usually participated in a World War One uniform and helmet that I had purchased. I chose World War One as a tribute to my Dad's service in "The Great War". Of course I wasn't born until the years of the great depression before World War Two but I remember one year when, after the ceremony, a little old lady came up to me and said in a most sincere way: "It's so nice that you can still get into your uniform"! Sincere, she was!

On a few occasions I had someone in a French and Indian War outfit; a couple of years there were two Buffalo Soldiers and every year a Civil War Confederate and Union uniform. The Confederate and Union uniforms were worn by a father and son. This so represented the tragedy of that war where, in some cases, father and son were on opposite sides of the front line. Most wars were covered to include the Iraqi and Afghan Wars. On some years I had Air National Guard F-16 pilots and Air Force Reserve C-130 aircrews participating; some of whom were Iraqi/Afghan War veterans. Additionally the local high school Junior ROTC usually provided me with six cadets in the school's collection of uniforms. By the time I gave up the annual Veterans Day uniform presentations, with my last participation in 2011 (16 years), I had an average of 30 participants with a high of 35; plus the six participating ROTC cadets. I thoroughly enjoyed the event, especially getting into a World War One uniform and reflecting on my Dad's war. But after 16 years I decided to give it up as being too demanding and stressful, and standing for long periods became more and more difficult; although I was still enjoying the participation. And as anyone who has ever tried to get a group of people together to march to the same drum-beat knows, it's *like herding cats.* Unfortunately I could not find anyone who was willing assume the tasks of continuing the presentations.

I mentioned above that one reason I began the "live uniform" presentations was as a tribute to my Dad's World War One service. Another reason was as a quasi-history lesson for our youth of today who seem to get little in the way of

American history; particularly the wars that America fought for our freedom and independence. You never know what gets through to our youth; but a few years after I "retired" from the uniform presentations, a tall, handsome and strapping young State Trooper came up to me at a luncheon and asked if I remembered him. I didn't. He looked sharp in his immaculate State Trooper uniform. He told me who he was and my recognition was immediate. He told me that his participation a few years previous in one of our Veterans Day Ceremonies wearing one of my collector World War Two uniforms opened his eyes about what America's wars, and the cost of freedom, was all about. He had joined the Montgomery Police force and later the Alabama National Guard and did a tour in Iraq as an army medic; and now was an Alabama State Trooper. It did me proud to hear him say that my Veterans Day uniform presentations caused him to understand the sacrifices that veterans make for our country. As I said, that was one of the reasons I started it all. One never knows what influence our lives and actions have on those around us – especially our youth!

Occasionally my Vietnam combat veteran friend Keith flies his Cessna 172 into Prattville for a few days. He is gracious enough to take me flying (and my friends too) and let me try my hand again. I can still land with the "rubber side" down!

I am also a member of the Prattville Lion's Club International, a charitable organization orientated toward assisting the sight impaired; plus other community charitable events.

First Aviation Cadet Reunion

In 1997 I learned of a first-ever all military Aviation Cadet/Flying Cadet reunion to be held at Kelly Air Force Base, San Antonio, Texas. As a former 1956 Air Force Aviation Cadet, the reunion caught my interest since I consider my aviation cadet pilot training to be a major and memorable experience in my life. Up until this time I was unaware of any aviation cadet reunions; nor the location of any of my pilot training classmates. This proposed first-ever all aviation cadet reunion kindled a desire to renew acquaintances with my classmates. So I began a search to locate members from my pilot training class. I started with my roommate in basic flying training whose hometown I remembered was in California. Through several phone calls I finally located him and learned of another classmate in California and one in Texas. Upon contacting them I informed them of the aviation cadet reunion at Kelly Air Force Base and got their agreement to attend. It had now been 41 years since any contact with either of them – or any of my classmates. The reunion was planned and organized by a former aviation cadet who had a dream of an Aviation Cadet Museum which he began and operates out of Eureka Springs, Arkansas. This individual was a member of one of the last Air Force aviation cadet pilot training classes before aviation cadet pilot training was phased out of Air Force.

The Air Force dismantled the aviation cadet program in mid-1965. In his effort to establish a lasting legacy for all aviation cadets, which began in World War One (called flying cadets), he established the museum and wrote a book about the training titled: "The Last of a Breed". The reuniting with my aviation cadet friends brought back many fond memories. The reunion with nearly 1000 former aviation cadets attending was a huge success. There were former aviation cadets from the pre-World War Two 1930s era to the mid-1960s when the Air Force Aviation Cadet Program was phased out. It was also the first time since my Aviation Cadet Class graduation in 1956 that Pat would see any of them again. I always told Pat, Norris and Robert that those were the guys that I "grew up" with; although some may question whether I've yet grown up.

At the reunion my aviation cadet friends and I discussed a reunion for our pilot class 56-V, which was composed of aviation cadets and officers (called student officers). After a discussion of how and whom we could get to coordinate a reunion of our class, the three of them said almost in unison: "George, you do it!" I said I would if I could have the reunion in Prattville, Alabama where I lived. They agreed and our first *all* 56-V Pilot Training Class reunion was born. There were nine training bases where 56-V trained and our class from one of those bases was already holding their *own training base* reunion. My reunion would be the first *all* 56-V reunion – aviation cadets and student officers alike – to be held September of 1999 (our graduating anniversary month). It was a great success; although we only had about 65 members, wives and friends attending. Pat, Norris, Gwen and Robert (my family) attended that reunion. Norris and Robert were a great help. A few members commented on how much they enjoyed meeting and talking with Norris and Robert. Pat was a great hostess hosting the class in our home. I also initiated the task of forming a class roster of the hundreds of members of our pilot training class. However, I was only able to locate about 135 members. Over the years we have had five reunions scheduled: The one I hosted in Prattville; one that I hosted at the Aviation Cadet Museum, Eureka Springs, Arkansas; one member-hosted reunion in Seattle, Washington and two scheduled reunions that were cancelled: One by Osama bin Laden's September 11, 2001 attack on America and the other by a hurricane threatening the reunion site. As long as I have my memory I will remember the day that Osama bin Laden's attack on America brought down the World Trade Center Towers! Robert was minutes away from leaving his home in Florida to board an airline flight to join me for our trip to the second Pilot Class 56-V reunion, which was to be held at Wright-Patterson AFB in Dayton, Ohio. Of course all flights throughout the United States were immediately grounded. Our reunion was cancelled. It was a most tragic day when nearly 3000 lives were lost in that cowardly attack: Military, civilian, women, children, rescue, law enforcement and other first-responder personnel.

Robert has attended some of my military reunions with me over the years since Pat died. We attended a squadron reunion at Fort Walton Beach, Florida and a Vietnam Forward Air Controller (FAC) reunion in Hawaii. On the way back from Hawaii we stopped for a few days in San Francisco to visit a couple of my 56-V buddies in the area. Robert always made a great impression on my friends. On my 70th birthday he did a surprise birthday party for me at a local restaurant. When he took me into the restaurant I almost jumped out of my skin when the lights came on and the crowd suddenly erupted into loud cheering. It was a great surprise!

Oh Happy Day, "Maggie May!"

My wife Margaret (Sometimes called "Maggie") is British, a registered nurse, and college lecturer. She had been working in the foreign medical missionary field, when I met her in Prattville, Alabama. She had served in many countries around the world, nursing and teaching, and was staying temporarily with my neighbor (a friend of mine and Pat's, who is blind) while she was waiting to go to China to continue her medical missionary work. She and I were introduced by my blind friend, who sat us together at a local banquet in May of 2003. Margaret was a very nice looking lady and I was taken with her charm. I have always admired missionaries who sacrifice so much to do God's work around the world. Since she was new to the area, I offered to show her around Prattville while she awaited her next assignment. The S.A.R.S epidemic caused a block on travel to China, so her departure was postponed. We began dating and were married on April 3rd, 2004. Since then, Margaret has accompanied me to many of my military reunions; one of which was a squadron reunion cruise out of Florida to Mexico. My Air Force Pilot Class 56-V members and their wives were impressed with her career, work and missionary experiences.

Margaret's first job out of nursing school was working with Dr. Meg Patterson and her world-famous journalist and adventurer husband, the writer George N. Patterson, both originally from Scotland. Meg Patterson was a pioneer of neuro-electric therapy (NET) for treating drug and alcohol addiction. Margaret worked with George and Meg in many subsequent projects on and off over the next two decades; and her work had brought her to the United States. George Patterson spent many years in Tibet carrying the Gospel to the Tibetan people. In doing so, he lived and worked with the Tibetans and sincerely endeared himself to them. One of his many books is his autobiography: "Patterson of Tibet" which I have read. It is a nail-biter! He tells of his harrowing travel over a Himalayan route, never before attempted during the brutal winter conditions, in order to bring news of the plight of the Tibetan people to the outside world. This he did in the days long before cell phones and internet. Imagine! Exciting reading! I believe this autobiography is where he describes how he was instrumental in arranging the escape and exile of the Dalai Lama, when the Chinese invaded Tibet.

When we were married in 2004, because Margaret's own Dad was already deceased, George Patterson came over from Scotland to walk her down the aisle and 'give her away' at our wedding. Of course, he wore his tartan Scottish kilt. *I did not peek!*

Margaret and I enjoy our outings together, and brief trips to fun places. She has even taken me to see the world famous Rockettes perform their Christmas dance routine in Nashville, Tennessee! Now I ask you, what wife would do that for her husband? She has taken me to meet her family in England. It was a great visit; her family is tremendous and great hosts. While there, we traveled across the Channel to visited France and some of my Dad's World War One sites. Margaret helped me find a World War One bivouac area in France where I believe my Dad had been during the war. I was unable to find that site when I was there in 1991. Her family and friends are great and showed me an enjoyable visit – except for the cold, damp and windy weather. We were there in August and I actually wore winter clothing – heavy coat, hat, scarf and gloves – and I was still freezing cold. The wind actually blew me off my feet at one time.

At home in Alabama we have traveled to lakes and beaches for weekends; one of her favorite things. Second to the beach is bargain-hunting at yard sales. As long as she doesn't pay the sticker price; she's very frugal. I've taken her to airshows around the country; one of my favorite things. I took her to visit my military college in the Blue Ridge Mountains at Dahlonega, GA: North Georgia College: The college is a 24/7 military college that I attended in 1950 and 1951. It was their annual alumni, family, and military parade weekend. We also spent some time antiquing, touring the mountains and looking for military collectibles – also one of my favorite things. My son Robert joined us there for the weekend's festivities. I always enjoy my visits with Robert as we reminisce about old times together.

In 2009 Margaret's brother Tim and their mother came from England to visit us in Prattville. It was a great time for all of us. At the age of 56, her brother Tim set a triathlon world record for endurance athletics in the 'Arch to Arc' triathlon Run / Kayak / Cycle category. It involved running 87 miles (the equivalent of three marathons) from Marble Arch in London to the Dover coast; kayaking 21 miles across the English Channel; and cycling 180 miles to L'Arc de Triomphe, Paris, in record time, to gain the title 'Enduroman'. He also represented Britain in the World Games and won a Gold and Silver Medal.

When the Olympic Games were held in London, Tim was one of the Torchbearers, chosen to participate in a relay round the coast of Britain, passing on the Olympic flame, before it ignited the cauldron for the opening ceremony of the Olympic Games in London. We were able to watch most of his exploits live, from the USA. When we had previously visited England, I went out in a boat with Tim and his friend Ben in Portland Harbour; we rowed out towards the English Channel. Later Tim and I paddled around the harbor in a two-man kayak.

Unfortunately, in 2010 Margaret had a heart attack. In the same week, we were informed that her Mother had died in England. Since Margaret was in the coronary intensive care unit, we were unable to attend her mother's funeral.

In 2014 her nephew Josh and his friend visited us for a few weeks. They have their own band in England (The Leggomen) and wanted to visit the music centers in New Orleans, Memphis, Nashville, and the beach at Pensacola. After those adventures Prattville probably seemed a "bummer". However, according to them they had a fantastic time. Now we're trying to get a couple of Margaret's friends, and her sister over to visit Alabama.

Subsequent to her heart attack Margaret developed serious health issues, which limit her activities. She also retired from any further foreign mission trips. We can still travel together but she requires a lot of rest and assistance. She does her best but it is distressing to see her unable to do the things she used to do and enjoy. She had been a great example of fitness and health. I have no doubt that Margaret's medical knowledge and expertise has saved my life during a couple of my medical emergencies. Thank you, Margaret!

In 2014, when I was diagnosed with an aggressive type of prostate cancer, Margaret researched the available options and I chose Proton Therapy, a type of radiation treatment available in only a few places in the U.S. So we packed our bags and we went to spend the summer at the world renowned M.D. Anderson Cancer Center in Houston, Texas for me to receive the treatment. We were blessed to have wonderful caregivers: Patty and Heather at our home, and Lauren who came over from England and stayed with us 24/7 in Houston. With the cancer treatment on top of my open heart multiple bypass surgery in 2006, subsequent stent implants and one heart attack, I too have very little energy and stamina thereby curtailing my activities severely.

There are so many things to be thankful for in my life; Margaret being only one of them; and my family another. I love Margaret; my son Robert; my family; my extended family; and all of my friends. Indeed I am blessed.

To Be Continued.........Eternally!

Although Margaret and I began to experience some very challenging health issues in the last few years – as I'm sure many of you have – we continue to enjoy life in spite of the scale-back. I am ending the writing of my story with this chapter. However, my life will continue here on this earthly planet until Jesus comes or He calls me Home! Regardless of which occurs first, this final chapter will continue eternally in Heaven! If you're not prepared to do your final chapter in Heaven, I sincerely encourage your getting to know Jesus as your Savior before it's too late.

Although I promised many years ago to write my story for my family – some of whom I have since lost – I sincerely hope that all who read my story enjoy my adventures as I have enjoyed living them. I would encourage everyone to write "your story" if for nothing more than for *your* family. I didn't know I had had so much fun until I put my story to paper. Writing my story brought back such fun memories and those of so many close calls in my life. It is by the grace of God that I have been spared and able to write my story. I want all of my family and friends to know that I am thankful for all of you and your being a part of my story. As I said early on: If our footprints have met, you are a part of my life and my story. Thank you! My love to all and I wish you God's Blessings!

George R. Partridge, Prattville, Alabama

*****

About the Author

Lieutenant Colonel Partridge was born to a Georgia share cropper on a small north Georgia farm during the Great Depression Era of the early 1930s. He grew up barefoot behind a plow *staring at the south end of a north-bound Georgia mule*; dreaming of flying those military fighters from a nearby military airbase always *dogfighting* overhead. His plan was to enter the aviation cadet pilot training program and win his wings; but to do so he needed two years of college in order to apply for aviation cadet flight training, required at that time. His mother feared for his wanting to fly. But realizing his dream was to fly, she used her meager savings (along with his summer work wages) to help him enter North Georgia College at Dahlonega, Georgia; a military college in the foothills of the beautiful Blue Ridge Mountains. Following the necessary two year of college, he enlisted in a local Marine Air Reserve Squadron during the Korea War. A few months later in March 1952, he enlisted in the United States Air Force. In June 1955 he entered the Air Force Aviation Cadet Pilot Training Program. Following graduation and commissioning, he completed 33 plus years of service before retiring. Along the way he married his boyhood *dream-girl* and together they raised two outstanding sons. His *adventures* include Labrador, The Philippines, Korea, and combat in Vietnam. In 1965 during a training mission he was forced to eject from his jet fighter and years later in 1998, survived a fiery crash in a 1950s vintage military trainer. He married his present wife Margaret in 2004, a lovely British nurse, three years after a seriously grievous loss of his mother-in-law, a son and his wife of 45 years; all within six months time. Margaret closely monitors his health and has probably saved his life during a couple of medical emergencies. Colonel Partridge is also quick to give God the praise for sparing him from several close calls during his lifetime and for his countless blessing. He and Margaret now live in Prattville, Alabama.

*****

ANNEX – PHOTO SECTION
My story in pictures.

Note: Some photos are old and of reduced quality – but so am I☺

Grandpa and grandma Partridge with Children: (L-R) Kate, Arthur, Percy and Agnes. Not shown: George, John, Dora, Annie Bell and Willie Mae (1918).

Seated: George and Annie Bell. Standing: Arthur, Agnes, Percy, Kate (1917).

Dad: George S. Partridge
US Army, WW I 1917

Mom: Lenna A. Gilbert,
Circa 1917

Dad and Mom with my brother
Harold and sister Oreese. (1930).

And then there was me. Cute Kid!
(1933)

Me(L), younger brother Richard(R).
(Circa 1940)

Me emulating my hero Gene Autry.
(Circa 1943)

Dad and Mom's old farm house on
Rockbridge Road. Me and some of my
model airplanes in the front yard.
(Circa mid 1940s).

Me with Butch in dog *obedience
school.* (Circa mid1940s).

Me(L) and Richard fishing(?)
(Circa 1943).

(L-R) Richard, Dad, Mom and me
(Circa 1949).

Above: High school basketball team. Me,
Jersey #9 next to coach (1949).

Me still making like my hero
Gene Autry. (Photo taken at
North Georgia College, 1950).

Piper J-3 Cub like George soloed at age 16.
(Photo taken at Old Reinbeck Airshow, NY).

Me; Airman First Class, NCCA, DE
(Courtesy Gold Craft Studio1954).

Me as crew chief on my F-94C #531 New Castle
County Airport (NCCA), DE (1954).

Me with my F-94C and my assigned pilot.
NCCA, DE (1953-55).

My "Chick Magnet" NCCA, DE.
(1953-55)

Aeronca "Champ" like I flew Pat
and Mom in at the Charlie Brown
Airport, Atlanta, GA 1954.
(Copied)

Me in Piper PA-18 at DuPont Airport.
Wilmington, DE (1954).

USAF Preflight aviation cadet pilot trainees
on the march. Lackland AFB, TX (1955).
(Photo courtesy 56-V)

Me: Aviation Cadet Lackland AFB,
TX. Preflight Pilot Training. (1955)

Upperclassman *instructs* lowerclassman "nub." (Photo courtesy of 56-V)

Project X. Note: There are no nets! (Photo courtesy of 56-V)

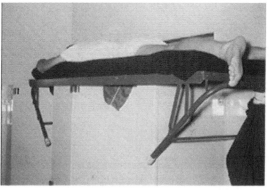

Some tigers must have their sleep; even on top of a refrigerator. Primary, Spence AB, Moultrie, GA 1955-56. (Courtesy of 56V)

Every Cadet a tiger! *I'm the one on the left.* Aviation Cadet Barracks in the background. Lackland AFB Preflight. (1955)

Cadet barracks living area ready for upperclass inspection. Mom would be proud. (Courtesy of 56-V).

Cadet barracks after upperclass inspection. Mom *would* recognize this. (Courtesy of 56-V).

USAF Primary Pilot Trainer
T-34 Mentor
Spence AB, Moultrie, Georgia. (1955-56)

First Solo Splash! (Unknown).
(Courtesy 56-V)

USAF Primary Pilot Trainer
T-28 Trojan
Spence AB, Moultrie, GA.
(1955-1956)

T-28 Instructor and students; (L-R)
Lt. William G. Baker (deceased),
Lt. Robert N. Johnson (deceased),
Mr. C. W. Weir, instructor, (deceased)
and Aviation Cadet George R. Partridge.

USAF Basic Pilot Trainer: T-33A
Shooting Star. Bryan AFB, TX.
(Courtesy of 56-V)

Aviation Cadet George Partridge.
Bryan AFB, Bryan, TX.
T-33A (1956)

Bryan AFB, TX: "C" Flight, 3531st Pilot Training Squadron (Class 56-V). Instructors front row. George R. Partridge third row, eighth from left (on wing of T-33). (USAF Photo)(1956).

2nd Lieutenant George R. Partridge
Graduation, September 1956
Bryan AFB, TX.
(Courtesy Bryan Studio)

My first fighter squadron assignment
97th Fighter Interceptor Squadron(FIS)
New Castle County Airport, Wilmington, DE.
(1957)

Norris, Pat with Robert, and George.
NCCA, Delaware 1957.

Pat en route NCCA to Hamilton AFB,
California 1958.

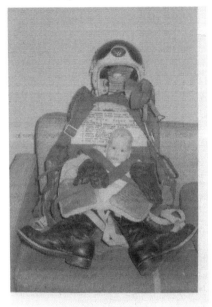

Robert: NCCA 1957.
My Flight Gear.

Norris: NCCA 1957.
My 97th FIS Helmet.

F-89J on 84th FIS Flight Line,
Hamilton AFB, CA 1958.

Family: Mom, Dad, Oreese;
Standing: Harold, Richard, George.
1958

Office: F-100 cockpit and instruments.
Best job in the world!

F-100 low-level bombing (copied).

Norris, Robert, Pat and me.
Rim of Grand Canyon. 1967

Pat, Easter 1964,
Cannon AFB, New Mexico.
1964-66.

Cub Scout Robert with his Mom, Pat
Luke AFB, Arizona. 1967

Norris, Gwen, Tessa & Robert A. 1990

Norris performing at 1968
Sweetheart Banquet, AZ.

Norris, Dysart High School, with his future wife
Gwenda Fackrell. May 1968 Arizona.

My Mom at Yellowstone National Park 1967.

Prettiest car in the world!
My 1964 Olds Starfire.

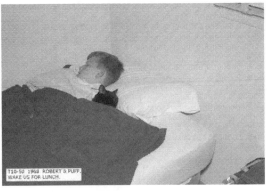

Exploring the AZ Desert. Indian Ruins.
1968

Buddies: Robert and Puff.
Arizona 1968

Somewhere over the Pacific on the way home from Misawa AB, Japan to Cannon AFB.
(Ctsy Ken McDaniel)

Mike Ryan, Al Doddroe, Geo. Partridge, Stan Wells (deceased), Kent Owen, John Rundell (deceased) Misawa AB, Japan 1965.

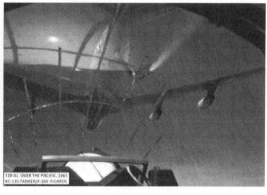

Rendezvous over the Pacific. A beautiful sight! 1965.
(Ctsy Ken McDaniel)

Move in slowly for contact. Note: Tanker's drogue is over-boarding fuel.
(Ctsy Ken McDaniel)

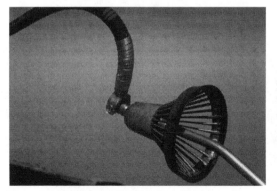

"Receiver Contact." "Tanker Contact."
(Ctsy Ken McDaniel)

Forward Air Control Aircraft: O-1 Bird Dog like I flew in Vietnam 1965.
Photo taken at Hulbert Field FL Airpark.

Geo. Partridge aboard USS Mann
en route to Vietnam.
1965

US Army First Div; 3rd Brigade Hqs;
Lai Khe, VN.
1965

AF TACP: Geo. Partridge & Keith Fabian
Battalion Hqs, Lai Khe, VN.
1965

Our TACP FAC Jeep dug in at
2nd Bn, 2nd Inf Hqs, Lai Khe, VN.
1965

3rd Brigade TACP's O-1 Bird Dog
At the Lai Khe Airstrip.
1965

Keith's and my home away from home.
FAC tent at Battalionn Hqs.
(Ctsy Keith Fabian)
1965

Battalion Hqs, Lai Khe rubber plantation,
Vietnam 1965.
(Ctsy Keith Fabian)

APC destroyed by VC/NVA rocket;
Battle of Bau Bang, VN 12 Nov 1965.
(Ctsy Keith Fabian)

Dustoff medical evacuation helicopter;
Bau Bang, VN 1965. (Ctsy Keith Fabian)

VC/NVA weapons captured; Battle
of Bau Bang, 1965. (Ctsy Keith Fabian)

George Partridge(L)/Keith Fabian; point of RPG Rocket explosion
in their faces at Battle of Bau Bang, VN 12 November 1965.

Our POWs return to a tremendous welcome at Clark AB, PI March 1973.

Cute small Pilipino girl inviting George to dance with her during Mayday Celebration 1973.

Robert: Carabao driving lessons. Philippines 1973.

Robert, University of Florida Graduation, 1980.

Robert with Cessna 152 that he flew his first solo in with Eglin AFB Aero Club, Florida, 15 Mar 1975.

Grandson Robert A. & Granddaughter Tessa, 1993.　　Norris and Gwen; Norris'
Graduation, University of Richmond
Virginia,1975.

George & son Robert, 2011.

Norris, Gwen Pat & George with Tessa and
Robert A. George flying family to visit
family in Cessna 210. Lawrenceville, GA.

George and Pat September 2000.
(Courtesy of Oland Mills Studio).

George's T-34 Crash, Maxwell AFB 14 May 1998.

George and Margaret, San Francisco, 2006   Margaret 2008

Three *really* cute Chicks
Margaret, Lauren and Donna.

George: Aerobatic Citabria Cockpit.
Ctsy Milton Livingston. (Circa 2000).

George and Margaret 2011

George in WWI uniform with *Donut
Dollie,* Margaret. Veterans Day 2008.

Margaret's orientation flight with
Maxwell Aero Club Flight instructor
September 2005.

Margaret trip to 2006 56-V reunion at
Eureka Springs, AR & Avn Cdt Museum.

George S. and Lenna's kids: (L-R)
Richard, George R., Oreese and Harold.(2002)

Melissa Harrelson (Harold's daughter).
(2017)

George S. & Lenna's Grand Kids:
(L-R) Hal (Harold), Robert (George R.)
Stuart (Richard). (Harold's daughter
Melissa not shown) (2002).

How did this cute kid...morph into.................*this!?*
...By the Grace of God!
*****

374

I hope you enjoyed reading my story.
George R. Partridge

2nd Edition
17 October 2017

Made in the USA
Columbia, SC
15 December 2017